In memory of Sean Body
and all those we lost along the way

PETER DOGGETT

You Never Give Me Your Money

The Battle for the Soul of The Beatles

VINTAGE BOOKS

London

Published by Vintage 2010

10

Copyright © Peter Doggett 2009

Peter Doggett has asserted his right under the Copyright, Designs and
Patents Act 1988 to be identified as the author of this work

First published in Great Britain by
The Bodley Head in 2009

Vintage
Random House, 20 Vauxhall Bridge Road,
London SW1V 2SA

www.vintage-classics.info

Addresses for companies within The Random House Group Limited
can be found at: www.randomhouse.co.uk/offices.htm

The Random House Group Limited Reg. No. 954009

A CIP catalogue record for this book
is available from the British Library

ISBN 9780099532361

The Random House Group Limited supports The Forest
Stewardship Council (FSC), the leading international forest
certification organisation. All our titles that are printed on
Greenpeace approved FSC certified paper carry the FSC logo.
Our paper procurement policy can be found at:
www.rbooks.co.uk/environment

Mixed Sources
Product group from well-managed
forests and other controlled sources
www.fsc.org Cert no. TT-COC-2139
© 1996 Forest Stewardship Council
FSC

Printed and bound in Great Britain by Clays Ltd, Elcograf S.p.A.

Contents

Picture Credits

Introduction

Fame is a curse, with no redeeming features.
Allen Ginsberg

The Beatles could be forgiven for doubting the value of celebrity. One of the quartet was shot dead outside his apartment building by a man who claimed to be a fan. Another was attacked brutally in his home; within two years, he too was dead. A third was involved in a marital breakdown that exposed every corner of his life to the public gaze. The fourth found it so difficult to survive outside the group that he lost himself in alcohol and cocaine.

These four men created music of such joy and inventiveness that it captured the imagination of the world, and has never lost its grip. Even a few bars of 'She Loves You' or 'Hey Jude' have the power to pull the listener out of the everyday, and into a fantasy world where every moment oozes with possibility, and love conquers pain. They have the magical ability to recreate the idealism that sparked their own creation, and open that source of inspiration to us all. The Beatles' songs seem to come from a time of dream-like innocence, and represent all the turbulence and splendour that we have learned to identify with their decade. The landmarks of their story have passed into myth, as familiar as the ingredients of a fairy tale. They provide a comforting collective memory – 'a universal gleam', as one observer noted, which could and still can illuminate the world.

Yet they were human, the heroes of this myth; stubbornly, sometimes distressingly human. Almost alone of their generation, they did not want the fantasy to continue. The public basked in the freedom that the Beatles evoked; the Beatles simply wanted the freedom not to be the Beatles. Through the late 1960s, while listeners mapped out their lives in their songs, the quartet plotted an alternative vision of the future in which they would be liberated from the four-man shackles that they had forged.

They soon realised that there could be no escape: they would always be the Beatles, and would always be judged against the peaks they had ascended in the past. Their individual efforts, no matter how inspired, would inevitably pale alongside the endless replays of their youth. John Lennon, Paul McCartney, George Harrison and Richard Starkey ('Don't call me by my stage name,' Starkey asked in a 2009 TV ad) are locked together for all time as the guardians of popular music's most enduring legacy. But their bonds don't end there. Since 1967, they (or their heirs) have been the co-owners of Apple Corps, a venture that was envisaged as a tax dodge, and refashioned as a revolutionary alternative to the capitalist system, but then corroded to become a magnet for lawyers and accountants. What was conceived as utopia turned out to be a prison.

The uncanny consequences of that fate – to be divided and yet eternally combined, separate but still together – are the subject of this book, which traces the personal and corporate history of the Beatles from the heights of 1967, through the relentless decay of their final months, to the endless aftermath beyond. Their ability to survive and sometimes prosper in the eye of a legal, financial and emotional hurricane is perhaps one of their greatest, and most underrated, achievements. Through it all, together and alone, at odds and at one, the Beatles somehow managed to create and preserve music that is as enduring as their myth, perfectly encapsulating its own time and enriching every time to come.

Prologue:
8 December 1980

It was almost 11 p.m. in New York City, and singer-songwriter James Taylor was at home in the exclusive Langham Building on Central Park West. He'd just placed a call to Betsy Asher, whose husband had signed him to the Beatles' Apple label twelve years earlier. 'She was in Los Angeles, and she was complaining that things were getting very crazy there,' Taylor recalled. 'Something was happening to do with the Charles Manson family, something mad going on. Then I heard these shots. I'd been told that the police would leave an empty chamber under the hammer of their guns, so when you heard a police shooting, it would be five shots of a large-calibre weapon in rapid succession, to empty the gun. What I heard was *bam-bam-bam-bam-bam* – five shots. I said to Betsy, "You think it's crazy out *there*. I'm just listening to the police shooting somebody down the street." We rang off. Then about twenty minutes later she called me back, and said, "James, that wasn't the cops."'

The police were on the scene in minutes, and news crackled across the radio of a shooting outside the Dakota Building, a block downtown from the Langham. The press agency UPI wired the initial reports: 'New York police say former Beatle John Lennon is in critical condition after being shot three times at his home on Manhattan's Upper West Side. A police spokesman said, "A suspect is in custody." But he had no other details. A hospital worker said – quote – "There's blood all over the place. They're working on him like crazy."'

ABC-TV trailed the bones of the story across the screen as the New England Patriots visited Miami Dolphins on *Monday Night Football*.

Five minutes later commentator Frank Gifford interrupted his colleague Howard Cosell: 'I don't care what's on the line, Howard, you have got to say what we know in the booth.' 'Yes, we have to say it,' Cosell said wearily, adding a warning that sounded almost sacrilegious in his sports-obsessed country: 'Remember, this is just a football game. No matter who wins or loses.' Then, with the portentous cadence of a man accustomed to translating sporting contests into drama, Cosell announced, 'An unspeakable tragedy. Confirmed to us by ABC News in New York City. John Lennon, outside of his apartment building on the West Side of New York City, the most famous perhaps of all of the Beatles, shot twice in the back, rushed to Roosevelt Hospital' – he hit each word slowly and carefully like a nail into wood – 'dead . . . on . . . arrival. Hard to go back to the game after that newsflash.'

Richard Starkey and his girlfriend, actress Barbara Bach, were drinking in a rented house in the Bahamas when he was contacted by his secretary, Joan Woodgate. 'We got some phone calls saying that John had been injured,' he recalled. 'Then we heard he was dead.' He was the first of the surviving Beatles to learn the news. 'John was my dear friend, and his wife is a friend, and as soon as you hear something like that . . .' Horror pierced the anaesthetic haze of alcohol that had become his protection against the world. 'You don't just sit there and think, What to do? It was just . . . We had to make a move, and we had to go to New York.'

First, Starkey phoned his former spouse, Maureen Cox, in England. Her house guest Cynthia Lennon was woken by screams. Seconds later Cox burst into her bedroom, and told her: 'Cyn, John's been shot. Ringo's on the phone. He wants to talk to you.' Cynthia rushed to the phone and heard the sound of a man crying. 'Cyn,' Starkey sobbed. 'I'm so sorry. John's dead.' She dropped the phone and howled like an animal caught in a trap.

George Harrison's elder sister Louise had just retired to bed in Sarasota, Florida when she was phoned by a friend telling her to turn on her TV. 'My first thought was that something was wrong with George,' she recalled. 'When I heard, I felt two things – a wave of relief that George was OK, and horror at what had happened to John.' She immediately tried to phone her brother at Friar Park, his unfeasibly expansive Gothic mansion in Henley, but nobody answered.

'They kept the phone under the stairs in those days,' she remembered, 'because George didn't like to be disturbed by it.' For the next two hours she dialled the number again and again, but heard nothing but the endless bleat of the ringing tone.

Around 5 a.m. UK time, an hour after the shooting, the BBC was ready to deliver the news to the world. In her home overlooking Poole Harbour 74-year-old Mimi Smith – John Lennon's aunt, who had raised him from the age of six – drifted in and out of sleep to the comforting drone of the BBC World Service radio broadcast. She had not seen her nephew for nine years, but two days earlier he had told her that he would be returning to Britain in the New Year. She heard his name, uncertain whether she was awake, and realised that the radio announcer was talking about Lennon. She just had time to register a thought familiar from his childhood – 'What has he done *this* time?' – before the newsreader confirmed the fear that had always haunted her. She lay alone in her bed and listened as hope and pleasure died in her heart.

An hour later Louise Harrison abandoned her attempts to call Friar Park and woke up her brother Harry, who lived in the gatehouse on his younger sibling's property. 'I blurted out that John had been shot,' she recalled. 'Harry said that there was no point in waking up George at that time of the morning, as there was nothing he could do about it. "I'll tell him when I take up the post after breakfast," he said.'

Gradually the news spread through the Beatles community. The group's longest-serving assistant, Neil Aspinall, shared an especially close bond with Lennon. When he was woken, his first impulse was to phone John's Aunt Mimi: his call persuaded the elderly woman that she was indeed experiencing a living nightmare. Then Aspinall went grimly through the Beatles hierarchy, calling Harrison's home, speaking to Starkey before he left for Nassau airport, but failing to reach McCartney, whose phone was disconnected at night.

In McCartney's Sussex cottage nobody turned on the TV or radio; Linda McCartney drove the couple's children to school as usual. While she was away, her husband plugged in the phone and learned that his songwriting partner and estranged friend, the man who had shaped and sometimes scarred his entire adult life, was dead.

Minutes later, his wife returned home. 'I drove into the driveway,' she remembered, 'and he walked out the front door. I could tell by looking at him that there was something absolutely wrong. I'd never seen him like that before. Desperate.' Linda described his face as 'horrible'. Then he told her what had happened. 'I can see it so clearly,' she said later, 'but I can't remember the words. I just sort of see the image.' Sobbing and shaking, the couple staggered back into the house. 'It was just too crazy,' McCartney said. 'It was all blurred.'

A year later Paul McCartney was asked how he had felt. 'I can't remember,' he said, though he could, all too clearly. He relived the clanging emotions of that moment: 'I can't express it. I can't believe it. It was crazy. It was anger. It was fear. It was madness. It was the world coming to an end.' Reeling with grief and unreality, he began to imagine that he too might become the target of an assassin. 'He started wondering if he was going to be next,' Linda McCartney revealed, 'or if it would be me or the kids, and I didn't know what to think.' 'You couldn't take it in,' her husband confirmed. 'I still can't.'

George Martin, who had supervised the Beatles' recording career with fatherly care, was woken by an American friend anxious to pass on the news. 'Not a good way to start the day,' he remembered. 'I immediately picked up the phone and rang Paul.' The two men were scheduled to meet later at Martin's London studio, where McCartney was making an album. Martin recalled: 'I said, "Paul, you obviously don't want to come in today, do you?" He said, "God, I couldn't possibly *not* come in. I *must* come in. I can't stay here with what's happened."' As McCartney explained later, 'We heard the news that morning, and strangely enough all of us reacted in the same way. Separately. Everyone just went to work that day. Nobody could stay home with that news. We all had to go to work and be with people we knew.'

As in the 1960s, 'we' was the Beatles, another of whom was scheduled to record that afternoon. Having been told that his latest album was insufficiently commercial, George Harrison had reluctantly agreed to submit four new songs. His collaborators included percussionist Ray Cooper, and American musician Al Kooper, an insomniac who, like Mimi Smith, had learned of Lennon's death from the BBC World Service. 'I called Ray and said, "Do you know about this?"' Kooper recalled. 'I said, "We should go and take [Harrison] in the studio and work and take his mind off it" as opposed to letting him stew. So he said OK, and we drove out there, and when we got to the gate there was like a million press people there, just standing there in the rain. I got out of the car and they started shouting at me. I said, "Don't you have anything better to do?"'

McCartney faced a similar gauntlet at Martin's AIR Studios in London. 'I did a day's work in a kind of shock,' he said later. Irish musician Paddy Moloney was there. 'It was a strange day,' he remembered, 'but playing music seemed to help Paul get through it.' George Martin recalled music taking second place to therapy: 'We got there and we fell on each other's shoulders, and we poured ourselves tea and whisky, and sat round and drank and talked and talked. We grieved for John all day, and it helped.'

Lennon's childhood friend Pete Shotton, who had worked for the Beatles in the late 1960s, 'decided I wanted to be with someone who knew John as well as I did'. He arrived at Harrison's home around midday. '[George] wrapped his arm around my shoulders and we went silently into his kitchen and had a cup of tea. We spoke quietly, just for a bit, not saying much, and George left the room to take a trans-atlantic call from Ringo.' Then Starkey left for his early-morning flight to New York. 'There's nothing else we can do,' Harrison told Shotton; 'we just have to carry on.' Al Kooper was taken into the kitchen, where he found Harrison 'white as a sheet, all shook up. We all had breakfast. He took calls from Paul and Yoko, which actually seemed to help his spirit, and then we went into the studio and started the day's work.'

In New York thousands of mourners had gathered around the Dakota Building. By 2 a.m. EST police had erected barricades, and armed guards were stationed at the site of the shooting. Lennon's widow, Yoko Ono, recalled, 'I came back here and went into our bedroom, which faces 72nd Street. All I could hear all night, and for the next few weeks, was the fans outside playing his records. It was so excruciating, just spooky. I asked my assistants to beg his fans to stop it.' Her staff informed the mourners that Ono was attempting to sleep and intercepted calls on her private line.

Lennon's 17-year-old son Julian told his mother Cynthia that he wanted to fly immediately from Britain to New York to join his step-mother and half-brother. 'We were put straight through to [Yoko],' Cynthia remembered, 'and she agreed that she would like Julian to join her. She said she would organise a flight for him that afternoon.

I told her I was worried about the state he was in, but Yoko made it clear that I was not welcome: "It's not as though you're an old school-friend, Cynthia." It was blunt, but I accepted it.'

When Ono spoke to McCartney a few hours later, her tone was more conciliatory. 'She was crying and cut up,' McCartney said that evening, 'and had no idea why anyone should want to do this. She wanted me to know that John felt warm about me.' For more than a decade Lennon and McCartney's relationship had been fragmentary and strained, and McCartney's self-confidence had clearly been shaken by their estrangement. Ono's reassurance helped to bolster his ego: 'It was almost as if she sensed that I was wondering whether the relationship had snapped.'

Lennon's death had robbed both McCartney and Harrison of someone with whom they felt a precious rapport. 'The consolation for me,' McCartney reflected in 1992, 'was that when [Lennon] died, I'd got our relationship back. And I feel sorry for George because he never did. George was arguing until the end.' Harrison and Lennon had not spoken for several years, and Lennon's final interviews revealed resentment towards his old friend. Yet Harrison's grief was flecked with fury rather than self-doubt. Derek Taylor phoned him that after-noon and found him 'shocked, dreadfully upset and very angry. He said he didn't want to give a statement at such a time, but [business manager] Denis O'Brien had said there ought to be one. After an hour or so I telephoned George again and this time we worked out a short statement based on his real response to the tragedy.' Harrison's deep sense of spirituality was masked by his rage. 'After all we went through together,' his statement read, 'I had and still have great love and respect for him. I am shocked and stunned. To rob life is the ultimate robbery in life. This perpetual encroachment on other people's space is taken to the limit with the use of a gun. It is an outrage that people can take other people's lives when they obviously haven't got their own lives in order.' Later he spoke to his sister in America. 'George phoned me,' Louise Harrison said, 'and he was obviously very upset. He just told me, "Stay invisible."' Then Harrison returned to his home studio. Al Kooper reported, 'We kind of got him drunk, and kept going as long as we could until we just ran out of stuff to do.'

While McCartney and Harrison soothed their grief with alcohol and companionship, Richard Starkey and Barbara Bach flew to New

York. 'You had to say hello to the guy's wife,' he explained, 'just to say "Hi" and "We're here."' They took a cab to the apartment where Bach's sister lived, and phoned Ono at the Dakota. 'Yoko didn't really want to see anybody,' he recalled. 'She was really up and down – she wanted to see someone and then she didn't. So we sat around for a bit and then she said, "Come on over." We got to the apartment, and she said she just wanted to see me – mainly because she's known me a lot longer, and she'd only met Barbara twice before.' A decade earlier Lennon and Ono had informed the world that they were now inseparable, indissoluble: 'Johnandyoko'. In an unconscious tribute to his friend, Starkey now mirrored this stance, telling Ono, 'Sorry, we go everywhere together.' Ono agreed to see them for a brief, traumatic meeting. 'Then we flew out,' Starkey said, 'because we didn't feel too partial to New York at that time.'

In London the numbing effects of McCartney's recording session had worn off, and he walked outside onto Oxford Street. A phalanx of reporters surrounded his limousine, asking obvious but unanswerable questions. McCartney remained polite but sullen, chewing gum determinedly as a distraction from his pain. To bring his ordeal to a close, he compressed everything he couldn't say into three words, tossed contemptuously towards the voracious microphones: 'Drag, isn't it?' Then, out of habit, he waved to the cameras and vanished into the safety of his car. 'I had just finished a whole day in shock,' he reflected later. 'I meant "drag" in the heaviest sense of the word. [But it seemed] matter of fact.' 'He was slated for that,' George Martin said. 'I felt every inch for him. He was unwise, but he was off his guard.'

That night the two British television networks treated the murder like the death of a minor royal. The BBC screened the Beatles' film comedy *Help!*, its pop-art playfulness adding a surreal veneer to the tragedy. ITV herded anyone with a faint claim to expert status into their studios: biographers, critics, ephemeral pop stars – 'all those people who were supposed to have been John's friends' McCartney raged later. 'Then the pundits come on, "Yes, so John was the bright one in the group. Yes, he was a very clever one. Oh well, he'll be sorely missed, and he was a great so-and-so." I said, "Bloody hell, how can you muster such glib things?" But they were the ones who came off good, because they said suitably meaningful things. I was the idiot who said, "It's a drag."' Powerless, bereft, stricken by the loss of the man whose approval he rated above all others', McCartney raged against the night. 'I did a lot of weeping,' he revealed. 'I remember screaming that [Lennon's assassin] Mark Chapman was the jerk of all jerks; I felt so robbed and emotional.'

Alcohol eventually calmed all of the surviving Beatles. Starkey flew to Los Angeles, where he dined at Mr Chow's in Beverly Hills with Harry Nilsson, the defiantly self-destructive singer-songwriter who had once been Lennon's companion-in-carousing. 'Ringo never brought up the events that had just transpired on the East Coast,' said fellow diner Ken Mansfield, 'and I found myself admiring the manner in which he handled the whole situation.' Yet such insouciance would become increasingly hard to maintain. Unbeknown to Starkey, his arrival at Los Angeles airport had been monitored by dozens of police, responding to a threat to his life made by a deranged man who arrived at the terminal building determined to rival Mark Chapman's sudden fame. Meanwhile, New York police informed Yoko Ono's staff that someone had been arrested at the Dakota entrance, seeking to kill her.

For some, the tragedy brought reward. David Geffen, who had just released Lennon's final album, watched in amazement as orders flooded his distributors' phone lines; cancelling all advertising for the album as a mark of respect didn't stem the flow. Lennon's attorneys were inundated with requests to license the musician's name. Workers at the EMI Records factory outside London were placed on emergency overtime to handle the demand for Lennon's back catalogue. In less than 24 hours he had been transformed from a musician into a global hero, and the three surviving members of the Beatles had joined the supporting cast of their own life stories.

'It is not difficult to imagine what a staggering blow his death inflicts on Paul, George and Ringo,' Daily Mirror columnist Donald Zec wrote after Lennon's death. 'Think of the sudden collapse of one of the steel stanchions supporting an oil rig. No answer to that kind of catastrophe.'

For all their stubborn talk that they no longer considered them-selves Beatles, McCartney, Harrison and Starkey knew that they would always be defined by the monolith that shadowed their lives. The loss of Lennon was existential: it affected every atom of their being. For McCartney, it ended all hope of reunion with the man whose name would forever be linked with his, and the familiar hierarchy of that link – Lennon/McCartney, never McCartney/Lennon – would become increasingly uncomfortable in the years ahead. He had not just lost a friend, but a man whose approval or disdain could determine his self-confidence. McCartney had been grieving for the loss of Lennon's love and esteem since Yoko Ono supplanted him as Lennon's chosen collaborator in 1968. Now that grief would become permanent, without hope of relief. Twenty-five years after Lennon's assassination, the memory could still cause McCartney to break down in public.

George Harrison's relationship with Lennon was rooted in the cosmic realm. During the two men's early experiments with chemical mind expansion in the mid-1960s Harrison had experienced a feeling of profound kinship with his often aggressive and sarcastic friend. They might have enjoyed little personal contact in the decade before Lennon's death, but in Harrison's eyes the bond could not be broken: it was a spiritual union, which would survive the grave just as it had weathered years of public and private tension. At their final meeting Harrison could still detect the unspoken link in Lennon's eyes.

'I was always worried about Ringo,' Lennon noted after the break-up of the Beatles. Lennon, McCartney and Harrison all carried proven songwriting skills into their solo careers; Starkey was forced to rely on charm and comradeship. They proved rich resources: in 1973 he had come close to engineering a Beatles reunion, and at the time of Lennon's death he was attempting to match that achievement on a new album. McCartney and Harrison had already contributed to the sessions, and Lennon was scheduled to complete the set in January 1981. But it was obvious that nothing less than the magical presence of all four Beatles could arouse significant interest in anything that Starkey did. His career had been in free fall since the mid-1970s, mirroring his decline into acute alcoholism, as Lennon had lamented to his friends. His relationship with Starkey was closer and less complicated than his dealings with Harrison or McCartney, not least because Starkey represented no artistic or financial threat. Lennon offered Starkey unconditional love and acceptance, qualities that the alcoholic millionaire was struggling to register in his own troubled heart.

Each of the surviving Beatles registered a uniquely personal loss in

December 1980, but emotion was only one of the levels on which Lennon's murder took its toll. Despite the annulment of their legal partnership, the four Beatles were still caught in a claustrophobic web of financial obligations. Literally dozens of companies created, managed and squandered their individual and corporate wealth. Some of their advisers had invented methods of steering their earnings from one tax jurisdiction to another, with cash speeding around the world from company to company, en route to an offshore resting-place in an idyllic haven. None of the Beatles comprehended the full implications of the hundreds of legally binding documents that they had signed since 1962. Once upon a time they had collected their money from Liverpool promoters in grubby notes and coins, and split it equally in the back of their van. Now they employed armies of financial specialists, whose purpose was to expand their clients' riches and their own commissions. Once the Beatles had dealt solely in music. Now their interests ranged from film production to dairy farming, plus that mysterious form of money broking available only to the obscenely rich.

In the beginning the Beatles' affairs had been entrusted to their manager Brian Epstein. He recruited a team of assistants with comforting Liverpool accents, who continued to serve them after Epstein's death in 1967. The loss of their naive but devoted mentor opened the gates to financial confusion and men with vastly greater business experience than Epstein but sometimes less loyalty. A struggle ensued to gain mastery of the Beatles' business interests, but no sooner had New York accountant Allen Klein triumphed than his prize dissolved before his eyes. By the mid-1970s, when their professional partnership was finally annulled, the Beatles had each assembled – exactly how they found hard to remember – his own rich entourage of corporate lawyers and advisers.

While their representatives threw themselves gleefully into legal battles and financial coups, the Beatles could at least feel secure that they held some vestige of control over their music. The exact extent of their stake in their timeless 1960s catalogue was open to costly legal dispute, and would remain so for years to come. But until the late 70s, when record companies first dared to say no to Starkey and then Harrison, the recording studio remained a fiercely guarded bastion of independence for the four men.

In personal and creative terms the Beatles had never been entirely equal, but when it came to matters that affected them all each man's vote carried the same weight. Yet as early as 1968 Lennon had introduced a fifth element to the quartet: his partner, the experimental film-maker and artist Yoko Ono. First he insisted on her presence while the Beatles were working; then he abandoned the group and collaborated solely with her. Finally, after the birth of their son Sean in October 1975, he made the fateful decision to appoint her his surrogate in business meetings and contractual negotiations. The other three Beatles and their extravagantly rewarded advisers were now forced to work with a petite, softly spoken, wilful and utterly unpredictable woman whom they had always regarded with suspicion and unease.

Until December 1980 McCartney, Harrison and Starkey could reassure themselves that their former colleague was still a party to the deals being made in his name. When he died, Ono was entrenched as the sole guardian of the Lennon legacy: the self-appointed 'keeper of the flame', protector of his interests, curator of his archive, spokesperson for his memory, and controller of 25 per cent of the Beatles and their business empire. There were no longer four Beatles, but there was always Yoko Ono, maverick in Manhattan. Her elevation to ersatz Beatle status presented a baffling conundrum to Lennon's former colleagues.

From the beginning the four men had commanded different levels of respect. Starkey was the drummer, with the saving grace of appearing lovable and self-deprecating, and being armed with a simple but droll wit. Harrison was 'the quiet one,' though 'If I was the quiet one,' he complained once, 'the others must have been *really* noisy.' A dedicated student of the guitar, he was in thrall to Eastern philosophies, possessed of dry humour and seriousness in equal measure, and incidentally the creator of what Frank Sinatra described as 'the greatest love song of the twentieth century'. (All of Harrison's humour was needed to ignore Sinatra's conviction that 'Something' had been penned by Lennon and McCartney.)

McCartney was an enigma. Fiendishly talented, driven to near-obsession by a work ethic implanted in early childhood, the proud owner of a pure seam of creativity almost unmatched in the history of popular music, he was also insecure, clumsy in front of the media, a natural entertainer and a born ham. Ex-employees dubbed him a control freak. But his melodic gift outweighed all his human frailty. So too did his determination, which sometimes overpowered his artistic judgement. This medley of traits and characteristics combined to make him the most commercially successful songwriter of all time. But at some level of his psyche none of this counted if he did not have the respect of John Lennon. With Lennon gone, he was locked into intimate financial partnership with a woman whom he had never understood, and who seemed never to have valued him or his talent.

In the years after his death Lennon was portrayed in vivid, clashing colours. Some observers claimed that his final years were shaped by creative bankruptcy, drugs and suicidal despair. Others – not least Lennon himself, in his final testimony – declared that he was at the height of his powers, fully re-engaged with his muse, ready to celebrate another dazzling chapter of the romantic saga he had once dubbed 'The Ballad of John and Yoko'. The obituary writers declared him 'a hero', who 'reached out beyond entertainment to offer a gentler philosophy of life'. His promise and stature were compared to those of the late President Kennedy: 'both represented, in their different ways,' *The Times* claimed, 'the aspirations of a generation'. In the editorial columns that still represented the voice of the British establishment, the same paper declared, 'Lennon was only one member of the group, but he was its most charismatic and interesting one, and perhaps its most important.' His death 'commits to history the decade that so utterly changed British society'.

How could Paul McCartney maintain his own career while his former partner was being canonised? How could he stake his claim to a proper share of the Beatles' artistic legacy when he was uncomfortably mortal and Lennon was up among the gods? Personal grief was only one of his curses; for the rest of his life McCartney would be battling Yoko Ono for his place in history. There were now three Beatles, and one saint. Perhaps that was McCartney's cruellest fate: he desired nothing more than to regain Lennon's love, but now he was condemned to compete with Lennon's memory for the recognition that, rightfully, should already have been his.

Two days before he shot Lennon, Mark Chapman spent several hours waiting fruitlessly outside the Dakota Building. Then he hailed a cab, which took him downtown to Greenwich Village. He told the driver that he was a recording engineer who had spent the afternoon working on an album that reunited John Lennon and Paul McCartney.

Chapman could not have known that McCartney had attempted to contact his ex-colleague during the making of Lennon's recently completed *Double Fantasy* album, but that communication had been prevented by a third party. Neither was he aware that New York City officials had been asked to undertake a feasibility study for a possible Beatles reunion concert in Central Park; nor that Lennon had just sworn in an affidavit that he was planning to collaborate with the group for the first time in eleven years.

All of these fantasies and schemes died with Lennon on 8 December 1980. The four Beatles had last worked together in August 1969; had effectively disbanded a month later and had announced the fact in spring 1970. A year later the tatters of their reputation were scattered around the London High Court when Paul McCartney sued his friends in an attempt to dissolve their legal partnership. The four Beatles had always squabbled like brothers; now their confrontations were worthy of a Mafia family. The moptopped idols still known as 'the boys' to their long-suffering staff were exposed as jaded, embittered men who had slipped inexorably out of time.

Throughout the 1970s their disagreements captivated the press and public, who charted their shifting positions like armies on a general's map. Hints of détente between the two main protagonists would be countered by a sudden surge of animosity from Harrison; one Beatle might suggest that a reunion would be 'fun', only for another to respond with contempt. Yet no matter how often the Beatles denied that they were about to regroup, there was a shared understanding – shared at least by their fans – that eventually they would be reconciled, and (equally contentious) that the reunion would be artistically valid. The commercial potential of a reformed Beatles was never in doubt, but it was not just money that sparked the offers of unimaginable sums for a single concert or tour. Nor was it music, the ostensible purpose of any reunion. Depending on their mood, the Beatles greeted the inevitable questions about their future with a mixture of supreme self-confidence ('If we did do something, it would be great') and insecurity ('Could we ever be as good as people expect us to be?'). Ultimately, as the collaboration between McCartney, Harrison and

Starkey in the 1990s proved, their artistic achievement was irrelevant; what counted was the symbolism.

'Sexual intercourse began in nineteen sixty-three,' the poet Philip Larkin wrote, 'between the end of the Chatterley ban and the Beatles' first LP.' And from 'sexual intercourse' you could infer every facet of that cultural phenomenon now known as 'the Sixties' – erotic liberation, flamboyant fashion, student protest, the anti-war movement, Carnaby Street, Grosvenor Square, the Prague Spring, Paris in May, acid, pot, free dope, free love, free music, freedom from the past and, as it turned out, the future. Numerous factors combined to place the Beatles at the heart of this cultural upheaval, or revolution, or whatever best described the collective sense that something in the world had changed irrevocably. There was the coincidence of the calendar: it was mere chance that led the group to split in the final months of the decade, not a keen eye for self-mythology. Their youthful exuberance and unwillingness to accept the status quo chimed with the restlessness of the baby boomers who were achieving demographic dominance. They displayed an uncanny ability to assimilate the enthusiasms of the artistic and cultural vanguard, from psychedelic drugs and Indian spirituality to *musique concrète* and pop art, and reproduce them for the mass audience. The Beatles didn't create the Sixties, but their music and charisma sold it to the world.

Beyond their active lifetime the Beatles were borrowed to support wildly varied depictions of the 1960s. Some commentators blamed them for the decade's cultural ills: lack of respect for authority, extramarital sex, drug use, swearing, the moral decay of society. Less controversially, the Beatles joined the era's other icons in an apparently seamless collage, as evocative and – in time – culturally empty as JFK, miniskirts, urban riots, flower power, the Vietnam War and the first landing on the moon. Reduced to a few seconds of matching suits and hysterical fans, the Beatles provided the smoothness of nostalgia with no unsettling jolts of reality.

There was indeed a sense that the group had passed through the 1960s immunised from history, as removed from the times as they were from the everyday necessity of feeding themselves. Wealth and fame exiled the Beatles from the youth revolution that they were supposedly leading, and one of the symptoms of their impending disintegration was their increasing clumsiness when they were confronted with life outside their bubble – notably in the creation of their utopian business empire, Apple. The group had imagined that they could bypass commercial necessities with the sheer power of their name. Theirs was not the child-like wonder of a generation coming to flower, but the naivety of men (no longer 'the boys') who had forgotten how to deal with reality. Like closeted princes faced with a high-street vending machine, they were clueless and confused. That left them prey to businessmen who were anything but starry-eyed, and who recognised earning potential when they saw it. As their empire decayed from within, the Beatles were forced to confront the things that separated them as individuals, and which gradually over-came the solidarity that had supported their dizzying rise to fame.

Much of this was forgotten when people talked about a Beatles reunion. Nobody dreamed of a return to the dark days of 1969, when Lennon and McCartney were often reluctant to occupy the same room, and Lennon ensured he was absent whenever a George Harrison song was due to be recorded. There was no heady glow attached to the memory of a court case that pitted the Fab Four against each other, or exposed their bitter recriminations to the world. Even the most unrealistic supporters of a reunion could not expect them to look or sound like they did in 1964, when their irrepressible energy conquered the world. No, what was required of a reunited Beatles was that they should make their audience feel as they had done when they first heard 'I Want to Hold Your Hand' or smoked a joint to the accompaniment of *Sgt Pepper*. What people wanted wasn't the Beatles; it was their own past, stripped of pain and ambiguity. But it was precisely the combination of pain and ambiguity which had already destroyed the dream.

Chapter 1

The Beatles were such profoundly artistic people that they gave themselves massive licence to be their own artistic selves. That was how it was possible to sustain the group, because they could say or do harsh things to each other. They could reject things in songs that were corny, and come out with this most superb finished work. They had this way of dealing with each other's weaknesses so that only the strengths came through.

Apple press officer Derek Taylor

As early as 1963 journalist Stanley Reynolds suggested that the Beatles were 'about to fade away from the charts, to the Helen Shapiro hinterland of the 12-months wonders . . . it was a good exciting sound while it lasted'. And it did last, despite persistent murmurs in the same vein, provoked when a record failed to reach No. 1 or empty seats were spotted in the arenas that the Beatles had once filled with ease.

The nine-month hiatus after their final live show in August 1966 disguised a transformation in the Beatles' lives. In the late spring of 1967 they completed work on an album widely acclaimed as a landmark in twentieth-century music. Almost simultaneously, they embarked on a business scheme that began as an exercise in tax avoidance, and became a sketch for utopia. The Beatles had conceived a daring fantasy: the idea that four pop musicians might be able to reshape the capitalist system. They dreamed of a world in which creativity would flourish without the shackles of commerce; in which art and business could be joined in joyous union; in which society could be transformed not by the bullet or the ballot box, but by the Beatles, and the cosmic power of their name. Instead, they built a corporate prison which would sap their vitality and their willingness to survive, and prove to be inescapable long after the utopian fantasies had been forgotten.

In the summer of 1967, the Beatles were the princes of pop culture. *Sgt Pepper*, released in June, presented the era in miniature: gaudy, extravagant, decadent, playful, solipsistic, alive. Only the closing minutes of 'A Day in the Life', with its threatening orchestral crescendo and atmosphere of surreal paranoia, greyed the technicolour pages of their dream. It was in just such innocent gaiety that the denizens of the counterculture lived that summer, in London, San Francisco and wherever the hippie trail might lead. It was possible, so misty-eyed veterans assure us, to wander up and down the Haight or the Kings Road, and hear nothing but the familiar melodies of *Pepper*, blasting joyously out of sync from every window.

If the young and privileged took comfort in their oneness, there was always the threat of pregnancy, a drugs bust, even (for young Americans) the arrival of a draft card. The flower-power uniform of bells, beads and body paint was a collective mask, the emblem of a conscious decision (in the most enduring cliché of the age) to 'Tune in, turn on, drop out.' The hope was that, in congregating together, young people might create and preserve the fantasy of their choice, banishing forever the straight world of obligations and employment, marriage and maturity, their parents' crushing inheritance.

The Beatles, so pop commentator Tony Palmer declared, were 'the crystallisation of the dreams, hopes, energies, disappointments of a countless host of others who would have been Beatles if they could'. There was no resentment of their wealth or fame: their apparently effortless journey from proletarian drabness to aristocratic gaiety promised a similar transfiguration for their admirers. Where the Beatles led, millions were content to follow. Moustaches, kaftans, military tunics, cannabis, Indian ragas, flowers, universal peace and love: none of these was invented by the Beatles, but the group were the conduit by which the symbols of the age reached the outside world.

No longer available on the concert stage, the Beatles now existed in image alone, via the promotional films that accompanied their single 'Penny Lane' and 'Strawberry Fields Forever', the peacock-rich cover of *Sgt Pepper*, the worldwide television premiere of 'All You Need Is Love' and the newsreel footage that captured them arriving at their recording studio, jetting to Greece or setting out for enlightenment with the Maharishi Mahesh Yogi in Bangor. Yet there were less exclusive opportunities to glimpse one of these fabled creatures in the flesh.

Paul McCartney was the only Beatle not to have bought a mansion in the 'stockbroker belt' of gated villages and secluded estates south-west of London. His relationship with actress Jane Asher had provided an entrée into upper-middle-class London society, where he learned to mix with minor royals, businessmen and the theatrical elite. Besides his training in etiquette, the Asher family – in the shape of Jane's pop-singer brother Peter – introduced him to London's burgeoning world of alternative arts. He had gained a taste for modern drama and poetry at school, and relished the opportunity to patronise exotic galleries and theatres. Soon he was encountering beat writers such as Allen Ginsberg and William Burroughs, attending concerts of atonal and electronic music, quietly financing underground papers and events, and assisting the Indica Bookshop, run by Peter Asher's friend Barry Miles.

As McCartney soon discovered, celebrity status allowed him access to all areas of metropolitan life. He utilised the power of his name to meet prominent figures who would otherwise have ignored the ephemeral world of pop. 'Paul would do that a lot,' Barry Miles said. 'He'd call people up and say, "This is Paul McCartney, would you like to have dinner?" Most people said yes.' Among those he sought out was the philosopher and veteran peace campaigner Bertrand Russell. 'He saw Russell because he realised that he wouldn't get the truth about the Vietnam War from the London press,' Miles explained. 'The thing to do was to go to the top, and as far as Paul was concerned, that was Russell.'

The polarising conflict in Vietnam was only one of the political currents preoccupying those who were prepared to engage with the outside world. There was the struggle for civil rights in America, global liberation movements seeking to overthrow colonial regimes, and apartheid in South Africa and its near-neighbour Rhodesia. Closer to home, the Beatles shared the common distaste among the young for censorship and the widespread contempt for the drug laws on the British statute books.

Their views were echoed by Brian Epstein, who had been managing the group since 1961 via his Liverpool company NEMS. But he was wary of letting political controversy endanger their appeal to the public. As their press officer Tony Barrow explained, 'Epstein asked the Beatles not to discuss their love lives, their sexual preferences, politics or religion with the media. But behind the scenes, the Beatles – particularly John and George – talked current affairs in general and topics such as Vietnam in particular. They were very much against war, having seen the results of bombing in Liverpool as kids. Talking about Vietnam at a press conference, as they started to do in 1966, was also a way of demonstrating to Epstein that they were beginning to resent being told what to do.'

Even McCartney realised the limits of the Beatles' power, however: 'What could we do? Well, I suppose that, at a Royal Command Performance, we could announce a number and then tell people exactly what we thought about Vietnam. But then we'd be thought to be lunatics.' Or they might, as John Lennon discovered, become the subject of virulent fundamentalist hatred after expressing perfectly intelligent views about the relative popularity of religion and music. When the Beatles arrived in Chicago on their final tour on 11 August 1966, Lennon was forced to defend his comments that the group were 'more popular than Jesus'. So heated was the debate that nobody thought to ask the group about the political crisis uppermost in the minds of Chicago's citizens: the campaign against segregated housing led by the Reverend Martin Luther King. Interpreting their silence as indifference, radical black activist LeRoi Jones complained that the Beatles were the epitome of 'exclusive white . . . isolated from the rest of humanity'. He added, 'The Beatles can sing "We all live in a yellow submarine" because that is literally where they, and all their people (would like to) live.'

As if to prove Jones right, the Beatles embarked the following year on an expedition that symbolised their isolation from the real world. 'We were all going to live together now, in a huge estate,' their past and future press agent Derek Taylor recalled. They initially set their sights on the windswept landscape of East Anglia, then a more attractive idea emerged: they would buy an island in Greece. Brian Epstein's long-time assistant Alistair Taylor was sent to the Mediterranean like a colonial governor seeking a winter retreat for a monarch. He returned to London with photographs of Leslo, a suitably idyllic setting for escapist millionaires, not least because it was surrounded by four smaller islands, one for each Beatle.

Three months earlier the democratic Greek government had been overthrown in a military coup, ostensibly to prevent any Marxist influences from corrupting the nation. The new regime tortured and executed its opponents with the minimum of judicial process. Nor did it overlook the young: the army colonels banned long hair, rock music and all criticism of their policies. Left-wing activists in Britain launched a campaign to dissuade tourists from holidaying in Greece. The regime unconsciously aided their efforts by deporting visitors who failed to achieve military standards of appearance and discipline. It was not, perhaps, the most promising of cultural climates for a group of young millionaires who lived by their own law. Yet the Beatles did not allow petty politics to impede their vision of nirvana. 'I'm not worried about the political situation in Greece, as long as it doesn't affect us,' Lennon declared. 'I don't care if the government is all fascist or communist.' Their more socially aware friends, such as Barry Miles, were shocked by their indifference. 'I was horrified,' he recalled. 'As I remember it, Paul was faintly embarrassed by it all, but John wasn't concerned.' Paul McCartney's political misgivings were, in any case, outweighed by more selfish concerns: 'I suppose the main motivation would probably be [that] no one could stop you smoking. Drugs was probably the main reason for getting some island.'

A few weeks earlier McCartney had confirmed that he had experimented with the psychedelic drug LSD, or acid. 'It seemed strange to me,' George Harrison recalled, 'because we'd been trying to get him to take LSD for about eighteen months – and then one day he's on the television talking about it.' Harrison complained, 'I thought Paul should have been quiet about it – I wish he hadn't said anything, because it made everything messy,' not least by raising the question of the Beatles' roles as moral exemplars for their fans. McCartney dismissed the problem by telling the interviewer that if he was so concerned about the welfare of the young, then he shouldn't broadcast comments. In the time-honoured tradition of the British media, sensation won out over common sense.

The latter quality was in short supply at Kenwood, Lennon's mansion, where the musician filled the Beatles' more relaxed schedule by escaping from the barrenness of his everyday life into a maelstrom of psychedelic chemistry. If Lennon's acid intake was an attempt to find unreality, Harrison was more specific, greeting acid as 'a blessing, because it saved me many years of indifference'. Though more cautious about his intake than his colleagues, McCartney recognised that LSD could focus and enhance his creativity if used in moderation. While Lennon sought to dissolve his ego and Harrison to transcend it, McCartney strolled through the mid-1960s as the captain of his soul, powered by self-belief and artistic certainty.

Sexual intercourse was so freely available to the Beatles that it hardly counted as a motivating force. Neither did wealth: virtually no luxury or experience was beyond their financial reach. Even the most insecure personality would have been satisfied by the overwhelming fame shared by these four young men. If anything, their celebrity was now a curse, keeping them from the uncomplicated pleasures of ordinary life. So what remained to keep the Beatles hungry for experience and achievement?

Richard Starkey's outlook was the least complex of the four. He had experienced poverty, isolation and prolonged illness as a child, and he still took simple pleasure in the freedom that stardom had brought him. He developed a talent for photography, though his pictures were rarely seen outside the family. He channelled some of his vast income into a short-lived building company, but took its failure in good heart; he still had his wife, his growing family, his pool table and the lavishly stocked bar that he installed in his den. Life had already provided more than he could ever have dreamed of; even acid did little to expand his horizons.

LSD had a far more profound effect on George Harrison, providing 'the awakening and the realisation that the important thing in life is to ask, "Who am I?" "Where am I going?" and "Where have I come from?" All the rest is, as John said, "just a little rock 'n' roll band". It wasn't that important.' This was said with the hindsight of almost thirty years, but as early as 1966, when pop's possibilities appeared limitless, Harrison reckoned that it seemed 'somehow dead'. He was also restricted by the persona that had been created for him by the media. 'They called him "the quiet Beatle",' recalled his sister Louise, 'but that was because the first time they went to America, he had a really bad strep [sore] throat, and so he didn't say much at press conferences, and that image just stuck. It's interesting, though, because our mum and dad never allowed us to go out and play with the other kids; we went everywhere with them instead.' A sense of isolation, and self-reliance, was built into Harrison's psyche from his early childhood, allowing plenty of space for his imagination to roam.

A chance encounter with Indian musicians on the set of the Beatles' movie *Help!* fired that imagination in a way formal education had never achieved. As a teenager, he had rejected academia in favour of the guitar. He lacked McCartney's intuitive musicality but substituted effort for natural ability. In 1965 he bought his first sitar, and was widely responsible for introducing the languorous hum of Indian instrumentation to the pop audience. Eager to experiment further, he took sitar lessons from the maestro Ravi Shankar, who became a lifelong friend and guru. Perhaps more importantly, Shankar's brother Ravu gave Harrison a book in which he found the philosophy that would dominate his subsequent life: *Autobiography of a Yogi* by Paramahansa Yogananda. This account of spiritual devotion, of miracles and meditation, of gurus and disciples, left an almost visceral mark. As Harrison described his reaction, 'Wow! Fantastic! At last I've found somebody who makes some sense.' With naive enthusiasm, he read every Indian spiritual text he could find 'by various holy men and swamis and mystics, and went around and looked for them and tried to meet some'.

His sister Louise recalled, 'As kids, we were always encouraged to find out for ourselves what we believed in, and what was right and wrong. Our family were Catholics, but we always had a global outlook. We were spiritual, not religious as such. George didn't change as a person after he went to India; he was the same as he'd always been. But he became a passionate apostle for what he had found there, and was very keen to spread the word.' Harrison's passion for all things Indian was revealed on the Beatles' albums, which now routinely included at least one excursion into ethnicity. Brian Epstein was relieved that the youngest member of the group – whose early efforts at songwriting had been ridiculed by Lennon, McCartney and producer George Martin – had finally found his métier. Unknown to Epstein or the wider world, however, Harrison was now comparing life as a Beatle with the way of the mystic, and finding his fame wanting. 'After what had happened [in India],' he recalled, 'everything else seemed like hard work. It was a job, doing something I didn't really want to do, and I was losing interest in being "fab" at that point.' He returned from India to work on the *Sgt Pepper* album, but remembered, 'It was difficult for me to come back into the sessions. In a way, it felt like going backwards.'

While Harrison was in India, McCartney basked in life as a man about town. In his well-cut jackets and colourful neckerchiefs, he paraded through society like a benevolent dandy, bestowing his bounty – a smile here, a few hundred pounds there – on every deserving soul who crossed his path. He had been raised to be kind, generous, polite and friendly, and that was precisely the impression he left upon those who enjoyed fleeting encounters with him at film premieres or in Chelsea salons.

McCartney was prepared to dabble in Eastern philosophy, as he was in *musique concrète* or experimental cinema. Acclaim from his peers and from the public at large fuelled his creativity; his exposure to the avant-garde refined his vision. During the final months of 1966 he composed a traditionally melodic score for a movie, prepared electronic collages for his own amusement and schooled himself in the extremes of contemporary classical music. He was the golden boy of the British counterculture, limited only by the boundaries of his imagination. When *Pepper* took shape, it was in his image.

The apparent richness of McCartney's life contrasted sharply with the emptiness that haunted John Lennon. During the mid-1960s 'I went through a terrible depression, I was going through murder,' Lennon revealed in 1969. His friend journalist Maureen Cleave penned a vivid portrait of his 'large, heavily panelled, heavily carpeted, mock Tudor house' filled with 'tape recorders, the five television sets, the cars, the telephones of which he knows not a single number'. She noted, 'He can sleep almost indefinitely, is probably the laziest person in England.' And she found him curiously dissatisfied: 'You see, there's something else I'm going to do, something I must do – only I don't know what it is. All I know is, *this* isn't it for me.' A few months later he said, 'I feel I want to be them all – painter, writer, actor, singer, player, musician.' McCartney shared his curiosity, and carried it into his working life. For the moment Lennon's aspirations and activities remained painfully out of register. He would listlessly attempt to compete with

McCartney's experiments in sound and vision, without ever quite believing in what he was doing. Occasionally, his labours would bear fruit: over several arduous weeks he channelled his confusion into 'Strawberry Fields Forever', while another burst of creativity produced the skeleton of 'A Day in the Life'. But his other contributions to the Beatles for the next six months were sporadic and forced. In the depths of his depression at Kenwood he had to recognise that the balance of power had shifted in McCartney's direction.

In an effort to imitate McCartney's lifestyle, Lennon allowed their mutual friend and gallery owner Robert Fraser to shepherd him through London's avant-garde. On 7 November 1966*, he was taken to the Indica Gallery, where a Japanese member of the experimental art group Fluxus was setting up her exhibition Unfinished Paintings. In a meeting that would assume mythological status, he spoke briefly with the artist, 33-year-old Yoko Ono, and established some form of rapport. Lennon wasn't the only enthusiastic visitor to the gallery: a few hours later film director Roman Polanski experienced Ono's work for the first time, exclaiming, 'This is the most beautiful apple I have ever seen,' and, 'That is the very essence of a needle,' when faced with exhibits comprising nothing more than an apple and a needle. Just over two weeks later Lennon and Ono met again at the opening of an exhibition by Claes Oldenburg at Fraser's own gallery, smiled and moved on. McCartney also met Ono that evening, and it was to his house that Fraser directed her when she sought a handwritten Beatles manuscript to include in a Festschrift for the composer John Cage. McCartney suggested she should contact Lennon instead, and the jaded Beatle and unsettlingly intense Ono struck up a distant, asexual friendship.†

By spring 1967, when the Beatles were ensconced in EMI's north London studios, Yoko Ono had become a minor celebrity. Her *Film No. 4*, colloquially known as 'Bottoms', was refused a certificate by the British Board of Film Censors, sparking protests outside their

---

* Convinced that 9 was his lucky number, Lennon rewrote history to place this meeting on 9 November, and all subsequent chroniclers have followed suit.
† One biography of McCartney, by Christopher Sandford, quoted a source claiming that McCartney and Ono had sex when she arrived at his London home. Though it would add delicious spice to the subsequent history of the Beatles and Apple, there is not the slightest shred of evidence to support this accusation.

office. *The Times* sounded surprised to discover that 'Miss Ono turned out to be an attractive young woman with long black hair and a soft, shy voice.' This proved to be the last occasion on which Ono won praise for her appearance in the British press. Eventually, in August, her 'film of many happy endings' received its world premiere in London and was exhibited at private clubs. Its Fluxus-inspired concept – a parade of anonymous backsides, accompanied by amused comments from the participants – attracted much humorous comment and a little forced outrage. Ono added to the later by writing a humorous essay for the underground magazine *International Times*, to which both Lennon and McCartney subscribed. After lampooning male genitalia, she declared, 'Men have an unusual talent for making a bore out of everything they touch.'

Lennon slowly opened a channel of communication with this placid but strangely provocative woman. In September she was invited to watch the group recording McCartney's 'Fool on the Hill'. Two days later she launched a conceptual event entitled *Yoko Ono's 13 Days Do-It-Yourself Dance Festival*. Postcards tumbled through the letter boxes of subscribers (including Lennon) every morning, bearing cryptic messages such as 'Draw a large circle in the sky' and (on Lennon's birthday) 'Colour yourself. Wait for the spring to come. Let us know when it comes.' Lennon was alternately exhilarated and infuriated, but never bored.

In another echo of McCartney's patronage of the arts, Lennon acted as sponsor for an Ono art exhibition, *Yoko Plus Me: Half-A-Wind*, in London. Entirely by accident, of course, Lennon's name appeared in the publicity for the show, despite earlier assurances that he could remain anonymous. Out of habit more than lust, he made a token pass at Ono after the exhibition opened, but Ono politely turned him down. As yet, no hint of scandal attended his involvement in her career, and Lennon (and McCartney) soon sponsored a second art show, by his college friend Jonathan Hague.

By then, Robert Fraser had introduced Lennon to the man he would describe as 'my guru', a young Greek inventor called Alexis Mardas, or as Lennon dubbed him, 'Magic Alex'. Derek Taylor, tongue very slightly in cheek, later described him as 'the genius who had arrived in England knowing only the Duke of Edinburgh and Mick Jagger'. Often dismissed in subsequent accounts as 'a television repairman' of no technical ability, Mardas had been recognised as a scientific prodigy as a teenager, and given the opportunity to study at a special academy, from where he was encouraged to travel around Europe to broaden his education. Perfectly mannered and utterly persuasive, he had amassed an impressive but ill-fitting set of acquaintances that stretched from the Rolling Stones to the exiled Greek royal family, and hence to other crowned and deposed heads of Europe. A keen follower of scientific innovation, he concocted inventions that might have been designed to attract the attention of the pop aristocracy: force fields that could prevent car crashes and repel burglars, or a camera that could take X-ray pictures. George Harrison, who was bitterly cynical about Mardas's abilities in later years, had the grace to admit that some of his inventions were 'amazing'. Lennon was willing to follow anyone who could carry him out of the mundane, and encouraged the other Beatles to offer Mardas financial support.

It was Mardas's good fortune to enter the Beatles' milieu at the very moment when they were seeking out methods of spending – 'investing' was the more hopeful term – extravagant amounts of money. Brian Epstein's inexperience as a manager perennially left him reacting to financial necessities, rather than anticipating them. He had explored a primitive tax-haven scheme in the Bahamas, but succeeded only in losing money there. Swiss bank accounts had been set up in the Beatles' names (though this was kept from the public, who preferred to think of their heroes as unassuming working-class lads at heart). But by late 1966 it was apparent to Harry Pinsker, the Beatles' chief contact at accountants Bryce Hamner, that immediate action was required if the musicians were not to face a potentially devastating tax bill from the British authoritises. 'I suggested to the boys,' the punctilious Pinsker explained, 'that they bought freehold property and went into retail trading.' Their reply, he recalled, was, 'We want to be like Marks and Spencer's.'

The Beatles had first been incorporated – as The Beatles Ltd – in 1963, when it became apparent to Epstein that their career might outlive the year. Within six months the company instigated its first lawsuit, against two manufacturers of unauthorised memorabilia based in Blackpool. The Beatles Ltd held the group's collective earnings, after Epstein's NEMS organisation had taken its 25 per cent. Without realising the implications, the Beatles had agreed a management deal with

Epstein in October 1962 that not only guaranteed NEMS a quarter of their income for the next five years, but maintained that percentage on deals negotiated during that period. They had effectively signed away 25 per cent of their lifetime earnings from their recording contract with EMI – whether or not their relationship with Epstein survived. Other companies handled specific aspects of their career. Lennon and McCartney's songwriting interests were controlled by Northern Songs Ltd; their income from Northern passed into another holding company, from which Epstein claimed director's fees as well as his subsequent 25 per cent. The less substantial money accrued by Harrison's songwriting went into Harrisongs Ltd – run, like Northern Songs, by opportunistic publisher Dick James. Epstein formed Subafilms Ltd in early 1964 to handle the Beatles' movie projects. After Lennon published two books of cartoons and writings, he was encouraged to form a separate company to receive his royalties. And there were similar companies in the USA, not least Seltaeb Inc., the organisation that notoriously signed away the Beatles' rights to 90 per cent of the earnings from memorabilia sold in their name.

The intricacies of this financial web had long since exceeded Epstein's comprehension. Nor did it help that during late 1966 and early 1967 the Beatles' manager was undergoing a process of psychological disintegration, fuelled by his drug use, his chaotic sexual habits and his fear that by quitting live performance the group were slowly moving beyond his control. But Epstein did manage to negotiate a new recording deal in January 1967, whereby the Beatles promised to deliver 70 recordings in the next five years, and a guaranteed flow of albums until 1976 – either collectively or individually. (It is intriguing to note that the possibility of the Beatles splitting up was already built into this deal.) At the same time, he tightened his grasp on his 25 per cent, ensuring that his cut was now enshrined in the recording contract.

Incapable of running NEMS with the efficiency that had once been his trademark, Epstein had recruited a partner, producer and entrepreneur Robert Stigwood, who soon showed signs of wanting to assume total control. The Beatles learned nothing of this until late August 1967, when Epstein's death from an overdose of sleeping pills first focused their attention on the contracts that they had signed.

It was Epstein's altogether more sober brother Clive who guided the formation of a company that would carry out Harry Pinsker's advice and save the Beatles from having to pay almost £3 million to the British government in income tax. Instead of being four individuals sharing their income in The Beatles Ltd, they would become employees of a new corporation, The Beatles & Co. They would each own a 5 per cent stake in the firm, the remaining 80 per cent being held by The Beatles Ltd – renamed Apple Music Ltd in 1967, and Apple Corps Ltd ('It's a pun, you see,' McCartney said helpfully) in January 1968. The financial benefits were obvious. Their earnings were now subject to corporation tax rather than income tax (currently running at 94 per cent for such high earners as the Beatles), and they could claim back their personal living expenses from the company.

The first public acknowledgement of the new order came with a cryptic reference to Apple on the sleeve of *Sgt Pepper*. By then, the Beatles were beginning to realise that their company could become a plaything as well as a tax dodge. Alexis Mardas had been delicately telling Lennon about the technological breakthroughs that would be possible if only funding were available. He was added to the Beatles' payroll in August 1967, and by the end of the year he was installed as a director of Apple Electronics Ltd. Like a child at Christmas, Lennon was entranced by the wizardry of Mardas's inventions. Derek Taylor noted that Mardas 'remained the least challenged' of all the Beatles' aides in the years ahead; after all, he was Lennon's protégé and – not to be understated in the year of acid – he was officially 'Magic'. Of all the Beatles, McCartney had the least interest in prolonging the Mardas mythology, but even he, thirty years later, conceded, 'We weren't being stupid, but we were probably overreaching . . . We were thinking this could happen in five years, whereas it's taken a little longer.' By January 1968 Mardas had been commissioned to build new recording studios for both the Beatles and the Rolling Stones, and to purchase a factory to facilitate the mass production of his magical inventions.

Despite the close friendship he built with Harrison, Mardas was always Lennon's guru; the Beatle even acted as best man at his wedding. The next addition to the Beatles' circle fulfilled the guru's role for the entire group. Early in 1967 Harrison's wife Pattie Boyd had attended a London seminar in Transcendental Meditation, given by the Maharishi Mahesh Yogi. The Maharishi might have been invented to fill the spiritual chasm in the Beatles' lives: gentle and serene, a baby-like giggle never far from his lips, he exuded a beguiling mixture of wisdom and playfulness, supported by a devilish awareness of business opportunity. His devotion to the practice of meditation was total and sincere; so was his eagerness to reach out to the affluent young of the West. By studying the teachings of the Lord Krishna in the *Bhagavadgita*, the Maharishi insisted, his disciples would attain a truly fulfilled life: 'When society accepts it, social well-being and security will result, and when the world hears it, world peace will be permanent.' Boyd was duly trained in the practice of meditation, and joyfully spread the word to her husband. The Maharishi returned to Britain in August 1967, and the Harrisons encouraged the other Beatles to attend his lecture. 'There was a collective consciousness within the Beatles,' Harrison recalled of this period. 'I assumed that whatever one of us felt, the others would not be far out of line.' The guru affected ignorance of their superstar status, and casually invited them to attend a course in Wales that weekend. It was there that they heard that Brian Epstein – the guru, if you like, of their early success – had died. It was, wrote Derek Taylor, 'the first crack in the marble of our wonderful temple of the mind wherein we would all dwell in perfect harmony'.

Having uttered some spiritual banalities fed to them by the Maharishi, who assured them that Epstein hadn't died, he'd just moved to another place*, the Beatles returned to London. There the implications of their 1962 contract with Epstein were spelled out to them: they were not managed by Brian, but by his company NEMS, which would now be jointly controlled by Stigwood and Clive Epstein. The Beatles felt a degree of family loyalty towards the Epsteins, but no personal bond with Clive. They had no affection for Stigwood: as an independent record producer, he had rejected the Beatles in 1962. And another recent recruit to NEMS, Vic Lewis, was also tainted: in 1957 McCartney had attended a rock 'n' roll show by Bill Haley in Liverpool, and was disgusted to discover that the first half of the performance would be given by Lewis's dance band instead.

There was an immediate announcement that 'no one could possibly replace Brian' and 'things will go on as before', mutually contradictory

---

* In Eric Idle's recasting of the Beatles' myth, *All You Need Is Cash*, their manager Leggy Mountbatten tragically moves to Australia.

statements that signalled trouble ahead. For a while the Beatles imagined that Clive Epstein might be able to supervise the launch of Apple without having power of veto over their actions, but that compromise could never have held. The naturally conservative Clive advised caution; the Beatles interpreted this as lack of faith. 'He didn't believe in us, I suppose,' Starkey complained. 'He thought we were four wild men and we were going to spend all his money and make him broke.'

The NEMS management deal expired in late September 1967, and the Beatles let it lapse. Instead, the four men decided that they would manage themselves and cast about for a suitable accomplice. It was at this point that Neil Aspinall, the trainee accountant who had become their road manager and personal assistant in 1961, broke one of life's cardinal rules, 'Never volunteer.' 'I said to them, foolishly, I guess, "Look, I'll do it until you find somebody that you want to do it."' Aspinall could appear sullen in the company of the Beatles, but his wit was as quick and scathing as theirs, and he enjoyed a particularly warm relationship with Lennon, while being trusted implicitly by all four. 'Neil was indivisible,' as Derek Taylor recalled. Aspinall rapidly discovered that the Beatles knew nothing about their financial and business obligations: 'We didn't have a single piece of paper. No contracts. The lawyer, the accountants and Brian, whoever, had that. Maybe the Beatles had been given copies of various contracts, I don't know. I know that when Apple started I didn't have a single piece of paper. I didn't know what the contract was with EMI or with the film people or the publishers or anything at all. So it was a case of building up the filing system, finding out what was going on.' It was only now, for instance, that they discovered NEMS was entitled to 25 per cent of the Beatles' income from record sales in perpetuity.

It was a moment for taking stock. Instead, the Beatles impulsively launched their business empire. A maze of new companies was established in London: Apple Electronics, boasting a scientific laboratory in Boston Place; Apple Music Publishing, run by former car salesman Terry Doran in Baker Street; Apple Retailing, which established a boutique below the publishing office; Apple Tailoring, funding the creations of designer John Crittle; and, after a few uncomfortable weeks squatting at NEMS, a corporate office for Apple Corps Ltd in Wigmore Street. Neil Aspinall's fellow road manager Mal Evans rapidly found himself called into service: 'We had a meeting to set up Apple, and we were all sitting round this big table eating sandwiches and drinking. Paul turns round to me and says, "What are you doing these days, Mal, while we're not working?" "Not too much, Paul." He says, "Well, now you're president of Apple Records." Thank you very much!'

All four Beatles were insistent that Apple should be run by their friends, regardless of their talents or experience. Fortunately, some of their choices had the group's best interests at heart. An early recruit was journalist and PR man Derek Taylor. He had ghost-written a newspaper column for George Harrison and an autobiography for Brian Epstein, and survived several turbulent months in 1964 as the group's press officer. Impossibly charming and possessed of a dry wit, Taylor had escaped his Fleet Street roots and moved to California, where the hardened hack of pre-Beatles days became the acid-fired doyen of Hollywood pop publicists.

I was a wild 1960s counterculture figure in California, and George felt that they couldn't run Apple without me. We had always been friendly and now that – in the phrase of the day – we were on the same trip, he had to have me there. There might not have been an Apple as we knew it if I hadn't come back, and it might not have been as mad. I had a phone call from all four Beatles, asking me to join, but it was probably George's idea. He said, 'We want you to come back and run Apple.' John said, 'I've asked Neil to run it.' And Paul said he'd asked Peter Asher. It never occurred to me to say, 'Well, if all these different people have already been asked to run it, why are you asking me?' It was that acid summer: it was a time of complete trust. I know now that we were foolish. We didn't come to any terrible harm, but when I look back at how we trusted everything would work out all right, it was folly. LSD did that to you.

* * *

The film is about the predicament of people [who] are trapped inside an image and a wealth machine which simply cannot express what they really feel.
Review of *Magical Mystery Tour*, *Guardian* 1967

On Boxing Day 1967 the Beatles' first self-produced, self-written, self-directed movie was premiered by BBC-TV. Shot in sumptuous colour, it was unfortunately screened in black-and-white. *Magical Mystery Tour* blended surreal imagery, avant-garde photographic techniques and jokes borrowed from English end-of-the-pier variety shows. Keith Dewhurst in the *Guardian* applauded its 'poetry beyond professionalism' and concluded that 'it redeemed in retrospect days of shallow rubbish', but his was a lonely voice. So vitriolic was the general reaction of the press that McCartney felt he had to apologise for having failed to meet the public's expectations.

Magical Mystery Tour was effectively a McCartney creation: he had devised the concept, supervised the filming, and been the only Beatle dedicated enough to endure the editing process. The film's reception introduced an unfamiliar sense of vulnerability into the group's morale, and threatened the unchallenged leadership that McCartney had assumed over the previous 18 months. 'John used to say, "I'm the leader of this group!" and we used to say, "It's only because you fucking shout louder than anyone else!"' McCartney noted thirty years later. 'Nobody cared as much as he did about being the leader.' It was precisely that Lennon no longer seemed to care, about the Beatles or anything else, that had allowed McCartney to seize control. 'Paul was always courageous,' Derek Taylor recalled. 'In a way he was braver than John.' In 1967 he masterminded the group's assumption of new identities on the *Sgt Pepper* album and the development of Apple into a commercial empire.

'Paul wanted to work,' reflected Beatles/NEMS press officer Tony Barrow; 'John hated to work. He had a MTV-level concentration span. He got bored very quickly, and pushed things aside, whether it was a song or a business deal. Paul was a much more methodical worker. He liked the discipline of coming into the office every day.' Lennon would be shaken by fits of passion, for Magic Alex or against men in suits, and would then subside into an inertia that bordered on depression. McCartney never quite lost control of his emotions. As Barrow noted, 'John was the noisiest of the four, and so he was accepted as being the leader. But it quickly became obvious that Paul was the most persuasive of the Beatles, and the one who wielded the real power with Brian Epstein. John would make a lot of noise, but not get his own way. Then Paul would go in and persuade Brian that what John had suggested was the right thing to do. Paul was very shrewd in the way he handled relations, both inside and outside the group.'

But now Brian was dead, and the buffer between Lennon and McCartney had been removed. In any case, the relationship between the two men was built upon shared recognition of Lennon's supremacy. 'I always idolised him,' McCartney admitted in 1987. 'We always did, the group. I don't know if the others will tell you that, but he was our idol. He was like our own little Elvis . . . always someone for us to look up to.' Elsewhere, McCartney revealed that he lived for those occasional moments when his idol would acknowledge his talent: 'He was older and he was very much the leader; he was the quickest wit and the smartest. So whenever he did praise any of us, it was great praise indeed, because he didn't dish it out much. If ever you got a speck of it, a crumb, you were quite grateful.'

McCartney's comments suggest that even at the height of his creative fulfilment he could still be deflated and undermined by Lennon. He seemed to require public affection more than his older partner, and even that reward could feel empty if it wasn't supported by Lennon's approval. Nobody else could ever have made him admit, 'I have always quite enjoyed being second . . . You're still up with number one. Number one still needs you as his companion.' Everywhere else in his life, McCartney demanded first position: from his lovers, from his employees, from the audience whose desertion might render his life meaningless. But subservience to Lennon gave him a sense of worthiness that he couldn't find elsewhere.

As the junior member of the Beatles – 'Paul was always eight months older than me, and he's still eight months older' – George Harrison sometimes displayed resentment towards his more successful colleagues. But he drew consolation from their willingness to share his explorations of Indian spirituality. When the Beatles travelled to the Maharishi's retreat in Rishikesh early in 1968, he took personal responsibility for their devotion. 'George actually once got quite annoyed and told me off because I was trying to think of the next album,' McCartney revealed. 'He said, "We're not fucking here to do the next album, we're here to meditate!" It was like, "Ohh, excuse me for breathing!" You know, George was quite strict like that.' And in those moments McCartney felt hurt and bewildered that the natural order of Beatles hierarchy – John, Paul, George and Ringo – had been disturbed.

Harrison's obvious admiration of Lennon did not mean that he felt inferior to his older colleague. 'After taking acid together, John and I had a very interesting relationship,' he explained. 'That I was younger or I was smaller was no longer any kind of embarrassment with John. Paul still says, "I suppose we looked down on George because he was younger." That's an illusion people are under. John and I spent a lot of time together from then on, and I felt closer to him than all the others, right through until his death.' This conviction allowed Harrison to transcend any petty aggravations in his dealings with Lennon and concentrate on what he saw as their mutual understanding.

Harrison and Lennon were certainly the two Beatles most prepared to immerse themselves in the spiritual waters of Rishikesh. Starkey famously returned home first, weary of his self-imposed diet of baked beans and his wife's aversion to the subcontinent's array of insect life. McCartney followed, having set his own limit – a strict four weeks – on the expedition from the outset. As he admitted later, he 'wondered what was going to happen with the other guys. For a week or so there I didn't know if we'd ever see them again, or if there ever would be any Beatles.' Even Starkey, normally the least imaginative and most level-headed of the quartet, was now philosophising like a mystic about 'the greater plan' that governed life 'with a pattern and a reason for everything you do'. Like the Christian conundrum about the extent of free will in a God-directed universe, his statements demonstrated a blend of fatalism and blind faith: 'I think that when you're born, there is a very complex pattern that is planned out for your whole life . . . The major decisions are yours, but if you decided to do one thing, then everything that happens to you because of that decision has been planned out in advance. I never worry about what's going to happen in the future, and I never plan too far ahead, because I know that things are planned to happen, whatever I do.'

In the face of such acceptance, at home and abroad, McCartney could only trust his own instincts and continue to shape his own future – and, he hoped, that of the Beatles. While Lennon and Harrison were away he was free to impose his will on the fledgling Apple organisation. He told Derek Taylor that Apple should exhibit 'controlled weirdness'. This chimed with Taylor's own mental state: 'I was completely out of control. I was as free as a bird, and if this thing was going to be weird, then it was going to be weird. But it didn't take me many hours to realise that Apple was not a dream world.' At the end of

Taylor's first day in the office McCartney turned to him and said, 'You've been pretty obnoxious. It must be living in America that's done it.' As Taylor realised, 'I was still an employee and the boys were still the bosses – especially Paul, the bossiest of the bossy. But still one's optimism survived.'

In India the two remaining Beatles were sucked into a drama about the Maharishi and his supposed preference for sexual rather than spiritual relations with his young female disciples. 'To tell you the truth, I think they may have used it as an excuse to get out of there,' McCartney reasoned. Lennon stormed home like a child who'd been promised Christmas and instead found himself at the dentist. Harrison refused to allow the squabbles in the Maharishi's camp to shake his faith in the power of meditation or the allure of the East.

Delaying his return to Britain by visiting Ravi Shankar allowed Harrison to distance himself from what was happening in London. 'I had very little to do with Apple,' he insisted. 'I was still in India when it started. I think it was basically John and Paul's madness – their egos running away with themselves or with each other.' At the heart of the madness, Derek Taylor became aware that

The Beatles weren't together: they didn't know what they wanted out of Apple. What Paul wanted was a publishing company, a record company, the Apple shops. I'm not sure that he wanted Apple Electronics and Magic Alex. John was the big sponsor there, but George liked Alex and Paul didn't dislike him. I don't know what Ringo's idea of Apple was. But back then I still saw the Beatles as one tight unit, one for all and all for one. I didn't realise the tensions underneath, until George came back from Rishikesh and reacted with real horror to what was going on in the building, particularly in my press office.

The legendary excesses of Taylor's hospitality, with the finest dope and whisky on offer to guests, paled alongside the magnitude of Apple's ambitions. Every week a new company was incorporated under the Beatles' umbrella – Python Music Ltd, Apple Publicity Ltd, Apple Management Ltd, even a financial subsidiary based in Jersey. There should also be, Lennon and McCartney decided, an Apple School, and their Liverpudlian pal Ivan Vaughan – responsible for the pair's first meeting, in 1957 – was recruited to mastermind this unlikely venture.

The most innocent of Apple's schemes was to solicit music, poetry and art directly from the British public, thereby evading the bureaucracy that had delayed the Beatles' rise to stardom. Paul McCartney conceived a series of advertisements which suggested that anyone with unheralded talent should send their wares to Apple's office in Baker Street. 'If you're a singer, sing for us,' McCartney wrote. 'If you're a writer, write for us. Send us tapes and picture.' The company's ethos was simple: 'WITH THE EMPHASIS ON ENJOYMENT'. Apple's reward was a torrent of packages containing tapes and manuscripts, few of which were ever opened, let alone enjoyed. 'It was a good idea to help the world,' Taylor said twenty years later, 'but you should do it quietly, and not try to save the whole world at once, because then you end up breaking your promises. What on earth made us think that we could pull off this stunt of opening the doors to the world? After all these years of the Beatles shopping in Harrods after hours, suddenly we threw all that out of the window and said, "Here we are, come and get us!"'

While the deluge descended upon Baker Street, Lennon, McCartney and a retinue of retainers – Taylor, Mardas, Neil Aspinall, Mal Evans and Ron Kass, who had been recruited to lend Apple Records a more professional edge than Evans could provide – flew to New York on 11 May 1968 to proclaim Apple to the New World. McCartney had already set the tone, declaring, 'Instead of trying to amass money for the sake of it, we're setting up a business concern at Apple – rather like a Western communism.' The Beatles' motives, he claimed, were purely altruistic: 'We've got all the money we need. I've got the house and the cars and all the things that money can buy.' No mention of the Beatles' tax burden was allowed to intrude on this idealistic scene.

In New York McCartney said that they wanted 'to see if we can't get artistic freedom within a business structure; to see if we can create things and sell them without charging three times our cost'. His comments betrayed a stunning naivety about the distribution network whereby art and artefacts reached the public, but also an almost Christ-like willingness to lay down his wealth and be as one with his audience. Lennon's message was more direct: he wanted to avoid the inevitability of creative people having 'to go on their knees in an office, begging for a break . . . You don't even get there, because you can't get through the door because of the colour of your shoes.' His perception of himself as a persecuted outsider would become entrenched over the years to come.

Taylor remembered the New York trip as 'a mad, bad week . . . frenetic with promises, explanations and small silver packages containing something called speed, which made me talk very quickly and which was probably methedrine'. McCartney liaised with a local photographer named Linda Eastman whom he had met in London the previous summer. The American media buzzed with Apple-related news: of the possibility that the Rolling Stones might join the company when their current contract expired; of the film soundtrack that George Harrison had recorded; of the enticing projects optioned by Apple Films; of the 72-track recording studio that Alexis Mardas would build in their newly acquired London HQ in Savile Row, at the heart of the city's tailoring district; of the 47 territories around the globe in which Apple had been trademarked. As a corporate ad boasted that week, 'A is for Apple: Beatles Film, Television, Electronics, Retail, Records, Publicity.' As an aside, Lennon trailed his intention to 'package peace in a new box'. Ending war, reshaping capitalism, rescuing artists, reinventing education: there were no limits to the Beatles' hubris and hope.

'Basically, it was chaos,' Harrison recalled of this era. 'We just gave away huge quantities of money. It was a lesson to anybody not to have a partnership, because when you're in a partnership with other people you can't do anything about it (or it's very difficult to), and at that point we were naive. Basically, I think John and Paul got carried away with the idea and blew millions, and Ringo and I just had to go along with it.' Harrison's estrangement from his older colleagues had been captured on celluloid a few months earlier when the Beatles filmed promotional clips for their single 'Hello Goodbye'. While Lennon and McCartney cavorted like ecstatic lovers, Harrison glowered through the entire shoot. Had he heard his comrades' extravagant rhetoric in New York, his sense of distance could only have increased.

Yet already McCartney was showing signs of being overwhelmed by the demands of the empire he had created. As Derek Taylor lamented, 'The weirdness was not controlled at the start. You can't control weirdness, anyway; weirdness is weirdness.' And weirdness was now seeping into McCartney's private life. He was notorious among Beatles aides as, in one's description, 'a cocksman', but that was simply a facet of his fame. What threatened his long-standing relationship with actress Jane Asher was her insistence on pursuing her own career, even if this entailed lengthy engagements in the United States. Having come close to ending their affair, McCartney overcompensated by asking Asher to marry him. Yet this show of commitment did nothing to quell his restlessness.

Lennon's problems were more existential, as his lifestyle was more extreme. In India meditation had freed his imagination. 'I wrote 600 songs about how I feel,' he noted. 'I felt like dying, crying and committing suicide, but I felt creative.' Restored to family life, however, he retreated into his familiar gloom. 'I spent years trying to destroy my ego,' he recalled the following year. Jet-lagged after the flight from New York, he medicated himself with anaesthetic doses of LSD and marijuana. Still afloat on some level of consciousness, he experienced an epiphany. 'I'm Jesus Christ; I'm back again,' he told his friend Pete Shotton. 'I've got to tell the world who I am.' He called an emergency meeting of senior Apple staff, invited McCartney to witness the second coming and made his revelation. There was a stunned silence, before Lennon's friends politely welcomed their messiah to the planet. 'I've never been frightened by insanity or eccentricity,' Derek Taylor recalled, and Lennon was certainly teetering between those two states.

Restored to a degree of normality after a night's sleep, Lennon shuffled morosely around his spacious home while Shotton attempted to distract him. Cynthia Lennon was out of the country, and her husband hoped that some novel female company might brighten his mood. Shotton no doubt expected his friend to order in some models or aspiring starlets, but instead Lennon announced, 'I'll call Yoko.'

Since his sponsorship of Yoko Ono's art exhibition, Lennon had maintained discreet communication with the artist and film-maker. He had been intrigued and entranced by intelligent, articulate, assertive women in the past – journalist Maureen Cleave, folk singer Joan Baez, actress Eleanor Bron – but he had never sought out those qualities in a lover, let alone a wife. 'The Beatles were, and probably still are, typical northern male chauvinists,' Cynthia Lennon reflected. 'The Beatle wives were supposed to be on constant call, but not to get in the way of their husbands.' An art student herself, she had briefly attempted to emulate her husband's passion for heightened creativity: 'I remember once that I painted a psychedelic design on the front of a cabinet at home, and then I came down the next morning to find that John had covered it over with posters. After that, I gave up.'

Ono would never have conceded so easily. 'She has a tendency to think of men as assistants,' Lennon joked shortly before his death. Both of her husbands – Japanese pianist Toshi Ichiyanagi and American artist Tony Cox – had begun as equal partners and then discovered that they were expected to support her creativity rather than their own. Despite separating in 1967, Cox and Ono continued to work together. On Boxing Day that year, as the British public prepared to sample *Magical Mystery Tour*, the couple were in the Belgian city of Knokke. A festival of experimental cinema was in progress, but the organisers refused to allow Ono's *Film No. 4* to be shown because it contained nudity. As a protest against this timidity, the French anarchist Jean-Jacques Lebel staged a satirical beauty contest to elect 'Miss Exprmnt'. The participants – Ono and Cox among them – danced naked in public, and were promptly arrested. Scotland Yard's International Division was enlisted to investigate Ono's activities in Britain. The artists were tried *in absentia* and sentenced to three months' imprisonment – though only if they were foolish enough to revisit Belgium.

For more than a year Ono had been concentrating her artistic efforts on Britain. 'The English people were very kind to me when I first arrived in London,' she recalled. 'I found the English so poetic and sensitive; I felt like, Oh, it's my kind of people. So I felt I didn't want to go back to New York. And the press was extremely kind to me – until one of their boys got together with me.'

Besides contributing to occasional celebrations of the Fluxus movement, Ono gave public performances of what she dubbed Music of the Mind, where she would appear on stage hidden in a large black sack (Bag Piece), allow audience members to snip away her clothing with scissors (Cut Piece) or invite them to leap from a stepladder (Fly). She staged concerts in universities and arts centres, offered 'a Perception Weekend with Yoko Ono' in Birmingham, and participated in the mostly conceptual Antiuniversity of London, offering a course entitled The Connection, which attempted 'to connect people to their own reality by means of brain sessions and ritual'. Occasionally, she reprised one of her early experiments in sonic collage, which she had formulated earlier in New York and Japan. Her instrument was her voice, which she used fearlessly as a means of communicating pain, pleasure and the unhindered expression of pure emotion. In February 1968 she appeared as a guest artist at a London concert by the free jazz pioneer Ornette Coleman, squawking and squealing while Coleman's band improvised in her wake.

Among the underground elite Ono was a celebrity. Her Fluxus comrades were suspicious of her uncanny knack of attracting publicity and undoubtedly jealous too, but nobody dared to question her ferocious commitment to her work or the energy she devoted to the cause of constant creativity.

Although some chroniclers have chosen to portray Ono as a monomaniac who relentlessly pursued Lennon for his wealth and fame, there is little evidence that she regarded him as anything other than that most valuable of assets for any experimental artist, a wealthy patron. She was nowhere near as innocent of his fame as she liked to suggest, but as she admitted later, 'I didn't find a lot of sympathy for, or interest in, rock music in the avant-garde scene that I was in. Quite the opposite, in fact. There was quite a pride in not becoming part of the rock scene, because it was too commercial. Fluxus was the furthermost experimental group of its time, and rock was just . . .' She waved her hand in a gesture of contempt.

Once established, the rapport between Ono and Lennon remained fluid and intense. She supplied him with a steady stream of schemes, manifestos and concepts that were dazzling in their simplicity and power, and Lennon responded in kind. As the Beatles were preparing their Indian expedition in February 1968, he allowed himself to envisage taking not only his wife, but also Ono, as an intellectual companion.

At Kenwood three months later Ono arrived in a taxi, Shotton paid the driver (Lennon, like the Queen, never carried cash) and the two artists muttered small talk until Shotton took the hint. At which point the Lennon/Ono mythology takes over, and we have only their word for the oft-told story that they retired to Lennon's home studio, recorded their first experimental music (subsequently released as the Apple album *Two Virgins*) and made love at dawn. 'It was beautiful,' Lennon always insisted. 'I was such a snob at the time,' Ono admitted decades later, 'and I thought [John's] contribution to *Two Virgins* tended towards not being abstract enough, the sounds that he made – it was more vaudeville, I thought.' Familiar with a milieu in which collaboration was commonplace, Ono failed to sense that anything unusual had occurred. Lennon felt like a prisoner reprieved from the gallows.

The next morning he told Shotton, 'This is *it*. This is what I've been waiting for all my life. Fuck everything. Fuck the Beatles. Fuck money. I'll go and live with her in a fucking tent if I have to.' Even allowing for poetic exaggeration, his liaison with Ono seems to have marked an epochal moment in his life. Aside from her erotic charms (and sexual imagery filled his songs for the next year, from 'Happiness Is a Warm Gun' to 'Come Together'), Ono liberated Lennon's creativity. 'She had a galvanising effect,' Shotton confirmed. 'She wasn't just the love of his life; she convinced him he was an artist, which he'd always wanted to be. You could even say that Yoko brought John back to life.' The effect was mutual.

Lennon had maintained a healthy scepticism towards experimental art, not least because it was McCartney's area of expertise. Though he never reached Harrison's level of cynicism – 'Avant-garde is short for haven't got a clue' – he harboured an innate distrust of any art that imposed a distance between its creator and its audience. He instinctively felt dishonest when masking his emotions behind word-play or surrealism (as on the deliberately obtuse 'I Am the Walrus'). What was remarkable about Ono was the accessibility and directness of her work. Her concepts were simple to grasp: you either accepted or rejected them. Moreover, Ono believed that creativity was a way of life, not a matter of waiting for inspiration. Under her influence, it was no longer enough to produce art: Lennon had to become an Artist, whose every act would betray his ethos and emotion.

First there was another betrayal to enact, as he allowed Cynthia to discover him and Ono in the kitchen at Kenwood. For a few days he avoided further confrontation by pretending that his marriage could be saved. Then, having encouraged Cynthia to leave the country for a recuperative holiday, he escorted Ono to the opening of a theatrical adaptation of his own books. 'Where's your wife?' reporters shouted at him. 'I don't know,' he replied, which wasn't strictly true, as he had paid for her to visit Italy, where she read reports of his public appearance with Ono and was then visited by Alexis Mardas, who told her that Lennon wanted a divorce on the grounds of *her* (non-existent) adultery. Lennon eventually relented, and admitted his own offence to speed the process of legal separation. It was not one of the most courageous episodes of his life.

Until now, no hint of the Beatles' exotic love life – the teenage conquests on tour, the casual infidelities – had appeared in the press. As Lennon noted in 1970, the media had a vested interest in letting the circus continue, as male journalists were often able to exploit the girls who had not made it as far as the Beatles' beds. The group's public image remained impeccable: Lennon and Starkey had married their teenage sweethearts (both of whom were pregnant at the time); Harrison had secured that talisman of the age, a blonde model; and McCartney was linked with one of Britain's most talented actresses. Ono's arrival punctured the illusion that the Beatles were eccentric but still dependably decent. Not only was Ono a married woman consorting with a married man, she was linked in the public imagination with nudity, she didn't match up to English conventions of beauty and, worst of all, she was Japanese at a time when that was virtually a synonym for the extreme cruelty inflicted on prisoners of war little more than twenty years earlier. Many British people who would have regarded themselves as tolerant made an exception for the Japanese, who were widely felt to be slitty-eyed, merciless and sadistic. 'I can understand how they felt,' Ono admitted in retrospect. 'It's just that I was totally naive about all that.'

When Cynthia Lennon saw Ono and Lennon in June, some of those stereotypes were inescapable. She remembered Ono 'beside him in the chair, shrouded by her hair, her face set in an expressionless mask', the epitome of the inscrutable oriental. Moreover, 'I barely recognised John. It had only been a few weeks since we last met, but he was thinner, almost gaunt . . . He was quite simply not the John I knew. It was as if he'd taken on a different persona.' Mrs Lennon asked the question that would soon be repeated around the world: 'What power does she have over him?'

Lennon would have welcomed the idea that he had taken on a different persona. He had thrown himself headlong into Ono's concept of art. They had staged a simple show, *Four Thoughts*, at the Arts Lab in London, and then clashed with the curators of Coventry Cathedral when they wished to contribute to an exhibition of sculpture within the cathedral precincts. As adulterers, they were forced to plant their symbolic acorns ('This is what happens when two clouds meet') outside consecrated ground. Lennon was using Ono's language in Ono's medium, his own ego submerged in hers. 'It brought out the child in him again,' Pete Shotton said of their relationship: both the child who sees the simple truth behind adult concealment, and the child who does as his parent asks. Ono was seven years older than Lennon, but age mattered less than character: for all her girlish inarticulacy in public, she had a core of steel and the courage of self-belief. Cynthia Lennon drew an obvious parallel: 'Aunt Mimi. John had grown up in the shadow of a domineering woman – it was what he knew and was most familiar with . . . Yoko offered the security of a mother figure who always knew best.' For Lennon, Aunt Mimi had represented security after the disappearance of his parents, but also rejection of the rebellious rock 'n' roller and satirical artist he became in his teens. Ono, by contrast, offered direction and approval; and Lennon reacted as if he had miraculously found his way home.

As the part-owner of his own (still dormant) record company, Lennon wanted to celebrate his love in public. He told EMI that he planned to launch Apple Records with an album of the tapes he had made with Ono. He was reminded that he had signed an exclusive recording deal with EMI. The album could appear under Ono's name alone, or under a pseudonym (Lennon suggested Doris and Peter). Still functioning mentally in the world of Fluxus rather than the Beatles, Ono said that she would prefer the record to appear in a signed limited edition for their friends. But she regretted that it would not find a wider audience 'because the message is going to be so beautiful that it could light up the world'.

The other Beatles had become used to Lennon's volatility, the abrupt changes of direction, the near-manic descent from exhilaration to despair, the competitiveness that could spill into open combat. 'They always had a very healthy rivalry,' recalls press officer Tony Barrow, 'but it turned vicious, more barbed. They always used to take potshots at each other, and at us. John vented his spleen with everyone, in and out of the group. They were like brothers: they had fierce fights, but they still loved each other. But in the late 1960s brotherly love went out of the window.'

Brotherly love in the widest sense was what sealed the partnership between Lennon and McCartney. Lennon might be the more aggressive and sarcastic of the pair, McCartney the more subtle, but as long as the partnership held, the Beatles could continue. Now, on 30 May 1968, the group reconvened at Abbey Road Studios to begin what proved to be a six-month process of chaos and creation. The result was a double album entitled *The Beatles* (alias the 'White Album'), which was their most diverse and, arguably, most rewarding work: a kaleidoscopic collage of reckless eclecticism which also operated as a history of 20th-century popular music, from vaudeville to the avant-garde. But the music, which sounded so zestful and anarchic, was the product of sessions so dispiriting that they sapped the Beatles of their collective identity.

Many factors combined to disturb the sessions. George Harrison was still convinced that Western music paled alongside the glory that was India. In addition, he resented being treated like an errant pupil by Paul McCartney. 'It was essential for me,' McCartney insisted. 'Looking back on it, I think, OK. Well, it was bossy, but it was also ballsy of me.' Yet his parental attitude, intended to benefit the music, left its scars. One observer reckoned, 'Ringo would rather have quit the band than go through Fat-Face McCartney's daily torture trip,' and Harrison only survived because 'he enjoyed teasing Paul'. In August Starkey left for two weeks, unwilling to face the pressure of constant sniping from McCartney and the heightened tension among his three closest friends. Recording engineer Geoff Emerick, who had worked with the Beatles for five years, also walked out ('the atmosphere was poisonous'), while producer George Martin – who had rarely missed a session until then – opted to take a prolonged holiday.

The tone was set at the first session, in May. Lennon arrived desperate to record 'Revolution', his commentary on the recent student protests in Paris. With him was Yoko Ono, silent and enigmatic. 'I remember being very freaked out,' Starkey recalled. 'The four of us had been through a lot together and we were very close, most of the time. We were very possessive of each other, in a way. Wives and girl-friends never came to the studio. *That* was when we were together. So Yoko came in. And that was fine when we all said hello to her, cos she was with John. But then she was sitting in the studio on his amp.' The amplifier assumed mammoth proportions in the other Beatles' minds. 'It was fairly off-putting,' McCartney said. 'You wanted to say, "Excuse me, love, can I turn the volume up?" We were always wondering how to say, "Could you get off my amp?" without interfering with their relationship.' The inference was that Ono was disturbing McCartney's intimacy with Lennon. 'It was our careers,' he insisted. 'We were the Beatles, after all, and here was this girl.'

'This girl', the one McCartney called 'love', began to assume that Lennon's entourage was also working for her. 'She was soon treating me like a servant to order about,' Shotton recollected. 'That's when it got hard. She rubbed lots of other people up the wrong way.' McCartney complained that Ono continually called the group 'Beatles' rather than 'The Beatles': 'We said, "*The* Beatles, actually, love".' It's tempting to imagine Lennon recognising McCartney's annoyance and goading Ono to say it again just for the pleasure of seeing anger flash across his colleague's face. Yet Ono picked up no hint of antagonism from McCartney. 'Paul has been very nice to me,' she confided to her tape recorder in May 1968. 'I feel like he's my younger brother or something. I'm sure that if he had been a woman or something, he would have been a great friend, because there's something definitely very strong between John and Paul.' That empathy would soon be put to the test.

'Suddenly we were together all the time,' Lennon said, 'sort of in a corner mumbling and giggling together, and doing *Two Virgins*, and there were Paul, George and Ringo saying, "What the hell are they doing? What's happened to him?" And my attention completely went off them. Now, it wasn't deliberate. It was just that I was so involved and intrigued with what we were doing. I understand how they felt.'

It suited Lennon's friends to blame Ono for the disruption. Harrison believed that 'she didn't really like us, because she saw the Beatles as something that was between her and John. The vibe I picked up was that she was a wedge that was trying to drive itself deeper and deeper between him and us, and it actually happened.' Shotton agreed: 'Unfortunately her possessiveness and jealousy or insecurity, call it what you will, meant that she couldn't bear to see John enjoying a close rapport with anyone but herself.' He witnessed her mutating 'from being a timid little mouse into a tiger, insisting on being with John at all times'. McCartney said, 'It was like we were her courtiers, and it was very embarrassing.'

Ono's account was very different. She recalled that Lennon was desperate to possess every moment of her day. 'If I go to the bathroom, he was upset that I closed the bathroom [door]. Is there anything

going on in there that he should not know?' She insisted that it was
Lennon's decision that she should come to the studio, not once but
every day from May 1968 until the final Beatles session 15 months later.
'I was just trying to sit there quietly without disturbing them,' she
says. 'John always wanted me there, and if I was not there, John might
not have gone to those sessions.' What frustrated her was that she
was not asked to participate in the sessions: 'I'm a composer. I want
to make my own music, and I'm just sitting there.' Lennon told a
record company executive that Ono ignored small talk: 'You must
understand that she communicates through the canvas. If you want
to talk with her, you have to take out a paintbrush and make a sketch.
If you knew her inner self, this would make sense to you.' The Beatles
could have tried to establish an artistic rapport with Ono, but this
strategy would have been fraught with difficulties. She recalled that
if she accidentally sat too close to one of the other Beatles, especially
McCartney, Lennon would immediately pull her aside and demand to
know what was going on. He was scared that the other Beatles might
seduce her away, while they simply wanted her to leave.

For anyone who regarded the continued creativity of the Beatles
as more important than the happiness and security of one of its
members, Ono's incursion into the recording process was a tragedy.
At a stroke it destroyed the delicate, battered but still viable working
relationship that had seen the Beatles through six years of unimaginable pressure and success. In the studio there was a hierarchy, with
Lennon at its peak. But each Beatle had an equal vote and could speak
his mind. Now there was an unspeaking fifth body in the room, her
face shadowed by her raven-black hair. Her silence and unwavering
expression of mild boredom rang like a damning verdict in the other
Beatles' ears. Her body language sang disapproval as her lips remained
tightly closed.* They could endure scathing ridicule from each other,
but this constant display of apathy was unbearable.

The most essential line of communication within the Beatles ran
between Lennon and McCartney, and now that was interrupted, in
both emotional and physical terms. McCartney felt judged, excluded,

---

* The scenario only altered when Ono mumbled quietly into the portable tape
recorder that she used as a diary. While the Beatles recorded, she confided her sense
of insecurity, and her erotic fantasies about Lennon, to her tape. One recording,
completed in private, ended with Ono masturbating to orgasm.

rejected. 'We could recognise [their love],' he admitted, 'but that didn't diminish the hurt we were feeling by being pushed aside.' His partnership with Lennon was non-sexual, but it ran deeper than anything he had experienced with a woman. It underpinned his self-belief and his status in the world. Seeing Lennon focus on Ono rather than him was as devastating as it would have been for Cynthia Lennon to witness the couple making love. Ono later dismissed the Beatles' attitude towards her as archetypally male: 'I didn't know about all this macho trip that they were on.'

McCartney's response was impulsive, almost childish. Within a week he had seduced an American woman named Francie Schwartz, who was working in the Apple office, and brought her into the studio to balance Yoko Ono's presence. This power play soured the working relationship between the group. 'We were trying to take photographs for *The Beatles Book* when they were recording "Revolution",' recalled the magazine's publisher, Sean O'Mahony, 'and the atmosphere was terrible. It was the only time when we were really made to feel uncomfortable, particularly by George, who looked very unhappy and obviously didn't want us to be there.' O'Mahony was surprised to see Schwartz and Ono with the Beatles. 'Wives and girlfriends weren't usually allowed in the studio. My first thought when I saw Yoko was that she must be a girl from a Japanese pop magazine. I didn't imagine for a second that she could be with John.'

McCartney may have hoped to shock Lennon into recognising that women weren't welcome in the workplace, or simply show his colleague that he wasn't the only Beatle with a new girlfriend. But his show of petulance was also an admission that his relationship with Jane Asher was dying. In mid-June 1968 he flew to Colorado, where Asher was working, and spent his 26th birthday in her company. Two days later he was in Los Angeles on Apple business, where he was joined by Linda Eastman. Back in London he renewed his liaison with Schwartz, making no effort to conceal her when Asher returned home. The actress discovered Schwartz in the bedroom she'd been sharing with McCartney, stormed off and requested her mother to remove all her belongings from the house. Then she used a television interview to announce that their engagement was over, and never spoke in public again about Paul McCartney. If their paths crossed in future, they would be civil, but any sense of intimacy had been destroyed forever.

'Paul was absolutely devastated,' Apple aide Alistair Taylor recalled. 'Jane's departure shattered him. It was the only time I ever saw him totally distraught and lost for words. He went completely off the rails.'

His misfortune was that he replaced Asher with Schwartz, an intelligent and literate woman who later penned an autobiography in which her relationship with McCartney provided the climax to a chronicle of sexual entanglements. She claimed that he demanded to know exactly where she was 24 hours a day; expected her to work full-time for Apple, cook, clean and score dope for him, and still be available on demand as a lover; and reserved the right to vanish without warning and sleep with other women. 'He was petulant,' she wrote, 'outrageous, adolescent, a little Medici prince, powdered and laid on a satin pillow at a very early age.' He became antagonistic towards the other Beatles and their songs, and after a session would often 'drink hideous Scotch–coke combinations, throw food at the dogs and cats, drop his clothes in a path from the door to the bed, and ignore me completely.'

The jilted Beatle hid this allegedly emotionally charged behaviour behind his customary facade of bonhomie. In his effort to distance himself from Lennon and Ono, he refused to participate in the recording of an experimental sound collage entitled 'Revolution 9'. Its assembly of effects tapes, 'found' sounds and random musical elements was an extension of the music that McCartney had been making at home for years and demonstrating to an envious Lennon. The avant-garde had been his London playground; now Lennon was claiming it as his own and choosing to collaborate with a genuinely alternative artist instead of McCartney. One can only assume that his only defence would be to deny his own past, to pretend that he had always found these experiments banal and pretentious, and to banish the avant-garde from his own repertoire for years to come.

In the midst of this turmoil McCartney invited Lennon and Ono to live with him and Schwartz in his home close to Abbey Road Studios while the Lennons' divorce was finalised. 'When John came over,' Schwartz recounted, 'all he could talk about was how much he loved Yoko. That disturbed Paul. In spite of John's obvious happiness, Paul stifled his jealousy with not-very-cute bursts of crap.' Schwartz remembered Lennon and Ono discovering an envelope on the mantel-piece one morning, addressed to them but not bearing a postmark.

Inside was a single typewritten sentence: 'You and your Jap tart think you're hot shit.' While they stood there in shock, McCartney entered the room and said, 'Oh, I just did that for a lark,' and smiled. As Schwartz recalled, 'That was the moment when John looked at Paul as if to say, "Do I *know* you?" It was over, it was completely and totally over at that moment. They may have been able to work together, but it was never the same.' Soon afterwards Lennon and Ono moved into a central London flat that was being rented by Starkey.

The venomous atmosphere inevitably affected the Apple office. Derek Taylor said, 'I don't think I ever hated anyone as much as I hated Paul in the summer of 1968.' He remembered McCartney gathering the staff together and saying, 'Don't forget, you're not very good, any of you. You know that, don't you?' Neil Aspinall was still struggling to make sense of the Beatles' legal commitments and maintain some form of control over Apple's daily operations. 'Neil would come to my room in Apple in the middle of the day and collapse on the sofa and sit staring and staring,' Taylor said. 'He tells me now it was fear.'

Essentially, Apple was a record company, with a global launch scheduled for late August. Although the Beatles were still contracted to EMI, they had been granted permission to use the Apple logo on their future releases, to maintain the fantasy of independence. The initial batch of singles was released on Aspinall's wedding day. 'There were only a few of us at Apple who knew anything about the record business,' Taylor admitted. 'The Beatles certainly didn't. When they were struggling, they just knew it as something that said no to them, and then when they were big, they knew it as a thing that didn't know *how* to say no to them.' Taylor hyped the first Apple records with typical elan: '[The Beatles] are confident and cheerful and the human condition will be thrilled by the coming results of their willing and enduring Beatle bondage. Unhampered by the pressures of world stardom, entranced by their opportunities, stimulated by the blossoming of Apple, they will give all of us new wonders to soothe our pain.'

As he wrote, Lennon and McCartney's estrangement was widening, Harrison preferred to lose himself in meditation rather than interact with his colleagues, and Starkey had chosen to abandon the group entirely for two weeks. But Apple's debut releases included the Beatles' best-selling record to date, 'Hey Jude', an anthemic McCartney song that glowed with optimism after a summer that had burned with anxiety and rage within the group and in the troubled world beyond. McCartney's production of a sentimental folksong, 'Those Were the Days', for teenage singer Mary Hopkin was equally successful, and when the Beatles' white-sleeved double LP was finally completed late in the year it surpassed the sales and receipts of any album in history. It didn't matter that, as Lennon complained a few weeks later, 'All of us were dissatisfied [with the album]. As a Beatles thing, as a whole, it doesn't work.' Taylor spun the yarn that the four Beatles were 'firmly united one for all and all for one as the Beatles . . . administering the Happy Apple complex of companies in London'. And the world wanted to believe him.

Chapter 2

Our main business is entertainment – communication. Apple
is mainly concerned with fun . . . We want to devote all our
energies to records, films, and our electronics adventures. We
had to zoom in on what we really enjoy, and we enjoy being
alive, and we enjoy being Beatles.
  Paul McCartney, July 1968

I can't talk . . . I daren't put my foot anywhere.
  Paul McCartney, January 1969

The summer of 1968 was a time of political ideals and wounded dreams.
In Czechoslovakia the rigid communist regime had been replaced by a
more liberal Marxist government which for the first time was prepared
to allow its citizens to sample the exotic tastes of freedom beyond the
Iron Curtain. In Chicago the American anti-war movement centred its
scattered energies on the Democratic Party's national convention, as if
protesting to the president would end the conflict in Vietnam. Then, in
late August, Russian tanks swept aside Czechoslovakia's 'communism
with a human face', and Chicago police clubbed demonstrators to the
ground outside the convention hall. Like the French union of strikers
and students that had briefly threatened to seize power in Paris that
spring, the crusades of East and West had ended in betrayal and despair.
  The Beatles' Apple organisation grew out of that same flowering

of hope and fantasy. 'If any of our dreams could come true,' Derek Taylor recalled, 'we would protect them as best we could.' 'There is no profit motive,' Paul McCartney's spokesman Barry Miles insisted that summer, 'as the Beatles' profits go first to the combined staff and then are given away to the needy.' Apple might be a corporation, he said, affiliated to the multinational EMI conglomerate, but it could still 'represent the workers seizing control of the means of production'. The Beatles' decision in July to close the Apple Boutique and give away its contents seemed to confirm the purity of their intentions. Yet the closure was a business move, not a political gesture, and suggested that the group were struggling to adapt to commercial reality. 'Everyone had their own autonomy,' Taylor said, 'and all of it cost money.'

Such qualms were overshadowed by the stunning debut of Apple Records. 'Hey Jude' and 'Those Were the Days' ensured that the company enjoyed instant success, but Apple's plans went far beyond mainstream pop. They were planning to launch a pioneering series of 'disposable records' – the aural equivalent of paperback books, which would offer readings or speeches by iconic figures of the age at a bargain price. There would even be albums of the Beatles in conversation, the company announced. McCartney and Harrison were prepared to spend half the year in California, to establish Apple as a truly transatlantic enterprise. As proof of the company's global reach, Apple even licensed a subsidiary operation in apartheid South Africa, where Mary Hopkin's hit was translated into Afrikaans by a local performer. Sensibly, this move wasn't publicised at home as Apple's political reputation would have been tarnished.

Far more damaging was the public reaction to Lennon's adultery with Ono. When the couple launched dozens of balloons into the sky as a gesture of peace, each carrying a postcard asking its finder to respond, they were shocked by the racist abuse that they received. But there was still enormous public goodwill towards the institution of the Beatles. Their cartoon animation *Yellow Submarine* may have been widely criticised, with one British newspaper referring disdainfully to a 'film flop' from this 'over-exposed quartet'. But the release of 'Hey Jude' suggested that the group had never been more committed to their music, and to each other. With its rousing chorus, McCartney's song encapsulated the widespread feeling among Western youth that political setbacks could never shake their solidarity.

Beyond their record sales, the Beatles' earning potential appeared to be limitless. 'Magic' Alexis Mardas had invented a telephone that would respond automatically to spoken commands. The American corporation AT&T tabled an offer of one million dollars for exclusive rights – which the Beatles rejected, instinctively feeling that Mardas's gadget was worth more. No further bids were forthcoming, and the telephone was never manufactured. There were even higher hopes for another Mardas scheme. In a strange precursor of the 'Home taping is killing music' campaign of the 1980s and the 21st century concern about illegal downloads, Lennon and McCartney feared that record sales would suffer if the newly devised cassette tape recorder went into mass circulation. Mardas developed an electronic signal that could be added to recorded sound to prevent it being copied. 'It seemed quite possible,' noted commentator Tony Palmer in 1969, 'that within a few years, every single record sold anywhere in the world would carry this device, and thus pay to the Beatles a royalty.' This invention would have generated more income than the group's music, but it was delayed while Mardas concentrated on the more immediate task of building the Beatles a recording studio. 'Nobody at Apple had any management skill,' Derek Taylor explained. 'We were all amateurs.' And not just amateurs, but under exotic influences. 'I remember going into Derek Taylor's office,' said publisher Sean O'Mahony, 'and the entire room was a haze of cannabis. It was ridiculous – you could hardly breathe. I asked Derek for some new photos of the Beatles, and he wandered around the room in a daze, and eventually gave me some – which turned out to be the same ones I'd given them. But that was what Apple was like.'

McCartney was the only member of the Beatles who took an active interest in Apple that summer. Aware that he was the part-owner of an organisation that wasn't organised, he felt compelled to intervene but was wary of assuming too much personal responsibility: 'I wanted Apple to run; I didn't want to run Apple.'

There was another problem: after his partial estrangement from Lennon, he had lost the self-confidence that had been his mainstay. He felt, he admitted later,

like I was in an *Alice in Wonderland* scenario. I would say, 'Now, what's to be done here? Ah, I know, cut spending.' That would start in my brain as a reasonable assumption but by the time it reached my mouth, it was like the devil was speaking. It was like a traitorous utterance. So I started to think my logic was suspect and that to try and make money was a suspect act. I really couldn't say anything without feeling I was being devious. And yet I knew I wasn't.

He decided, in one of the few sober assessments of that tumultuous summer, to seek help. The Beatles had rejected the idea of appointing a successor to Brian Epstein, but now McCartney discreetly approached senior business figures, none of whom had any sympathy for the counterculture. After consulting EMI boss Sir Joseph Lockwood and former Conservative Party chairman Lord Poole, he met Lord Beeching, infamous in Britain as the man charged with slashing the rail network into economic shape. Beeching offered to impose similar sanctions at Apple but advised McCartney to search for a full-time manager.

Little assistance was offered by McCartney's colleagues. 'I was getting fed up with the Beatles by that time,' Harrison remembered, 'let alone anything else around it.' Starkey had never wanted to be a businessman in the first place. Lennon, meanwhile, was pursuing his own agenda: art exhibitions, experimental films, all of them alongside Yoko Ono, not McCartney. The most notorious of his projects was the *Two Virgins* album. Its whimsical musical content was irrelevant; all attention focused on the cover artwork, which featured nude portraits of Lennon and Ono.

Every member of the Beatles' entourage remembered seeing these photos for the first time, and reacting with shock or hysterical laughter. Neil Aspinall snapped, 'I don't like it, and Paul doesn't like it, and none of the others are going to like it, and I don't care what the fuck [John] says, I don't want it coming out.' Derek Taylor was more tolerant: 'I was very broad-minded, and my attitude was, if that's what John and Yoko want, that's fine, this is a far-out building. But I knew that it would cause problems with certain sections of the press, and it did.' Not only the press; EMI refused to distribute the album, and its chairman advised Lennon to put someone prettier on the cover. He suggested McCartney, who according to Lennon 'gave me long lectures about [the cover], and said, "Is there really any need for this?" It took me five months to persuade them.' McCartney finally contributed an enigmatic sleeve note snipped at random from the pages of the *Daily Express*.

'All of us thought, why did he do it?' he remarked to Starkey the following year. 'It ended up that the answer was, why not?' For George Harrison, *Two Virgins* merely confirmed Lennon and Ono's arrogance. 'They got involved with each other and were obviously into each other to such a degree that they thought everything they said or did was of world importance, and so they made it into records and films.'

Two Virgins tipped the balance of public opinion so firmly against Lennon and Ono that they became easy targets.* After attending a 24-hour session for the Beatles' new album in October, the couple returned to Starkey's flat in Montague Square and were woken by the Metropolitan Police drugs squad. The officers and dogs found a small quantity of cannabis resin, which Lennon swore had been planted. The couple were arrested, and he pleaded guilty to possessing illegal drugs to save Ono – who was now pregnant – from deportation. Nobody at Apple realised that his conviction would threaten his ability to enter the United States. Soon after the bust, Ono was hospitalised, and on 21 November, 1968, she suffered a miscarriage.† In keeping with their open-ended philosophy of art, Lennon had taped the unborn baby's heartbeat. It was included on the couple's second album, *Life with the Lions*, which – as if to support Harrison's view – also featured photographs of their court appearance and Ono's hospital bed.

As the euphoria of their early months together evaporated, Lennon and Ono felt less like Edenic virgins than survivors of a medieval siege. Apple staff muttered racist comments about Ono just out of earshot;

---

* So was anyone who owned the album. US shops that stocked it were raided; thousands of copies were seized at Newark Airport; and an antique dealer in Doncaster was convicted of staging an indecent exhibition after he placed the cover in his shop window. Police were concerned by the fact that his shop was close to a primary school. In Canada an MP decried the importation of 'foreign-made pornographic material'.

† During her hospital stay, Lennon's divorce from Cynthia was finalised. She claimed to have phoned her husband to discuss the settlement. He told her, 'There's nothing to talk about. My final offer is £75,000. That's like winning the pools.' She eventually received £25,000 to purchase a house and £75,000 maintenance for herself and their son. A further £100,000 was placed in a trust fund, to be shared by Julian with any subsequent Lennon children. Cynthia Lennon remained bitter about the settlement, though her counsel acknowledged that Lennon had made 'generous and proper provision' for his wife and child, who were also allowed to keep 2 per cent of the shares in the music publishing company Northern Songs.

the press and public despised her; Lennon's fellow Beatles, with the exception of Starkey, barely attempted to engage with her. Lennon penned a satirical poem in which he complained about 'some of there beast friends' and wrote songs that reflected his depression: 'A Case of the Blues' and 'Everyone Had a Hard Year'. The pair even composed an epitaph for their lost baby: 'You had a very strong heartbeat, but that's gone now. Probably we'll forget about you.'

Within days of Ono's miscarriage, she and Lennon were using heroin. 'George says it was me who put John on heroin,' Ono said later, 'but that wasn't true – John wouldn't take anything he didn't want to take.' McCartney claimed that he had never seen Lennon on heroin, but that simply meant he didn't want to see. 'Unfortunately, he was drifting away from us at that point,' he conceded, 'so none of us actually knew. He never told us; we heard rumours, and we were very sad.' Even in the more innocent climate of 1968 heroin was considered decidedly more perilous than any substance the Beatles had sampled in the past. Lennon was entranced by the romantic image of the junkie/artist, and was in sufficient pain not to care how it was relieved. He would be battling against addiction for the next five years.

With Lennon distracted and Harrison uninterested, McCartney was left to maintain control. He had split from Francie Schwartz, who flew home with McCartney's parting words in her ears: 'Don't cry, I'm a cunt. I'm going out for a while, will you make dinner?' After completing work on the Beatles' double album, he contacted photographer Linda Eastman in New York and spent the final weeks of the year there. He left behind plans for the Beatles to make their first public appearance for more than two years. Even the reluctant Harrison was briefly enthusiastic: 'I'd like to be resident in a club, with the amps there all the time so you could just walk on stage and plug in.' Initially planned as a showcase for their new album, the concert was soon reshaped as the climax of a documentary film, to be made in January 1969, which would portray the Beatles creating and performing an entirely fresh set of material. With Lennon's approval, McCartney arranged for Twickenham Film Studios in London to be booked for the entire month, with sessions scheduled to begin every morning at ten o'clock. Just four weeks after the 30-track White Album was released, the Beatles – Lennon and McCartney, effectively – were now under pressure to compose another dozen songs.

The Beatles prepared in vastly different ways. Lennon snorted heroin, shot films and participated in a Rolling Stones TV special. Harrison experienced a more democratic form of music-making in the bucolic company of Bob Dylan's former backing musicians The Band, before staying with Dylan and his family in Woodstock. He was touched that Dylan, one of the few Western musicians he admired, did him the honour of helping him write a song – something that Lennon or McCartney had never been prepared to do.

Meanwhile, McCartney was living anonymously with Linda Eastman and her almost-six-year-old daughter Heather in Manhattan. He grew his first luxuriant beard and prowled through the city without attracting hysterical attention. He enjoyed acting like a father to Heather, having already astounded Lennon with his carefree ability to entertain his son Julian. Almost casually McCartney asked Eastman to marry him, but she refused, still wary after a short but unhappy marriage in the early 1960s.

What intrigued him was her ability to move in different worlds: she had been raised as the daughter of a successful lawyer and the heiress to a supermarket fortune, and had attended the same prestigious New York college as Yoko Ono; but despite her wealthy background she eased effortlessly through the rock scene, where a combination of looks and unscrubbed talent had gained her acceptance as a photographer. Like McCartney, she had experienced an active love life; but being a woman rather than a Beatle, she was maligned as a groupie, who pursued stars for sex rather than professional reasons.* Eastman knew who and what she was, and unlike McCartney she wasn't ashamed about it. What excited him most was her cool resistance to his stardom: it became obvious that she was more attracted by his rapport with her daughter than his membership of the Beatles.

Late in the year McCartney met Eastman's family: her father Lee, stepmother Monique, and brothers, the eldest of whom, John, worked alongside his father in the law firm of Eastman & Eastman. Lee's music business clients had included bandleader Tommy Dorsey and songwriter Harold Arlen. When Linda was three years old her father's friend Jack Lawrence had penned a song in her honour ('Linda', later

---

* As late as the mid-1970s *People* magazine referred to Eastman as 'the Park Avenue groupie'.

recorded by Frank Sinatra), which was a chart-topping hit for singer Buddy Clark in 1947. Beyond his dexterity with entertainment law, Eastman prided himself on being able to squeeze 'missing' royalties out of publishing and recording companies. For example, he had championed R & B composers Jerry Leiber and Mike Stoller in 1964, winning them a royalty payment of $18,000 (but in the process severing their ties to the company with whom they'd enjoyed most success). His relationship with his daughter had been strained since the late 1950s, when it became apparent that she didn't intend to marry for status and wealth. Her friend Robin Richmond recalled, 'She adored her father so much; she was in awe of his intelligence, his success, his confidence. But it was very hard for Linda, because he was cold to her, and disapproved of what she was doing, very obviously.'

Lee Eastman was both impressed and repelled by the idea of his daughter dating a pop superstar. Under the circumstances, it was only natural that McCartney would discuss the Beatles' affairs with his girl-friend's father and brother, who was just a year older than Lennon; and equally natural that they would suggest how they might stabilise Apple's assets. By the time McCartney returned to London – with Linda and Heather in tow – he had agreed that he would invite the Eastmans to disentangle the Beatles' jumbled affairs.

On New Year's Day 1969 George Harrison made his first appearance at Apple for several weeks. He was exuberant: his time with Dylan had fired his creativity, and he was enjoying the frisson of sharing his home with two beautiful women – his wife Pattie and the French model Charlotte Martin, who had just ended her relationship with his friend Eric Clapton. 'She was always flirtatious with George,' Pattie Boyd recalled, 'and he, of course, loved it.' At Apple he spent time with Derek Taylor, who suggested that the two of them should write a musical about life at the company. 'Often this office is like *Alice in Wonderland*,' Taylor commented a week later. 'Since Apple is constantly surrounded and involved in music, it seemed a natural subject to base a musical around. George has already written an outline and some of the music. I'm in charge of ideas and lyrics.'

A day later Harrison and the other Beatles were woken around eight o'clock and chauffeured to Twickenham Film Studios. The set was cavernous, frosty and lacking in atmosphere. 'I don't dig under-estimating what's here,' McCartney told his colleagues, suggesting that the scaffolding was more interesting than conventional scenery. But the other Beatles stared balefully around the hangar-like space and adopted an attitude of sullen resentment, which quickly enveloped the project.

For the next week the four Beatles acted out a drama with no movement or character development. McCartney played the boss, haplessly patronising towards his colleagues, desperately trying to prolong the agony in the hope that it might miraculously ease. Wary with Lennon, he focused his awkward encouragement on Harrison, who responded with the undisguised resentment of a persecuted child. Lennon sat virtually speechless and usually stoned, never more than a few feet from the equally uncommunicative Ono. Starkey stared ahead in an appearance of utter gloom, wondering why he was still trying to provide a rhythmic backbone for this divided body. McCartney chivvied the others through fragments of new songs. Lennon diverted them onto the safer ground of the rock 'n' roll standards that had comprised their repertoire a decade earlier. Harrison unveiled an array of freshly composed material, only to be met with polite boredom from McCartney and open derision from Lennon. Fragments of their conversations capture the full horror:

McCartney: I'm only trying to help you, and I always hear myself trying to annoy you.

Harrison: (*sarcastically*) You're not annoying me. You don't annoy me any more.

McCartney: We've only got twelve more days so we've got to do this methodically. I just hear myself saying it. I never get any support.

(*silence*)

McCartney: What do you think?

Lennon: About what?

Harrison: Hear no evil, speak no evil, see no evil.

Starkey: I'm not interested.

McCartney: I don't see why any of you, if you're not interested, get yourselves into this. What's it for? It can't be for the money. Why are you here? I'm here because I want to do a show, but I really don't feel an awful lot of support.

(*silence*)

McCartney: I feel terrible. (*to Lennon*) Imagine if you were the only one interested. (*silence*) You don't say anything.

Lennon: I've said what I've been thinking.

McCartney: There's only two choices. We're gonna do it, or we're not gonna do it. And I want a decision. Because I'm not interested in spending my fucking days farting about here, while everyone makes up their mind whether they want to do it or not. I'll do it. If everyone else wants to do it, great. But I don't have to be here.

(*silence*)

McCartney: We should just have it out. If this one turns out to be like [*the previous album*], it should definitely be the last – for all of us. There's no point hanging on.

Harrison: The Beatles have been in the doldrums for at least a year.

Harrison: Maybe we should get a divorce.

McCartney: Well, I said that at the last meeting. It's getting near it.

Relations had soured to the point that when McCartney sang 'Get Back' Lennon was convinced that he was aiming the chorus at Yoko Ono. After the Beatles attempted Lennon's song 'Across the Universe' McCartney complained, 'There's an oriental influence that shouldn't really be there' and pretended that he was talking about music.

For Harrison, there was no relief from the tension, as his wife had become convinced that he was having an affair with Charlotte Martin. Harrison denied it, but Pattie left to stay with friends. A couple of days later, on Friday 10 January 1969, after another morning of rejection from Lennon and bickering with McCartney, he cracked. He argued violently with Lennon over lunch – the two men supposedly came to blows – and then told him, 'I'm leaving the group.' 'When?' Lennon asked. 'Now,' Harrison replied. 'You can replace me. Put an ad in the *New Musical Express* and get a few people in.' He drove home to Henley, where Charlotte Martin was ejected and Pattie reinstated. But the bond between husband and wife had been broken. 'George would start to say something, then stop,' Pattie recalled. 'He appeared unable or unwilling to share his thoughts with me. He kept his hurt, frustration, anger, or whatever it was, to himself. At times I couldn't reach him.' He would often sit hunched over his prayer beads, muttering to himself, resolutely ignoring anything that was said to him.

Harrison's departure came as a shock to McCartney and Starkey, who debated whether they could continue without him. That afternoon they 'started jamming violently', Starkey remembered. 'And Yoko jumped in, of course, she was there.' While Ono unleashed a series of screams, McCartney rubbed his bass guitar suggestively along his amp, Lennon corralled feedback from his amplifier, and Starkey 'was playing some weird drumming that I hadn't done before'. Later, when a guitar solo was needed, Lennon called out, 'Take it, George,' to Harrison's empty chair. While the Beatles closed ranks to avoid reality, Apple boss Neil Aspinall talked to the film crew about 'the box George is in. A few months of that would be enough for me. But eight years . . .' Lennon wandered into the conversation. 'I think that if George doesn't come back by Monday or Tuesday, we'll have to get Eric Clapton to play with us,' he said. 'The point is: if George leaves, do we want to carry on the Beatles? I do. We should just get other members and carry on.' The suggestion was relayed to Starkey, whose friendship with Harrison was steadfast. But he wasn't prepared to argue. 'Do it,' he said dismissively.

'It was unbearable to me that they should break up,' Derek Taylor recalled. But that was the agenda when all four Beatles gathered at Starkey's home that Sunday. 'George said, "What we need is just the four of us,"' Neil Aspinall reported after the meeting, 'and I think John knew what he was talking about.' But Lennon professed ignorance, telling Harrison, 'I don't understand you.' 'I don't believe you,' Harrison retorted and left. 'George in the presence of all of us said that another reason for walking out was that he could not get on with Yoko,' McCartney explained in 1971. 'Yoko was doing all the talking,' Linda Eastman recalled. 'I'd just tell her to shut up,' Aspinall insisted, though he hadn't when the opportunity arose.

By the time Harrison left, the quartet had already agreed that they should split up but not when it should happen. Starkey and McCartney reported for work the following morning, and in Lennon's absence McCartney felt able to criticise the hold that Ono had established over him. Posterity would find it ironic, he noted, if the Beatles split up because Lennon insisted on bringing his girlfriend to the studio. Lennon and Ono arrived later, but a phone call to Henley established that

Harrison had driven to see his parents in Liverpool. So Lennon and McCartney agreed that if unity had not been restored by Friday, then the Beatles were finished. 'It's a festering wound,' Lennon admitted. 'It's only this year that [George] has realised who he is. And all the fucking shit we've done to him.'

The charade continued on Tuesday, though the tedium was broken by a visit from actor Peter Sellers. Lennon boasted to his comic hero about his heroin use. 'Showbiz people need a form of relaxation,' he said. 'It's that or exercise, and drugs win hands down.' 'Shooting [heroin] is exercise,' Ono added proudly. Then Lennon sat down with a Canadian TV crew and promptly vomited on the floor. 'John had escalated to heroin and all the accompanying paranoias,' McCartney recalled, 'and he was putting himself out on a limb. I think that as much as it excited and amused him, at the same time it secretly terrified him.'

Harrison was persuaded by Derek Taylor to meet the other Beatles at Apple on Wednesday. 'Brian Epstein, I knew, would have fought and fought to keep them together,' he explained, 'and so I was bolder than I had ever been or ever would be again, and demanded passionately and at length that George not let Paul carry the weight of keeping the film and the Beatles going. I felt that George's sense of decency could be touched, and it was.' Taylor's reward was a postcard in McCartney's handwriting, with the stamp carefully torn in half and the simple Northern injunction, 'Up yer.'

The Beatles agreed to abandon Twickenham and their live concert, and resume filming the following week at Apple. It was time for Alexis Mardas to unveil his recording studio, which, Harrison recalled, 'was the biggest disaster of all time. He was walking around with a white coat on like some sort of chemist, but didn't have a clue about what he was doing. It was a 16-track system and he had 16 little tiny speakers all around the walls. The whole thing was a disaster and had to be ripped out.' Every account of this episode – with one exception – is in agreement: Mardas installed the studio; George Martin's team of EMI engineers declared it unworkable. The dissenting voice belongs to Mardas. His memory was that he was in Greece during January 1969, and that someone from Apple or EMI broke into his Apple Electronics workshop and transported his work-in-progress to the Savile Row basement. It was never intended as a working studio, he insisted, but merely as a demonstration of how a multitrack studio might operate. And he claimed, moreover, that the EMI staff had a vested interest in belittling his work, as they were afraid of losing the opportunity to work with the Beatles in the future. Whatever the truth, portable recording equipment had to be ordered and installed.

By then another crisis had emerged. During a heroin-fuelled monologue Lennon had told journalist Ray Coleman that Apple was in deep financial trouble. 'We haven't got half the money people think we have,' he declared. 'We have enough to live on, but we can't let Apple go on like it is.' He admitted that he and McCartney had been foolish to promise artistic liberation before the company was running effectively, and he concluded, 'If it carries on like this, all of us will be broke in the next few months.' He was clearly not in PR mode. He also told Coleman about his obsession with pornography, and his desire to raise chickens on a macrobiotic farm. But his comments forced Neil Aspinall to issue a hasty rejoinder, to the effect that the Beatles were far from broke and were considering a face-saving merger with the Epsteins' NEMS company.

On January 22 the Beatles walked into the basement of their company HQ, gazed suspiciously at the film crew and prepared to rejoin the battle they'd interrupted twelve days earlier. But Harrison, who had least to gain from the reunion, had stacked his own hand in advance. He had invited the American keyboardist Billy Preston, whom the Beatles had befriended in 1962, to visit Apple that afternoon. It was only polite for Preston to be asked to play. 'I think Billy saved the *Let It Be* album and film,' Derek Taylor commented, 'because he put all the Beatles on their best behaviour. To be difficult with each other after that would have been to abuse their guest. That Liverpool slagging-off would not have been OK in front of Billy. His enjoyment at being there filtered through into the Beatles. I remember thinking, Thank Christ that someone has done something, because the atmosphere at the time was so bad.' Within a few days Lennon was proposing that Preston become a permanent member of the band. 'It's bad enough with four [Beatles],' McCartney joked. 'But with five, it's creating havoc.' Still, Preston remained an honorary Beatle until the end of the month. He was there on 30 January 1969, when the group solved the riddle of how to end their documentary film by performing on top of the Apple headquarters. 'You had a sense of a rare and odd occasion,' recalled film director Michael Lindsay-Hogg. 'You were at a Beatles concert with nobody up there except yourself. And probably because they didn't have the burden of an audience, they really did play for each other.' With Ono sidelined, sheltering by a chimney rather than interposed between Lennon and McCartney, the pair's instinctive rapport was restored, if only for 40 minutes. Then the police intervened to stop the noise, as everyone had secretly been hoping. 'The Beatles,' Lindsay-Hogg reckoned, 'kind of wanted to go to jail. You know, "Police bust the Beatles", that sort of thing. They were very contentious.' A day later the group returned to the Apple basement to tape finished versions of several McCartney songs. 'The next day there wasn't much talk about [the live show],' Lindsay-Hogg recalled, 'other than it had been fun, there was newspaper coverage, and it was better down in the studio because it wasn't as cold as it was on the roof.' The Beatles were no longer impressed by their own mythology. As Derek Taylor noted, 'It was not insignificant that they chose a rooftop, their own private rooftop, out of reach and for the most part out of view, to do their last show together.'

There was little jubilation when the documentary project ended; merely relief that the cameras were going to leave the Beatles in peace. Engineer Glyn Johns was commissioned to sift through the countless hours of tapes, most of them desultory and discordant, and translate them into an album. But all his attempts were rejected, and while editors slowly reviewed the accompanying film footage the Beatles did their best to forget that January 1969 had ever happened. Certainly George Harrison backed down from his commitment to leave the group, perhaps because Preston remained on call for the next few weeks. With no clear intention in mind, the Beatles found themselves back in the studio within days, as if drawn by some Pavlovian reflex. And if they were making music, no matter how lacklustre, they could avoid dealing with the latest incursion into their increasingly dented sanctum. The Beatles had barely survived the arrival of Yoko Ono; now, like shop workers arriving one morning to find an unfamiliar logo over the door, they seemed to be under new management.

> Klein is essential in the pantomime as the Demon King. Just as you think everything is going to be all right, here he is.
> Derek Taylor

There were countless assistants and collaborators in the Beatles' story, and the affection that surrounded the group encompassed almost all of them. Each has his or her role in the saga: Brian Epstein, their naive but loyal guide; Neil Aspinall, their eternally faithful servant; George Martin, their kindly musical chaperon; Derek Taylor, purveyor of dry wit and wisdom; wives, girlfriends, roadies, photographers, sidemen, school friends; each loved by those who loved the Beatles, for enabling them to flourish and their story to become the fairy tale of the age, endlessly repeatable and open to infinite interpretation.

And then there were the intruders: more controversial figures whose names can still provoke a sharp intake of breath from true adherents of the Beatles cult. Suspected for their motives, hated for their disruptive power, they all arrived from America and were all regarded as suspects for the crime of breaking up the Beatles, on the assumption that without them the group would have continued happily in each other's company until their dying days. The first of these intruders was Yoko Ono; the second was Linda Eastman; and the third was Allen Klein.*

With the possible exception of Alexis Mardas, who occupied a less central role, nobody in the Beatles' milieu has received a more damning verdict from historians than Allen Klein. He was, one said, 'a tough little scorpion'; for another, 'fast-talking, dirty-mouthed . . . sloppily dressed and grossly overweight'; again, 'short and fat, beady-eyed and greasily pompadoured'. Beatles aide Alistair Taylor said, 'He had all the charm of a broken lavatory seat.' Yet he inspired awe. In Eric Idle's satirical recasting of the myth he became (as impersonated by John Belushi) Ron Decline, so terrifying that his employees would hurl themselves out of skyscraper windows to avoid meeting him. So consistent was the vilification that when biographer Philip Norman merely described Klein as 'a little tubby man', it sounded like a compliment.

Ono's sin was to be Japanese and to marry a Beatle; then, as it became apparent that she had dared to infiltrate the recording studio, she was maligned for interfering in their music and destroying their

---

* One of the ironies of this reading of Beatles history is that three months after he invited Klein into the drama Lennon was still quite confident that the group would last forever. 'Wait and see,' he said in April 1969. 'We'll be around, we'll be together when we're 60. But we won't be following each other around like sheepdogs.'

rapport. There was much sympathy in the late 1960s for the idea that she had turned Lennon 'weird'. Later, she was hated for her music, and for forcing that music upon Lennon's audience. Only after his death was she allowed to assume a milder role, as the grieving widow. Likewise, those who were appalled by McCartney's decision to marry Linda Eastman and then shocked to see wife on stage with husband, were mollified when Linda McCartney proved a caring mother, champion of animal rights and best-selling author of cookery books.

No such rehabilitation was available for Allen Klein, who entered the Beatles' story as a villain from central casting, and never escaped that role. Yet we are asked to believe that three of the four Beatles found this 'beady-eyed' 'grossly overweight' 'scorpion' such an attractive figure that they were prepared to trust him with their futures. Clearly the Demon King didn't always exude the stench of sulphur.

'Allen Klein could be the most charming and interesting person you'd ever met,' said Allan Steckler, who worked for him throughout this period. 'He knew more about music than most – he *loved* music. And he would have been the most brilliant psychologist of all time, because in ten or fifteen minutes he could get you to do anything he wanted. But he could be crude, rude and very uncaring. That's a strange mixture of qualities, but it was what made him a brilliant businessman.'

'I brought him to Apple,' Derek Taylor admitted, 'but I did give the Beatles certain solemn warnings. I told them to ask around, and said that he had various reputations, that he might get them a good financial deal, but might not be someone you would want to take home to your mother.' Klein's 'reputations' included an undeniable ability to squeeze cash out of record companies; like Lee Eastman, he excelled at locating royalty underpayments and other 'accidental' errors. It was a skill he had honed in the late 1950s, when he had persuaded Morris Levy, an entrepreneur with Mob connections, to pay singers Buddy Knox and Jimmy Bowen some belated royalties. His secret was meticulous examination of company accounts and an accountant's eye for loopholes. But his ability to conjure sizeable cheques out of entertainment corporations enabled him to appear as magical as Alexis Mardas to his famous clients (Bobby Darin and Sam Cooke among them), and with more justification.

Belying his subsequent image, Klein became a financial mentor to Cooke, treating him more like a brother than a client. Not that he overlooked opportunity: in March 1964 he agreed to represent the New York office of RCA Records in an audacious bid to steal the Beatles' recording contract from EMI. He offered Brian Epstein $2 million as a signing fee, plus a 10 per cent royalty, which would then have been the most lucrative deal in history. But for Epstein loyalty counted more than money. Klein approached Epstein again in 1966, when he heard that the EMI contract was being renewed, but this time he was refused a meeting. A year later Epstein was dead. 'I was driving a bridge out of New York and I heard on the radio that Epstein had died,' Klein admitted later, 'and I said to myself, "I got 'em!"'

Other elements of the British pop scene were more malleable. Between 1964 and 1967 Klein collected a financial interest in many of the era's most successful acts, among them the Rolling Stones, the Kinks, the Animals, Herman's Hermits, the Dave Clark Five and Donovan. He let their managers – the likes of Rolling Stones mentor Andrew Oldham – have the fame, and raked in his percentage as business manager. He was so diligent that he ended up owning many of the catalogues he represented. Among those who lost out was Oldham, who nonetheless retained fond memories of his ex-partner: 'He was in his early thirties, casually dressed in sports shirt and slacks, and I liked him. He was not greasy; he did not have three chins. He did not swear like a trooper or a gangster. He spoke calmly, invitingly and warmly and had eyes that pierced through you.' According to Klein, it was Oldham who embellished his image: 'Andrew liked having me portrayed as this shadowy American who could take care of anything. That was Andrew; he just created it, that I was like a gangster. He said they'd love it in England.'

The fact remains that, in Oldham's words, 'He started out representing us and ended up owning us.' Klein founded a US company with the same name as the Rolling Stones' UK publishing firm. Oldham and the Stones innocently assumed that when the US firm took over the rights to the Stones' catalogue in America, the band would end up in control. Instead, Nanker Phelge's US operation rested solely in the hands of Klein. When Oldham and the Stones fell out in 1967, Oldham had to sign over the UK Stones catalogue to Klein in order to finance his court battle. As Apple staffer Ken Mansfield recalled, 'Klein was virtually unbeatable in negotiations. His business dictionary had only one word in it: win! A picture of Klein's smiling face followed as the definition.'

Klein was still operating as the Rolling Stones' business manager in January 1969, when he read Lennon's admission that Apple was collapsing. He tried in vain to reach Lennon from New York, and then asked Tony Calder, Oldham's business partner in London, to intervene. Calder persuaded Derek Taylor to speak to Lennon. On 27 January, after another inconclusive day in the studio, Lennon and Ono met the American in the Harlequin Suite of the Dorchester Hotel on Park Lane. The following day Lennon wrote to EMI boss Sir Joseph Lockwood: 'I've asked Allen Klein to look after my things. Please give him any information he wants and full co-operation.' Five years after his first attempt to carve himself a slice of the Beatles, Klein had secured a quarter of the group in a single evening.

'Everyone knew that Klein wasn't a pleasant guy,' contended Apple aide Tony Bramwell. 'Don't get me wrong. I liked Klein, and I still do. But John had this attitude of dumb blindness as far as Klein was concerned.' Ignorant about business, and not interested in adding to his knowledge, Lennon relied solely on instinct. Klein, he decided, was a charming bruiser, a tough but vulnerable bear who had lost his mother young, like Lennon, and been raised in an orphanage. Lennon instantly warmed to Klein's earthy humour, his obvious passion for music, his gratifying awareness of Lennon's own work, all qualities that marked him out from other businessmen. Ono too was flattered that Klein appeared to treat her seriously as an artist, and not just as an inconvenient adjunct to a Beatle. Klein told Lennon stories about the music business and Hollywood (he'd produced three Westerns, and a musical starring Herman's Hermits), and gossip about the Stones. Wary of meeting an accountant, Lennon was won over by Klein's humanity. Reputation counted for nothing: Lennon felt that Klein understood him, and that was enough. In any case, as Klein recalled, 'Yoko said that when she and John came to me, they were looking for a real shark – someone to keep the other sharks away.'

Lennon arrived at Apple the following day and told his colleagues that they had to meet this guy – he was great; he could solve all their problems. But there was an immediate complication. Clive Epstein had recently told the group that he wanted to sell his brother's company NEMS, in which the Beatles held a 10 per cent stake. McCartney had asked the Eastmans for advice, and they recommended that the Beatles buy NEMS outright, thereby ending the company's claim to commission on their record sales. To finance the deal, the Beatles should borrow the money from EMI. The Eastmans believed that they were acting on behalf of all four Beatles, but now they had to secure Klein's approval as well.

On the night of 28 January, Klein came to Apple, where he held a lengthy meeting with the entire group – so lengthy, in fact, that McCartney cried off shortly before midnight, complaining that there was more to life than business. The others remained, and by 2 a.m. both Harrison and Starkey had agreed to let Klein represent them too. He advised them not to proceed with the NEMS purchase, pointing out that to repay EMI's £1 million loan, they would have to earn many times that figure for the company. McCartney had already insisted that he was not prepared to discuss the problem unless John Eastman was present, and so a further meeting was scheduled after the Beatles' filming was completed.

'We met with Allen Klein,' Starkey recalled, 'and were convinced by him. Well, I was convinced by him, and John too. My impression of him when I first met him was brash – "I'll get it done, lads." Lots of enthusiasm. A good guy, with a pleasant attitude about himself in a really gross New York way.' Harrison concurred. 'I thought, Well, if that's the choice, I think I'll go with Klein, because John's with him, and he seemed to talk pretty straight.' And, like Lennon, Harrison could be swayed by social status: 'Because we were all from Liverpool we favoured people who were street people. Lee Eastman was more like a class-conscious type of person.' By 'class-conscious', Harrison meant precisely the social niceties that had always impressed McCartney (but never Lennon). 'Eastman wasn't a polo-neck and chinos kind of guy, like Allen,' said Tony Bramwell. 'The Eastmans were always in suits.'

Unlike Harrison and Starkey, McCartney was no longer prepared to follow Lennon's leadership without challenge. Mick Jagger, he decided, would tell them the truth, but when the Rolling Stones vocalist came to Apple, he was uninformative, saying only, 'He's all right if you like that kind of thing'.* Klein's presence at the meeting presumably encouraged Jagger to guard his tongue. Lee Eastman, who could glimpse his potential stake in the Beatles ebbing away, was more forthright. Klein, he said, could not be trusted. The financial regulators of Wall Street had been investigating the operation of Cameo-Parkway, the company that Klein now ran. Eastman was convinced that Klein had been guilty of insider trading, though he had been cleared of any wrongdoing. Within a matter of days, Klein renamed Cameo-Parkway ABKCO – ABK denoting Allen and Betty Klein. Moreover, Eastman informed McCartney that Klein was being investigated on charges of failing to file tax returns; the implication was that Klein had been caught evading tax.† John Eastman agreed to fly immediately from New York to present the facts to the other Beatles.

'Apart from the fact that John Eastman [became] my brother-in-law, I trusted him,' McCartney recounted. 'I distrusted Klein.' It was against this background that the Beatles played their rooftop concert. 'This was the first time in the history of the Beatles that a possible irreconcilable difference had appeared between us,' McCartney said in legal testimony two years later. 'I was most anxious not to stand out against the wishes of the other three except on proper grounds. I therefore thought it right to take part in discussions concerning the possible appointment of Klein, though I did not in the least want him as my manager.'

The day after the Beatles had recorded McCartney's conciliatory ballad 'Let It Be', the group returned to Apple to discuss their future with Allen Klein and John Eastman. Lennon immediately took offence because Lee Eastman had sent his son rather than attending the meeting himself; of course, if the senior Eastman had appeared, Lennon would have accused him of being old and out of touch. Lennon noted later, 'John Eastman gave me the impression of being an inexperienced and somewhat excitable and easily confused young man.' Klein had spent the intervening days on his favourite turf, scouring the small print of the Beatles' accounts. The ostensible agenda

---

* Jagger's girlfriend at the time, Marianne Faithfull, insisted that Jagger wanted Klein to take over the Beatles, in the hope that he might then lose interest in the Stones.
† 'No allegation was made of failure to pay any tax,' Klein explained in 1971, claiming that the problem related to paperwork that had inadvertently not been filed by 'a member of my staff' between 1959 and 1962.

for the 1 February meeting was the possible purchase of NEMS, but that was merely the ground on which Lennon and McCartney had chosen to exhibit their show ponies. Eastman opened the contest by setting out the case for the Beatles owning NEMS, as they would thereby regain a crucial stake in Lennon/McCartney's publishing firm Northern Songs. Aside from the 2 per cent of shares that Lennon had given to his son and first wife, he and McCartney held equal quantities of Northern Songs shares – or so he thought. In fact, the Eastmans had been encouraging McCartney to buy shares held by outside parties, to boost his negotiating power.

Klein responded by advising caution: he had been asked by three of the group to look into the Beatles' financial affairs, he said, and his work was not yet complete. 'It was agreed by all four Beatles that I should be the person to look into the financial position of those companies,' he recalled. But Eastman wasn't about to leave his supremacy unchallenged. In Klein's words, he 'launched an attack on my personal integrity' and 'alleged I had a bad reputation in general'. It was a grave tactical error. Eastman hoped he might loosen Klein's grip on Lennon by showing him cuttings about the unusual trading in Cameo-Parkway shares, but his assault merely solidified Lennon's sympathy for his victimised champion. Eastman may have expected Klein to launch a volley of New York street rhetoric, but Klein calmly defused the row, and the meeting was adjourned for two days. When it resumed, both sides had a trophy to display: Apple announced that it had asked Allen Klein – 'a New York business expert' in the words of *The Times* – to 'look into all their affairs, and he has agreed to do so'. Klein promised to produce a full statement of the Beatles' financial situation. That night he persuaded Clive Epstein to delay the sale of NEMS for three weeks, and then booked a flight to New York, so he could investigate the group's US income. Meanwhile, the Eastmans were appointed Apple's legal advisers. Music business analysts took their appointment as proof of 'a stepped-up campaign to maximise the act's business potential on a world level. Eastman's office will act as a clearing-house for all deals involving the Beatles and their activities in recording, writing, filming and other matters.'

To an outside eye it appeared as if the Beatles had solved their financial crisis. The Eastmans promised to bring security to the group's affairs, with a conservative integrity reminiscent of the Epstein era.

The more mercurial Klein, meanwhile, would terrify the Beatles' commercial partners, especially EMI and its US arm Capitol Records, into producing any unaccountably delayed royalties. Meanwhile, the Beatles could continue their 'recording, writing, filming and other matters', convinced that they would no longer be exposing themselves to ruin.

This settlement depended on several assumptions, however: that Klein and the Eastmans could work in harmony; that neither had any aspirations towards assuming total control of the Beatles' management; and, most important, that the Beatles could still function as a creative unit. All three were soon in doubt.

The arrangement between Klein and the Eastmans depended on mutual communication and co-operation, and both principles swiftly collapsed. 'We co-operated with Klein for about two weeks,' John Eastman said. 'It was agreed that both of us would see all the Beatles' documents, but Klein took out all the important stuff and sent along a huge bundle of documents containing nothing of importance.' Klein was unapologetic: 'I ripped off those documents, damn right! But Eastman and McCartney had already gone behind our backs buying Northern Songs shares.'

A more immediate problem was NEMS. On 14 February, Lee Eastman wrote to Clive Epstein to suggest a meeting at which they could discuss not only the state of Beatles affairs, but also 'the propriety of the negotiations' that Brian Epstein had conducted with EMI on the group's behalf in 1966. 'Propriety'? As far as Clive Epstein was concerned, the language was incendiary: this American was calling his late brother a crook. He demanded an explanation and then authorised the sale of his mother's stake in NEMS – 70 per cent of the company's shares – to a merchant banker, Leonard Richenberg of Triumph Investment Trust. A quarter of the Beatles' earnings from EMI would now effectively be controlled by financiers with no personal interest in the group. Hastily recalled from New York by a panicked phone call from Neil Aspinall, Klein was quietly elated: in his eyes Eastman had just damaged his credibility. There was a conference at the Dorchester Hotel, and the group signed a memo to EMI demanding that all their future royalties – including the 25 per cent intended for NEMS – now be sent to the Beatles' own merchant bankers. Confused about exactly where the money should go, EMI decided to retain it and wait for a clinching legal opinion. The new alliance of Eastman and Klein was already in disarray.

Klein returned to New York on 12 March 1969. As his flight left Heathrow, crowds of crying teenagers gathered at Marylebone Register Office in central London, where Linda Eastman had finally agreed to become Paul McCartney's wife. Now it was McCartney's turn to worry: was it still possible to separate his personal life from his business problems? The Eastmans had been eager to see the wedding proceed, but was that because it suited their professional purposes? On the eve of the marriage the couple quarrelled, and the event was nearly cancelled. Beatles aide Mal Evans recalled, 'He was saying to me, "Look, I'm scared stiff of getting married. Do you think I should?"' But the McCartney marriage proved to be a remarkable success story.

One of Evans's colleagues had misgivings about the match. To Alistair Taylor, Linda was 'a hard-faced star-chaser from the United States' who had 'set out to get Paul' and who was determined to divide her husband from 'anyone who had been close to Paul, especially during his relationship with Jane'. But despite the catcalls of disappointed fans that greeted the newly married couple, Linda's position was hardly enviable. She was acutely aware that her husband's future and her family's business reputation were now mutually dependent. 'You can't know how hard it was,' she told her friend Danny Fields. 'I was suddenly in the middle of a situation where the Beatles were breaking up; Paul was really upset; there was a whole business and legal thing happening which took everyone's energy; and I hated it. I thought it was going to be all peace and love and music, and it was wartime. Plus, everyone hated me, those horrible groupies always in front of the house, calling me names, spitting at me.'

None of the other Beatles attended the ceremony: Lennon and Ono were at Abbey Road Studios, Starkey was filming with Peter Sellers and Harrison remained at Apple, where his wife phoned to report that they were being raided by the drugs squad. 'Tell them where it is,' Harrison said, and a minimal amount of marijuana was shown to the police. Two of the Beatles had now been targeted by the same officers; could further visits be ruled out? The landlords of Starkey's London flat, where Lennon had been staying, took the hint, instituting proceedings to have Lennon and Ono banned from entering the premises.

Within days of McCartney's wedding, Lennon and Ono flew out of the country in search of a venue for their own marriage. They couldn't wed in Britain without negotiating with immigration officials about Ono's status, and as usual Lennon wanted to act immediately. France was their first choice, and the couple spent 'four days shopping, eating and doing things. Just being in love, in the spring in Paris, it was beautiful.' But legal barriers remained until Apple executive Peter Brown discovered that the British colony of Gibraltar would permit them to marry without any legal delays. In those unlikely surroundings, on 20 March 1969, Lennon and Ono became man and wife. 'I broke down, and John nearly did too,' Ono said. 'Marriage is so old-fashioned, it's like dressing up in old clothes.' In fact, both bride and groom were dressed in virginal white, though her minidress and his unkempt beard and plimsolls weren't orthodox. Neither was the couple's vision of the ceremony as an art event. 'We are going to stage many happenings and events together,' Ono declared, 'and this marriage was one of them.' Lennon added, 'Everything we do we shall be doing together. I don't mean I shall break up the Beatles or anything, but we want to share everything.' The full implications soon became clear, when the couple devoted their honeymoon to a 'bed-in' for peace in front of the world's press. For the remainder of the year, global peace dominated the Lennons' lives. With almost obsessive fervour, they gave literally hundreds of interviews, each devoted to the same well-intentioned but simplistic message.

The Lennons' crusade distracted attention from the Beatles' future and cemented the public perception of the couple as two people with one identity. Yet even in bed the past tugged remorselessly at their pyjama sleeves. One reporter wondered what Lennon made of Starkey's recent comments that he had no intention of performing in public with the Beatles again. 'I don't miss being a Beatle any more,' the drummer admitted. 'You can't get those days back. It's no good living in the past.' From Lennon or McCartney, his statement would have been front-page news. Instead, it was trumped by Lennon's conviction that the group 'will give several public shows this year'. As Derek Taylor told the press, 'It would be indelicate for us to comment whilst John and Ringo are so obviously in disagreement.' But promoter Sid Bernstein, who had staged the first US shows by the group in 1964, felt this an appropriate moment to offer them $4 million for four North

American shows. George Harrison offered a typically convoluted verdict on the Beatles' current status: 'We've got to a point where we can see each other quite clearly. And by allowing each other to be each other, we can become the Beatles again.'

Four was no longer their magic number, however. In 1968 the problem had been creative: how to function as four Beatles plus one avant-garde artist. Now their financial crisis dominated all thoughts of art, and the Beatles had to balance the two factions vying to control them.

Meanwhile, a new legal front had opened. While Klein and Eastman were distracted by the situation with NEMS, chaos was advancing from another direction. On 28 March, Dick James, managing director of Lennon/McCartney's publishing firm Northern Songs, agreed to sell his shareholding and that of his fellow director Emmanuel Silver to ATV, the entertainment conglomerate run by Sir Lew Grade. Sir Lew, a character in the great British storybook noted for the length of his cigars and the brevity of his wit, was one of three brothers who dominated show business in the 1960s. The Beatles had no time for them: they were the old-school impresarios who had first scorned Brian Epstein, and then embraced him as soon as the group became successful. For both symbolic and financial reasons, they were adamant that Grade should not win control of their songwriting catalogue. But with James's portion Grade now held around 35 per cent of the shares; the Beatles and their associates could only muster 30 per cent. The race was on to achieve a majority shareholding, and control of the company.

'They are my shares and my songs and I want to keep a bit of the end product,' Lennon declared from his Amsterdam bedroom. 'I don't have to ring Paul. I know damn well he feels the same as I do.' Both Lennon and McCartney phoned Klein at the Puerto Rican hotel where he was enjoying a brief holiday, and asked him to come to London and save their publishing copyrights.

For the next few months these two legal battles dominated the Beatles' landscape. Even with a completely united team – musicians and businessmen alike – it was unlikely that they could outbid Triumph Investments and gain control of NEMS, while the balance of power in the Northern Songs dispute was delicately weighted. But rather than cementing their relationships, these legal complexities drove the Beatles and their defenders further apart.

Underlying both issues was a stark reality: the four musicians were running short of cash. 'I had many meetings with the Beatles,' Klein testified in 1971, 'and I made it clear to them that their financial position was perilous. I took the view that my first task was to help them generate enough income to alleviate this situation.' He decided that their recording deal was still the most stable, and potentially most lucrative, aspect of their empire. 'I wanted to negotiate a new recording arrangement with EMI,' he declared, aware that the group had already fulfilled their part of the 1967 deal. 'Discussions were held with the Beatles and John Eastman as to how EMI should be approached and who should go to a meeting with them.' Though Eastman insisted that legal matters were his affair, all four Beatles agreed to let Klein represent them – thereby causing McCartney some embarrassment with his in-laws.

The focus then shifted to the battle for Northern Songs. Lennon and McCartney confronted Dick James at McCartney's house on 2 April, as the publisher tried to explain why he had broken his word and sold his shares without warning them first. 'He wrapped it up in silver paper,' Lennon said afterwards. 'But it doesn't matter how you wrap it up, it's still a bomb.' To counter Grade's bid for control, the Beatles attempted to raise nearly £2 million to buy the 14 per cent of the company held by an independent group known as the Consortium; if this was added to the Beatles' existing shares, victory would be almost certain. These negotiations endured for months, and at various times both the Beatles and Grade claimed victory, only for an embarrassing retraction to be issued the following day. Two key questions remained. Could the Beatles muster the business acumen to run Northern Songs successfully, given the confused state of Apple's finances? And could Allen Klein be trusted?

Consortium members who saw the *Sunday Times* on 13 April 1969 might have felt that they knew the answers. The paper's celebrated 'Insight' team of investigative reporters had prepared a damning portrait of 'The Toughest Wheeler Dealer in the Pop Jungle'. As Derek Taylor recalled, the article said Klein 'was a liar, a self-publicist, said he was involved in tax-evasion charges, said he went to see Mr Morley Richenberg [of Triumph Investments] wearing a dirty polo-necked sweater'. Klein objected. 'He is funny that way,' Taylor noted ironically. The inevitable consequence was a libel suit.

With the scene switching from bed-in to boardroom, honeymoon to High Court, the Beatles' musical career – the supposed focus of this scattered, frantic activity – seemed strangely irrelevant. Their January 1969 film project was stagnant, although a single ('Get Back') had been extracted to give the impression of business as usual. No sooner had it reached the shops than Lennon wanted to cut another single for immediate release. Entitled 'The Ballad of John and Yoko', it chronicled the Lennons' wedding and honeymoon. As neither Harrison nor Starkey was available, just two Beatles entered Abbey Road studio on 14 April, McCartney playing drums and Lennon lead guitar. 'I didn't mind not being on the record,' Harrison recalled, 'because it was none of my business. If it had been "The Ballad of John, George and Yoko", then I would have been on it.' A film clip was prepared to promote the song, mixing newsreels of the Lennons with footage from the January 1969 sessions. A drum skin showing the familiar Beatles logo was shown upside down for a few seconds, as if to reflect Ono's impact on the group. In America the single was packaged in a sleeve that pictured all five Beatles: Lennon, McCartney, Harrison, Starkey and Ono. 'Yoko used to sit in on the photos, and we didn't really know how to tell her to get out,' McCartney complained later, 'because she was John's bird. You couldn't really say, "Excuse me, John, can you get her out?" George wasn't too happy about it, but then none of us were.'

Engineers at that recording session reported that Lennon and McCartney had rarely seemed happier. But any hint of rapprochement was quickly dispelled. Lennon veered between fascination at the machinations of the business world ('Businessmen play the game the way we play music, and it's something to see') and contempt ('I'm not going to be fucked around by men in suits sitting on their fat arses in the City'). McCartney simply felt out of his depth. 'This was like playing Monopoly on a very large scale with lawyers,' he recalled. 'I never used to be very good at the game, anyway; I used to get real tense. And when it was real houses and real money and real Park Lanes and real Savile Rows, it got very fraught.'

Then something happened that polarised the two Beatles so dramatically, the rift was impossible to repair: Lee Eastman came to town, to lend his weight to his son's struggle against Allen Klein. At 59, he was twice as old as Lennon, and 21 years the senior of Klein.

He represented Park Avenue privilege, old-school values, tailored conservatism and, as Harrison had already noted, 'class-consciousness'. When Klein and John Eastman insulted each other – as they had, after the 'propriety' letter to Clive Epstein in February – the invective was raw but somehow equal, Klein's 'piece of crap' and 'shithead' being matched scatologically by Eastman's 'perfect asshole'. The confluence of imagery seemed to suggest some form of grudging mutual respect.

There was no rapport, however, between Klein and the senior (and more voluble) Eastman. As Lee remarked later, 'I won't do business with him; he's a swine. When you go to bed with a louse, you get lousy.' At two successive meetings, Klein reported, Eastman 'launched into an emotional tirade against me' and 'created another unpleasant scene'. He claimed, 'I thought it best not to retaliate.' Klein was a shrewd judge of human frailty. He reckoned that Eastman senior was operating on a short fuse, and that sarcasm would provide the spark. Klein chipped away at Eastman's dignity, and Eastman duly exploded. Lennon had just learned that Eastman had been born Lee Epstein, but had changed his name to aid his assimilation into smart New York circles, so he pointedly called him 'Mr Epstein' throughout. When Eastman bit back, Ono asked him, 'Will you please stop insulting my husband? Don't call my husband stupid.' Eastman yelled at Klein, 'You are a rodent, the lowest scum on earth.' It was effectively an admission of defeat. Lennon goaded Eastman, telling him that *he* was the 'fucking animal', not Klein. Through it all, McCartney watched in horrified silence, feeling a grim sense of responsibility for both his colleague and his father-in-law. Lennon showed no such sensitivity: to him, McCartney was now merely another member of the Eastman family.

On 18 April, four short days after the apparent rebirth of the Lennon/McCartney partnership, the two men came close to blows at Apple. The Eastmans advised McCartney not to add his block of Northern Songs shares to Lennon's as collateral for the loan the Beatles needed for their takeover bid. Allen Klein offered to make up the shortfall with his £750,000 worth of shares in the film company MGM, but the symbolism was inescapable: the Eastmans wanted McCartney to treat himself as a separate entity from the other Beatles. Then Klein informed Lennon that McCartney had secretly been increasing his stake in Northern Songs. 'John flew into a rage,' recalled Apple executive Peter Brown. 'At one point I thought he was really going to hit Paul, but he managed to calm himself down.' One unconfirmed report of this meeting had Lennon leaping towards Linda McCartney, his fists raised in her face.

After the meeting Lennon, Harrison and Starkey signed a letter officially banishing Lee Eastman: 'Dear Mr Eastman, This is to inform you of the fact that you are not authorized to act or hold yourself out as the attorney or legal representative of "The Beatles" or of any of the companies which The Beatles own or control.' McCartney could only interpret this as a personal rejection.

Incredibly, the Beatles continued to collaborate during this traumatic week, laying down the initial track for a new George Harrison song, 'Something'. Its opening line – 'Something in the way she moves' – was lifted from a song on a James Taylor album Apple had issued the previous year. 'I was pleased to think that I'd had an impact on the Beatles,' Taylor remembered. 'Anyway, the end of my song was just like "I Feel Fine". So I didn't think of what George had done as plagiarism, because I had already stolen from them.' Harrison seemed to have been unaware of the borrowed lyric; maybe he simply regarded the theft as an employer's prerogative. In either case, Lennon found an excuse to leave the studio, as he often did when Harrison's material was recorded in 1968 and 1969.

Lennon was a master of compartmentalisation during this period: he retained the ability to scream at McCartney in meetings, insult his wife and her family, and then expect to work with him as if nothing had happened. So it was that on 30 April Lennon and McCartney completed work on a playful song left unfinished in 1967: 'You Know My Name (Look Up the Number)'. It was no more than a collage of musical pastiches, but McCartney remembered this as his favourite Beatles session – perhaps because it only involved him and Lennon, or because it represented the final occasion on which the two men worked as an authentic partnership.

In public the pair still presented a united front. Lennon later presented himself as a vigorous opponent of the legendary 'medley' that dominated Side 2 of their *Abbey Road* album, but he was the first member of the group to boast about the idea. In the same interview he revealed that he and McCartney were enjoying a ferocious creative spurt, and claimed that 'the outcome of this whole financial business doesn't matter. We'll still be making records, and somebody will be copping some money and we'll be copping some money, and that'll be that.' The more practical McCartney channelled his frustration into a melodious song entitled 'You Never Give Me Your Money'. Looking back in 1996, he explained that the song wasn't directed 'to the other members of the band. I didn't really feel like they were to blame. We were kind of all in it together, and it wasn't really until Allen Klein came in that we got really divisive and started getting our own lawyers and stuff. Cos he divided us. It was basically him that divided us.' The role played by the Eastmans, and McCartney's preference for them over Klein, was conveniently forgotten.

Certainly McCartney lacked Lennon's knack for separating his personal and professional lives. Lennon was proclaiming that he had finally rediscovered himself: 'I got lost in the Beatles, and now it's John Lennon again. I'm always John and Yoko, that never stops, we're a 24-hour couple. So whatever I'm doing as Beatles, Yoko's sitting on my shoulder like a parrot.' But McCartney believed in himself as a Beatle, first and foremost, and an equal partner with Lennon, and he understandably felt each assault from his colleague as a thrust to the heart. Gill Pritchard, one of the so-called Scruffs, the fans who stood patiently outside Abbey Road Studios and Apple's HQ waiting for the Beatles to appear, remembered the night when 'Paul came racing out of the front door of the studio in tears, went home and didn't come back. The next day he didn't turn up at all even though the studio was booked.' Another fan, Wendy Sutcliffe, continued the story:

John was really angry because they were all waiting, and he came storming out of the studio and made off towards Paul's house. We followed and when he got there he stood outside and just banged on the door again and again, calling for Paul to open up. Paul didn't answer so John climbed the gate and hammered on his door. Then they had a screaming match. He was shouting that George and Ringo had both come in from the country and Paul didn't even bother to let anyone know he couldn't make the session.

While the Beatles' erratic progress towards a new album continued, Allen Klein sought to consolidate his position. He believed he was about to achieve the ambition that he had first revealed in 1964: becoming the Beatles' manager. He had already established dominion over their Apple headquarters in March, with permission from all four of the group to impose the redundancies that McCartney had wanted the previous year.

'On a bad day,' Derek Taylor conceded, 'Apple could look as if it was being trespassed upon. We might run into one of our paymasters on the stairs, holding what John described as a steak sandwich. Then they would say, "Who are these cunts? We're paying for them all." But a certain amount of extravagance was necessary, because we had invited the great and near-great to come to Apple.' Among the acts who approached the company that spring were two of the best-selling groups of the next decade, Fleetwood Mac and Crosby, Stills and Nash, although eventually neither was signed. Taylor understood, however, that 'if you are one of the Beatles, paying for it all, it doesn't matter that this is an institution that you have created, you can still be bad-tempered about it. And all of them finally said, "I didn't mean it to be like this." No one was in charge. Everyone had their own autonomy, and all of it cost money. But people did turn up to work every day, and work. The work never stopped.'

Apple had become notorious for its 'generosity': you could walk in, and if someone liked your looks you could leave with a set of Apple albums, and without any money changing hands. Besides the drinks and dope that constituted legitimate business expenses, private cars and holidays were now being charged to the company in the well-founded expectation that nobody would notice. From mid-March, when Klein established an office at Apple's Savile Row base, the climate changed. Alexis Mardas arrived at his workshop one morning to find a chain and padlock around the door handle. He remained on salary until August, and was close enough to the Lennons to share a cruise around the Greek islands that autumn, but the days when Apple Electronics could function without a clear commercial end in sight were over.

So too was the air of suave hippie majesty that emanated from Derek Taylor's impeccably stocked press office. 'When I think of going through it all again,' Taylor said twenty years later, 'well, I could just about stand parts of it, but I couldn't stand living through the arrival of Klein. That was miserable. I've never been so unhappy. But there was no alternative that could deal with this writhing thing that was Apple, that could put it in a container and hold the lid down.' Besides Taylor's budget, more savage sacrifices were made. Ron Kass had masterminded the early commercial success of Apple Records, which in Klein's eyes made him dangerous, so he had to go. Paul's old friend Peter Asher, employed effectively as a talent scout, jumped ship, taking with him the young singer-songwriter James Taylor. The Beatles verbally tore up James Taylor's deal, which didn't prevent Klein from attempting vainly to sue him for breach of contract in 1970, when his first album for Warners became a best-seller. 'Klein was a terrible idea,' the singer recalled, 'but nobody at Apple had any business sense at all. Somebody needed to come in, and it was ripe for someone like Klein to take over.'

Among the casualties was Alistair Taylor, who had faithfully served the Beatles as a general factotum since 1962, and was, so a colleague recalled, 'a cheerful cove who knew what the boys needed'. When the axe fell, Taylor tried to speak to his employers. 'Not one of them took my call. I got excuses from embarrassed wives and secretaries. I heard nervous Beatle voices in the background. But not one of my four famous friends came to the phone. And that hurt a hell of a lot more than getting the sack.'

The group only intervened when Klein attempted to oust their two closest aides, Neil Aspinall and Mal Evans. But what really mattered to Klein was official recognition that he now controlled the Beatles and their empire. At the end of April 1969 he drew up the rough draft of a formal agreement. One of the Beatles' legal advisers said it would be crazy for any artist to sign such a deal. But he had not reckoned on Lennon's willingness to commit himself to Klein.

The contract appointed ABKCO (Klein's company rather than the man himself) 'exclusive business manager' to Apple Corps Ltd 'on behalf of The Beatles and The Beatles Group of Companies' – a phrase that soon provoked much legal debate. Under its terms, ABKCO would receive 20 per cent of all Apple's income, before tax, and the percentage would continue indefinitely for any deals signed while the contract was in force. There were two important exceptions to this rule: Klein would not receive any portion of the Beatles' record royalties unless he negotiated a new deal for the group, and then he would only receive 20 per cent of the increased royalty, not the full rate, and he could only claim 10 per cent of the gross income generated by the Apple Records label. In return, Apple would agree to pay expenses for Klein and other ABKCO staff working on their behalf. As this deal stood, then, it was in Klein's interest to negotiate an improved royalty rate for the Beatles from EMI, and particularly to persuade the Beatles to perform in public, as often and as lucratively as possible. The contract would stand for three years, although either party could terminate it after each year, if sufficient notice were given.

On the surface Klein's percentages seemed modest: the Beatles had paid Epstein 25 per cent, for example, while Elvis Presley's manager Colonel Tom Parker took no less than 50 per cent of his client's earnings. Yet there was a profound difference: Epstein and Parker had masterminded their clients' rise to fame, so their percentage rewarded their original faith and the energies they had invested. Klein was simply inheriting the most famous entertainers in the world.

On Wednesday 7 May 1969 Klein, Lennon, McCartney, Harrison and Ono met EMI executives at Lincoln's Inn to discuss where the Beatles' royalties should be paid. EMI insisted that they would retain the money until the dispute with NEMS was concluded. After lunch Starkey joined his colleagues. Klein and his lawyer were asked to leave the room while the managerial contract was discussed. The Beatles took advice from a lawyer acting on behalf of all but McCartney, and also a legal counsel. At this stage none of them queried the percentages, let alone the intention to appoint Klein manager. The deal was agreed in principle, and then Klein and his lawyer Harold Seider were invited to rejoin the gathering while minor changes were negotiated, with Harrison and McCartney the most vocal of the four musicians.

Thursday morning brought another legal conference, at which the group's advisers inserted an extra clause, effectively transforming the contract from a binding deal into a basis for further discussion. Lawyer Peter Howard took this revised document to Lennon at Apple, explained why it had been changed and obtained his signature. Howard then drove to Harrison's home in Esher. Meanwhile, Lennon had visited Klein at the Dorchester Hotel and proudly showed off the revised deal he had signed. Klein retorted that the agreement was now meaningless – nothing more than a piece of paper. 'I was not prepared to accept a document in this form,' he recalled, complaining that its effect was 'to make it doubtful whether the contract would be binding'. He phoned Howard to say that he would only sign if the new clause were deleted and replaced by something that affirmed the binding nature of the deal.

With typical ebullience, Lennon completely changed his mind and supported Klein's view. He spoke briefly to Harrison, who declared that he also preferred Klein's revision. At this point the saga nearly slipped into farce, as Howard discovered that he had left behind the document that Lennon had signed at Apple. Fortunately, Harrison agreed to sign a carbon copy. Before he did so, he felt obliged to tell McCartney what was happening. But he was unable to get through. McCartney had changed his phone number and neglected to tell the man who had been his friend since he was 15 years old. So Harrison felt he had no alternative but to sign. Howard then drove to see Starkey at his home in Elstead. Like Harrison, Starkey agreed to sign whatever Lennon had approved.

Alone of the three Beatles, however, Starkey seems to have made some attempt to wrestle with the financial implications of the contract. Suppose Klein negotiated a more lucrative recording contract for the Beatles, he said, and received his 20 per cent of the increased royalty. Wasn't there a danger that he could also claim 10 per cent of the entire royalty when it arrived in the coffers of Apple Records? Howard admitted that the current wording was ambiguous, but reassured Starkey that both sides had agreed verbally that the Beatles' royalties would not qualify as part of Apple Records' income. The lawyer also advised Starkey, as he had his colleagues, that it was possible – more than possible, in fact – that McCartney would choose not to sign the deal. Starkey told him that wasn't a problem: he, Lennon and Harrison wanted the American to manage them, and McCartney could look after himself.

There were now two versions of the document: one signed by Lennon alone, the other by Harrison and Starkey. So Howard returned to London, where Lennon was waiting in Klein's hotel room. Lennon added his signature to the carbon copy, and so did Klein. Eventually, in the early hours of 9 May, Howard's arduous day of negotiations came to an end. The document was now legal, but for one thing: it needed to be officially ratified by the Apple board of directors.

Around twelve hours later all four Beatles assembled at Olympic Studios in south-west London, as Glyn Johns made another forlorn attempt to salvage their January recordings. But the session quickly dissolved into a fractious business meeting. 'It was like a divorce,' said original Beatles press officer Tony Barrow, 'where you don't like what the lawyers are doing, but you have to go along with it. Lots of rash things were said and done on both sides.' As McCartney testified later, 'It became clear to me that the other three had already signed the agreement on the previous day without my knowledge.' He was informed that he wasn't told because he had not bothered to give his colleagues his phone number. Neil Aspinall and Peter Howard listened as the four men argued. McCartney recollected that he disagreed with the percentage Klein was being offered: 'I said, "He'll take 15 per cent. We're massive, we're the biggest act in the world, he'll take 15 per cent." But for some reason the three of them were so keen to go with him that they really bullied me and ganged up on me.' Crucially, though, McCartney did not reject outright the idea of being managed by Klein; he merely wanted his lawyer, who was not present, to draft a rival agreement.

By this time Klein was at London airport, where he was about to board a plane for New York under the impression that the negotiations were over. He was paged and called to a phone, where he heard Lennon tell him, 'Paul's making trouble. You have to come back to Olympic.' So Klein returned to the studio, where he explained to McCartney that the ABKCO board insisted that he obtained the Beatles' approval that day. This was merely a tactical move: Klein had single-handed control over ABKCO. McCartney told his colleagues that he would present them with an alternative document to sign on Monday, and the other Beatles agreed that if they preferred his version, they would sign it. But, with the innocence of rich young men, they insisted that the document they had already signed should be ratified by the Apple board. McCartney objected, and was told, 'Well, we'll do it without you.' 'They couldn't,' he insisted years later, but the minutes of the board meeting that followed proved otherwise. Officially only three directors were required to form a quorum, and just before 8 p.m. on 9 May 1969 Aspinall, Lennon and Harrison signed a resolution noting that the agreement with Klein had been ratified, and was now binding on the Beatles, their company and their new manager. With a final fierce exchange of words, the Klein faction exited the studio, leaving McCartney to face the reality of his separation. He wandered through the Olympic complex and stumbled across the American rock musician Steve Miller. After McCartney had poured out his troubles, Miller suggested that work might distract him from his rage. So

McCartney thrashed his drums while Miller recorded a song with the symbolically appropriate title of 'My Dark Hour'.

Regular legal missives were exchanged over the next few weeks. One side insisted that neither McCartney nor any of his companies could be held to an agreement he hadn't signed; the other conceded that Klein did not seek to manage McCartney as a single artist, or any companies that he solely owned, but that the deal was binding for Apple, as it had been signed by the requisite number of Beatle directors. It was like two colour-blind men arguing about a rainbow: destined to end in disharmony. From this point on McCartney rejected Klein and all his works, while Lennon, Harrison and Starkey stayed loyal to their financial guru. As Apple aide Tony Bramwell noted, 'Allen Klein had achieved his ambition of managing the Beatles, but in doing so, he blew them apart.' There were still – just – four members of the Beatles in May 1969. But the unity that had sustained them for the previous decade had vanished forever.

Chapter 3

Why will people underestimate the Beatles and refuse to take
them seriously? They're not four little boys who don't know
what they are doing, they're four grown men. If all this business
happened to anyone else, no one would take any notice of it.
But because it's the Beatles, everything they do is magnified.
   Allen Klein, July 1969

The girls who lived on the steps of Apple's office at 3 Savile Row –
the Apple Scruffs, as George Harrison immortalised them – were old
enough to have fallen for the Beatles in 1963. They no longer screamed
when they saw them, as they would have done when they were twelve.
Their trademark was a cool demeanour: only newcomers acted like
the teenyboppers that the Scruffs had once been.

Their younger sisters accepted the Beatles as a fact of life, but
beards and dour faces made the former Fab Four unlikely objects for
pubescent ardour. The pre-teens of 1969 had idols with smoother
faces: Davy Jones of the Monkees, Andy Fairweather-Low of Amen
Corner, Bobby Sherman and Oliver. That summer, the airwaves were
dominated by 'Sugar Sugar', a candy confection prepared by producers
who predated the Beatles, and credited to a group who existed only
as cartoon characters.

Between 1965 and 1967, pop had become a playground for musicians
eager to expand their imaginations with psychedelic drugs, Eastern

spirituality and an array of 'high art' influences that stretched from T.S. Eliot to Charles Ives. But in 1967, between the Monkees' calculated recreation of Beatlemania and the release of the *Sgt Pepper* album, pop split into two ideologically divided streams – one aimed at its traditional market, of kids from eight to fifteen, the other targeting precocious teens, students and young adults, who preferred music that was serious and progressive, but still hissed with the spirit of rebellion.

The Beatles were still unchallenged as the most popular musicians in the Western world; via illicit dubs and cross-border radio, they had even reached behind the Iron Curtain. But their appeal was now balanced precariously between the audiences for pop and rock. McCartney songs such as 'Hello Goodbye' and 'Get Back' retained enough naive enthusiasm to attract the pop children, but few pre-pubescent fans could identify with the darker corners of their White Album. Neither could the parents and grandparents who had tapped their feet to 'A Hard Day's Night', but who had been alienated by the symbols of the Beatles' current lifestyle – drugs, police raids, meditation and full-frontal photographs. Even the dependably attractive Paul McCartney had abandoned his British girlfriend and married an American.

Within the culture of rock, which treated its heroes as seriously as any students of literature or art, the Beatles occupied an ambiguous place. They were still the stuff of legends, but they no longer led a generation or formed its taste. Famous for as long as most rock fans could remember, Lennon, McCartney, Harrison and Starkey seemed to share little with the pilgrims who flocked to vast outdoor festivals such as Woodstock. The Beatles had intended Apple as a bridge between them and their audience, but its failure as an idealistic enterprise – already apparent before the arrival of Allen Klein – merely widened the divide. If rock fans wanted to feel at one with their heroes, they looked elsewhere – to the brazen vulnerability of Janis Joplin, the enigmatic presence of Bob Dylan, the confessional openness of Crosby, Stills and Nash, and the Rolling Stones, who were accepted as the most perceptive guides to the treacherous currents now flooding through the counterculture.

So what were the Beatles in the summer of 1969, except a phenomenon that sold records in suitably phenomenal quantities? It was a question that clearly puzzled and concerned John Lennon. 'He has refused to become the prisoner of his special talent as a musician,' observed critic Leslie Fiedler, 'venturing into other realms where he has, initially, at least, as little authority as anyone else.' Yoko Ono encouraged him to explore every possible mode of creative expression, from filming his penis in a state of mild excitement (*Self Portrait*) to fiddling with the dial of a radio and calling it music ('Radio Play'). He immersed himself in her vision of art as a state of heightened existence that deserved constant documentation. In December 1968 Lennon and Ono had appeared on the stage of the Royal Albert Hall in London, doing and saying nothing while enveloped in a black bag. This was 'bagism', an Ono concept enabling total communication, the couple explained, because it hid the individual and thereby undercut any kind of prejudice (except irrational dislike of people in bags). The event was filmed, and the Lennons' silent act of performance art thereby became a second artwork as part of a documentary; and then a third, as the London Arts Lab filmed the Lennons watching their bagism footage – a process that could have been continued ad infinitum and ad nauseam.

Such solipsistic art could never touch anyone who wasn't already captivated by Lennon's fame. Of the four Beatles, he was in most danger of alienating himself from his public. To his credit, he soon realised that self-centred art wasn't enough. To be worthwhile, art had to reach a global audience and change lives, the way that the Beatles' music had once done. In 1968 Lennon had declared his ambition to 'package peace in a new box'. In 1969 he and Ono opted not to sell peace, or preach it, but to become its human incarnation. They would sing, talk and breathe nothing but peace; they would take their message to the world, and war would inevitably end, 'if you want it', as a poster event would proclaim.

Their honeymoon bed-in was merely the beginning. Now they intended to carry the message of peace to the heart of the US anti-war movement. They embarked with Derek Taylor on a transatlantic liner and, barred from entering the US by Lennon's recent drugs conviction, headed for the Canadian city of Montreal, an hour's drive from the US border. Once again they donned their pyjamas and entertained press representatives from across North America. 'For hours, they would do nothing but interviews about peace,' recalled Gail Renard, a local teenager who talked her way into the Lennons' suite. 'I asked John, "What do you do when everyone goes home?" He said, "Tiredness and loneliness, my dear." He was only half-joking.'

Writing about 'Revolution' a year earlier, Lennon couldn't choose between his visceral urge to overthrow the 'system' and his fear of physical injury. Now, he declared, 'We believe violent change doesn't really accomplish anything in the long run, because in the over 2,000 years we've been going, all the violent revolutions have come to an end, even if they've lasted 50 or 100 years. The few people who've tried to do it our way, unfortunately, have been killed, i.e. Jesus, Gandhi, Kennedy and Martin Luther King. The way we might escape being killed is that we have a sense of humour and that the worst, or the least, we can do is make people laugh.'

By selling peace, Lennon believed he was operating beyond the spectrum of politics. But he soon manoeuvred himself into a political controversy 3,000 miles away, in Berkeley, California. Community activists and students had proclaimed a three-acre area near the University of California campus as People's Park. It was a symbolic act, reclaiming land that had once held public housing but was now earmarked for college sports facilities. As radical historian Todd Gitlin explained, 'People's Park amounted to the spirits of the New Left and the counterculture in harmonious combination: it was a trace of anarchist heaven on earth.' University officials failed to appreciate the symbolism, and a bloody contest ensued between activists and police, resulting in the death of one demonstrator and the blinding of another.

A protest march was scheduled for 30 May, and two days earlier the cream of California's psychedelic rock bands staged a fund-raising concert, firmly aligning the musical community with those who wanted to preserve People's Park for the people. Activists approached Lennon for a gesture of support. Instead, he preached his new philosophy of non-violent disobedience. 'I don't believe there is any cause worth getting shot for,' he told the Berkeley dissidents. 'You can do better by moving on to another city or moving to Canada. Go anywhere – then they've got nothing to attack and nobody to point their finger at.' Then he lapsed into hippie clichés: 'You can make it, man; we can make it, together,' and so on. It was not what the Berkeley protestors had expected: rather than fighting the system, Lennon preferred to ignore it and give it free rein. In the eyes of Village Voice columnist Robert Christgau, Lennon was 'firming up his newfound status as a pompous shit'. Abbie Hoffman, one of the leaders of the anarchic protest movement the Yippies, accused Lennon of propounding 'an establishment form of pacifism'. He believed that the Beatle and his wife, whom he racistly dubbed 'Oko Nono', were in the pay of the American government. 'Lennon wrote to the [US] State Department,' Hoffman complained, 'and said, "I will do a good service here, I will speak to the young people, I will tell them not to be violent, I will tell them not to shout, 'Kill the pigs.'"' His postscript exposed the widening gulf between Lennon and his more politically aware fans: 'I ain't gonna buy his records any more. I'm not interested. He doesn't say anything to me any more.'

Anyone offended by Lennon's pacifism would have been equally bewildered by George Harrison's philosophy. The focus of his life wasn't with the Beatles, or at home, where his wife Pattie found him increasingly withdrawn, not depressed but simply elsewhere. Although he was prepared to support pet projects at Apple – Billy Preston's gospel tunes, or a spiritual chant by the London members of the Radha Krishna Temple – his imagination was directed high above this material world. On this spiritual level such petty concerns as war and peace were irrelevant. Through meditation, he declared, you should 'be able to conjure up that peace in the middle of Vietnam . . . There is no problem if each individual doesn't have any problems . . . The problems are created more, sometimes, by people going around trying to fix up the government, or trying to do something.' These, then, were the political role models on offer to the increasingly radicalised generation who had grown up with the Beatles: one hero who declared it was better to flee than fight oppression, and another who believed that oppression was merely an illusion.

No wonder Beatles fans were confused about what the group stood for, and where they were heading. The pop newspaper *Disc* asked its readers, who had recently voted the Beatles the world's best group, how they really saw them. Some interpreted Lennon's peace crusade in the spirit that he intended, referring to him as a 'saint', but one drew a vivid distinction between the Beatles as men and as musicians. 'If Lennon raped a 10-year-old girl,' he commented, 'it would make no difference to the next single.'

In any case, the next single was a deliberate blurring of music and message: a simplistic chant recorded in the Lennons' Montreal hotel room entitled 'Give Peace a Chance'. The US magazine *Billboard* announced that it would be a Beatles release, an understandable error given that their last single had been exclusively about Lennon and his wife. But instead Lennon chose to issue it under the pseudonym of the Plastic Ono Band, an open-ended entity which offered a refuge from the restrictive dimensions of the Beatles.* For the moment, he chose to maintain the fantasy that he was still collaborating actively with Paul McCartney, whose name duly appeared on the record as co-writer. 'Give Peace a Chance' matched the sales of recent Beatles releases, and achieved its intended purpose as an anthem during a major anti-war rally in Washington DC.

While Lennon transformed his music into a vehicle for social commentary, Harrison had more profound ambitions. 'The first thing in my life is music,' he insisted that summer, 'but now I just want to sing songs that give me some benefit. I've come to understand that music should be employed really for the benefit of God-perception, like chanting, that sort of thing.' His work with the Radha Krishna Temple solidified his image as a disciple of one of God's oriental incarnations, and carried the holy refrain of the 'Hare Krishna Mantra' into the Top 20. The temple's shaven-headed disciples became regular visitors to the Apple office. 'Paul didn't relate to the Krishnas,' Derek Taylor recalled. 'You'd hear them coming down the street, chanting and ringing their bells, and when the bells stopped outside, you'd think, Oh no, the fucking Krishnas are coming upstairs. They could be as disruptive as anyone.'

The four Beatles had not attempted to make music together since early May, but their cottage industry at Savile Row continued merrily without them. Apple proudly announced that they would shortly be issuing an album from the ill-tempered January 1969 sessions, entitled *Get Back*. Its cover photograph would echo their first LP, *Please Please Me*, but with the bearded Beatles replacing their more conservative predecessors. The photograph would demonstrate how much had changed in those six years and provide a symbolic farewell if the Beatles were unable to work together again. But the *Get Back* album didn't appear, despite frequent promises. Instead, the raw tapes leaked onto the new underground market for unauthorised bootleg records. Several American radio stations aired the recordings, and this illicit distribution of the Beatles' music was widely interpreted as a triumph of the people over the greed of big business.

Paul McCartney had remained uncharacteristically quiet after Allen

*Besides its symbolic importance, the Plastic Ono disguise had financial implications: Lennon earned a higher royalty rate than he would have done with the Beatles.

Klein's appointment. But he was clearly in elegiac mood. 'Paul called me,' Neil Aspinall recalled, 'saying, "You should collect as much of the [film] material that's out there, get it together before it disappears." So I started to do that, got in touch with the TV stations around the world, checked what we had in our own library, the promo clips. I got newsreel footage in, lots and lots of stuff.' The Beatles had never been sentimental about where they'd been: in 1965, for instance, they had refused to help the owners of Liverpool's Cavern Club, where they had performed nearly 300 times, to keep the venue alive. But now they could envisage a future in which they would no longer be Beatles. As Aspinall's archive expanded, all four of the group authorised him to compile a documentary film about their career.

Their relationship with the film industry remained uneasy. The success of their first two features, *A Hard Day's Night* and *Help!*, was tainted by their embarrassment at their gauche appearance on screen. Lennon's experience in the satirical comedy *How I Won the War* proved equally unsatisfying. Their misgivings weren't merely artistic: Brian Epstein had signed a contract committing the group to make a third film with United Artists, and lawyers were uncertain that the *Yellow Submarine* animation had fulfilled the deal. Rather than risk a costly court case, the Beatles continued to search for an appropriate vehicle for their talents. They had recently attempted to obtain the rights to J.R.R. Tolkien's mythic trilogy of fantasy novels *The Lord of the Rings*, but Tolkien's lawyers refused to let their property fall into such unruly hands, and the project was abandoned. So attention was focused on the documentary footage that the Beatles had shot in January. By July director Michael Lindsay-Hogg had prepared a rough cut that ran for some 210 minutes, barely shorter than *Gone With the Wind*. Allen Klein invited the Beatles to a screening, after which he proposed that the project – entitled *Get Back* at this stage, like the accompanying album – should be aimed at the cinema, not television.* The four musicians were asked for their comments, and McCartney, Harrison and Starkey each complained that too much screen time was devoted to Lennon and Ono. Rather than confront Lennon directly, Klein cunningly asked Lindsay-Hogg to concentrate on the Beatles and their music,

* Unbeknown to Klein, Lee Eastman was keen to negotiate his own deal for the *Get Back* film, and was entreating senior Apple staff to back his efforts rather than Klein's.

rather than the surrounding milieu. If Ono's role thereby became less prominent, that was merely an unfortunate side effect of a purely artistic decision.

Klein's primary purpose remained 'to make for each one of [the Beatles] in cash, after tax, as much money as everyone felt that they ought to have and should have'. Slowly he began to exert pressure on EMI boss Sir Joseph Lockwood, pointing out that the Beatles had effectively fulfilled the terms of their 1967 contract and might choose to express themselves in other fields if their deal were not improved. Lockwood replied that the Beatles had known what they were signing in 1967 – 'They had a year to consider it. They knew their rights' – and that 'They have done jolly well.' He was prepared to negotiate a revised contract that would benefit both parties. But he believed that the Beatles themselves were perfectly satisfied with the existing deal: the objections, he suggested, emanated from Klein not his clients.

Both Klein and the Beatles understood that Lockwood would never agree to improve the terms of the contract if the group was no longer active. Partly to prove that they still existed, partly out of habit, all four Beatles agreed to return to the familiar surroundings of Abbey Road Studios on 2 July 1969. The previous day McCartney taped a lead vocal for 'You Never Give Me Your Money', perhaps feeling it would be easier to express his ambivalent feelings towards the group if none of the others was present. Meanwhile, Lennon, Ono and their two children (Lennon's son, Ono's daughter) were holidaying in Scotland. Lennon was at the wheel as they headed to the airport: never a confident or competent driver, he ran their car off the road. The family escaped with comparatively minor injuries, but Lennon and Ono were kept in hospital under observation. So it was a three-man Beatles who regrouped at Abbey Road, with George Martin once more at the controls, and made significant progress towards a new album. The most telling contribution came from Harrison. 'Just to be singing, "It's a lovely day today," and all that, it's a waste of energy,' he declared that summer, but his beautiful song 'Here Comes the Sun' proved him wrong. Engineers noted the lack of tension among the three musicians, and waited anxiously to see how the atmosphere might change when Lennon and Ono returned.

Business remained a potentially divisive subject, no matter how many Beatles were present. The future of Northern Songs was still uncertain, and Lennon and McCartney heightened the stakes by promising to take their publishing interests elsewhere if the company fell into the hands of Sir Lew Grade's ATV corporation. By mid-May neither the Beatles nor ATV controlled the majority of shares, and stalemate was reached. Both sides claimed victory, but neither could clinch it.

The relationship between the Beatles, their former management company NEMS and the banking consortium Triumph Investments was equally taxing. EMI maintained its neutrality by holding back the royalties earned by the Beatles' records – a grievous blow at a time when Apple was struggling to achieve financial stability. In late June the dispute escalated when Clive Epstein and NEMS issued a writ against the Beatles, Klein, Neil Aspinall and anyone else with an interest in the group's film company Subafilms. The focus was the income generated by the *Yellow Submarine* animation: should the money be going to NEMS or directly to the Beatles?

Legal arguments now shadowed the Beatles' earnings from records, songwriting and films. Klein's urgent priority was to solve the dispute over NEMS, and thereby release their EMI royalties from captivity. A prolonged series of meetings with Triumph banker Leonard Richenberg produced a peace agreement, officially announced to the press on 9 July. 'The situation has been resolved to the satisfaction of both sides,' the press release said with the gravitas appropriate for a treaty between warring nations. 'New arrangements have been made which will give the Beatles the independence they desire.' Under the terms of the deal, NEMS dropped all its claims to represent the Beatles. In return, the Beatles agreed to sell their 10 per cent interest in NEMS to Triumph. NEMS was offered compensation of around £750,000 for the earnings it might have gained as the group's managers up until 1972, while the company was also promised 5 per cent of the Beatles' record royalties from 1972 until 1976.* There were two immediate benefits for the Beatles: first, EMI released the £1.3 million it had been safeguarding during the dispute; second, the Beatles acquired the NEMS shareholding in Northern Songs, which seemed to give them a decisive edge in the battle with ATV.

---

* The Beatles were giving up less from this deal than it might seem, as Klein agreed that the 5 per cent of North American royalties, around three quarters of total global revenue, would come from his commission rather than from the Beatles' pockets.

Inevitably, perhaps, this settlement was not reached without sniping behind the Beatles' lines. The final agreement had to be signed by all four of the group, and the documents were duly sent to Paul McCartney via his lawyers. He signed without argument, while Klein obtained the other three signatures on a separate copy of the agreement. On 7 or 8 July Klein was visiting John Lennon, who had just returned from Scotland, when he was called by one of Apple's lawyers. Klein alleged that McCartney threatened to pull out of the deal unless Klein agreed not to take any payment for negotiating the agreement over the previous five months. Klein couldn't believe what he was hearing, so he checked with McCartney's lawyer, who confirmed the news. It was a gesture of almost adolescent defiance but very little potency. Klein hurried to Abbey Road, where the other three Beatles were working. In front of Harrison and Starkey he told McCartney what his lawyer had said. McCartney was cornered: he could either refuse to pay Klein, scupper the deal and probably sabotage any chance of the Beatles completing their album, or he could back down. He chose the politer option, telling Klein that what he'd heard was 'ridiculous', and phoning his lawyer to authorise the exchange of contracts. 'So far as I am concerned,' Lennon said later, 'Paul did accept Klein as the Beatles' manager, though he may not have liked him.'

It was perhaps just as well that Lennon was not a witness to this scene. He returned to the fray on 9 July and, for a few seconds, it appeared that he had come alone; but then Yoko Ono hobbled into the studio, followed by four porters from Harrods department store, wheeling in a bed. Ono was still suffering severe whiplash after the car crash in Scotland, but Lennon insisted that she should attend the sessions. 'Jaws dropping, we all watched as it was brought into the studio and carefully positioned by the stairs,' engineer Geoff Emerick recalled. 'More [porters] appeared with sheets and pillows and sombrely made the bed up. Then, without saying a word, Yoko climbed in, carefully arranging the covers around her.' And there she remained for the next few days, as if she was staging some magnificently comic piece of performance art, a third bed-in, perhaps, for the benefit of a very carefully selected audience. As McCartney noted, it was 'not the ideal way for making records'.

Perhaps in an unconscious attempt at revenge, McCartney subjected Lennon and the other Beatles to several days of hard labour, trying to transform his novelty song 'Maxwell's Silver Hammer' into a possible single – 'which it could never have been', as Lennon said bitterly. Somehow the group managed to rise above their petty squabbling for the next four weeks, regaining their collective identity to the extent that Lennon, McCartney and Harrison were able to devote almost twelve hours to recording the most choirboy-perfect harmonies of their entire career, on Lennon's composition 'Because'. But this show of unity disguised the fact that the group's two main creative forces now had completely different agendas. While McCartney retained his almost freakishly inspired command of melody, Lennon was only interested in music that was an unvarnished expression of emotion. At its most extreme, this gulf was demonstrated by the weightless trickery of 'Maxwell's Silver Hammer', from McCartney, and Lennon's relentlessly direct love song 'I Want You (She's So Heavy)'. Both men, meanwhile, chose to underestimate the flowering talents of George Harrison, whose best work – such as his two contributions to this album, 'Something' and 'Here Comes the Sun' – combined the most attractive qualities of his elder colleagues. The Beatles had always been a blend of talents, but now the fusion could only hold if the four men were prepared to restrain any creative impulses that didn't fit the mould. For Lennon, this degree of compromise was no longer bearable.

Fortunately he was able to submerge his passion for the avant-garde long enough for this final album, entitled *Abbey Road*, to be completed. The name was a description rather than an expression of love for a studio complex that the Beatles felt they had long since outgrown; it also enabled them to shoot a cover picture quickly and comfortably. On the morning of 8 August 1969 they marched back and forth across the zebra crossing outside the studio to create one of the most famous album sleeves in history. Lennon became increasingly impatient as a crowd of onlookers gathered: 'I was muttering, "Hurry up", you know, "Keep in step,"' he admitted afterwards.

It had become increasingly difficult for the Beatles to keep in step for longer than it took to click a camera shutter. At Apple aides such as Tony Bramwell experienced the daily fluctuations of power.

People like myself and Neil Aspinall and Mal Evans would constantly be getting calls from one of the Beatles, asking us to do something but not tell the others. Paul would want us to book him a recording session at Morgan Studios, but not let John know, while John and Yoko had their own reign of terror. John got completely negative about everyone else's projects. He would only be interested in himself and Yoko. One week Paul would be in the office, the next it would be John and Yoko ruling the roost. It was difficult for those of us who'd grown up being faithful to them, and who suddenly found ourselves having to play them off against each other, behind each other's backs.

For Lennon, Apple no longer offered even the illusion of freedom. 'The problem is that two years ago our accountants made us sign 80 per cent of all our royalties to Apple,' he explained. 'We can't touch any of it, and it's a ridiculous situation. All the money comes into this little building and it never gets out. If I could get my money out of the company, I'd split away and start doing my own projects independently. I'd have much more freedom and we'd all be happier. I still feel part of Apple and the Beatles, and there's no animosity, but they tend to ignore Yoko and me.' In fact, Lennon and Ono were difficult to ignore at Apple. 'They tended to be very demanding,' recalled Derek Taylor, 'but I was used to being demanding myself, so that didn't worry me. But Yoko did tend to come into my office and expect a thousand different things to be done immediately, which presented something of a challenge.'

Money was uppermost in Lennon's mind in August 1969, as he faced a bill for three months' building work on Tittenhurst Park, the Ascot mansion he had bought in May. (In fact, the property had been purchased by Maclen Ltd, which handled Lennon and McCartney's songwriting income, opening up another financial problem for the future.) The grounds, which had been open to the public for decades, were expansive; the house was a perfect example of rock star grandiosity. The Lennons proudly invited the other Beatles to visit, on 22 August 1969. Photographer Monty Fresco documented the occasion in a series of shots that comprised the group's final photo session. Inevitably, Ono found her way into the frame more often than not. Perhaps sensing this was a historic occasion, Pattie Boyd took some silent-film footage of the four musicians as they would never be seen again.

Now there was no reason for the Beatles to meet except business. While they completed work on *Abbey Road*, Allen Klein continued to negotiate a takeover of Northern Songs. The block of shareholders known as the Consortium, who had refused to choose between the Beatles and ATV, remained an enticing target for Klein, who learned in late summer that they might finally be prepared to sell. He invited John Eastman to fly to London so that McCartney's interests would be fully represented. The relationship between the two men had recently descended into open enmity. 'Dear John,' Klein wrote to Eastman on 2 September, 'I am on a diet, so please stop putting words in my mouth. Your misuse and abuse of the truth is almost without parallel.' Eastman arrived on 15 September, and a day or two later all four Beatles endured a turgid discussion about voting rights and share options, which broadened into a desultory fight between Lennon and Harrison about the latter's right to equal exposure on any future Beatles record. Though nobody realised it at the time, this was an epochal moment: it was the last occasion on which Lennon, McCartney, Harrison and Starkey would be together in the same room. A saga that had begun in passionate commitment to rock 'n' roll music ended in a life-draining argument about the consequences of that passion.

On 19 September, Klein, Eastman and the Beatles (except Harrison) met again at Apple. To assure the Consortium that the Beatles' camp was speaking with one voice, a series of photographs was taken by Linda McCartney, showing the Beatles and Klein apparently signing a document together. Klein stood at the centre of the shots, with McCartney playful, coy and sheepish alongside the man who had outflanked his in-laws.

The mood changed abruptly as they turned their attention to business. Heading the agenda was the question of who should sit on the board of Northern Songs when it fell into the hands of the Beatles. According to Klein, John Eastman threw the meeting into confusion when he 'insisted that Paul should have as many votes as the other three Beatles put together. Mr Starkey looked incredulously at John Eastman and said, "I cannot believe what you are saying. Do you mean that Paul should have as many votes as all of us?" [McCartney] then looked at John Eastman and said, "John, that can't be right, why should I have as many votes as all of them?"' Eastman's reply – 'If we become unhappy, we should want to be able to vote with the other side' – didn't satisfy Lennon or Starkey, who told him, 'Look, the more and more we talk, it seems like you're trying to split us, not keep us together.'

The argument was soon rendered irrelevant by the discovery that the Consortium had thrown in its shares with ATV: the battle for Northern Songs was lost.* And at least two of the people at that meeting knew that another fight was nearly over: the struggle to preserve the Beatles. On 13 September Lennon and Ono attended a rock 'n' roll festival in Toronto with a hastily assembled group of musicians answering to the name of the Plastic Ono Band. George Harrison was among those invited to take part, but he told Lennon that he didn't have any interest in performing Yoko Ono's avant-garde music. There was a strict hierarchy among the musicians, as guitarist Eric Clapton discovered: 'It was raining, and we were standing around waiting for the luggage when a huge limo rolled up, and John and Yoko jumped into it and drove away, leaving the rest of us standing in the rain without a clue as to what to do next. Well, that's nice, I thought.' The Plastic Ono Band was booked to appear alongside many of Lennon's 1950s heroes, and to control his nervousness he inhaled a vast quantity of cocaine. The combination of nerves and stimulant took its toll, as the event's compère Kim Fowley recalled: 'John threw up. And he started to cry. He said, "I'm terrified. Imagine if the Beatles were the only band you've ever been in, and it's the first time you are going to step on stage with people who aren't the Beatles."' As bass guitarist Klaus Voormann noted, "John stood in the dressing room, which was admittedly rather tatty, saying, "What am I doing here? I could have gone to Brighton."'

Wearing the white suit that had become his public uniform, Lennon eventually led the Plastic Ono Band on stage for an ill-rehearsed but charismatic set of rock 'n' roll standards and his own recent compositions – notably 'Cold Turkey', a graphic account of heroin addiction that he had offered to the other Beatles as a potential single. Then he turned the stage over to Ono, who delivered two lengthy fusions of rock and performance art, culminating in a series of guttural shrieks, superseded by the relentless howl of guitar feedback. 'People were surprised when I suddenly used to start screaming during our concerts,' Ono said. 'But they didn't realise I had vocal training.' Press reports suggested that her uncompromising performance was greeted

---

* Lennon and McCartney were contractually bound to the company until 1973, and almost all of their Beatles copyrights are still held by Northern.

with howls of derision, but she demurred: 'I was completely wrapped up in the music. I did not feel any of that hostility, even though I'm sure it was there.'

Performing rock 'n' roll without the Beatles was a profoundly symbolic action. All that remained was the deed itself. On the flight to Toronto, between bouts of unamplified rehearsal, Lennon told Clapton and Voormann that he intended to quit the Beatles, and would be forming another band, if they were interested. Allen Klein was the next to be informed. He didn't attempt to change Lennon's mind; he simply said that contractual negotiations with EMI had reached a delicate stage and might be endangered if the record company learned that the Beatles could no longer work together.

Klein can scarcely have been surprised. He knew that Starkey and Harrison had walked away from the group in the past, and he was aware of the tensions aroused at Apple by the conflicting demands of the Beatles and the Lennons. He may have hoped – indeed, assumed – that Lennon was merely voicing a passing fantasy, and that once he was safely back on British soil he would resume his place as the group's fiercest internal critic. Securing the Beatles as his clients, Klein knew, would mean nothing if they disintegrated as soon as he assumed control.

The meeting on 19 September confirmed to Klein that the problem was not Lennon's commitment to the group, but the increasingly obvious split between McCartney and the rest. For once it was Starkey rather than Lennon who most vehemently opposed Eastman's proposals. The overriding impression left by Eastman's arguments was that McCartney should always be able to match the voting power of the other three, even if – as he was perennially in 1969 – he was in a minority of one. Starkey was outraged, rejecting each of Eastman's arguments in turn. 'Eastman is representing *him*,' he said, pointing at McCartney. You' – he indicated Klein – 'represent *us*.'

The following day, 20 September 1969, the same parties regrouped at Apple. They were there to authorise and sign the new recording deal that Klein had secured from Capitol Records, the North American arm of EMI, which was responsible for 75 per cent of the group's global record sales. Although John Eastman had originally wanted to stall the negotiations, going so far (according to Klein) as to tell Capitol that Klein did not represent McCartney in the talks, he had finally agreed to the deal. So too had McCartney, who could not fail to be impressed by the unprecedented terms of the agreement, which saw the Beatles awarded a higher royalty rate (25 per cent of the wholesale price) than any other recording act. The rate would rise again in 1972, as long as the last two Beatles-related albums issued at that point had each sold more than 500,000 copies in the USA, a clause that would become a subject for debate three years later. Derek Taylor summarised the negotiations: 'Klein takes EMI and Capitol to the cleaners and to hell and back and it is Stanley Gortikov, a senior executive at Capitol, who says a lot later that year that, OK, Capitol paid up, but did Klein have to be so hard about it?' Klein noted, 'I did Capitol a great favour. I delivered them product. These boys want to work, but you have to motivate them. They won't work when they're being screwed by a record company. But when somebody gets rid of the bullshit, and they're getting a fair deal, they'll work.' But would they work together?

In his official chronicle of this meeting, delivered to the London High Court in 1971, Klein testified, 'Everyone was in a very cheerful frame of mind and regarded this as a good deal, and a great occasion in the life of The Beatles.' Lennon, McCartney and Starkey duly appended their name to the contract; Harrison, who had just discovered that his mother was suffering from terminal cancer, signed later.

But Klein's account omitted the crucial fact that before the contract was signed John Lennon had left the Beatles. There was a long, circular conversation: as McCartney lamented later, 'We started talking about the future of the group, not knowing that there wasn't to *be* any future to this group.' It was a throwback to the dead-end discussions of January 1969: Lennon virtually silent, McCartney self-consciously enthusiastic, aware that the more optimism he displayed, the more he opened himself up to his former partner's contempt. There was sullen agreement from Lennon and Starkey that the Beatles should continue, but neither of them could muster a vision of how that might work. It was then that McCartney – not for the first time – unveiled his concept of how they could function in the decade ahead: they should return to their roots and turn up in small clubs unannounced, maybe billed under some pseudonym such as Rikki and the Redstreaks. They could reconnect with their audience, and themselves, and rediscover the commitment that had so clearly been missing from their relationship since the death of Brian Epstein.

Lennon's response was curt and abusive: 'I think you're daft.' Then, while McCartney looked on aghast, he smiled and said, 'Look, I might as well tell you. I wasn't going to say anything until after we'd signed the Capitol deal, but I'm leaving the group.' In McCartney's recollection, 'Our jaws – me, Ringo, George and Linda, because she happened to be nearby – dropped.' But Harrison wasn't there, and in later years Starkey couldn't remember any sense of shock, only relief. McCartney stuttered something like, 'What do you mean?' and Lennon hammered in the final nail: 'I've had enough. I want a divorce, like my divorce from Cynthia. It's given me a great feeling of freedom.' And then the three ex-Beatles signed their Capitol Records contract under the pretence of total unity, 'in a bit of a daze,' McCartney remembered, 'not quite knowing why we'd done it', though that was obvious: the deal ensured that whether they worked together or alone, they would earn much more from their record sales. 'I was reluctant to enter into the Capitol deal since it had been negotiated by Klein,' McCartney testified in 1971. He could not bring himself to admit that his enemy had secured such a lucrative agreement. For McCartney, money was no longer a priority. 'I would have liked the Beatles never to have broken up,' he admitted later. 'But the really hurtful thing to me was that John was really not going to tell us.'

As far as Starkey was concerned, it didn't matter whether Lennon had spoken or not: 'You could see it coming, but we all held it off for a while.' Elsewhere, he remembered that when Lennon made his announcement, 'We all said yes, because it *was* ending – and you can't keep it together, anyway, if this is what the attitude is.' The decision made so little impression on Harrison that he couldn't remember hearing about it; clearly it paled in his memory alongside the diagnosis of his mother's cancer. 'Everybody had tried to leave, so it was nothing new,' he said later. 'Everybody was leaving for years. The Beatles had started out being something that gave us a vehicle to be able to do so much when we were younger, but it had now got to a point where it was stifling us. There was too much restriction. It had to self-destruct, and I wasn't feeling bad about anybody wanting to leave, because I wanted out myself.' Starkey concurred: 'It was a relief once we finally said we could split up. I just wandered off home, I believe, and I don't know what happened after that.' He saw Lennon's decision as a moment of integrity: 'As anyone will tell you, if we had wanted we could have just carried on and made fortunes, but that was not our game.'

To celebrate, Lennon, Ono and Klein adjourned to a West End restaurant, the Peppermill. There Lennon took a decisive step into the future, appointing Klein manager of his Bag Productions company for the next three years. Perhaps the most important part of the deal for Lennon was that ABKCO would instantly transfer £20,000 to his account, enabling him to pay off the builders working at Tittenhurst Park. Over the next few days Lennon recorded his second Plastic Ono Band single, 'Cold Turkey', and its B-side, Ono's 'Don't Worry Kyoko', which he later described as the 'best fucking rock 'n' roll record ever made'. He also sat down with his friend Barry Miles for a lengthy interview that was syndicated across the underground press, ostensibly to promote *Abbey Road*. Even with Miles, he was careful to avoid any mention of his departure from the Beatles, although in retrospect there were hints: 'I don't write for the Beatles. I write for myself.' How had his relationship with Ono affected the group? 'You'll have to ask them.' More telling was his account of how his life had changed over the past two years: 'I'm more myself than I was then, because I've got the security of Yoko. That's what's done it. It's like having a "mother" and everything.' Friends had noticed that he had been calling Yoko mother since the summer; it was both an acute psychological summary of their relationship and a colloquialism familiar in the north of England. And, of course, for Lennon 'mother' meant not only protector and carer; it meant the carefree spirit who had abandoned him as a small child and then reappeared in his teens, sparking a confused medley of emotions that ran from primal love to forbidden lust. 'It all came back to me like I was back to age 16,' Lennon said, not realising exactly what he was revealing. 'All the rest of it had been wiped out. It was like going through psychiatry, really.' And the interview closed with a line that would have meant so much if its readership had known what had just happened: 'It's like starting my whole life again.'

The same realisation struck Richard Starkey. He was perfectly capable of rationalising the split: 'The break-up came because everyone had ideas of what *he* wanted to do, whereas everyone used to have ideas of what *we* would do, as a group. We weren't really fulfilling John's musical ambitions or Paul's or George's or my own, in the end, because it was separate.' Understanding why the Beatles could no longer function was one thing, dealing with the emotional consequences quite another. 'I sat in the garden for a while wondering what the hell to do with my life,' he admitted later. 'After you've said it's over and go home, you think, Oh God – that's it, then. Now what do you do? It was quite a dramatic period for me – or traumatic, really.'

Rather than finding solace in alcohol, as he would in later years, Starkey invented something to do. His solution echoed Lennon's: he would return to mother – not by marrying a dominant woman, but by recording songs that his own mother loved, a throwback to the days of crooners and big bands. Aware that his voice was an acquired taste, he enlisted the help of George Martin, who commissioned a set of arrangements from talents old and new. The sessions, which began in October 1969, were engineered by Geoff Emerick, who had always felt distant from Starkey and now found him more difficult than ever. 'Ringo was just uptight all the time, or perhaps it was just an act to keep me at a distance. The problem was that I never knew if I was talking to the actual person underneath the veneer or not.' For Starkey perhaps more than the other Beatles, the gulf between his lovable public image and his authentic self would grow increasingly difficult to bridge. Some fundamental sense of insecurity had always shone through his Beatle persona, where it appeared as self-deprecation, and boosted his appeal with fans. Now he had no obvious role, no reliable showcase for the musical talent of which he was so proud. But neither had he been seen to develop as a personality since 1963, in the way that his colleagues had. Their maturity was expressed through their songwriting; Starkey said little and wrote less*, so he remained a mystery to his audience, who chose to believe in his simple decency.

Like Starkey, McCartney was now forced to face himself, as an individual, beyond the safety of the Beatles and without the self-assurance he had always gained from Lennon's love and approval. In

* Surviving tapes of Starkey composing in the mid-1960s illustrate the limits of his songwriting talent: two guitar chords and melodies borrowed from Johnny Cash country hits.

later years he would admit that the shock of Lennon's announcement had first numbed him, and then left him fearful and uncertain. He was the one Beatle who had a guaranteed future as a soloist: critics had been applauding his innate talents as a songwriter ever since they became aware that Lennon and McCartney worked as two separate entities. But success only seemed meaningful for McCartney in the context of Lennon: most of his actions in the months ahead seemed to be designed to demonstrate his independence, and to demonstrate it to Lennon most of all.

By contrast, Harrison was already so removed from the Beatles that he was barely touched by the split. He went through the motions of promoting the *Abbey Road* album in October 1969, though his technique was unorthodox. 'To me, listening to *Abbey Road* is like listening to somebody else,' he announced. 'It doesn't feel like the Beatles.' Nor did *he* feel like one of the Beatles: he was already assembling songs for a solo album, thrilled to have escaped the restrictive gaze of his elder colleagues.

None of this alerted the public to the possibility that the Beatles had disbanded. 'I was at Apple,' recalled journalist Ray Connolly, a close friend of the group during this period, 'and Derek Taylor came in and said, "Well, that's it, we're all fucked." But he wouldn't say why. It was only later that I discovered that was the day when John announced he was leaving. Then a few weeks later I was in Toronto with John, and he pulled me aside and said, "Ray, I want to tell you something. I've left the Beatles. But you mustn't tell anyone. I'll let you know when it's OK to tell people." Every so often I'd ask John and he'd say, "No, not yet."' Harrison could still talk blithely about a future record on which 'we're going to get an equal rights thing, so we all have as much on the album'. Allen Klein authorised the release of a single, combining two songs from *Abbey Road*: Lennon's 'Come Together' (the subject of an immediate claim for copyright infringement by the publishers of Chuck Berry's 'You Can't Catch Me') and Harrison's 'Something'. There was a promotional film for the latter track, which featured footage of all the Beatles with their wives – but individually, never as a group. Lennon and Ono maintained their fiendish work schedule: they released a *Wedding Album*, an extravagantly packaged box set in which the record was one of the less intriguing items; 'Cold Turkey' carried the subject of withdrawal from heroin into the Top 30 for the first time; they prepared a live album of their Toronto performance; and they screened their experimental films in London, including the infamous *Self Portrait* of Lennon's penis.

Perhaps sensing that there was something awry, a pair of American DJs let their minds free associate and decided that the answer was simple: Paul McCartney was dead, and had been replaced by a lookalike in 1966. The 'news' broke in mid-October, boosting sales of the Beatles' back catalogue and encouraging idle minds to scan the group's recordings for clues. Music was played backwards; photographs examined for evidence of the imposter; album covers interpreted. There were obvious flaws in the theory. If McCartney's death was a secret, why were the Beatles offering clues in their songs? And how had they managed to find a doppelgänger who could write 'Hey Jude' and 'Blackbird'? But the story tapped into the global sense of distrust that had greeted the assassination of John F. Kennedy. At their most extreme the JFK conspiracy theories asked US citizens to accept that their president had been replaced in a *coup d'état*. The notion that one of the Beatles was a fake offered a safer route to that satisfying frisson of paranoia.

What's ironic is that the Beatles were indeed conspiring to keep a secret from their fans; the theorists had simply identified the wrong target. Yet the clues were there, all the same: the conspirators could not restrain their tongues. Starkey distanced himself from his friends: 'I'm sorry, but I'm just not like them'; 'I don't particularly dig what John and Yoko are doing'; 'We are four completely different people. We have all stopped doing things together.' McCartney was unearthed at his Scottish farm by a reporter from the US magazine *Life*. The magazine trumpeted the fact that McCartney was alive, but missed the barely concealed subtext: 'The Beatle thing is over. It has been exploded, partly by what we have done, and partly by other people. We are individuals – all different. John married Yoko, I married Linda. We didn't marry the same girl.' It was an intriguing way to describe the break-up, deflecting his disagreements with Lennon onto their choice of partners.

Inevitably, Lennon was the least restrained of the four. In a radio interview he referred to 'the Beatles, so-called'. Under the headline BEATLES ON THE BRINK OF SPLITTING, the *New Musical Express* reported his observations in detail: 'Paul and I both have differences of opinion on how things should be run. But instead of it being a private argument about how an LP should be done, or a certain track, it's now a large argument about the organisation of Apple itself.' There was no mention of wives, and Lennon added gracefully, 'I don't really want to discuss Paul without him here.' He concluded, 'The Beatles split up? It just depends how much we all want to record together. I don't know if I want to record together again. I go off and on it, I really do.'

For McCartney, and maybe Harrison and Starkey as well, this signified hope. 'For about three or four months,' he recalled years later, 'George, Ringo and I rang each other to ask, "Well, is this it, then?" It wasn't that the record company had dumped us. It was just a case of: we might get back together again. Nobody quite knew if it was one of John's little flings, and that maybe he was going to feel the pinch in a week's time and say, "I was only kidding." I think John did kind of leave the door open. He'd said, "I'm pretty much leaving the group, but . . ."' McCartney testified in 1971, 'I think all of us (except possibly John) expected we would come together again one day.' Yet it's hard to imagine him reading some of Lennon's other comments in late 1969 without a stab of pain – for example, 'The Beatles can go on appealing to a wide audience as long as they make nice albums like *Abbey Road*, which have nice little folk songs like "Maxwell's Silver Hammer" for the grannies to dig.'

Of course, the Beatles were still locked together as the reluctant controllers of 'the Beatles Group of Companies' under the supervision of Allen Klein. Although they had failed to secure control of Northern Songs, there remained the dilemma of what to do with their substantial shareholding. Klein negotiated for ATV to buy the Beatles out, only for negotiations to be disrupted when ATV received a letter from John Eastman claiming that Klein did not represent McCartney in any way. This surprised Klein, to say the least, as he had been negotiating regularly with McCartney about exactly that subject. There was a crisis meeting at Klein's apartment in Mayfair at which McCartney spoke to Eastman by telephone, scolded him for contacting ATV, and told him that he supported what Klein was doing. McCartney said that Eastman's final words were, 'Well, I don't understand it. You're all crazy.' Klein then recalled that McCartney phoned ATV chief Sir Lew Grade and told him, 'Allen Klein is coming over and he speaks for me.' The deal was concluded, and Klein registered it as a decisive victory in his battle of wills with the Eastmans

On the same day that ATV bought the Beatles' shareholding, Klein held another screening of the *Get Back* film. He invited the entire group and their wives, but Lennon and Ono did not attend. The movie now ran around 100 minutes, about half its original length, and McCartney, Harrison and Starkey agreed that it was fit to release. Klein claimed credit for suggesting that it should be retitled *Let It Be*, enabling the McCartney-penned song of that title to be issued as a single at the same time, alongside a soundtrack album.* At dinner Klein told the three Beatles about another proposal, which Lennon had already approved: Apple Records should invite the American record producer Phil Spector to join its staff. The group had met Spector on several occasions in 1963 and 1964, and Harrison in particular was an admirer of his work. 'They were all enthusiastic,' Klein recalled.

Apparently random events filled the landscape of the Beatles' new world. While McCartney and Starkey struggled to imagine how they might survive outside the group, Lennon ran fearlessly into the future. He outraged many right-thinking British citizens by returning the MBE medal he had been awarded in 1965, complaining about the government's inaction in the face of famine and civil war in Nigeria, and, as if to annoy anyone who wasn't already ruffled, adding a sly comment about the fact that 'Cold Turkey' was now sliding down the Top 30. His action spurred one gesture of solidarity, as Nigerian boxer Dick Tiger also returned his MBE, and a flurry of protests from those who felt that Lennon was insulting both the Queen and the decaying British Commonwealth. The next day Lennon prepared fresh edits of two songs he'd recorded earlier, 'What's the New Mary Jane' and 'You Know My Name', and announced that they would be rush-released as a Plastic Ono Band single. Just as quickly, the project was cancelled,

---

* This was probably the only occasion on which Harrison and Starkey saw the film before its release in 1970. At this stage it still included footage of Ono jamming with the three-man Beatles on the day of Harrison's departure. Discreet pressure ensured that the clip was removed, but both Harrison and Starkey later talked as if it still featured in the final edit.

with Apple explaining, 'It was mutually decided by the Beatles that it sounded more like the Beatles themselves than the Plastic Ono Band' – not least because both songs were indeed Beatles recordings. McCartney's reaction to Lennon's attempted theft can easily be imagined.

A clear sign that the times had changed came with the December 1969 publication of the final edition of *The Beatles Book*, which had appeared every month since 1963 with the group's increasingly distant approval. 'The Beatles have lost interest,' publisher Sean O'Mahony complained to the *Guardian*. 'They won't co-operate, let us have new pictures, or give interviews.' In his last editorial he attacked the group for their willingness to encourage young people to take drugs. 'I didn't think that the pop world had done young people any favours,' he recalled later. 'It was fine for them: they were rich, and had someone to pick them up if they fell over. But their fans didn't have the same support network if things went wrong.'

With the timing that would become his trademark, US promoter Sid Bernstein chose this moment to offer the Beatles another substantial payday, if only they would come to their senses and perform together: $1 million for an appearance at a Dutch festival in August 1970. Lennon had similar plans of his own. Fired by his recent appearance in Toronto, he proposed a much more ambitious project: a peace festival in the city that would not only involve the Beatles but Elvis Presley, Led Zeppelin, the Who and virtually every other artist whose name came to Lennon's mind. The idea was doomed from the start, as Lennon was insistent that (a) the artists should be paid and (b) it should be a free festival. This equation proved impossible to solve, and after much hype in the underground press Lennon and his fellow organisers acrimoniously parted company. Stranger still was the idea, also given credence by Apple, that Lennon might sit on the board of a United States peace festival – to be staged not by hippies and peaceniks, but by the United States government. Even Lennon realised that this might endanger his image, and the proposal disintegrated in the wake of heightened protests against America's involvement in the Vietnam War.

'When we're not working, we get pretty depressed,' Lennon admitted, and his activities had taken on a frantic quality – demonstrations, films, records, every aspect of his life translated into performance art. Surprisingly, Harrison echoed his work rate, having signed up with the touring band of US rock soul duo Delaney and Bonnie alongside Eric Clapton. On 6 December the musicians appeared in Liverpool, where Harrison allowed himself a rare moment in the spotlight. Unknown to him, Clapton had developed a passionate attachment to Pattie Boyd, who attended the Liverpool show with her younger sister Paula. According to Clapton, Harrison took him aside afterwards 'and suggested that I should spend the night with Pattie so that he could sleep with Paula . . . but at the last moment he lost his nerve and nothing happened. The end result was not the one George wanted, as I ended up spending the night with Paula instead.' Clapton began to live with Paula Boyd while continuing to court her sister.

Harrison also found time in Liverpool to tell a journalist, 'I'd like to do the Beatles thing, but more like Delaney and Bonnie with us augmented with a few more singers and a few trumpets, saxes, organ and all that.' The closest that his dream came to fruition was nine days later, when Lennon, Ono and the Plastic Ono Band were joined by the entire Delaney and Bonnie troupe, including Harrison, for a 30-minute charity performance in London. The impromptu 'supergroup', as the pop papers named it, played extended versions of the songs from Lennon/Ono's latest single, hitting almost supernatural peaks of what Lennon regarded as the music of the future, but confusing as many fans as it delighted.

It was easy to imagine that Starkey might have appeared alongside Lennon and Harrison that night, but McCartney would never have been invited. He continued to isolate himself from his colleagues and from Klein, despite being happy to benefit from the contracts that Klein had renegotiated. He secretly began work on a solo album, instructing his confidants at Apple that Lennon should not be told. That month he phoned Klein early one New York morning, and (so Klein alleged) 'said something about my not giving interviews to newspapers, and leaving his in-laws alone'. Meanwhile, Lennon was describing Klein's impact on Apple as 'really marvellous . . . He's swept out all the rubbish and the dead wood, and stopped it being a rest house for all the world's hippies. Klein's very good.'

Derek Taylor had the unfortunate task of interpreting the Beatles' actions for the outside world. As 1969 came to a close, the Apple press officer was invited to speculate about the year ahead. He clearly knew nothing about McCartney's recording activity, as he said that the musician was 'the only one who doesn't seem to have an outlet for whatever he gets together'. He hoped that McCartney would return from his winter holiday prepared to spur the reluctant Beatles back to work. 'We can expect a Beatle meeting to be called in January,' he said. But Taylor revealed that the Beatles might now be a more elastic concept than in the past. 'Yoko's really one of them,' he claimed. 'Without Yoko, there wouldn't be the Beatles. [Lennon] and Yoko are 50 per cent of each other, so if John's a Beatle, that makes her a Beatle too.'

One of Taylor's predictions was proved right, although not in the fashion he might have anticipated. On the afternoon of 3 January 1970 the Beatles gathered in the familiar setting of Studio Two, Abbey Road Studios. This was not a quartet, however, or even quintet, but the three-man group that had worked together so successfully in July. John Lennon was absent, undergoing hypnosis treatment in Denmark in an effort to quit smoking, cropping his hair and telling the press that all his future record royalties would be donated to the peace movement. (Allen Klein's 10 per cent share of Bag Productions was suddenly looking less attractive.) Without Lennon, the Beatles recorded Harrison's 'I Me Mine'. The song was featured in the *Let It Be* film, and Klein was anxious that it should appear on the soundtrack album. The following day the trio applied various overdubs to McCartney's 'Let It Be', and Linda McCartney was persuaded to flesh out the background harmonies with her naive, untutored voice. Eighteen months after Lennon had first invited Ono to participate in a Beatles session, McCartney had finally secured his hollow revenge.

Once again the luckless Glyn Johns was asked to assemble an appropriate album; once again the four Beatles turned it down. *Let It Be* was now scheduled for cinema release in May, and Klein was desperate to seize the commercial opportunity that the film represented by issuing a new record. He had already asked Apple Records' US head, Allan Steckler, to compile an album for the American market entitled *Hey Jude*, which the Beatles condoned as it represented a way of earning money without any effort. Klein must have been tempted to overrule his infuriatingly indecisive clients and authorise his own version of the *Let It Be* soundtrack. But even he could not have imagined that the Beatles' record company could release a new album by the group without their unanimous consent. As it turned out, his imagination was about to be stretched to its limit – and so was Paul McCartney's patience.

Chapter 4

You mustn't pretend that brothers don't fight, because they fight worse than anybody.

Richard Starkey

At Christmas 1969 John Lennon and Yoko Ono launched a worldwide poster campaign to announce 'War Is Over (If You Want It)'. It was a stunningly simple and effective message, placing the responsibility for peace on the whole of mankind. It also removed the couple's self-imposed burden of saving the world. There was little more talk of donating their earnings to peace or carrying their bed-in tactic behind the Iron Curtain. Their priority now was personal freedom: physical, chemical, existential. 'We've been through the post-drug depression,' Lennon explained when they returned from Denmark in mid-January. 'Now we've resurrected hope in ourselves.'

Yet the world was closing in on the Lennons: their marriage was disintegrating, so was the Toronto Peace Festival; Ono's health was delicate after a series of miscarriages; and there was the perennial problem of Apple. Since May 1969 two ravenous sets of lawyers had been debating the legality of the management agreement that Lennon, Harrison, Starkey and Klein had signed. As Paul McCartney reflected ruefully, 'We put every lawyer's kid through school.'

During a meeting at Apple in mid-January, Lennon, Harrison and Starkey agreed an expanded management contract with ABKCO and Klein designed to cover the gaping loopholes in the original draft. (Significantly, McCartney was not consulted about the deal.) They signed on behalf of a web of companies that month – not just the various Apple subsidiaries, but such concerns as Singsong Ltd (handling Harrison's music publishing), Startling Music Ltd (likewise for Starkey) and Ono Music Ltd. There were Apple offices in Switzerland, Canada, Australia, the Netherlands, Sweden, Italy, France and Germany to consider; twin incarnations of Apple Records Inc. in New York and Los Angeles; Bag Music Inc., for some far-flung outpost of the Lennon/Ono empire; and Joko Films Inc., which looked after the Lennons' US film interests. A total of 33 companies sheltered under the Apple umbrella, each now owing allegiance to Klein's ABKCO.

The meeting was held a few hours after Lennon and Harrison had completed a recording session at Abbey Road – not for the Beatles, but for the Plastic Ono Band. The previous day Lennon had woken up with a song, which he titled 'Instant Karma!'.* Impatient as ever, he wanted to record it and release it immediately. He contacted George Harrison, who was in London with Phil Spector discussing his first solo album. 'I said to Phil, "Why don't you come to the session?"' Harrison recalled. With characteristic brio, Spector transformed the ambience of the track, which crackled with tension as Lennon delivered his deconstruction of stardom over ominous piano and whiplash drums.

Lennon was ecstatic: in a few minutes Spector had concocted a fervid, almost claustrophobic sound beyond anything the Beatles could have achieved. The producer was erratic and prone to frequent explosions of temper and ego, but Lennon was smitten. He told Klein that he wanted Spector to produce his next album as well as Harrison's. 'Why don't we get Phil to listen to the Let It Be tapes?' he added.

The decision required the approval of all four Beatles, and for several weeks it proved impossible to pin McCartney down. He had finally decided to accept Lennon at his word: the Beatles were over. 'I started thinking, Well, if that's the case, I had better get myself together,' he recalled. 'I can't just let John control the situation and dump us as if we're the jilted girlfriends.' He closed the doors to the outside world

---

* Karma Productions was the Canadian company promoting the Toronto Peace Festival; the song may have been a subtle message to them.

and worked in an environment where there was no one to question his judgement. His first solo album took shape in his home studio, before he ventured into Morgan Studios in north-west London – removed from the hub of the London recording industry. Even so, he reserved all his session time under the pseudonym Billy Martin, a ruse that continued when he finally felt brave enough to stroll round the corner from his home to Abbey Road Studios in February.

Eventually, McCartney answered the string of messages he'd received about Phil Spector. A soundtrack album was definitely required, but McCartney must have wondered whether someone who had already worked with Lennon, and was about to produce Harrison, could deliver an impartial appraisal of *his* material. Eventually he agreed, on the same proviso as the other Beatles: the album could not be released until all of them had approved Spector's work. Meanwhile, McCartney completed his own record, a charming if insubstantial collage of fragments, including rejects from the Beatles' January 1969 sessions, instrumentals and two hauntingly beautiful love songs, 'Every Night' and 'Maybe I'm Amazed'.

All four Beatles were now promising solo albums. Harrison had a stockpile of at least 20 songs, some of which had been rejected by the Beatles in January 1969, while others had been carefully retained for his own use, notably his collaboration with Bob Dylan 'I'd Have You Anytime'. Yet he was still torn between the spiritual and the secular. He had recently bought Friar Park, a Gothic mansion on the outskirts of Henley-on-Thames, formerly occupied by an order of nuns. Built by the Victorian eccentric Sir Francis Crisp, it was surrounded by grounds that encompassed not just ornamental lakes but a network of underground caves that could be explored by boat and extravagant gardens that had been allowed to slip into disrepair. Harrison's plans ran to a complete refurbishment of the property and its surroundings, and the installation of a lavish recording studio. Even by the standards of rock star grandeur, it was an epic enterprise in consumerism, but Harrison also envisaged the house as a spiritual haven.

He soon invited several members of the Krishna Temple to live with him, to his wife's muffled horror. She felt more and more isolated from her husband. 'He became increasingly obsessive about meditating and chanting,' she recalled. 'He would do it for hours.' After several months dedicated to the spirit, Harrison would relapse: 'As if the pleasures of the flesh were too hard to resist, he would stop meditating, snort coke, have fun flirting and partying.' As Boyd explained, 'I didn't want to chant all day. George did it obsessively for three months, then went crazy.'

It was Harrison the chanter who travelled to Paris in March 1970 with the acolytes of the Krishna Temple on a mission to spread the word of God. 'It was rather like throwing a mountain into a puddle,' said his Krishna friend Shyamasundar, 'because about 330-odd Frenchmen, photographers and pressmen met him at this restaurant and almost smothered him. We didn't get too much Krishna consciousness propagated.' The same observer noted that Harrison's 'future plans were to become Krishna conscious . . . He's got everything that the material world can offer, but still there's no satisfaction in it, so he knows that to understand Krishna and actually associate with the supreme personality of God is the highest and rare-most [sic] achievement of man.' And Shyamasundar confirmed that Krishna also dominated Harrison's musical ambitions: 'He has said that from now on he only wants to sing mantras.' Yet Harrison knew that wasn't an appropriate dish to set before Phil Spector, so he kept the producer waiting.

So did John Lennon, despite Apple confidently announcing in March 1970 that he was about to begin an album. (Meanwhile, George Martin was promising that the Beatles would record together in June, a triumph of hope over reality.) Several obstacles remained, not the least of which was Lennon's lack of songs. After the deluge of inspiration he'd experienced in India, his creativity had been spasmodic, although the quality of his material, from 'Come Together' to 'Instant Karma!', obscured his difficulties. He continued to insist that his relationship with Yoko Ono had unleashed his full capabilities as an artist, but to write songs it seemed he needed the Beatles and the stimulus of McCartney's competitive instinct, or else the intervention of an irresistible force from outside. The Toronto Peace Festival certainly wasn't the answer: it collapsed in early March 1970, after Lennon sent the promoters a telegram that ended, 'We want nothing to do with you or your festival. Yours in disgust, John and Yoko.' Harrison might have found Lennon's vision of the festival sympathetic: 'Our latest idea was to have everyone at the festival singing only "Hare Krishna" . . . Can you imagine what we could achieve together in the one spot

– singing and praying for peace – one million souls?' But his final words to his global audience were more despairing. 'We are sorry for the confusion. It is bigger than both of us . . . We still believe. Pray for us.' It sounded like a last telegram from the *Titanic*.

Still prepared to engage with the outside world, Lennon found a fresh hero in Trinidad-born black-power activist Michael Abdul Malik (known professionally as Michael X), founder of a London collective known as the Black Eagles, inspired by the Black Panther Party of California. Malik stumbled upon every radical's dream, a rich and guilt-ridden patron. 'Michael was a persuasive guy,' recalled Lennon's friend Barry Miles. 'He became whatever people wanted him to be. He would spin these rich people a yarn, and how could they not write him a cheque? John Lennon was bound to be impressed by him. It was inevitable.' Malik talked his way into Apple's offices and fearlessly accused Lennon of cultural larceny. 'You have stolen the rhythms of the black people you knew in Liverpool,' he said. 'You might have done it consciously or unconsciously. Anyway, now you owe us a debt.' Lennon offered him cash from the Bag Productions account, ostensibly as an advance on a book deal, although no contract was ever signed or manuscript delivered.

When he and Yoko Ono had cut their hair in Denmark, he had saved the cuttings in a plastic bag, aware that in a world still prone to Beatlemania there were few things more valuable than true fragments of a Beatle. Now he had found a cause worthy of his sacred offering. On 4 February 1970 Lennon, Ono and Derek Taylor climbed to the roof of Malik's HQ, watched by a crowd of photographers. Lennon handed over the bag of hair, Malik offered a pair of bloodstained shorts once worn by boxer Muhammad Ali, and Lennon grinned inanely at the cameras. 'It was such an ugly meeting. Nobody printed anything,' recalled Derek Taylor. 'There was a massive press turnout, with photographers clambering over the roofs, and then nothing in the papers. I definitely should have had the wisdom to call a halt to the daily press conferences they were giving. Every day there was a new campaign, a new cause. This was the final proof that they were overexposed.'

Lennon's desire for publicity seemed to have reached manic proportions. Even the Valentine's Day gift of his psychedelic Rolls-Royce to Allen Klein was accompanied by a press advert and a statement:

'Believe it or not, Allen Klein is a soul brother from way back – a few incarnations ago. We went out to eat with him, and it was revealed unto us, and I was sorry for the thoughts I'd had about him, even the paranoia I'd had laid on me by other people. There'll be no more of that, and I wanted to give him this to surprise him. He's just fantastic, and I know there's a lot of shit going around about him. About us too.'

More pressing was what Lennon in a notorious 1971 letter would call 'shit from the inside, baby': the psychological turbulence that was corroding his relationship with Ono. In January 1970 Lennon received a book in the mail. Entitled *The Primal Scream*, it was the work of radical psychotherapist Arthur Janov. '[John] read it,' Janov recalled, 'and he came to me.' The book represented a profound break from orthodox psychotherapy. 'I believe that the only way to eliminate neurosis is with overthrow by force and violence,' Janov wrote, 'the force of years of compressed feelings and denied needs; the violence of wrenching them out of an unreal system.' These feelings and needs, he declared, were the accumulation of primal pain, first experienced in the earliest stages of childhood, perhaps even during the birth process itself. They represented rejections by fathers, mothers and other authority figures, all the agony of life in the cauldron of everyday cruelty. 'Just as neurosis results from a gradual shutting-off process, becoming healthy involves a gradual turning-on again,' Janov wrote. 'Primal Therapy is like neurosis in reverse. Each day in a young child's life, hurt after hurt closes off more of his feelings until he is neurotic. In Primal Therapy the patient relives those hurts, opening himself up until he is well.' The final breakthrough of recovery, Janov said, would come in an outpouring of emotion so urgent and unrestrained that it would emerge as a piercing shriek of pain.

Instinctively repelled by intellectual theory ('bullshit'), Lennon still devoured *The Primal Scream* with the same excitement that *The Autobiography of a Yogi* inspired in George Harrison. He immediately phoned Janov and asked him to come to England. By mid-March the therapist was at Lennon's Ascot home, encouraging him to scream for his mother's love. 'John had about as much pain as I've ever seen in my life,' Janov recalled. 'He was a very dedicated patient. Very serious about it.' A measure of Lennon's commitment is the fact that he did not immediately run to the press, like an excited schoolboy, to alert the world to his new discovery. He had become a compulsive enthusiast, for drugs, for the Maharishi, for Ono, and for Klein, but Primal Scream Therapy affected him too profoundly to be translated into a poster event. Soon he would be dragged back into the material world, however, as the more recent past demanded his attention.

Nearly six months after Lennon had quit the group, the Beatles continued to pretend that they were still a functioning unit. Any concerns to the contrary were calmed by the imminent arrival of the *Let It Be* film, and by statements from Starkey and Harrison suggesting the quartet would soon work together. 'We've got unity through diversity,' Harrison explained cryptically. It was an epigram that would soon be exposed as wildly optimistic.

There was a series of Beatle landmarks on the horizon. The *Hey Jude* album was released on 26 February 1970. Starkey's *Sentimental Journey* was scheduled for 27 March. The *Let It Be* film was meant to premiere in New York on 28 April, then in London a week later. And the 'Let It Be' single was rush-released on 6 March, though tellingly it failed to top the British chart. Nevertheless, McCartney's elegant, gospel-inflected tune* whetted the global appetite for the soundtrack album, which still awaited completion.

Suddenly there was another item to squeeze into the agenda, an album entitled *McCartney*. Its creator believed that, as a co-owner of Apple, he could impose his own schedule: the record, he said, would be issued on 10 April. Neil Aspinall politely asked if he would mind postponing the album for a week, to allow Starkey's record a little longer in the spotlight. McCartney agreed, prepared a final mix on 23 March, handed over the tapes and artwork, and discovered on 25 March, when his brother-in-law John Eastman visited EMI, that Allen Klein had already postponed his album's release. McCartney immediately phoned Harrison, who told him that there was no question of delay, confirming this in a telegram that he sent to the other Beatles, Klein and Aspinall.

McCartney triumphantly showed the telegram to EMI, but his victory was short-lived. On the same day he finished his record, Phil Spector had begun work at Abbey Road on the *Let It Be* album. By

---

* According to Mal Evans, McCartney was inspired to write the song not by his late mother, whose name appeared in the final lyric, but by a vision he had experienced during meditation of Evans walking towards him, saying 'Let it be, let it be.' 'Mother Malcolm' became 'Mother Mary' for public consumption.

the end of March Spector was confident that the project would be completed within a couple of days, so Klein alerted EMI that the new Beatles LP would be issued before the end of April, to accompany the premiere of the film. But the most suitable date was just one week after *McCartney* was due to be released. Now the Beatles would effectively be competing for sales with Paul McCartney.

Klein visited EMI executives, and 'discussed with them the problem of two long-playing records coming out together. They agreed that it was undesirable from a selling point of view.' Once ego was removed from the equation, the solution was obvious. *McCartney* was only a record; *Let It Be* was a multimedia package, albeit chaotically assembled and still, less than a month before release, unfinished. Besides, *Let It Be* was a group project, and should automatically take precedence over that of an individual. And so McCartney might have agreed, had the decision not followed eighteen months of acrimony.

Lennon and Harrison certainly had no qualms about delaying *McCartney*. On 31 March Lennon informed EMI of their decision, writing, 'We have arrived at the conclusion that it would not be in the best interests of this company for the record to be released on that date.' Meanwhile, Harrison wrote to McCartney:

> Dear Paul, We thought a lot about yours and the Beatles LPs – and decided it's stupid for Apple to put out two big albums within 7 days of each other (also there's Ringo's and *Hey Jude*) – so we sent a letter to EMI telling them to hold your release date til June 4th (there's a big Apple-Capitol convention in Hawaii then). We thought you'd come round when you realized that the Beatles album was coming out on April 24th. We're sorry it turned out like this – it's nothing personal. Love John & George. Hare Krishna. A Mantra a Day Keeps MAYA! Away.

Harrison's religious references sounded almost aggressive; McCartney must have wondered whose side Maya, the Hindu goddess of illusion, was on.

Harrison's letter to McCartney was sealed in an envelope labelled 'From Us, To You', and left at the Apple reception desk for a messenger to carry to McCartney's home. But Richard Starkey agreed to deliver the bad news in person. 'I didn't think it fair some office lad should take something like that round,' he explained. He drove to St John's Wood, handed over the letter and told McCartney that he agreed with what it said. 'He went crazy; he *was* crazy, I thought,' Starkey recalled. 'He just shouted and pointed at me. He was out of control, prodding his finger towards my face. He told me to get my coat on and get out. I got brought down, because I couldn't believe it was happening to me.' McCartney explained: 'I really got angry . . . I said, in effect, this was the last straw, and "If you drag me down, I'll drag you down." What I meant was, "Anything you do to me, I will do to you."' Lennon felt that 'Paul's was just an ego game . . . Ringo had not taken sides or anything like that . . . he attacked Ringo and he started threatening him and everything, and that was the kibosh for Ringo.' As Starkey admitted, 'I'm very emotional; things like that really upset me at the time.' The Beatles weren't strangers to the raised fist – it was an instinctive reaction from Lennon when he felt he was being challenged – but none of the group had ever physically confronted Starkey, who was its most diminutive and vulnerable member.

The immediate victor was McCartney: the distraught Starkey reported back to Apple, and the decision was taken to let the bassist's album go ahead. But the incident had a grievous effect on the relationship between the two men. Throughout the disputes over Apple and Klein, Starkey had never let business decisions affect their friendship. Now he felt disgusted, alienated, crushed, battered, the whole range of negative emotions that McCartney had experienced when Ono and then Klein disrupted his perfect universe.

The next day John Eastman wrote to United Artists Films to say that McCartney had not yet agreed that the film should be released, and that Klein's word could not be trusted. Meanwhile, Phil Spector was close to completing the soundtrack album. The day after his confrontation with McCartney, the luckless Starkey faced another psychodrama. Spector had commissioned orchestral and choral decoration for three songs, and Starkey was there to overdub his percussion tracks, which might otherwise be obscured. For the last five years nothing had been added to a Beatles track without the approval of its composer. Now songs by Lennon, McCartney and Harrison were about to be augmented, and none of the three was there to watch it happen.

Richard Hewson's* arrangement for McCartney's 'The Long and Winding Road' was by far the most radical, and controversial, of the revisions. As originally recorded, the song was a self-consciously maudlin affair, overflowing with sentimentality. Rather than subverting this mood with a touch of atonality, Hewson boldly decided to accentuate it. He delivered a score that was almost claustrophobic, like the ill-ventilated sick room of some *ancien régime* noble. On another day Starkey might have insisted that McCartney was consulted. But he was still in shock after their confrontation and also faced a more immediate problem: attempting to prevent the overwrought producer from treating the studio staff and orchestra so badly that they walked out. 'Phil had a style of humiliation that was part of his humour,' recalled Leon Russell, veteran of many Spector sessions.

With Spector's work complete on 2 April, copies of the *Let It Be* album were forwarded to the Beatles for their approval, with a letter from Spector. 'If there is anything you'd like done to the album,' the producer told them, 'let me know and I'll be glad to help. Naturally little things are easy to change, big things might be a problem. If you wish, please call me about anything regarding the album tonight.' 'We all said yes,' Starkey recalled. 'Even at the beginning Paul said yes. I spoke to him on the phone, and said, "Did you like it?" and he said, "Yeah, it's OK." He didn't put it down.' Starkey himself agreed: 'I like what Phil did, actually.' So did Harrison: 'I personally thought it was a really good idea.' And Lennon: 'He always wanted to work with the Beatles, and he was given the *shittiest* load of badly recorded shit – and with a lousy feeling to it – ever. And he made something out of it. It wasn't fantastic, but I heard it; I didn't puke. I was so relieved.' And finally, not exuberant but phlegmatic, McCartney: 'When I got the finished record there were loud ladies' voices wailing. It wasn't terrible . . . I preferred it the way it was.' But he raised no immediate objections. Harrison sent Spector a telegram of congratulations; Starkey phoned with the same message. It had taken fifteen months from first arrival in the chilly halls of Twickenham to the high-tension finale at Abbey Road, but it seemed as if the saga of *Let It Be* was over.

Throughout this period of Apple intrigue, Lennon and Ono remained

* Spector claimed that it was McCartney who recommended Hewson for the job. He also informed the Beatles in April 1970 that he thought this song would be a more appropriate title track for their album than 'Let It Be'.

under the care of Arthur Janov. The therapist had persuaded the couple that they would only gain lasting benefit from their screaming if they were separated. Reluctantly, they moved into luxury London hotels and were only allowed to communicate by letter. Janov scuttled from one suite to the other, returning Lennon to the pain of separation from his parents, Ono to the turmoil of Tokyo under American air assault.

McCartney was experiencing his own vision of hell. 'I was going through a bad time,' he recalled, 'what I suspect was almost a nervous breakdown. I remember lying awake at nights shaking.' Six months earlier he had felt bereaved by Lennon's departure from the Beatles. Now his tie to the group that he had joined in 1957 was strangling him. Since the arrival of Klein he had been reacting, not acting. The time had come for him to assert control over his own professional life in the hope that he could also lift the darkness closing around his soul.

The initial declaration of independence came from Eastman and Eastman. On 7 April they announced the formation of McCartney Productions Ltd. Its first two projects, they declared, would be the *McCartney* album and an animated film based around the strip cartoon character Rupert Bear. Meanwhile, copies of *McCartney* were prepared for the press. Derek Taylor rang McCartney to ask whether he was prepared to talk to journalists about the record. He replied, 'I can't deal with the press. I hate all those Beatles questions.' According to McCartney, he suggested that Taylor send him a list of questions, and he would provide answers. 'So he asked me some stilted questions and I gave some stilted answers,' McCartney recalled in 1984, 'that included an announcement that we'd split up.'

Taylor, however, insisted that the questions were entirely McCartney's invention: 'He was only supposed to write out information explaining how he made his album. Instead he hands us this interview with himself asking questions such as would he miss Ringo. It was entirely gratuitous. Nobody asked him that question. He asked that question of himself.' This edited version of the questionnaire gives a flavour of the topics McCartney chose to raise.

Q: Will Paul and Linda become a John and Yoko?
A: No, they will become Paul and Linda.
Q: Will the other Beatles receive the first copies?
A: Wait and see.

Q: Is it true that neither Allen Klein nor ABKCO will be in any way involved with the production, manufacturing, distribution or promotion of this album?

A: Not if I can help it.

Q: Did you miss the other Beatles and George Martin? Was there a moment, e.g., when you thought, Wish Ringo was here for this break?

A: No.

Q: Are you planning a new album or single with the Beatles?

A: No.

Q: Is this album a rest away from the Beatles or the start of a solo career?

A: Time will tell. Being a solo album means it's the start of a solo career . . . and not being done with the Beatles means it's a rest. So it's both.

Q: Have you any plans for live appearances?

A: No.

Q: Is your break with the Beatles, temporary or permanent, due to personal differences or musical ones?

A: Personal differences, business differences, musical differences, but most of all because I have a better time with my family. Temporary or permanent? I don't know.

Q: Do you foresee a time when Lennon/McCartney becomes an active songwriting partnership again?

A: No.

Q: What do you feel about John's peace effort? The Plastic Ono Band? Giving back the MBE? Yoko's influence? Yoko?

A: I love John and respect what he does – it doesn't give *me* any pleasure.

Q: Were you pleased with *Abbey Road*? Was it musically restricting?

A: It was a good album. (No. 1 for a long time.)

Q: What is your relationship with Klein?

A: It isn't. I am not in contact with him, and he does not represent me in *any* way.

Q: What is your relationship with Apple?

A: It is the office of a company which I part-own with the other Beatles. I don't go there because I don't like offices or business, especially when I'm on holiday.

Q: Have you any plans to set up an independent production company?

A: McCartney Productions.

Q: What are your plans now? A holiday? A musical? A movie? Retirement?

A: My only plan is to grow up.

The script was duly returned to Apple, where Derek Taylor read it, raised a weary eyebrow and sent it to the press. The packages arrived on Thursday 9 April 1970. 'I received one at the *Evening Standard*,' recalled journalist Ray Connolly, 'but the story was embargoed until the next day, so I didn't print anything. But Don Short at the *Mirror* did.' The result was a *Daily Mirror* exclusive under the headline PAUL IS QUITTING THE BEATLES. Early copies were available in the West End of London that evening, and Apple staff were immediately disturbed at home by fevered enquiries from other papers. The result was that the *Mirror*'s report was accompanied the following morning by an altogether more sober story in *The Times*, MCCARTNEY SPLIT WITH BEATLES DENIED. One of Taylor's assistants, Mavis Smith, was quoted as saying, 'This is just not true.' The paper added, 'She knew that Mr McCartney intended issuing a statement today on the release of a new recording, but denied that any critical statements meant a real break-up of the group. She said she hoped that the group would get together for another recording after the summer.'

Allen Klein had flown into London on Thursday. He was due to meet executives from the British arm of United Artists the following day, at a board meeting of Apple Films Ltd. George Harrison would attend in his role as company director, and Paul McCartney had also signalled his intention to be there, so that he could raise his misgivings about the deal between Apple and UA. But later that day McCartney informed Apple that he would not, after all, be present at the meeting. It was only when the story of a Beatles break-up appeared the next morning that Klein understood why his opponent had pulled out.

On Thursday afternoon McCartney called Lennon, who was in therapy with Arthur Janov. 'I'm doing what you did,' he told his colleague. 'I'm putting out an album, and I'm leaving the Beatles as well.' 'Good,' Lennon replied. 'That makes two of us who have seen sense.' The following morning, when Lennon heard about the *Mirror*'s story, he realised that he had been trumped. 'I phoned John,' explained Ray Connolly, 'and told him what Paul had said. He was furious and said, "Why didn't you write the story when I told you?" I said that he'd asked me not to, and he said, "You're the fucking journalist, Ray!" In retrospect, I think he was setting me up. He thought I wouldn't be able to resist breaking the story first, and then he could turn around to the others and say, "I told him not to say anything," and he'd be the innocent party.'

'John had made it clear that he wanted to be the one to announce the split,' Linda McCartney explained years later, 'since it was his idea.' 'He wanted to be first,' her husband confirmed. 'But I didn't realise it would hurt him that much or that it mattered who was first.' Lennon commented later, 'We were all hurt that he didn't tell us what he was going to do. I think he claims that he didn't mean that to happen, but that's bullshit.' Envy also entered the equation. 'I was cursing because I hadn't done it. I wanted to do it and I should have done it . . . I was a fool not to do what Paul did, which is use it to sell a record.'

With a mixture of admiration and contempt, Lennon described McCartney as 'a good PR man . . . about the best in the world, probably. He really does a job.' But in the years to come McCartney felt apologetic enough about the statement and the way it was released to spin defensive webs around himself: 'The way it came out, it looked like it was specially engineered by me'; 'It was going to be an insert in the album. But when it was printed as news, it looked very cold, yes, even crazy'; 'I figured it was about time we told the truth. It was stupid, OK, but I thought someone ought to say something. I didn't like to keep lying to people. It was a conscience thing to me'; 'It was a nasty little period, all of that. Looking at it now, it looks very callous.'

A 'conscience thing' that 'looks very callous': by his own admission, McCartney's credibility as a 'good PR man' had been shaken. His clearest summary of what he wanted, and what he achieved, came in 1986:

I think John thought I was using this press release for publicity – as I suppose, in a way, it was. So it all looked very weird, and it ruffled a few feathers. The good thing about it was that we all had to finally own up to the fact that we'd broken up three or four months before. We'd been ringing each other quite constantly, sort of saying, 'Let's get it back together.' And I think me, George and Ringo did want to save things. But I think John was, at that point, too heavily into his new life – which you can't blame him.

The circularity of his argument was obvious: I broke up the Beatles because John had already broken up the Beatles, although I wanted to save the Beatles . . . And yet one truth was inescapable: by staging a media event as shocking and effective as anything in Yoko Ono's imagination, McCartney achieved two purposes that did not have to be mutually exclusive. He publicised his new album, and he told the world that the Beatles were finished. Forty years later the question remains: did McCartney actually mean to split up the Beatles? 'Paul told me he was devastated when that was the story that the papers printed,' recalled Ray Connolly.

Contemporary commentators certainly noticed that 'Nowhere does he actually say he's leaving the group. Or that he will never record with them again.' As journalist Richard Williams observed, 'What else is new? All these facts existed at the time of *Abbey Road*, but it didn't stop that album being made . . . There's bound to come a time when they won't be the Beatles any more, but no one, probably not even themselves, will recognise it when it comes.'

Imagine an alternative script. The *McCartney* album is released, and its creator merely issues a cryptic comment about the Beatles, along the lines of 'Who knows what will happen?' Lennon is isolated in his room of primal screams at the Inn on the Park and says nothing. Later in 1970, with the 'split' still not made public, Lennon undertakes one of the frequent changes of heart that litter his career, and invites the Beatles to help him record the songs inspired by his experience with Janov. The Beatles stumble, or stride, into a new decade, and then . . . ? It's a tempting scenario, which begs a further question: did McCartney capsize the Beatles in a fit of pique because of the letter he received from Lennon and Harrison? Twenty years later Harrison would accuse McCartney of using the rumour of a Beatles reunion to sell his own records. But in 1970 this method seems to have worked in reverse: McCartney publicised his record by making it impossible for the Beatles to reunite. It's true that Lennon had already quit the group, but by not making that decision public he had left room for compromise. McCartney was the last of the four Beatles to leave the group but he chose to take the credit – or, as it turned out, the blame.

Once his statement was launched, and then not contradicted or clarified, the resulting turbulence had to be navigated. Derek Taylor opted for a denial that spoke more about his personal distress than his grasp of reality. 'Spring is here and Leeds play Chelsea tomorrow and Ringo and John and George and Paul are alive and well and full of hope. The world is still spinning and so are we and so are you.

When the spinning stops – that'll be the time to worry. Not before. Until then, the Beatles are alive and well and the beat goes on. The beat goes on.' It was the weakest pronouncement that this strikingly articulate man ever made. As he admitted later, 'The wording was no clearer then than it is now and somehow it had to do. We couldn't write the final words. We didn't want to, and we didn't know they were final, and really it wasn't any of our business, we thought in our escalating insecurity.'

Taylor then had to face the press in person, alongside Allen Klein. Here he was more realistic: 'They do not want to split up, but the present rift seems to be part of their growing up . . . At the moment they seem to cramp each other's styles. Paul has called a halt to the Beatles' activities. They could be dormant for years . . . It is no secret that Klein and Paul have never hit it off. Paul has been into this building just twice since Klein came here.' Klein did his best to rid himself of any hint of the demonic. 'I like Paul. We've had many meetings, but it's never pleasant when someone appears not to like you. I think his reasons are his own personal problems.' It was a subtle allusion to McCartney's binding links to the Eastman family. As Richard Williams wrote that week, 'On the face of it, Paul's distrust of [Klein] is irrational, and the only visible motive is family loyalty, honourable but scarcely characteristically hard-headed.' Klein added that McCartney's announcement was 'a permanent maybe' and insisted that it merely reflected a situation that had existed for the past six months. For the first time someone was prepared to acknowledge that there had been a decisive move inside the Beatles' camp the previous year, but the protagonist wasn't named. In his only statement on the affair John Lennon certainly didn't admit that he had already quit the group: 'I was happy to hear from Paul. It was nice to find that he was still alive. Anyway, you can say I said jokingly, "He didn't quit, I sacked him!"' His comments exposed the difference between the two men's PR techniques. If the roles had been reversed, McCartney would probably have insisted that 'I did it first.' But Lennon sat back and allowed McCartney to become the focus of the world's anger.

'I had so much in me that I couldn't express, and it was just very nervy times, very very difficult,' McCartney recalled of the weeks that followed. 'One night I'd been asleep and awoke and couldn't lift my head off the pillow. My head was down in the pillow and I thought,

Jesus, if I don't do this I'll suffocate. I remember hardly having the energy to pull myself up, but with a great struggle I pulled my head up and lay on my back and thought, that was a bit near! I just couldn't do anything.' His symbolic severance from the Beatles had done nothing to liberate his spirit.

A year after McCartney's wedding had brought sobbing fans onto the streets, reporters found it easy to procure equally shocked comments from those who didn't want the dream to end. It was too soon for any claims that this event marked the death of the 1960s; such theorising, applied to any number of apparently epoch-defining moments, would come later. For the moment the response was immediate, a reflex reaction to an unseen punch. Besides the devastated fans, the most obvious victims were the businessmen who feared the end of a financial bonanza. Allen Klein reminded the press that McCartney was 'obligated to Apple for a considerable number of years'. An official announcement followed, insisting that no member of the Beatles was allowed to 'offer his services without the approval of his colleagues'. Back in 1962 the prospect of a split had been built into the Beatles' managerial contract with Brian Epstein: 'The Artists jointly and severally agree that should two or more of them desire to remove one or more of the other Artists, then with the consent in writing of the Manager they shall give notice in writing by registered post.' But that was in the days of innocence, when the Beatles were merely a pop group, not a corporation with dozens of global subsidiaries to feed.

Those corporations still needed fuel, and while McCartney's statement was being digested, Richard Starkey and George Harrison attended a board meeting of Apple Films, after which Starkey signed a letter to United Artists, informing them that 20 per cent of the Beatles' earnings from *Let It Be* should be paid directly to Klein's ABKCO company. Over the next week the dramatic focus switched from the Beatles to the soundtrack album that would shortly be issued in their name.

When he received the acetate copy of *Let It Be* from Phil Spector, Paul McCartney had grudgingly agreed to its release. Now, with the furore surrounding the Beatles' split filling his ears, he kept returning to the album, like a dog obsessively licking a wound. As he listened again to 'The Long and Winding Road', with its grandiose arrangement obscuring his original design, he became increasingly disturbed.

There was no longer any need to conciliate his fellow Beatles; now truth must speak. But his prevarication was fatal. McCartney was imbued with the spirit of Hamlet, neglecting to act until only failure could follow.

On Tuesday 14 April, ten days or more after he first heard the album, McCartney rang Apple and demanded to speak to Klein. When he was told Klein wasn't there, he insisted that Apple staff member Bill Oakes take down a letter to the manager. The letter, which was to be copied to Spector and John Eastman, read:

> Dear Sir,
> In future no one will be allowed to add to or subtract from a recording of one of my songs without my permission. I had considered orchestrating 'The Long and Winding Road' but I decided against it. I therefore want it altered to these specifications: 1. Strings, horns, voices and all added noises to be reduced in volume. 2. Vocal and Beatle instrumentation to be brought up in volume. 3. Harp to be removed completely at the end of the song and original piano notes to be substituted. 4. Don't ever do it again.

McCartney complained to Ray Connolly a few days later, 'No one asked me what I thought. I couldn't believe it. I would never have female voices on a Beatle record.' He had chosen to forget adding his wife's vocals to *Let It Be* a few months earlier, and indeed the presence of Lennon and Harrison's wives on the White Album in 1968. Yet his central point was impossible to deny: 'It just goes to show that it's no good me sitting here thinking I'm in control, because obviously I'm not.'

The situation was laced with irony. McCartney had envisaged Apple as an artistic haven, but now the company had restructured his own work without his permission. Worse still, it was McCartney who had recognised the need to bring in a manager to trim the company's wildest excesses, and now that manager was committing excesses of his own in the one area that McCartney had imagined was safe from interference. Under the circumstances, his letter was comparatively mild. He made no threats, delivered no ultimata; he didn't even ask for Spector's overdubs to be removed, merely reduced in volume; he seemed to assume that, at some level of Apple, the McCartney name would still be powerful enough to ensure that his wishes were satisfied. Yet he was wrong.

The response from Allen Klein was also rational, within his own world view. Spector had invited comment from McCartney, who had chosen not to speak. Now that the production process of the album had begun, McCartney had finally decided to object. Klein's motive was to safeguard the company against interference, no matter what the source, and on 14 April, the company needed to push ahead with the album, to ensure that the release date was met. The time for remixing was over. Klein attempted to phone McCartney but discovered that the musician had once again changed his number. So, Klein recalled, 'I sent a telegram to the effect that I did not understand his letter, and asking him to call me or Phil Spector direct. I added a postscript that Mr Starkey wanted his telephone number. The following day a message was relayed to me that the letter spoke for itself. By this time it was too late to do anything about altering the record, in view of the time required for its production before release.' A few days later McCartney ingenuously told a reporter, 'I've sent Klein a letter asking for some of the things to be altered, but I haven't received an answer yet.' But by then he must have known what the answer would be.

So McCartney took his case to the people. He used an interview with Ray Connolly of the *Evening Standard* to expose the full palette of his objections to Klein, the *Let It Be* album, the bizarre restrictions that he now faced from his own company, but not, at least overtly, the other Beatles. Even Klein was spared savage criticism. McCartney presented his case as a lament, not an accusation: 'The party's over, but none of us wants to admit it . . . Allen Klein keeps saying that I don't like him because I want Eastman to manage the Beatles . . . I thought, and still think, that Linda's father would have been good for us and I decided I wanted him, but all the others wanted Klein. Well, all right . . . that's up to them . . . but he doesn't represent me.' As an illustration of the gulf that had opened within the Lennon/McCartney partnership, he explained, 'We don't do harmonies like we used to. I think it's sad. On "Come Together", I would have liked to have sung harmony with John, and I think he would have liked me to, but I was too embarrassed to ask him.' He was a scared child, alone in the dark forest of intrigue. 'I don't work to the best of my abilities in that situation.' He ended with a Lennonesque cry from the heart: 'Give us our freedom, which we so richly deserve. We are beginning now only to call each other when we have bad news . . . We're all talking about peace and love, but really, we're not feeling peaceful at all. There's no one to blame, we were fools to get ourselves into this situation in the first place.' It was a clear gesture of conciliation: there was no one to blame, not even Klein; the responsibility was owned collectively by the four 'fools' and their advisers; all they needed to do was obey their inner longing for 'peace and love'. While he was undoubtedly hoping to appear as a man of reason and goodwill, these were not the words of someone who had issued a triumphant manifesto of liberation less than two weeks earlier. He wanted détente followed by reconciliation, but like his effort to alter the Beatles' album, he had – by accident or unconscious design – left it too late.

In any event his most important audience was scattered. His relationship with Richard Starkey had been scarred by the confrontation of 31 March. In late April John Lennon and Yoko Ono left England for Los Angeles, to pursue a summer of Primal Scream Therapy during which they were effectively out of contact with Apple, the Beatles and the attendant disputes. Harrison took the same flight, intending to work with Bob Dylan. Just before he left, McCartney phoned him in Henley, and as Harrison recalled, 'came on like Attila the Hun. I had to hold the receiver away from my ear.' Once again McCartney had let emotion sway his judgement. As Harrison would soon reveal, he was still open to the prospect of reconciliation, but rather than negotiating McCartney had poured out all the vitriol he'd been repressing, all the anger he felt about the way that his friends had gone behind his back and distorted his work, all the bitterness and grief.

Harrison retained a sense of objectivity. The youngest Beatle, he was now the group's wisest spokesman. 'We all have to sacrifice a little in order to gain something really big,' he explained as he arrived in New York. 'And there is a big gain by recording together, I think musically and financially and spiritually. For the rest of the world, you know, I think that Beatle music is such a big sort of scene, that I think it's the least we could do, to sacrifice three months of the year, at least, just to do an album or two. I think it's very selfish if the Beatles don't record together.' Could the Beatles work together again? 'It's easy,' he replied. 'We've done it for years. We all know that we're all separate individuals, and all we have to do is accept that we're all individuals and that we all have as much potential as each other.'

The message was universal, but the implication was specific: for Harrison the Beatles could only function if the group was accepted as a partnership of four equals, and three equal songwriters, rather than a power base of two. 'There was a point in my life when I realised anybody could be Lennon/McCartney,' Harrison reflected. 'The point is, nobody's special.' And the particular 'nobody' he had in mind was his school friend Paul McCartney. 'Everybody changes, and sometimes people don't want other people to change, or even if you do change they won't accept that you've changed, and they keep in mind some other image of you.' Harrison didn't need to add that musicians beyond the Beatles were prepared to accept him as a creative artist. He was about to go into the studio with Bob Dylan, perhaps the only contemporary artist all four Beatles were prepared to recognise as their superior, and Dylan accepted him on a basis of equality, not polite sufferance or open derision. Their relationship had none of the jagged competition that had marked Dylan's sporadic friendship with Lennon. Dylan recognised the depth of Harrison's spirituality and found a gentle humour and heart in the Liverpudlian that ensured their relationship would survive for decades to come.

The creative freedom offered by the Dylan sessions and the prospect of an epic recording adventure with Phil Spector allowed Harrison to separate the Beatles as an institution from his repressed role in the group. Yet he still found it difficult to avoid pinpointing McCartney as the source of any conflict or tension. He could describe the 'bitchiness' between Lennon and McCartney as 'childish' and then say, 'I get on well with Ringo and John, and I try my best to get on with Paul.' It was McCartney, he said, who 'wouldn't let me out of the bag' and recognise his flourishing creativity. 'The conflict musically was [with] Paul,' he admitted, 'and yet I could play with any other band or musician and have a reasonably good time.'

The launch of Apple marked the moment when McCartney went off the rails, Harrison believed. 'Really it was his idea to do Apple, and once it started going Paul was very active in there, and then it got really chaotic and we had do something about it. When we started doing something about it, obviously Paul didn't have as much say in the matter.' And then the battle between Klein and the Eastmans had begun. Harrison said that he wished Klein had been their manager from the beginning, but that McCartney didn't agree – 'that's only a personal problem that he'll have to get over . . . It's a difficult one to overcome because – well, you can think of the subtleties. He's really living with it. When I go home at night, I'm not living there with Allen Klein, whereas in a way Paul's living with the Eastmans.' What McCartney failed to recognise was the power of democracy:

The reality is that he's outvoted, and we're a partnership. We've got these companies which we all own 25 per cent of each, and if there's a decision to be made, then, like in any other business or group, you have a vote, and he was outvoted three to one, and if he doesn't like it, it's really a pity. Because we're trying to do what's best for the Beatles as a group, or best for Apple as a company. We're not trying to do what's best for Paul and his in-laws.'

The Harrison quote that went around the world that spring was purely optimistic: 'Everyone is trying to do his own album, and I am too. But after that I'm ready to go back with the others.' No one doubted that Starkey would go along with the majority. Now even Lennon was prepared to hint at a positive outcome: 'I've no idea if the Beatles will work together again, or not. I never really have. It was always open. If somebody didn't feel like it, that's it! It could be a rebirth or a death. We'll see what it is. It'll probably be a rebirth.'

For McCartney it felt more like asphyxiation. 'It was murderous,' he recalled. 'I was having dreams, amazing dreams about Klein, running around after me with some hypodermic needle, like a crazy dentist.' But the nights paled alongside the days. 'I was impossible,' he admitted in 1984. 'I don't know how anyone could have lived with me. For the first time in my life, I was on the scrap heap, in my own eyes.' Since the age of 15 he had been John Lennon's friend, collaborator, partner, confidant; from 18 he had been a Beatle; from 20 he had been a star. His artistic abilities weren't in doubt, but what use was McCartney without the Beatles? His account of the spring and summer of 1970 reads like a textbook description of clinical depression: 'It was just the feeling, the terrible disappointment of not being of any use to anyone any more. It was a barrelling, empty feeling that just rolled across my soul . . . I really was done in for the first time in my life. Until then I really was a kind of cocky sod. It was the first time I'd had a major blow to my confidence.' The effect on his wife, he said, was devastating: 'She had to deal with this guy who didn't particularly want to get out of bed and, if he did, wanted to go back to bed pretty soon after. He wanted to drink earlier and earlier each day, and didn't really see the point in shaving, because where was he going? And I was generally pretty morbid.' He lingered in a state of psychological self-destruction, pointless, endless, inescapable.

Only one avenue promised relief: full legal separation from the rest of the Beatles. If they didn't want him any more, why did they insist on keeping him locked into this financial and spiritual prison? The Eastmans couldn't soften his despair, but they could spar with Klein, parry his blows and hope to land a punch. John Eastman made the initial assault, inviting Klein to a meeting at the University Club in midtown Manhattan. The venue, perhaps the grandest of New York's private rooms, might have been designed to intimidate Klein. Eastman negotiated with the *politesse* that the venue demanded. Was there a way, he wondered, in which McCartney might be able to secure the fruits of his own labour, rather than adding them to the Beatles' collective pot? Klein didn't reject Eastman's proposal; he merely pointed out the potential tax liability that might be accrued if, as Eastman suggested, the individual Beatles exchanged some of their assets within the Apple group. Then Lee Eastman entered the ring with characteristic bluntness. He drafted a letter to Klein demanding that McCartney be freed from his partnership with the other Beatles immediately. Klein didn't bother to reply. Next McCartney suggested that he should cover all his own expenses in future in return for being allowed to take £1,500 per month from the Beatles' account. The reply was predictably negative.

'Eventually,' McCartney recalled, 'I went and said, "I want to leave. You can all get on with Klein and everything, just let me out."' Having not spoken to Lennon for several weeks, he sent him a letter that summer, pleading that the former partners 'let each other out of the trap'. As McCartney testified, Lennon 'replied with a photograph of himself and Yoko, with a balloon coming out of his mouth in which was written, "How and Why?" I replied by letter saying, "How by signing a paper which says we hereby dissolve our partnership. Why because there is no partnership." John replied on a card which said,

"Get well soon. Get the other signatures and I will think about it."'
Communication was at an end. Yet the press continued to believe,
fired by hope more than evidence, that it was only a matter of days
before the four men healed their wounds. The stories taunted
McCartney, who fired off a letter to the prime offender, *Melody Maker*:
'Dear Mailbag, In order to put out of its misery the limping dog of
a news story which has been dragging itself across your pages for the
past year, my answer to the question, "Will the Beatles get together
again?" . . . is no.' He had finally pronounced the verdict that was
missing from his self-interview in April: the Beatles were no more.

There had been little evidence to the contrary during the intervening months. Apple released the *McCartney* album on 17 April 1970,
and Klein couldn't resist a public riposte to the musician's jibes. In US
music trade magazines Apple took out their standard advertisements
for the record, to which Klein affixed an incendiary statement of fact:
Apple, it said, was 'an ABKCO-managed company'. McCartney was
incensed, and booked rival ads for his album which featured photographs of him looking inappropriately coy or mock-serious, but carried
no mention of Apple, let alone ABKCO. The clear victors were the
advertising salesmen, able to sell space for the same record to both
sides.

In an effort to reinforce McCartney's separation from Klein, the
Eastmans contacted EMI to insist that all royalty payments for his
album should be sent directly to them, not paid to Apple. EMI executive Len Wood replied apologetically that this was impossible: the
company had a contract with Apple not the Eastmans.

Sales of *McCartney* soon outstripped those of the *Hey Jude* compilation album assembled by Klein, but in turn were overtaken by the
Beatles' *Let It Be* in May. NEW LP SHOWS THEY COULDN'T CARE LESS,
trumpeted Britain's best-selling pop paper, the *New Musical Express*.
Reviewer Alan Smith characterised *Let It Be* as 'a cheapskate epitaph,
a cardboard tombstone, a sad and tatty end to a musical fusion which
wiped clean and drew again the face of pop music'. And there was
more: 'narcissistic pin-ups and chocolate box dressing', 'contempt for
the intelligence of today's record-buyer', 'lost their self-respect', 'sold
out all the principles for which they ever stood', 'hype in a pretty
packet'. There were complaints about the cost of the package, with
its elegant paperback book chronicling the January 1969 sessions in

enigmatic words and sumptuous photographs. In keeping with the Beatles' current level of cohesion, the binding of the book soon disintegrated: 'a cheapskate epitaph' indeed.

There were harsh words too for the *Let It Be* film, and its 'pseudo-*cinéma-vérité* attempt to canonise' the Beatles. One US reviewer, *Billboard*'s Ed Ochs, pronounced sentence on the Beatles and the age they represented with a contemptuous demolition of their appeal: 'four moppet dolls who, for the good part of a decade, have danced and squealed as the creative playthings of a great mass who built an economy around their pleasant music'. And this from a magazine that still depended on Apple's advertising dollars. Was the Beatle decade nothing but collective self-deception?

Apple's beleaguered managing director Neil Aspinall hoped not. As *Let It Be* was premiered, the company announced that Aspinall was compiling a second documentary, which would span the Beatles' career from Liverpool to the London legal offices where their future was decided. It was assumed that the four members of the group would be interviewed for the project, which would in any case be released before Christmas 1970. Its working title was borrowed from McCartney's controversially abused song 'The Long and Winding Road'.

While the film did little more than mediocre business, the *Let It Be* soundtrack – symbolically packaged in a sleeve that featured separate portraits of its creators, with a fatuous note claiming that it was 'a new phase Beatles album' – was a remarkable success, as fans rushed to experience what they believed would be their final taste of the Fab Four. Allen Klein proudly announced that he had ordered four million copies of the album to be pressed in the USA, and that 3.2 million of those had been sent out to stores. The gulf between those two figures would become the subject of legal arguments several years later. For now, the album topped the American charts, and so did the two singles that accompanied it: the title track followed by a sardonic choice from Klein, the much-maligned Phil Spector production of 'The Long and Winding Road'. If the track was so lousy, he could have asked McCartney that summer, why had it reached No. 1?

This commercial success could not disguise the fact that Klein's empire was precariously placed. He had arrived at Apple when the company was unprofitable but still steaming ahead on idealism. 'Apple was an astonishing place to come into from the outside world,' press officer Derek Taylor commented twenty years later. 'All the rooms were different, but none of them was at all conventional, or like anything that anyone had known before. And it was all done unself-consciously; it wasn't as if we were all walking around showing off, we were all free spirits.' Any spirit of freedom had vanished with the sackings, the checks on expenses, the ABKCO accountants monitoring the Liverpool insiders who had served the Beatles since the beginning. 'We were working for people who were so famous that there was really no precedent,' Taylor said. 'It was like a bizarre royal court in a strange fairy tale. But nothing should have turned out like that, should it?'

The first public recognition of how things had turned out came in July 1970, when disc jockey and pop pundit Anne Nightingale visited the Apple office on a particularly lethargic day. Her findings were presented in the *Daily Sketch* newspaper under the heading APPLE COMING APART AT THE CORE. When Klein heard about the story, the phone line from New York to Savile Row glowed with incandescent heat. By the end of the month the press office was closed and the staff had been dismissed – with the exception of Derek Taylor, who was regarded too affectionately by three of the group and, with certain reservations, by Klein to be sacrificed immediately.* As another London paper reported glumly, 'Since the break-up of the Beatles, their Apple empire has diminished to little more than a centre for collecting their royalties, and dealing with their private affairs.' There was still an Apple Records, defiantly throwing occasional releases into the market-place by artists such as Badfinger and Mary Hopkin. But there was no talk of unearthing talent, changing the working methods of the industry, subverting capitalism or any of the proud boasts of 1968.

Not that Klein's ABKCO company was any more secure, it seemed. For a year or more he had been unchallenged as the most influential manager in the rock universe, controlling the affairs of not just the Beatles but also, despite their misgivings, the Rolling Stones. The Stones' agreement with Klein officially expired at the end of May 1970, however, and two months later the group announced that he would

---

* Taylor left at the end of the year, to pursue a career as an executive at Warner Brothers Records.

no longer be operating as their business manager.* The inevitable legal manoeuvring would follow soon enough, and Klein was left with effective control over all the music the Stones had recorded plus a vital share in their music publishing. Financially his position was enviable, but the end of his active involvement in their career compounded the feeling that Klein was more careful with columns of figures than with people and their fragile emotions.

Remarkably, Klein had not abandoned hope that the Beatles might resume their career. In July 1970 he contacted his accountants to check the potential tax implications of a grandiose project: a worldwide tour by the group with a documentary film to chronicle it for posterity. If a tour had taken place, he would have been eligible for 20 per cent of the proceeds. Given the distance between McCartney and the others, Klein can only have been anticipating that Lennon, Harrison and Starkey would recruit a replacement and carry on regardless.

Meanwhile, Klein's clients were still creating music. Richard Starkey's debut album had been greeted fondly as an indulgence from a national treasure. In June 1970, however, he recorded something more substantial in Nashville. Producer and steel guitarist Pete Drake assembled a crack session band and a bunch of previously unrecorded songs, and guided the nervous but soon exuberant Starkey through an album of country material ideally suited to his lugubrious voice. Meanwhile, Starkey was considering the possibility of making an album of experimental music. Suddenly the least creative of the Beatles was acting like the first graduate of the Lennon/Ono school of artistic expression. 'What I really wanted to do was confuse everyone,' he explained. 'I wanted the standards album, a country one, and I've done an electronics album which I haven't put out yet. I wanted to put all these albums out and people would say, "Shit, what's going on here! Electronic, country, standards, pop records!"' The country record, *Beaucoups of Blues*, duly appeared in late 1970, but sadly Starkey lacked the momentum to pursue his multidimensional scheme. His most significant artistic decision of this period, however, was only recognised much later: he was responsible for championing the classical

---

*Repeating a ruse that had worked perfectly with Paul McCartney, Klein took out ads for the final Rolling Stones album issued under the deal, *Get Yer Ya-Ya's Out*, which claimed that the band were 'an ABKCO-managed company'.

composer John Tavener, whose first two albums were issued by Apple. 'The next thing I want to do with him,' Starkey said excitedly, 'is get a rock group together, just a crowd of friends, and I'm [going to] put his stuff on top of what we play.' It was another tantalising but unfulfilled vision of Starkey as the Renaissance Beatle.

Starkey was among a dozen musicians assembled at a variety of London studios that summer by Phil Spector and George Harrison. Spector was responsible for forcing Harrison into the most inspired vocal performances of his career, and also for the intense, almost decadent quality of the three-LP box set that resulted, titled *All Things Must Pass*. In later years Harrison would compare these sessions to 'a case of diarrhoea', as he poured out the songs that had been held back for so long. Only one tune, 'My Sweet Lord', matched Harrison's determination to record nothing but spiritual chants, but many of the songs were pitched perfectly between the romantic and the divine.

More intriguing were the glimpses of Harrison's Beatles inheritance. 'Apple Scruffs' was a playful tribute to the fans who littered the doorstep of their London HQ, one of whom subsequently wrote a book documenting how close the Beatle came to crossing the divide between hero and lover.* 'Wah-Wah' was both a celebration of a guitar effects pedal and a response to Harrison's exile from the group in January 1969. 'Isn't It a Pity' was a remarkably non-judgemental commentary on the disintegration of the Beatles' spirit. But the most compelling testimony to the recent past was provided by 'Run of the Mill', a title that perhaps reflected a comment about his songwriting from one of his fellow Beatles. Certainly they inspired the song, which was both a rejection of the culture of recrimination that had scarred the Beatles' final months and a lament for lost love and respect. In a flashback to the *Let It Be* sessions, Harrison recalled 'another day for you to realize me, or send me down again', perhaps remembering how Lennon had unfeelingly criticised his songs. When he sang 'you've got me wondering how I lost your friendship' the sentiment was more apposite for his decaying relationship with McCartney. 'Even before I started,' he recalled, 'I knew I was gonna make a good album, because I had so many songs and I had so much energy. For me to do my own album after all that, it was joyous, dream of dreams.'

* Carol Bedford, *Waiting for the Beatles*, Blandford Press, 1984

In retrospect, critic Simon Leng astutely noted 'the self-referential nature of many of the solo Beatle songs' that emerged over the next couple of years. 'It's as if "the Beatles" were an everyday fact of life,' he wrote, 'as much a natural subject for a song as the weather or walking the dog. Such was the celebrity status attached to the group that the public and media longed for these further instalments of "The Beatles soap opera".' The Beatles were not alone in this self-obsession; it became a hallmark of the singer-songwriter movement that was emerging in the USA, fuelling the increasingly insular work of Crosby, Stills, Nash and Young, Joni Mitchell and James Taylor. But Harrison's work offered a teasing glimpse into an intimate world that had previously been off-limits to the public.

No Beatle project would ever match the self-exposure of the songs written by John Lennon during 1970. They were an unfiltered and uncensored portrayal of an artist who was shedding his past and uncertain of his future. Lennon had been eager to excise poetic imagery from his writing. There would be no more of the self-consciously psychedelic verbiage that filled his songs in 1966/7. The visceral roar of his wife's voice, which he viewed as an outpouring of pure emotion, had inspired him to search for words that would fulfil the same impulse. The songs he wrote under the spell of Primal Scream Therapy represented the apotheosis of that technique.

In lyric after lyric on the album that became *John Lennon: Plastic Ono Band* he scratched at the scars of the past, from the desertion of his parents ('Mother', 'My Mummy's Dead') to the inadequacies of his education ('Working Class Hero', 'I Found Out'). During his sessions with Janov he had laid bare his core of pain, which fuelled songs such as 'Remember' and 'Isolation'. While some of his writing was little more than a digest of Janov's theories, the most effective used the doctor's therapeutic techniques to reveal the shape of his soul, undecorated and unashamed.

None of Lennon's new songs was as blatantly a cleansing of the spirit as 'God', which presented a relentless list of divinities and heroes in whom he had lost belief. As the parade went by, icons and idols were brought to their knees, from Jesus and Buddha to Elvis Presley and Bob (Dylan) Zimmerman. But the most shocking disavowal, at least for Lennon's audience in 1970, came in the final line, followed by a suitably awed silence: 'I don't believe in Beatles.' Lennon later explained that he was denying 'Beatle' as a symbol, as a disguise, a deception; but it was hard for anyone who heard the song not to feel that he was pronouncing sentence on the group he had formed in his teens.

Initially his audience amounted to just three people: Yoko Ono, of course, plus Janov and his wife Vivian. He presented the Janovs with a handwritten set of his new lyrics on 6 August 1970. Janov wanted the Lennons to undergo his therapy for at least a year, but Lennon was convinced that he was under threat from the US immigration service. 'He said, "Could you send a therapist to Mexico with me?"' Janov recalled. 'I said, "We can't do that, John." We had too many patients to take care of. They cut the therapy off just as it started, really . . . We had opened him up, and we didn't have time to put him back together again. I told him that he had to finish it, but it wasn't possible.'

When Lennon returned to England in August he was around 30 pounds heavier than he had been in the spring. He had been living, he said, 'on chocolate and Dr Pepper'. He would soon refer back to his 'fat Elvis period' of the mid-1960s, when a combination of fame and lethargy had affected his physique. Now he had regained all the weight that he had found so contemptible. 'Part of [Primal Scream Therapy] was not to self-control in any way,' he explained, 'so I would just eat and eat and eat. And it was all very well for the mind, but for the body it was terrible. But the idea was, Well, I am an artist, not a model, so fuck it, I wonder who I'm trying to please? It was me I was trying to please, I found out – too late.'

Having embarked on the process of casting out idols, he found it difficult to stop. Lennon's espousal of a new passion, followed quickly by total rejection, formed a pattern in his adult life. It stretched from fame, which had been the initial impetus for all four Beatles, through sex (too many groupies), drugs (too many bad trips), Maharishi (disillusionment) and Magic Alex (further disillusionment). Only Yoko Ono and Allen Klein remained intact, because even a fully cleansed Lennon needed someone to lean on. Janov was the latest addition to the list. The therapist recalled that when Lennon left he 'wanted to put an ad in the *San Francisco Chronicle* saying, "This is it: Primal Therapy." I said to him, "I don't want you to do that. This therapy's far more important than the Beatles in the long run of history, and I think it's got to stand on its own."' Slowly, though, Lennon's familiar process of doubt set in. The power of Janov's therapy was unmistakable, but could its creator be trusted? Lennon started to wonder why all his sessions had been taped (standard practice, Janov said) and some of them filmed (not true, according to Janov). Could he trust another father figure when so many had let him down? Eventually he decided to distinguish between the man and his message, claiming, 'Janov was an idiot, but he was not bad. His therapy was good. It was just that he was a pain in the neck.'

In late September 1970 Lennon entered a recording studio for the first time in almost eight months. Phil Spector had already agreed to produce the album, but nobody at Apple could contact him, and eventually Allen Klein had to book a full-page ad in *Billboard* magazine, which read simply, 'Phil! John is ready this weekend.' By the time Spector appeared, the album was virtually complete, and the producer did little except supervise the mixing process and play piano on one song. Lennon was insistent that the sound should be as sparse and compelling as the lyrical content, so there was no call for Spector to demonstrate his flair for lavish orchestration. Indeed, Lennon recruited just three musicians for the project: Billy Preston, who made a fleeting appearance at one session, Klaus Voormann and Richard Starkey. Musical simplicity aside, the choices reflected Lennon's awareness that he could only record such revelatory material if he was with close friends.

The impact of Janov's therapy was soon clear to both Voormann and Starkey, who recalled that 'suddenly we'd be in the middle of a track and John would just start crying or screaming – which freaked us out at the beginning'. Voormann added, 'He was very vulnerable in a way. Very up and happy a lot of the time – but really emotional, crying a lot. He was still living those experiences out. He would cry in the control room, listening to the songs, talking to Yoko, remembering the kind of things in the lyrics. You could see that he was moved.' And though Starkey never let down his guard, Voormann revealed that the drummer found the sessions disturbing: 'Ringo was very sad. The old John had gone; it was a different John. It wasn't the old one he was used to. For him, that was quite a thing. Ringo told me that after one session – that it was hard for him.'

Midway through the sessions Lennon celebrated his 30th birthday – a cultural event of sorts, although no fanfare had greeted Starkey's arrival at the same landmark a few months earlier. Various rock luminaries were approached by Apple's Mal Evans to record musical greetings, among them Starkey and George Harrison, both of whom delivered their gifts in person.* That same day Lennon's estranged father, Freddie, visited him unexpectedly with his teenage wife and new baby. The visit might have been designed to trigger an immediate primal scream, and it ended with Lennon howling violent threats at his father, threatening to have him killed. Freddie Lennon was sufficiently disturbed to lodge an account of what had happened with a solicitor, in case he was murdered.

A few days earlier Lennon, Voormann and Starkey had laid down the skeleton of a song that its drumming composer called 'When Four Knights Come to Town'. Starkey completed the song with Harrison's help a few days later, and it was released the following year under the title 'Early 1970'. In four simple verses Starkey painted a vivid miniature of each of the Beatles: Lennon staying in bed for peace, Harrison escaping his 40-acre grounds to play endless sessions, McCartney keeping his 'plenty of charm' hidden away on his farm, Starkey exposing his own limited musical skills. The message was simple: Starkey knew that when Lennon and Harrison came to town, they would be happy to work with him, but would McCartney? He didn't know. But he was certain about one thing: 'When I come to town, I want to see all three.' It was a rough draft of a peace treaty, and for the handful of people who heard the track in October 1970 it must have signalled that a reunion was still not impossible, and that Lennon's 'rebirth or death' equation might have a positive solution. That was October, however, and the song wasn't released until March. By then, 'Early 1970' would seem like a false memory of a mythic past, its Arcadia tangled with weeds.

---

* In an era clouded by legal controversy, it was perhaps inevitable that Harrison's contribution, 'It's Johnny's Birthday', should spark the threat of a lawsuit when it was included on *All Things Must Pass* later in the year. Harrison had 'borrowed' the melody of the 1968 Cliff Richard hit 'Congratulations', and was forced to give its authors due credit. More costly accusations of plagiarism would soon follow.

Chapter 5

[The Beatles] are not children. They know what they are doing.
One forgets that, I think, sometimes.
  Apple counsel Morris Finer, the High Court, 1971

'America is where it's at,' John Lennon said in December 1970. 'You know, I should have been born in New York, man, I should have been born in the Village! That's where I belong. Why wasn't I born there?'

Once the Beatles belonged to Liverpool, then England, then the world. Apple had anchored them in the English capital, but for a year or more the office had meant only stress. Freed from responsibility to each other, three Beatles made their way to New York as the year closed. George Harrison followed Phil Spector to his hometown for the final sessions on his solo album. Lennon was drawn by the city's reputation as an artistic hub: 'Everybody heads towards the centre, that's why I'm here now. I'm here just to breathe it . . . this is where it's happening.' New York was also where Allen Klein plied his trade, but that didn't prevent Paul McCartney from travelling there in November. The move marked a symbolic break from the depression that had burdened him in Britain. For all three men New York represented liberation. Only Lennon admitted to being overwhelmed by the city: 'I'm such a fucking cripple that I can't take much of it; it's too much for me. I'm too *frightened* of it. It's so much, and people are so *aggressive*.'

Like Linda McCartney, Yoko Ono was effectively a New Yorker, and she walked her husband through the city's art world, where she had acquired her maverick reputation a decade earlier. In her domain the couple inevitably adopted her style, quickly assembling two conceptual films: *Fly*, in which an insect crawled across the drugged body of a naked woman and was encouraged to dwell near her more exotic curves and crevices, and *Up Your Legs Forever*, a logical sequel to *Film No. 4* ('Bottoms').

The McCartneys were in New York to inaugurate their own creative partnership, in which the balance of power was tipped decisively in Paul's favour. Linda's contribution to the *McCartney* album had been ephemeral, but when he began his first ever sessions in America the goal was a 'Paul and Linda McCartney' record. Not that the nature of the partnership was obvious: 'Linda didn't have much to do in the studio; she just took care of the kids,' revealed session guitarist David Spinozza. 'I really don't know what she did aside from sit there and make her comments on what she thought was good and what she thought was bad. I don't know where she's coming from. Now she thinks she's a producer.' In a tone that Harrison might have recognised, Spinozza complained, 'There was no freedom. We were told exactly what to play. He knew what he wanted, and he just used us to do it.'

Harrison and his wife Pattie were in New York when *All Things Must Pass* was released. A three-record set – the first in rock history – it was greeted as 'an extravaganza of piety and sacrifice and joy, whose sheer magnitude and ambition may dub it the *War and Peace* of rock and roll' by *Rolling Stone* magazine. The airwaves resounded to the spiritual chanting of Harrison's single 'My Sweet Lord'. 'Every time I put the radio on, it's "Oh my Lord",' John Lennon noted. 'I'm beginning to think there must be a God.' The *Rolling Stone* reviewer was among the first to note that 'My Sweet Lord' sounded like the Chiffons' 'He's So Fine', a 1963 hit built around an almost identical structure and melody line. Harrison later admitted that he had set out to rewrite another song, 'Oh Happy Day', but had taken the precaution of altering the melody. It is remarkable that neither he nor Phil Spector recognised the similarity to a record that had been a sizeable hit on both sides of the Atlantic. On 14 February 1971 Bright Tunes, the publisher of 'He's So Fine', filed a lawsuit claiming that

Harrison had plagiarised their song and demanding financial resti-
tution. By then, 'My Sweet Lord' had swept the world like the Beatles
hits of old, topping the sales charts in the UK and US. Though it
retailed for more than twice the price of a single album, *All Things
Must Pass* was a worldwide No. 1 hit by January. The comparison with
the therapy-inspired *John Lennon Plastic Ono Band* was telling. Despite
being the first album of new Lennon songs since the demise of the
Beatles, it sold no better than the *audio-vérité* recording of his Toronto
performance a year earlier.

The knowledge that he had been outstripped by his supposedly less
talented friend ensured that Lennon took a jaundiced view of
Harrison's work. 'I wonder how happy George is?' he said dismissively.
He complained that Harrison was 'not the kind of person I would
buy the records of. I don't consider my talents fantastic compared with
the fucking universe, but I consider George's less.' Harrison recalled,
'I remember that John was really negative at the time. I was away, and
he came round to my house, and there was a friend of mine living
there who was a friend of John's. He saw the album cover and said,
"He must be fucking mad, putting three records out. And look at the
picture on the front, he looks like an asthmatic Leon Russell." There
was a lot of negativity going down.'

That may explain why Harrison and Lennon avoided each other in
New York, despite both making regular visits to Allen Klein's office
on Broadway.* But the Harrisons did find time for the McCartneys,
the first time the two men had met since McCartney's publicity coup
in the spring. Though the encounter began peaceably enough, the mood
soured – as it so often would over the years to come – when the conversation turned to business. McCartney recalled, 'I said, "Look, George, I
want to get off the [Apple] label," and George ended the conversation,
and as I say it now I almost feel like I'm lying with the devil's tongue,
but I swear George said to me, "You'll stay on the fucking label. Hare
Krishna." That's how it was, that's how the times were.'

Ironically, when the press learned of the meeting between the two
Beatles, they treated it as a sign of détente. Knowing that Lennon had
been in the same city, they embellished the story to the point where

---

* While he was in New York, Harrison signed over more than £650,000 of Apple
money to Klein, as management commission.

the conversation became a summit conference. The pop paper *Disc* trumpeted its 'exclusive' a few days later: 'Come Together! The Beatles may play again – live!' Journalist Mike Ledgerwood proclaimed that the group were planning a concert in Britain 'following reports that Paul McCartney's "rift" from John, George and Ringo is about to be patched up'. He quoted an anonymous 'friend', who told him, 'They certainly seem serious about working together. There have been definite discussions in that direction.' The *New Musical Express* caught the same whispers in the breeze: 'The Beatles are said to be closer than at any time for the last 18 months.' Harrison did nothing to dispel the rumour, saying coyly, 'Stranger things have happened.' The reality was that Lennon had arranged a meeting with McCartney in Manhattan, but McCartney had cancelled the appointment. Just as well, Lennon revealed later, as he hadn't planned to turn up either.

After his argument with Harrison, it was obvious that McCartney would investigate other ways of escaping from the Beatles' partnership agreement. So a scheme was hatched to narrow his options. According to Lennon, 'Paul would have forfeited his right to split by joining us again. We tried to con him into recording with us too. Allen came up with this plan. He said, "Just ring Paul and say, 'We're recording next Friday, are you coming?'" So it nearly happened. It got around that the Beatles were getting together again, because EMI heard that the Beatles had booked recording time again. But Paul would never, never do it, for anything, and now I would never do it.' The result was the recording session for Starkey's song 'Early 1970', which – if McCartney had accepted the bait – would have been the symbolic focus of a manipulative Beatles reunion.

Once the rumour had been let loose, it proved impossible to contain. Within two weeks the story had changed: now McCartney was the outsider, and his colleagues had supposedly enrolled their mutual friend Klaus Voormann in his place. Voormann found the subsequent media attention so oppressive that he escaped to Harrison's Friar Park home. Once he went into hiding, the press decided that the new Beatle must be another bass guitarist, Lee Jackson (formerly with the Nice). The details were irrelevant: it was an open secret that the Beatles were about to re-form.

Coincidentally, both Lennon and McCartney chose to puncture the fantasy. They were working independently, to separate agendas, in starkly different ways. But their actions in December 1970 effectively ensured that there could be no Beatles reunion, then or in the years ahead. Lennon moved first. On 8 December, he and Ono submitted to the longest interview he had ever given, with *Rolling Stone* editor Jann Wenner. The encounter took place at the ABKCO office, where Klein's staff were instructed to provide Lennon with laxatives and headache medicine – corroborating later claims that, despite the benefits of Primal Scream Therapy, Lennon had relapsed into heroin use. On the aural evidence of the tape, his drug of choice could just as easily have been cocaine, as his voice displayed the manic enthusiasm and aggression of the habitual user.

Designed to promote the *Plastic Ono Band* album, the *Rolling Stone* interview (published in two issues of the magazine and subsequently in book form) broadened into a virtual manifesto of the post-Beatle Lennon. He set out his credo: he believed in himself, Yoko, art as creative expression and total honesty, in whatever proportions suited him best. Everything could be judged by these criteria, and aside from the Lennons' work outside the Beatles and the primitivism of 1950s rock 'n' roll, everything was found wanting.

Intrinsic to his philosophy was rejection of the past, which in the arithmetic of Primal Scream Therapy equalled pain. If, as he believed, Janov's therapy had liberated him from his inner torment and the defence mechanisms he'd erected to conceal it, then he needed to rid himself of all the other encumbrances he'd gathered in recent years. None of them weighed or imposed more than the Beatles. After initially diverting Wenner away from that subject, as if he was frightened how much he might reveal, Lennon tore ferociously into the myth, exposing the group's internal warfare, their debauchery on tour, their manager's homosexuality and their individual failings. He raged against the way that Harrison and McCartney had treated Ono, dismissed George Martin's claim to any credit for the Beatles' music and attacked his most loyal friends at Apple for not realising that they weren't Beatles, merely hangers-on.

'That was a pity,' Derek Taylor noted years later,

because the one thing Neil Aspinall and I did know was that there was a difference between us and them. At that time John was very oppressed by fame, and he was a terrific one for lashing out. We at Apple weren't feeling good anyway, because Apple had failed, and here was one of our friends telling everyone who reads *Rolling Stone* that we were cunts. In the end we had to say, 'Well, we're not.' John later retracted some of it, and we became friends again. And I forgave him. He would forget he'd said it, and expect to be forgiven, as he always was.

During his final meeting with Lennon, George Martin also confronted him about the *Rolling Stone* confessional.

We spent an evening together, and I said, 'You know, you were pretty rough in that interview, John.' He said, 'Oh Christ, I was stoned out of my fucking mind.' He said, 'You didn't take any notice of that, did you?' I said, 'Well, I did, and it hurt.' I was very incensed about that interview. I think everybody was. I think he slagged off everybody, including the Queen of England. I don't think anyone escaped his attention.

Lennon's account of his final years in the Beatles was profoundly shocking for anyone still clinging to the image of the four buccaneers who had captured the world's hearts. Layer by layer, he exposed the frail humanity beneath their fame. 'We took H [heroin] because of what the Beatles and their pals were doing to us,' he alleged. Asked to pinpoint the reason for the split, he identified a familiar target: 'We got fed up with being sidemen for Paul . . . Paul took over and supposedly led us, you know. But what is leading us when we went round in circles?' But McCartney was not the sole culprit, he claimed. 'I presumed I would just be able to carry on and just bring Yoko into our life, but it seemed that I either had to be married to them or Yoko. I chose Yoko, you know? And I was right.'

His denial of the Beatles was devastating enough for his audience, but Lennon was only just beginning. In the magazine that prided itself on being the voice of the counterculture, read by the people who had grown up with the Beatles and followed them into expanded consciousness, spiritual exploration and political idealism, he delivered the death knell for the whole fantasy that would become known as the Sixties. 'The dream's over,' he repeated. 'I'm not just talking about the Beatles is over. I'm talking about the generation thing. The dream's over, and I have personally got to get down to so-called reality.' None of that utopian spirit was relevant any longer; all that mattered was the pain that stretched back to his childhood, when his teachers and guardians failed to notice the genius that was sitting in front of them. 'Fuck you all!' Lennon screamed as if he were still in the therapy room. 'If nobody can recognise what I am, fuck them!'

Lennon still adhered to the concept of art as life and life as art. 'That's the way the genius shows through any media,' he explained. And on those terms the *Rolling Stone* interview, a sustained barrage of invective, profanity, humour and compulsive truth-telling, was as fully realised and uncompromising as the album he had just released. Indeed, it had claims to being his last great piece of concept art, the final occasion on which he would focus every ounce of his being onto a single purpose without losing concentration or lapsing into self-parody. At last, John Lennon was fully John Lennon; and in the process he destroyed almost every close relationship in his life. From now on Yoko Ono would have to carry the weight of being Lennon's companion, co-creator and saviour, a burden that left precious little space for her own artistic ambition and ego.

The *Rolling Stone* interview stood as his testament, for the next decade at least, defining his attitude to his fellow Beatles long after he had mellowed his views. For Paul McCartney, who had already endured the loss of Lennon as musical partner and friend, the interview represented the end of the affair. 'It's just like divorce. It's that you were so close and so in love that if anyone decides to start talking dirty – great, then Pandora's box is open. That's what happened with us. In the end it was like, "Oh, you want to know the truth about him? Right, I'll tell you."' As McCartney reviewed this trauma in 1987, he revealed how the episode had haunted him. 'Obviously, I go over this ground in my mind. I was one of the biggest friends in his life, one of the *closest* people to him. I can't claim to be the closest, although it's possible. It's contentious, but I wouldn't . . . I don't *need* that credit. But I was certainly among the three or four people who were closest to him in his life, I would have thought, and obviously it was very hurtful.' He might not have needed the 'credit', but his answers revealed how deeply he needed the acknowledgement – a moment, in private or public, when Lennon could drop his guard and confirm an obvious truth, that McCartney had occupied a key role in his life.

McCartney later conceded that there was 'one good thing' about the *Rolling Stone* interview: 'I'm glad I never answered a lot of John's stuff. I thought, No, I can't handle a big battle in the media with John. I think part of it was that I knew he'd do me in.' Yet he hated the sense of powerlessness, of being assaulted without the freedom to retaliate. He took the unwise step of replying in a medium in which Lennon had already proved himself a master of aggression. Hidden in a song entitled 'Too Many People', was a reference to 'too many people preaching practices'. 'He'd been doing a lot of preaching,' McCartney explained later, 'and it got up my nose a little bit.' It was hardly character assassination, but it briefly made McCartney feel empowered. For the moment though, 'Too Many People' remained a private joke.

Harrison's contemptuous dismissal of McCartney's plea for freedom had decimated his options. He hated to imagine the other Beatles as his enemies and would have preferred to target Allen Klein. But Klein wasn't his manager and so couldn't be fired. Likewise, Klein couldn't release McCartney's earnings from the Beatles partnership. This wasn't about money; if it was, then McCartney could have read the sales figures for Harrison's new records and relished the unearned 25 per cent that would soon be added to his account. What he wanted was to be a Beatle, and if that wasn't possible, then he wanted *not* to be in the Beatles, rather than being lost in this no-man's-land of phoney partnership. And it was the legal enactment of that partnership that fenced him in. The only valid escape routes from the agreement were expulsion by his colleagues or death. One was not available to him, the other not an attractive option. He was no longer prepared to go through the contortions required by the contract that all four Beatles had signed in April 1967, which bound them as business partners if not friends. It was, he said later, the most difficult decision he had ever made.

On 31 December 1970 McCartney's legal advisers filed a writ at the London High Court, 'A declaration that the partnership business carried on by the plaintiff and the defendants under the name of The Beatles and Co., and constituted by a deed of partnership dated 19 April 1967 and made between the parties hereto, ought to be dissolved and that accordingly the same be dissolved.' The plaintiff also wanted Klein's control over the partnership's affairs to be restricted, and an official receiver appointed to safeguard the Beatles' collective earnings. The plaintiff in case M 6315 of the Chancery Division of the High Court of Justice was James Paul McCartney; the defendants were John Ono Lennon, George Harrison, Richard Starkey and the company that McCartney had conceived and once controlled, Apple Corps Ltd. Though the basis of the case was financial, the symbolism was unmistakable. McCartney, already regarded as the protagonist in the break-up of the Beatles, was now suing his three closest friends.

In an affidavit lodged on the same day, McCartney laid out his case:

I have been driven to make this application because (a) The Beatles have long since ceased to perform as a group, (b) the defendants have sought to impose upon me a manager who is unacceptable to me, (c) my artistic freedom is liable to be interfered with so long as the partnership continues, and (d) no partnership accounts have been prepared since the Deed of Partnership was entered into.

As he told the press, 'We've split, and everything that we've ever earned should now be split. They don't agree. They think it should continue exactly as planned. But if the three of them want to, they could sit down today and write a little bit of paper saying I'll be released.' McCartney made that 'little bit of paper' sound so simple, but for Klein it signified 'horrendous tax problems', as it would expose to the taxman a set of massive individual payments that could no longer be offset against Apple expenses. Klein presented himself as the voice of reason: 'It doesn't accomplish anything, except bringing out into the public a lot of dirty laundry within the life that they live.' He also pointed out that McCartney had been happy to share the money that the Beatles earned from the song 'Yesterday' despite the fact that he had written it alone and performed it without the help of his colleagues. But Klein's argument undermined itself: in 1965, when they released 'Yesterday', the Beatles had been a unit; in 1970 they were four individuals with starkly different agendas.

The three defendants received their first notification of the impending writ (a 'letter before action') four days before Christmas. 'I just could not believe it,' Harrison testified a few weeks later. 'I still cannot understand why Paul acted as he did.' Starkey concurred, adding that he had been under the impression that all four Beatles would meet in London during January 1971 for the first time in almost eighteen months. 'I know Paul,' Starkey said, 'and I know we would not lightly disregard his promise [to meet]. Something serious, about which I have no knowledge, must have happened between Paul's meeting with George in New York, and the end of December.' Neither man understood that it might have been the confrontation between McCartney and Harrison that had tipped the plaintiff's hand.

Three days before the court case became public knowledge, the Beatles' film *A Hard Day's Night* was broadcast on British TV for the first time. Among the audience was John Lennon, freshly returned from New York. To him, the movie felt like a postcard from a previous century: there he was, acting out the role that had become his life, effortlessly confident and happily ensconced with the musicians whose reputations he had just undermined in *Rolling Stone*. Clearly shaken by what he'd seen, he began to sketch out a song with the sarcastic title 'I'm the Greatest'. Captured on tape in embryonic form a few days later alongside a painful revision of the Beatles' 1965 hit 'Help!', it provided little evidence of the arrogance that Lennon had displayed to Wenner. His therapy had uncovered a storehouse of pain that he had been able to channel into song, but where was his inspiration when the past ran dry? One answer came in another partially completed lyric, 'I Promise', the first in a long series of uncomfortably revealing ballads that spelled out the depth of his dependence on Yoko Ono.

Anxious to escape the court case, Lennon and Ono fled to Japan. 'I didn't tell anybody I'd arrived,' Lennon recalled. 'We just pissed off up in the hills and nobody could find us. Then suddenly I get these calls from the lawyer, fucking idiot. I didn't like his voice as soon as I heard him, you know. A sort of upper-class Irish–English voice. Fuck! And then he insisted I come home. I could have done it all on the fucking phone.'

Meanwhile, the McCartneys returned to work on their album in America. In their absence the first court hearing took place in London before Mr Justice Stamp. McCartney's chief lawyer, Queen's Counsel David Hurst, presented the fundamentals of his client's case. Although Allen Klein was not a party to the action, it soon became clear that he would be at the heart of the dispute. Hurst told the court that Klein 'is a man of bad commercial reputation. Mr McCartney has never either accepted him or trusted him, and on the evidence his attitude has been fully justified'. He reflected McCartney's complaint that Klein had never supplied him with accurate accounts for Apple or the

Beatles' partnership. A bewildering array of figures was thrown at the court: $7 million of record royalties here, £1.56 million of assets there, a tax deficiency of £450,000, the suggestion that Klein had so reduced the group's corporate finances that they would be unable to meet their tax liabilities. The judge heard the initial evidence and ruled that the action should proceed. In the meantime, both sides agreed that the Beatles' current and recent income should be frozen for the duration of the case, tying up almost four million pounds.

Klein defended himself in New York. 'I wish to make it clear that the partnership is solvent,' he told a news conference, 'and has more than sufficient net current assets to meet all income tax and surtax liabilities.' But he knew that fate was working against him. A local court was about to convict Klein of ten offences of 'unlawfully failing to make and file returns of Federal income taxes and FICA taxes withheld from employees' wages'. He immediately appealed but knew that the verdict was bound to shadow the London court hearings. As David Hurst noted with typical legal irony, the convictions had 'obviously not enhanced Mr McCartney's confidence in Mr Klein'.

For the next few weeks the Beatles existed simultaneously on two parallel but utterly distinct planes. In London the court case that would determine their future rumbled slowly through late February and early March, before halting for Mr Justice Stamp to reach his verdict. All four Beatles searched for distraction in the comfort of work. McCartney continued to wrestle with his second solo album, having been disappointed by the reaction of friends to the rough mixes he had played them. On 19 February 1971, the day the court case resumed, he issued his first single since leaving the Beatles, the charmingly lightweight 'Another Day'. Symbolically, it was credited to 'Paul and Linda McCartney'.

Starkey was preparing to issue his own single, 'It Don't Come Easy'. The song was co-written by Harrison, who spent much of February in the studio with Phil Spector, while his records continued to dominate the world's sales charts. Lennon was an occasional visitor to those sessions, and recorded several blues-inflected songs of his own. His priority, however, was 'Power to the People', a radical political anthem far removed from the non-violent philosophy of his peace campaign. On his return from Japan he had arranged a lengthy interview with two activists from the Trotskyist newspaper *Red Mole*. The pair approached him as a potential sponsor and benefactor, recognising that they might have found a kindred spirit in the self-confessed 'Working Class Hero'. Lennon kept silent about his distinctly bourgeois background and engaged in a righteous debate with the Trotskyists about the class struggle, racism and the workers' route to power. Perhaps he felt guilty about his conspicuous wealth, as immediately after the interview he composed his simplistic but undeniably rousing chant as a gesture of political commitment. As with the Maharishi and Janov, he had found a crusade, and instantly remade himself in its image. Soon he and Ono were sporting army fatigues and Japanese riot helmets, and posing for photographs with their fists raised in solidarity with the global revolution. Meanwhile lawyers argued over the most suitable distribution of his riches.

As Lennon complained later, his political subversion was interrupted by the demands of the legal system: 'We were having meetings all the time with these counsels, every other day, and it went on for weeks and weeks. George and Ringo were getting restless and didn't want to do it any more. George would say, "I've had enough. I don't want to do it. Fuck it all. I don't care if I'm poor."' Harrison diverted his exasperation into a song, 'Sue Me, Sue You Blues'. Money and the lure of the material world had been a constant theme of *All Things Must Pass*, representing the ultimate distraction from the contemplation of divinity. But, as Lennon noted sarcastically, Harrison could be as materialistic as any working-class hero: 'George goes through that every now and then. "I'll give it all away." Will he, fuck! He's got it all charted up, like Monopoly money.'

None of the three Beatles named as defendants in McCartney's action appeared in court, but John Eastman persuaded the plaintiff to attend. 'I realised it was make or break,' McCartney recalled. 'And it was, it really was. The Beatles' fortune was on the line. Not just mine, but theirs as well.' He strode into Court 16 on 19 February wearing a dark suit but no tie – a self-conscious throwback to teenage rebellion. As Lennon once noted, 'Paul's idea of being different is to look almost straight but to have one ear painted blue.' He sat with his lawyers, glanced around the court and noticed only one familiar face: Allen Klein 'in a brown turtleneck sweater . . . I just looked at him, then turned away.'

As proceedings began, Klein could have been forgiven for imagining that he was in the dock. David Hurst set out to demolish the American's reputation, accentuating his convictions in New York and linking them to his handling of the Beatles' corporate finances. He alleged that Klein had claimed commissions on projects with which he was not involved, including the *McCartney* album, and that these claims were not only erroneous but also excessive. The following day Apple's QC, Morris Finer, defended Klein. 'He inherited a situation,' Finer insisted, 'and rightly or wrongly – we say rightly – took the view that the vital thing from his point of view, having regard to the total mess – almost total bankruptcy – of their affairs, was to generate income.' Then he reeled off the ways in which Klein had maximised that income.

All four Beatles gave written evidence, which ensured that they were saved the potential embarrassment of cross-examination. Lennon's affidavit expressed his horror at the way Apple had been besieged by 'hustlers' and 'spongers', and his gratitude that Klein had imposed financial order on the company. Far from hiding information, 'Klein told me, George and Ringo almost daily what he was doing or trying to do, to the point almost of boring us.' And he insisted that, as far as he knew, Klein had never attempted to extract any money from the Beatles and Apple to which he was not fully entitled.

His most revealing testimony concerned the group's internal democracy. He admitted that there had been regular arguments since they stopped touring in 1966, particularly between McCartney and Harrison. 'From time to time we all gave displays of temperament and threatened to walk out. Of necessity, we developed a pattern for sorting out our differences, by doing what any three of us decided.' This was a crucial point, hotly contested by McCartney, who insisted that had only happened once, when Klein was appointed. Lennon continued, 'It sometimes took a long time and sometimes there was deadlock and nothing was done, but generally that was the rule we followed, and until recent events, it worked quite well.' Only two issues had been contentious: McCartney's enthusiasm for appointing the Eastmans as the Beatles' managers, to which Lennon objected because they were 'related to one of the group', and the group's music. 'From our earliest days in Liverpool, George and I on the one hand and Paul on the other had different musical tastes. Paul preferred "pop type" music and we preferred what is now called "underground". This may have led to arguments, particularly between Paul and George, but the contrast in our tastes, I am sure, did more good than harm, musically speaking, and contributed to our success.' The truth was being stretched beyond the laws of physics. The contrast of 'musical tastes' was not only inaccurate and intended to denigrate McCartney's work, but Lennon's claim that he welcomed the mix of styles was sharply at odds with his scathing comments about his partner in his recent *Rolling Stone* interview. Fortunately for Lennon, the magazine's distribution network did not extend to the High Court.

The affidavits from his colleagues were less contentious. Harrison focused on 'the superior attitude which for years past Paul had shown towards me musically' and reprised the story of his walk-out during the January 1969 sessions. 'Since Paul agreed that he would not try to interfere or teach me how to play,' Harrison testified, his sarcasm evident even in this legal statement, 'I went back. Since the row Paul has treated me more as a musical equal; I think this whole episode shows how a disagreement could be worked out so that we all benefited.' Starkey praised McCartney as 'the greatest bass player in the world', echoing a postcard he had received from his colleague at the end of the January 1969 filming: 'You are the greatest drummer in the world. Really.' He continued, 'He is also very determined. He goes on and on to see if he can get his own way. While that may be a virtue, it did mean that musical disagreements inevitably arose from time to time. But such disagreements contributed to really great products.' Starkey may have concluded by claiming that 'all four of us together could even yet work out everything satisfactorily' but his testimony, like those of Harrison and Lennon, consolidated the view that within the Beatles there was a unified trio, and then there was McCartney – ego-driven, spiky, difficult to please and ultimately divisive. By defending Klein, they had accentuated the gulf between them and McCartney and inadvertently aided his case for dissolution.

Unable to testify in person as he was not named as a participant in the case, Klein still made his presence felt. First Apple's QC, Morris Finer, read into court an affidavit by an accountant who testified that Klein had increased the Beatles' income by a factor of five in two years, and that Apple was finally solvent. 'This is why my clients don't want the man interfered with,' Finer added, 'and would not have thought that Mr McCartney would either.' This was merely a warm-up for the main event: Finer's recitation of an epic 46-page affidavit from Klein, which commanded several hours of the court's time. Klein introduced himself as a 'record manufacturer, music publisher and entertainment business manager', and set out to defend himself against McCartney's attacks on 'my commercial integrity', and 'to demonstrate that the assets of The Beatles' partnership are not in any sense now in jeopardy'. He rebuffed allegations about the legality of his trading activities in the United States, his recent tax convictions and his handling of the Apple empire. He claimed that his priority was always 'to sort out the confusion which I found at Apple and to negotiate commercial arrangements for The Beatles much more advantageous to them than those previously subsisting'. He viewed the possible appointment of an official receiver to handle the Beatles' partnership as being likely to 'undermine the financial and commercial status of The Beatle companies. It will make it impossible to recruit new artists, and it will create enormous confusion in the minds of companies and individuals having dealings with Apple as to whom they should account and with whom they should deal.' Apple, he concluded, would be 'gravely damaged' by such a move.

Throughout, Klein presented himself as a man of great patience and understanding who had withstood a barrage of opposition and invective from the Eastmans and McCartney. At every point of conflict he had been proven right; even McCartney, Klein claimed, had been forced to recognise the logic of his arguments and actions. Yet there was one gaping hole in his testimony: at no point did he acknowledge that the Beatles had broken up. He presumably knew that the central arch of McCartney's case was unanswerable: the partnership was dead. By ignoring that fact, he was effectively acknowledging that he had lost the battle. Klein's best hope was that he might emerge from the debris with his integrity intact.

Finer consolidated Klein's affidavit with another wash of figures designed to demonstrate that the manager had not only restricted his share of the Beatles' income to that laid down in his contract, but that he had actually chosen to forgo some potential earnings. He also reminded the judge of the disparity in earnings between the recent McCartney and Harrison albums, under which McCartney would benefit at Harrison's expense. 'No one is getting at Mr McCartney in this,' he noted.

That, however, was exactly what McCartney had experienced for more than two years: sniping, insinuations, kidney punches while the referee's back was turned, a full repertoire of snide remarks from Lennon and Harrison, from Klein, and more recently from the fans who didn't want their dream to end and were searching for a convenient scapegoat.

On 26 February his response to his colleagues' claims and accusations was read in court. For the first time the court picked up a flavour of the American's character, as McCartney recalled how Klein would exaggerate his power. Faced with the challenge of obtaining control of NEMS, he remembered Klein boasting, 'I'll get it for nothing.' It was swagger, bluster, ego, and it wasn't the McCartney way. 'I became more and more determined that Klein was not the right man to be appointed manager,' he declared.

The Beatles' relationships dominated his testimony. He denied the claim in Lennon's affidavit that 'We always thought of ourselves as Beatles,' reminding the court of Lennon's outright rejection of the group in the song 'God'. 'One has only to look at recent recordings by John or George to see that neither thinks of himself as a Beatle,' he insisted. He rejected another Lennon suggestion, that quarrels within the group had always been solved on the basis of a majority verdict. Nonsense, he said. Nothing was done unless the group was unanimous. 'I know of no decision taken on a three-to-one basis.'

Aware that Klein would be watching, McCartney couldn't resist the opportunity to twist the knife. Lennon had denied his original claim that Klein had instigated much of the personal conflict within the Beatles. McCartney remembered a phone conversation in which Klein had told him, 'You know why John is angry with you? It is because you came off better than he did on *Let It Be*.' He also alleged that Klein had told him, 'The real trouble is Yoko. She is the one with ambition.' He added, 'I often wonder what John would have said if he had heard the remark.' It was designed to suggest that Klein's apparent loyalty to the Lennons was only a negotiating tactic.

McCartney deserved his moment of public retaliation. He landed his firmest blow when he recounted that Harrison had once told him, 'If I could have my bit [of Apple] in an envelope, I'd love it.' What else, McCartney might have added, was *he* trying to achieve? His closing comments were poignant and decisive. He admitted that none of the other Beatles appeared to know why he had taken the drastic step of launching this court action; after two years of arguments and explanations, they still didn't understand him. So he repeated the reasons he had stated in his original affidavit: there were no more Beatles, merely four solo artists; Apple's accounts were in disarray; and none of the group knew what his tax liability might be. These were the issues that underlined his case, he said, and none of the others had attempted to answer them.

McCartney's testimony closed the first full week of hearings. The rest was lawyers, secure in their fees, arguing for their pride. But there were occasional sunbursts across the legal landscape – such as the moment when Morris Finer, for Apple, said dryly, 'Mr McCartney, through his counsel, seems to live in a world where everyone is either a seraphim or angel, or ape or viper – where there is precious little room for the intermediate atmosphere in which most people live.' He complained that McCartney's entire case boiled down to a simple instruction: 'You must appoint a receiver because of this wicked man.' Finer continued, 'The whole object of this operation is to poison the court against Mr Klein and say that he is dangerous, and it is for the benefit of everybody to get him out.'

His opponent, David Hurst, did little to refute Finer's claim, devoting much of his final summary to Klein's iniquities: 'Having regard to his record and his performance since he became manager, and what we now know of what has happened in America, and having regard to his evidence, we say he is not a suitable person to bear these responsibilities.' The key phrase was 'what we now know': Klein's tax convictions were like the tragic flaw afflicting a Shakespearean hero. The manager must have wondered how this case might have proceeded if he had taken better care of his bookkeeping a decade earlier.

On Friday 5 March, Mr Justice Stamp adjourned hearings for a week to consider his initial judgment. The following Wednesday there was a late-night meeting at Richard Starkey's house in Highgate, attended by all the Beatles except McCartney, plus Klein, Ono, Maureen Starkey and lawyers Peter Howard and Raymond Skilling. The conference would not have been called had Apple's legal team enjoyed any hope of victory: this was a summit of the soon-to-be-defeated. The verdict was delivered on 12 March, the day, ironically, on which Lennon's political anthem 'Power to the People' was released. In this instance, however, the power rested entirely with McCartney. The judge appointed Mr James Douglas Spooner, a partner in a London firm of accountants, as the official receiver and manager of the Beatles' assets until such a time as the partnership should be legally dissolved. Apple's lawyers had one week to lodge an appeal.

Mr Justice Stamp confirmed what David Hurst had hoped: the deciding factor in the case was the judgement and behaviour of Allen Klein. He stated the reality that Klein had refused to acknowledge: 'The Beatles have long since ceased to perform as a group.' He remarked, 'Apple is not, as it were, a Frankenstein set-up to control the individual partners'; it would be unjust for McCartney to be forced to remain in such a restrictive situation. The condition of their accounts was 'quite intolerable'; of their business affairs in general he said simply, 'Confidence has gone.' Equally intolerable was the idea that McCartney should submit to Klein's management, especially as the American had received 'grossly in excess' of what his work deserved. That this was a moral verdict as well as a financial one was emphasised by Stamp's reaction to Klein's statement that he had actually taken less commission than he was owed. This, Stamp said, 'reads to me like the irresponsible patter of a second-rate salesman'. (Even Morris Finer was forced to admit that his client's claim was 'a silly paragraph'.) Klein's testimony carried 'the flavour of dishonesty' and was in part 'untrue'. The judge stooped to offer a brief word of consolation to Klein, recognising that he had been forced to listen to his opponents' allegations without the legal right of reply. But he negated the gesture by declaring that nobody at Apple – even Klein, he might have added – had the financial knowledge and dexterity to manage the Beatles' affairs. It was a damning conclusion.

There have been lurid accounts of what happened next – of Lennon, Harrison and Starkey storming out of the court, brushing past reporters and driving immediately to McCartney's house, where Lennon allegedly took two bricks from his car and threw them through the nearest window. Then they are supposed to have returned to Apple to face the press. But none of the Beatles, victor or loser, was in court that day; there was no press conference; and the bricks remain an urban myth. Challenged on a similar tale, McCartney said, 'I recently read that I was supposed to have given John a painting, and he was supposed to have come around to my house and put his foot through it. I never did give John a painting, and if I did he never put his foot through it.' Even in the more reserved media climate of 1971 it seems unlikely that three of the Beatles could have vandalised the home of the fourth without a hint of the incident reaching the press.

As Lennon told his friend Kenny Everett two weeks later, 'We see more of each other now with the court case going on, so in a way it has brought Ringo, George and I closely together again.' Lennon also confirmed, 'It's like 90 per cent [probable] that George, Ringo and I would record together again, but maybe not as the Beatles.' Confusion between enforced and voluntary reunions sparked a press story that the three ex-Beatles had gathered at Apple with Klaus Voormann to discuss the formation of a new band. In fact, the Apple meeting was a legal conference, after which it was announced that Lennon, Harrison and Starkey were appealing the recent verdict. News that Paul McCartney had just attended the Grammy Awards ceremony in Los Angeles to collect a trophy for *Let It Be*, the album he hated, must have entrenched their position.

McCartney chose the US news magazine *Life* as the vehicle for his public defence. For the first time he revealed his reaction to Lennon's decision to quit the band, his rage at Klein's decision to slap the ABKCO logo on the adverts for his album and the misgivings he'd felt about suing the other Beatles. 'All summer long in Scotland I was fighting with myself as to whether I should do anything like that. It was murderous. I had a knot in my stomach all summer.' In vague, almost inarticulate terms he came close to thanking Lennon for forcing him to exist outside the Beatles: 'I've changed. The funny thing about it is that I think a lot of my change has been helped by John Lennon. I sort of picked up on his lead. John had said, "Look, I don't want to be that any more. I'm going to be this." And I thought, That's great. I liked the fact he'd done it, and so I'll do it with my thing. He's given the OK.'

He was asked how he had reacted to Lennon's already infamous interview with *Rolling Stone*. For once in his life McCartney found an adult persona in himself that held no hint of victim or persecutor – an acceptance of the entirety of Lennon's personality, from cruelty to love. 'I ignored John's interview,' he said.

I looked at it and dug him for saying what he thought. But to me, short of getting it off his chest, I think he blows it with that kind of thing. I think it makes people wonder why John needs to do that. I did think there were an awful lot of inconsistencies, because on one page you find John talking about how Dylan changed his name from Zimmerman and how that's hypocritical. But John changed his name to John Ono Lennon. And people looking at that just begin to think, Come on, what is this? But the interview didn't bug me. It was so far out that I enjoyed it, actually. I know there are elements of truth in what he said. And this open hostility, that didn't hurt me. That's cool. That's John.

To emphasise the point, he wrote a song entitled 'Dear Friend', a pained but still affectionate acceptance of their emotional divide.

For the first time one of the Beatles recognised that the group now existed beyond the four individuals who had brought it to life. 'Of course, we aren't just four fellows,' McCartney told *Life*. 'We are part of a big business machine. Even though the Beatles have really stopped, the Beatle thing goes on – repackaging the albums, putting the tracks together in different forms, and the video coming in.' It was a premonition of the decades to come, as the story was told and retold, and the myth hardened into false memory. 'I like fairy tales,' McCartney admitted.

The battle seemed to be over. 'My clients now consider, in the unhappy circumstances which have arisen,' Morris Finer told the High Court on 26 April, 'that it is in the common interest to proceed to explore as a matter of urgency a means whereby the plaintiff may disengage himself from the partnership by agreement. My clients feel that the continuance of this appeal would be inimical to establishing an atmosphere best suited to negotiation of this kind. They have therefore decided not to prosecute this appeal and ask for it to be dismissed.' The judge concurred: 'I can only express the court's hope that the parties will come to some amicable and sensible arrangement.' The hearing was over in five minutes. As a pledge of good faith towards his clients, Klein asked for ABKCO to be added to the official list of defendants, which ensured that he would share in the costs of the proceedings.

'My friend Johnny Eastman won the first round,' Allen Klein conceded later that summer.*

---

*The two men were photographed together around that time, in a line-up of dignitaries in New York. Eastman looked correct, Ivy League-attired and slightly pained; Klein resembled a man who'd just stumbled in from his neighbourhood bar.

But it was a victory in PR. The trouble was the establishment was against us. The establishment, the fucking courts, the government, they can all exercise what's known as direction, when they don't wanna face the facts. I knew the partnership would be dissolved. I know the English law. The only reason for opposing it was the horrendous tax consequences that could result. But that old judge, Stamp, he didn't understand what it was all about. He got lost. He got Beatlemania.

Another version of Beatlemania was apparent that spring, as singles by all four of the group competed for sales. In Britain and America Harrison's 'My Sweet Lord' easily outsold its competitors, with the McCartneys' 'Another Day' and Starkey's 'It Don't Come Easy' close together behind, and Lennon's less mellifluous 'Power to the People' trailing in fourth. With Harrison's *All Things Must Pass* already having outstripped Lennon's *Plastic Ono Band*, a decisive shift in power was under way. Admirers of the group could console themselves with a future in which the struggle for commercial supremacy might provoke the quartet to new creative heights. Optimists could taste the scent of reconciliation too, as Starkey and Harrison performed on each other's hits and played separately on Lennon's sessions, while a gulf was bridged at Mick Jagger's wedding in May, when McCartney and Starkey met for the first time since March 1970. 'That was a bit strange,' Starkey explained, 'but we both knew that everything was OK. We had to get *warm* together.' EMI Records, whose profits had sagged alarmingly over the previous year, hoped that eventually the temperature might rise enough for a four-man reunion.

The resolution of McCartney's case against the other three offered only a brief respite in the schedule of consultations, briefings and court appearances. Debates about the detail of ABKCO's earnings from the Beatles would continue well into 1972, for example. The day after Jagger's wedding McCartney's legal team were scheduled to meet representatives of Apple to discuss the ongoing dilemma of how to break up the Beatles' partnership without incurring massive tax liabilities. When Apple's lawyers failed to show up, McCartney's representatives continued without them but effectively endorsed what Klein had been saying for the previous year: if McCartney sold his share of Apple, the taxman would take almost all of the proceeds. 'Paul's probably cost us a million since he started this thing,' Lennon commented, 'and his tax counsel's just come up and given us exactly the tax advice we gave him two years ago, to tell him exactly not to do all that he's done.' Klein had suggested that the Beatles sell Apple to ABKCO; now the McCartney camp proposed that EMI take over the company. They would then be free from each other, but have no more control over their work than any other recording artists – scant reward for their bold attempt to remodel the music business three years earlier.

Other legal matters required more urgent consideration. Lennon and Ono were in hot pursuit of her ex-husband Tony Cox and their daughter Kyoko Cox. The search led them to Majorca, where the Lennons found Kyoko at a meditation camp and took her away without her father's knowledge. Cox told the police that the girl had been kidnapped, and the Lennons were brought in for questioning. In the mid-1940s Lennon had been placed in the appalling position of having to choose between his parents. Now nine-year-old Kyoko faced the same dilemma. Scared by the police intervention and the chaos caused by the Lennons' arrival, she declared that she wanted to be with her father. To secure right of access, the Lennons flew to the US Virgin Islands, where Ono and Cox's divorce had been registered, and back to Majorca, where the two sides reached a short-lived truce. Within a couple of weeks, however, Cox had slipped back to the USA, which is where the Lennons headed in June. Lennon would never see his stepdaughter again.

Two plagiarism suits continued to run, the first concerning two lines of lyric from Chuck Berry's 'You Can't Catch Me' that reappeared in John Lennon's 'Come Together'. The second was the problem surrounding Harrison's 'My Sweet Lord' and 'He's So Fine', handled by the US firm Bright Tunes. Klein met the company's president and suggested Harrison buy the entire Bright Tunes catalogue, including the song he was accused of plagiarising. Bright's president declined, and said that his company and Harrison's music publisher Harrisongs should share all the income from 'My Sweet Lord'. With neither side willing to concede, the legal machine began to gather evidence for another courtroom battle.

Publishing was at the heart of another case that June, filed in the Supreme Court of New York County. At stake were the potentially lucrative publishing royalties from *Ram*, the Paul and Linda McCartney album released in mid-May. Lennon and McCartney's deals with Northern Songs stated that the company would retain 100 per cent ownership of every song they wrote, regardless of whether they were composed with any other party. McCartney had decided to list his wife as co-writer of more than half the songs on *Ram*, plus the hit single 'Another Day'. Despite her lack of musical pedigree, he insisted that Linda had been an active collaborator, making valuable suggestions about lyrics and melodies. Northern Songs, however, believed he was effectively robbing them of half their potential income. Lennon was an amused observer. 'The thing with Paul is, he wants all the action.' Another set of lawyers prepared to prosper at the Beatles' expense.

Briefly it appeared that the album would be delayed until the dispute was resolved, but the warring sides recognised that they would both suffer from this decision. After his unassuming debut album, *Ram* demonstrated that McCartney had lost none of his skill as a melodist since the demise of the Beatles. Lushly orchestrated and full of the playful verve that had long been his trademark, it was a richly enjoyable record, culminating in a mini-suite ('Back Seat of my Car') that was a triumph of pop arrangement. Yet alongside the emotional honesty of Lennon and Harrison's work, *Ram* appeared lightweight, empty, meaningless.

Lennon's first reaction was 'Fucking hell, it was awful. In general I think the other album he did was better, in a way. At least there was some songs on it.' Besides the people 'preaching practices' and the 'first mistake' on 'Too Many People', Lennon thought he could find sarcastic references to himself and the other Beatles throughout *Ram*. There was the three-legged dog who couldn't run; the 'Dear Boy' who never knew what he had found (McCartney explained later that the song was about his wife's ex-husband); the noxious friend in 'Smile Away'; and the defiant proclamation in 'Back Seat of my Car', 'we believe that we can't be wrong'. As Linda McCartney recalled, 'They thought the whole album was about them. And then they got very upset.' The truce was over: forgetting what he had said about McCartney in *Rolling Stone*, Lennon treated *Ram* as an unprovoked attack and responded the only way he knew: openly and viciously.

Where McCartney had wielded a stiletto, Lennon opted for the axe. 'I always got angry,' he admitted later. 'If there was a game going on between Paul and me, I was the one who would get furious and emotional about it, and he would just do it subtly. There was stuff on his previous album and we were all annoyed by it, George, Ringo and me, but I answered back.' On 22 May 1971 Lennon began to record a song entitled 'How Do You Sleep'. Across three acerbic verses, Lennon mutilated McCartney's reputation, his lifestyle, his music and – ironically, given Lennon's own mother/lover complex – his dependence on his wife. 'I remember when he was writing, he was a bit tongue in cheek,' Ono recalled, 'like, "Wait until they see this."' 'We didn't take it that seriously,' Lennon confirmed. Other observers reported the relish with which he unleashed gratuitous insults at McCartney. George Harrison smiled indulgently as Lennon went to work, but Richard Starkey watched for a while and attempted to calm Lennon down. Underground journalist Felix Dennis watched the session. 'I remember Ringo getting more and more upset by this . . . I have a clear memory of his saying, "That's enough, John."' Lennon and Ono competed to come up with the most insulting lines, Dennis said. 'Some of it was absolutely puerile. Thank God a lot of it never actually got recorded because it was highly, highly personal, like a bunch of schoolboys standing in the lavatory making scatological jokes.'

'John would forgive himself, and expect Paul to forgive him,' Derek Taylor recalled. As Lennon said later, 'I'm entitled to call Paul what I want and vice versa – it's in our family.' But he must have calculated the impact of such lines as 'those freaks was right when they said you was dead' and 'the only thing you done was Yesterday'. Allen Klein joined in, querying Lennon's original line about 'Yesterday' ('you probably pinched that bugger anyway') and suggesting a more subtle reference to McCartney's recent single.

Amusing or sadistic, depending on one's distance from the line of fire, 'How Do You Sleep' was impassioned, armed with a string arrangement that cut as deep as the words, and more revealing than Lennon ever intended. Shortly before his death he hinted at a deeper knowledge of what lay behind the song: 'I used my resentment against Paul that I have as a kind of sibling rivalry resentment from youth.' Felix Dennis glimpsed a different relationship: 'It's quite obvious that Paul must have been some sort of authority figure in Lennon's life, because you don't take the piss out of somebody that isn't a figure of authority . . . As I felt it, they were taking the piss out of the headmaster.' The reference to an 'authority figure' was ironic, as that was exactly how McCartney viewed Lennon: 'It was just a bit [like] the wagging finger, and I was pissed off about it.'

By 1973 Lennon was prepared to admit, 'I'm talking about myself in that song. I just know it.' And so he was. McCartney was the ostensible subject, but the song was actually about Lennon's psyche, not McCartney's. It would have required a tough soul to find solace in that if you were Paul McCartney, however, and although he insisted, 'I don't have any grudge whatsoever against John,' he never claimed that he hadn't been wounded. In fact, he admitted in 1994, 'I have to say that the most hurtful stuff came from John. It was like a mate betraying me.' Elsewhere, he added, 'I think he was a sod to hurt me. I think he knew exactly what he was doing, and because we had been so intimate he knew what would hurt me, and he used it to great effect.'

There was a sense that Lennon's emotions were running out of control. In the same month that he wrote 'How Do You Sleep' he came across a publicity booklet about the Beatles compiled by a hapless member of the Apple staff. Lennon went berserk. When he couldn't find anyone willing to claim responsibility, he grabbed a felt pen and began to deface the booklet. 'This is so prejudiced against John, [and] Yoko and slightly against Ring[o] and Mo [Maureen] and G[eorge] and P[attie] that I want to know who put it together and fire them,' he scrawled. He added a speech bubble to a shot of the 21-year-old McCartney: 'I'm always perfect.' Alongside a reference to a McCartney visit to Hollywood, he wrote bitterly, 'Cuts Yoko and John out of film!' There was a line about the McCartneys' wedding, which Lennon altered to read 'funeral'. It was the work of a jealous child rather than an artist who had been freed of pain by Primal Scream Therapy. Asked incessantly about McCartney in interviews, Lennon insisted that the pair would never work together again, and couldn't become friends until their business quarrels were mended. 'Maybe about a year or two after all the money thing's settled, we might have dinner or forget about it,' was as friendly as he was prepared to be. He was still willing to work with Harrison and Starkey, and perhaps Klaus Voormann, as

Starkey conceded that summer: 'We keep having laughs about it. Not yet, though.' But sooner than any of them realised, the opportunity would come for all four Beatles to unite for a cause greater than ego or money.

Chapter 6

Imagine how we've flowered since [the split]. George is suddenly
the biggest seller of all of us. I think my music's improved a
million-fold, lyric-wise and everything. I think we're much better
than we ever were when we were together.
John Lennon, July 1971

I don't think Linda is a substitute for John Lennon, any more
than Yoko is a substitute for Paul McCartney.
George Martin, August 1971

More than eight million people – the population of London or New
York – fled their homes in 1971, as civil war racked Bangladesh. The
territory comprised the eastern section of the divided nation of
Pakistan, a geographically illogical entity formed after the partition
of India 24 years earlier. One thousand miles of India separated West
and East Pakistan, rendering equal distribution of resources impossible. An appalling cyclone in November 1970, which killed around
250,000 people in the East, emphasised the divide. Demonstrations
against the government were harshly repressed, and by March 1971
the result was a civil uprising – a bid for independence which was
crushed with merciless brutality. Millions fled the violence in search
of sanctuary across the Indian border. Instead, they found famine and
dehydration, and thousands began to starve. Another 300,000 citizens

were killed in the fighting. It was a humanitarian catastrophe, widely ignored in the West. ·

One of Bangladesh's most famous sons was sitar maestro Ravi Shankar. Early that summer he explained the dire state of his home-land to George Harrison and told him that he was planning a fund-raising concert. Wary of imposing, he asked if Harrison would compère the show. 'Why don't I play?' Harrison replied. By the end of the conversation, one of rock's most spectacular displays of altruism was born.* Allen Klein booked New York's premier concert venue, the 20,000-seater Madison Square Garden, for an appearance by 'George Harrison and Friends'. Demand for tickets was so intense that Harrison agreed to play two full shows on 1 August 1971. There had been rock benefits before, but never on this scale, encompassing not just live performances, but an album, film and accompanying single, all devoted to raising the consciousness of the world to the tragedy of Bangladesh. The challenge was enormous, not least because Harrison had been the Beatle least enthusiastic about touring in the mid-1960s and the first to suggest that the group should quit the road. Since then he had only performed as an unannounced guest with Delaney and Bonnie and John Lennon's Plastic Ono Band. Now he had to command an audience on the strength of his own name, with much more than his reputation at stake.

Though it was only four months since the Beatles' disunity had been exposed in the High Court, many fans assumed that they would be the 'Friends' promised on the concert posters. It was a bittersweet moment: was Harrison prepared to be overshadowed by the Beatles when he had just established himself as a viable solo artist? 'George lacked confidence,' recalled his friend Leon Russell. 'I worked on some of his records, and it was not uncommon for him to do 180 takes of a song before he felt he'd got it right. He never thought what he was doing was good enough.' For reasons of self-protection, or simply to boost the impact of the concerts, Harrison eventually asked all three of his ex-colleagues to perform. Starkey immediately agreed, as did Russell, Eric Clapton and Billy Preston. Harrison entered into lengthy

---

* To make room for the concerts in his schedule, Harrison abandoned his produc-tion work for Apple band Badfinger, and was replaced by Todd Rundgren, who recalled, 'He didn't finish any of the songs, though he was perfectly willing to take the credit for the songs that I finished.'

negotiations with the recalcitrant Bob Dylan which resulted in his first major appearance in two years. 'Everyone wanted to play,' recalled Apple Records' US head Allan Steckler. 'I had to turn down Crosby, Stills and Nash, and the Rolling Stones.' But neither Paul McCartney nor John Lennon was able to place the lives of starving people before their own egos.

'Klein called a press conference,' McCartney complained, 'and told everyone I had refused to do it for the Pakistani refugees. It isn't so. I said to George the reason I couldn't do it was because it would mean that all the world's press would scream that the Beatles had got back together again, and I know that would have made Klein very happy. It would have been an historical event, and Klein would have taken the credit. I didn't really fancy playing, anyway.'

Lennon's rationale was strikingly similar: 'I told George about a week before that I wouldn't be doing it. I just didn't feel like it. I just didn't want to be rehearsing and doing a big showbiz trip. And anyway they couldn't have got any more people in, if I'd been there or not. I get enough money off records and I don't feel like doing two shows a night.'

Neither man had grasped that there was more at stake here than the balance of power between the ex-Beatles. What did McCartney or Lennon's feelings matter alongside the chance to rescue people's lives? It was an ethical dilemma that haunted them for the rest of the decade: how could the Beatles refuse to play together for just one night, when they knew that they could help to feed the hungry and cure the sick? The group had never wanted to be messiahs, but did that entitle them to refuse the role? Did the Beatles have a moral duty to save the world?

Still caught up in the drama of their own lives, they were preoccupied with pettier concerns. It was only after Lennon's death that the real reason for his absence from the Bangladesh concerts was revealed. He insisted that he would not perform without Ono; Harrison told him that this was a gathering of rock superstars, not an avant-garde festival, and that she couldn't appear. Lennon was outraged, and decided that Harrison's inability to appreciate Ono's genius was symptomatic of his limited intelligence. 'There's no telling George,' he said. 'He's very narrow-minded, and he doesn't really have a broader view. Paul is far more aware than George . . . he's got an inferiority complex working with Paul and me . . . George doesn't really know what's happening.'

At a press conference Harrison was asked, 'Are there ever times when you wish you were back together again as a group?' It would become the opening gambit for every journalistic encounter with an ex-Beatle. Harrison handled it diplomatically: 'Yeah, there are times. But there are times also when we all appreciate not being together.'* Lennon was asked the same question in London. 'I never wanted them [the Beatles] to slide down and sort of make comebacks and things like that. I said, when I was 20 [sic] in the Beatles, that I'm not going to be singing "She Loves You" when I'm 30. Well, I was 30 this year and I didn't force it to happen. It just happened naturally. I guessed that by the time I was 30 I would have just grown out of it. And I have, you know.'

But the world wasn't ready to grow out of the Beatles. When the Bangladesh concerts took place, much of the media attention centred on the 'reunion' of Harrison and Starkey. The shows were a personal triumph for Harrison, who appeared serious, almost stern, in his crisp white suit and guru beard, but who delighted the crowd by dipping briefly into his Beatles repertoire. Starkey's appearance also rekindled the past. Shaking his head to the rhythm as he had in 1964, he seemed like a living incarnation of the Beatles of old, spreading their ageless magic throughout the hall.

The Bangladesh concerts confirmed Harrison's elevated status among the rock aristocracy. Bob Dylan might wield more enigma, and the Rolling Stones more charisma, but Harrison had proved himself the most successful of the solo Beatles and arguably music's most influential figure. His charitable gesture – $243,000 would reach UNICEF from ticket sales alone, with much more to follow – raised hopes that the rock elite might display a deeper sense of maturity in the decade ahead. For years rock had been interpreted as the soundtrack of dissent, channelling the political ideals of the counterculture and providing anthems for the revolution that would surely follow. But the heroes of the new decade, from Grand Funk Railroad to Led

---

* Leon Russell recalled that Harrison still felt nostalgic enough about the Beatles that summer to compile an album of the best cuts from their recent solo work, to play to friends in his car.

Zeppelin, showed little interest in politics and no messianic zeal. Where their predecessors had sparked opposition to the status quo, the icons of the new age were selling nothing more significant than their own stardom. Harrison's efforts suggested another way for rock to progress, as a standard bearer of idealism that wasn't tied to a strict political manifesto.

Yet just as rock was shedding its radical agenda, Lennon chose to remodel himself as a revolutionary. To prove that the 'Power to the People' single was more than a gesture, he had appeared at political rallies in aid of everyone from the postal workers' union to the underground magazine *Oz*, then facing trial on censorship charges. His campaigning soon crossed the Atlantic. On 1 June, the Lennons flew to New York to complete the album he had begun in February. Within 24 hours they were contacted by Jerry Rubin, from the anarchist protest group the Yippies. Like his comrade Abbie Hoffman, he had viewed Lennon as a traitor after 'Give Peace a Chance', but then he studied the *Plastic Ono Band* album, and found that it soothed his despair at the decay of the revolutionary American left. That weekend, Rubin, Hoffman and the Lennons met in Greenwich Village, where Lennon had stumbled across David Peel, a hippie street singer who had become a local legend, and promised to attend one of his recitals in Washington Square Park. 'I really didn't think they would come,' Peel recalled. 'But there they were. I sang them "Have a Marijuana" and a new song I'd written called "The Pope Smokes Dope".' The troupe of radicals strode around the East Village, singing the simple refrains of Peel's dope anthems. Lennon had found a peer group that represented rebellion and danger, and also a new musical direction. 'I'm pretty movable as an artist,' he recalled later. 'They greeted me off the plane, and the next minute I'm involved.' Rubin, Hoffman and Peel believed that the revolution could be reborn with a Beatle at the helm, and for the next year Lennon played the role of a radical activist with such zeal that he persuaded both them, and the US government, that he was in deadly earnest. Meanwhile he was withdrawing large sums from Apple's Swiss bank accounts to finance his bohemian lifestyle.

While Harrison and Lennon confronted the outside world, and Starkey pursued a career as a movie actor, McCartney seemed to be floundering. 'He disappoints me on his albums,' Starkey said. 'I don't think there's one tune on the last one, *Ram*. I just feel he's wasted his time. He seems to be going strange. It's like he's not admitting that he can write great tunes. I just feel he's let me down.' Under assault from his colleagues and the critics, McCartney could not even trust his fans. Insulting graffiti appeared regularly on the wall around his London home. 'Someone had written the words "Fuck Linda",' one innocent admirer recalled. 'Just as we decided to leave, a car started up and the doors to the yard opened. There we were, face to face with Paul and Linda. We all smiled and waved, and he pulled out of the driveway like a madman and gave us all the finger.'

In late July McCartney was at Abbey Road Studios with drummer Denny Seiwell and singer/guitarist Denny Laine. 'I missed playing in a band,' he explained. He chose not to dip into the same pool of session men as the other Beatles: 'I felt that it was a bit too predictable, that everyone would leave the Beatles and go with old Phil Spector, or the drummer Jim Keltner. It was like a clique, and I just didn't want to join that clique.' Instead, he opted for Seiwell, who had proved himself on *Ram*, and Laine, a reticent underachiever who had sung one major hit ('Go Now' with the Moody Blues) and written another (Colin Blunstone's 'Say You Don't Mind') without establishing a public profile. Laine offered his boss undoubted musical talent and no risk of competition. Yet safety was forgotten as McCartney completed his new band with someone who had no musical experience: his wife. Comparisons with Lennon and Ono were inevitable, but Ono had classical piano training and a history of avant-garde musical perform-ances to her name. Forcing his wife to carry one quarter of the burden of Wings, as McCartney named the band, was an act of enormous courage, defiance and possibly folly. The reaction from his peers was incredulous laughter. 'Everybody can be artists,' Lennon had said a few days earlier, but he drew the line at Linda McCartney*.

To symbolise that the past was past, McCartney became the first Beatle to withdraw from the group's official fan club. 'I don't want to be involved with anything that continues the illusion that there is such a thing as the Beatles,' he announced. His three former colleagues

---

* Lennon rarely displayed respect for Linda McCartney. Earlier that year, he had written her a vicious letter, attacking her 'petty little perversion of a mind' and 'insane family'.

echoed his thoughts by disputing EMI's right to issue an album of the Beatles' 1964 concert at the Hollywood Bowl. Apple claimed they owned the tapes; EMI insisted that they had paid for the recording and could do what they liked with it. This was not the moment for a public display of nostalgia: Neil Aspinall completed a rough cut of the Beatles documentary movie that he'd begun the previous year, but shelved the project after sending each of the group a copy. Meanwhile, Harrison insisted that the story of Apple was 'only just beginning'. To prove the point, the company's recording studio was now open for business, nearly three years behind schedule. Harrison admitted, 'It's a bit sad now that Apple is in the position all four of us planned three years ago. I just wish Paul would use the studio. It's silly not to.' But neither Lennon nor McCartney would ever set foot on the premises.

Indeed, Lennon was about to leave Britain for the last time. In August 1971, he recalled the abuse that he and Ono had received from the British public, and said, 'If I hadn't bought that fucking house, I'd leave – I'd go and live in New York. It's fucking great over there, the people are as hip as shit. Britain is at least 200 years behind.' On 3 September the couple flew to America for what was intended as a short visit. 'I only decided to live there after I'd moved,' he later said. 'I left everything in England. I didn't even bring any clothes. I just came for a visit and stayed. I should have informed the British government: I'd have got an amazing tax refund. If I'd only thought of it, I would have made a million pounds or something.'

In New York the Lennons took a hotel suite for six weeks and then rented a loft in Greenwich Village, home of the city's artists and radicals. Among them was David Peel, who had recently formed an organisation called the Rock Liberation Front with A. J. Weberman, a Village eccentric who had devoted himself to 'proving' that Bob Dylan was both a junkie and an enemy of the people. Now Weberman and Peel widened their sights to include 'rip-off people in the world of rock'. To Lennon's delight, their first target was Paul McCartney. 'We figured McCartney could use some liberating,' Weberman explained. 'It was around the time he released that album that was really inane and said nothing about what was happening on the street. He was supposed to be a representative of youth culture, but he was just a businessman. We reckoned he could use a wake-up call.' Weberman, Peel and a dozen supporters staged a mock funeral outside the Eastmans' law office. As Weberman proclaimed afterwards, 'I felt he's a good example of the capitalist, non-involved egotistical rock star which seems to dominate the hip culture.' 'I hope they're not after me,' Lennon quipped.

He was soon sporting a Rock Liberation Front badge and spouting their propaganda. 'I don't want that big house we built for ourselves in England. I don't want the bother of owning all these big houses and big cars, even though our company, Apple, pays for it all. All structures and buildings and everything I own will be dissolved and got rid of. I'll cash in my chips, and anything that's left I'll make the best use of.' It was two years since he had promised to give all his future royalties to peace, only to renege on his pledge immediately. 'John was not trying to make money out of the revolutionary movement,' insisted his friend film-maker Steve Gebhardt. 'He was not trying to turn it into a Rolls-Royce.' Indeed, Lennon now determined that his life and work would be devoted to the overthrow of the capitalist system that had made him rich.

'Imagine' became a hit single, although not yet an anthem. The album included songs of unfocused political anger, alongside declarations of love for Yoko and his demolition of McCartney's reputation 'How Do You Sleep'. The cover of *Ram* had featured McCartney holding a sheep; Lennon included a postcard-sized photo of himself wrestling with a pig. It was noticeable, however, that the *Imagine* LP represented a significant move towards the commercial mainstream. ABKCO's promotions manager Pete Bennett, who was a staunch supporter of US President Nixon, explained: 'We told John he had to go more commercial if he wanted to get a big smash. An artist has to put out what he feels, but I'm sure an artist wises up, and that's why John put out this new type of album.' Conceding the point, Lennon later told McCartney that *Imagine* was '"Working Class Hero" with sugar on it for conservatives like yourself'. The album duly followed *All Things Must Pass* and *Ram* to the top of the American charts.

The clash of ideology between radicals such as Rubin and Hoffman and Klein's team at ABKCO merely amused Lennon. He'd already warned Klein that he might be earning '20 per cent of nothing' if the Lennons kept to their plan of 'taking a really far-out show on the road, a mobile, political, rock and roll show'. Klein replied, 'I don't mind,' though as Lennon noted, 'Maybe he thinks he'll sell some comics on the side. He'll have thought of something.' He knew that McCartney was planning to tour with Wings. 'When Paul's going out on the road,' Lennon explained, 'I'd like to be playing in the same town for free next door! And he's charging about a million to see him. That would be funny.'

None of the three Beatles under Klein's supervision doubted his abilities, and they relished his reputation as a troublemaker. At worst, they saw him as someone who in Lyndon Johnson's immortal phrase was safer 'inside the tent pissing out'. So they weren't troubled by the $29 million lawsuit filed against their manager by the Rolling Stones on 1 September 1971 that alleged he had 'made false or fraudulent representations with intent to deceive and defraud'. Klein complained that the Stones' claims were 'at best ludicrous and at worst malicious', and 'an attempt to rewrite history'. (The case was settled out of court in May 1972.) Yet by November Paul McCartney was able to suggest that although 'the others really dig [Klein] . . . I think they might secretly feel that I am right'.

McCartney's comments followed three months of delays that threatened to sabotage Harrison's charity crusade. The principle was simple: all the proceeds from the Bangladesh benefits should go directly to the victims of famine and civil war. But between cause and effect was a landscape of obstacles. For example, Klein and Harrison had neglected to apply in advance to the US government for the concerts to be given tax-exempt status. Now the proceeds were automatically liable to tax, unless the government agreed to set a precedent. There were problems in Britain as well. Before the concerts Apple's official receiver wrote to Harrison, noting that he was planning to donate all the profits from the live album (and his 'Bangla Desh' single) to charity. 'This does place me in some difficulty,' the receiver explained, because 'the court order imposed on me the obligation to hold for the court the royalties not only on Beatle group recordings, but on any individual recordings made by individual partners.' Harrison needed to obtain the approval of the other Beatles before any donation could be made. Lennon and Starkey were in agreement, but Peter Howard at ABKCO suggested that the receiver should ask McCartney himself – evidence of how strained relations between the two ex-Beatles had become. McCartney eventually consented five weeks later, whereupon the receiver raised the possibility that Harrison might be asked to pay income tax on the proceeds, even if he immediately gave them to charity.

Harrison expected that the concert record would be released by October, and the film by Christmas. But the British government was now claiming its own share of the proceeds. In late September Harrison met the financial secretary to the Treasury, Patrick Jenkin, and asked 'if it would be possible to reduce, or even scrub completely, the purchase tax on the record. Unfortunately, he seemed to think that it was more important for this country to get the tax on the record than for the extra money to go to the starving people of Bangladesh.' Harrison even threatened to become a tax exile from Britain, but Jenkin could not be swayed.

By now almost everyone's motives were open to suspicion. It was reported that ABKCO/Apple 'picked up the approximately $100,000 tab' for staging the concerts, presumably as a charitable donation. But soon it became clear that the money would be reclaimed from the profits of the record. (Klein did make a personal donation of $50,000 to the relief fund, however. 'Has Eastman ever donated?' Lennon asked McCartney.) Record companies were also jostling for the small change. Klein entered lengthy negotiations with Capitol Records president Bhaskar Menon about distribution fees, while Columbia Records (who owned Bob Dylan's contract) also wanted a share. By the time the two labels and Klein had cut a deal, wholesalers were complaining that their margins had been sliced so savagely that they would lose money on every copy they shipped. So the album was delayed again, while illegal bootleg recordings of the concert went on sale without any charitable benefit. *The Concert For Bangla Desh* – Harrison's second three-record box set in twelve months – finally reached the stores at Christmas 1971. Radical journalist Mick Farren greeted it as 'the greatest achievement ever by its organisers – a group headed by George Harrison, Ravi Shankar and Allen Klein'. It would be the last time the press referred to Klein in such heroic tones.

Lennon continued to defend Klein, almost without reservation: 'I don't think he deserves the shit he gets thrown at him, and if time proves me wrong in the end, so be it. I think he deserves what he earns.' Removed from the Bangladesh charity fracas, he concentrated on his radical agenda. 'Repression is bad for you,' he had recently proclaimed, and there was little sign of restraint in his songwriting during the final months of 1971. First he penned a banal protest tune about the shooting of prisoners at Attica State jail in New York State, then he focused on the downtrodden Catholic minority in Northern Ireland. 'It became journalism and not poetry,' he later admitted of his work during this period. 'I was making an effort to reflect what was going on. Well, it doesn't work like that.' But in the reflected glory of revolutionaries such as Jerry Rubin, Lennon believed he had found his calling.

Klein had helped him organise a retrospective exhibition for Ono's art in upstate New York* – her first such showcase in two years – and now Lennon envisaged a future in which they could both function as full-time artists, removed from the expectations of the past. Ono, however, was less optimistic. 'After my exhibition,' she recalled, 'I stopped, because the crowds who came to the show came to see the Beatles. It was pandemonium, and my work is quiet.' She refused to place barriers between her art and the spectators, in a bid to sharpen the sense of communication and vulnerability, and was rewarded with accidental breakages and deliberate damage. When Lennon penned a one-line note for Ono's *Fly* album late that year – 'Love means having to say sorry every five minutes' – he was not only parodying the sales pitch for the hit movie *Love Story*, but acknowledging that his wife's creativity was being submerged beneath his own.†

All of Yoko Ono's creative enterprises – exhibitions, films, albums – were being paid for by ABKCO. 'Klein was in a difficult situation,' remembered Apple Records' US head Allan Steckler. 'I remember him saying to me, "Steckler, what can I do? She's spending a fortune. But she's the guy's wife! How can I say no to her?" Klein wasn't thrilled by the Janov album, let alone when they started making political records, but we had to keep funding them.'

---

* The opening coincided with Lennon's 31st-birthday party, celebrated with a drunken evening of song featuring Phil Spector, Allen Ginsberg and Richard Starkey. 'Spector insisted on making fun of Paul McCartney's songs,' recalled Steve Gebhardt, another guest at the party. 'But John didn't really want to go along with it.'

† Not everyone in Lennon's life was treated so sensitively. He did not inform his ex-wife Cynthia or son Julian that he had moved to New York. When she tracked him down, she was only allowed to speak to Ono. Lennon did not see Julian for another three years.

Jerry Rubin now imagined that Lennon and Ono would lead a revolutionary cavalcade to disrupt the 1972 presidential election. 'We would launch a musical, political caravan, tour the United States, raise money to feed the poor and free prisoners from jail,' he recalled. 'The shows would combine music and fun with political consciousness-raising, and all the money would go to the people!' So Rubin was surprised when the Lennons returned to the studio with Phil Spector, not to record one of their new political statements, but for a Christmas single built around their two-year-old peace slogan, 'War is over if you want it.' It was completed too late to catch the seasonal market, but survived to become a perennial favourite.* During the sessions Spector asked Lennon if he had heard McCartney's new album, adding, 'It's really bad. Just four musicians, and it's awful.' 'Don't talk about it,' Lennon replied. 'It depresses me . . . whenever anybody mentions his name, I don't think about the music – I think about all the business crap. Don't talk about him.'

Just seven months after releasing *Ram*, McCartney had completed *Wild Life*, the debut album by Wings. He penned some twee sleeve notes under a pseudonym to hype the record's magical qualities, but it was a severe embarrassment. Among its few highlights was 'Dear Friend', which as McCartney explained later was addressed to Lennon: 'Let's lay the guns down, let's hang up our boxing gloves.' But he could not stop himself dwelling on the past. 'He's talking about money now,' said his assistant Shelley Turner ruefully. 'That's one of his pet points. He'll never stop.' If he could have maintained the detachment of 'Dear Friend', the quarrel with the other Beatles might have been mended. Instead, McCartney let months of resentment and pain pour from his lips.

His obsession was the group's business partnership, no closer to being broken eight months after he had won the court case. 'I just want this thing settled,' he said. 'We just can't get at the money.' He repeated the demand he'd been issuing for two years: 'I just want the four of us to get together somewhere and sign a piece of paper saying it's all over, and we want to divide the money four ways. No one else

---

* The single wasn't released in Britain for another year, because Northern Songs refused to recognise that it had been co-written by Ono. Lennon ordered thousands of 'War Is Over' T-shirts to be printed, Allan Steckler recalled, 'but we couldn't sell them, so they rotted in the office'.

would be there, not even Linda or Yoko or Allen Klein. We'd just sign the paper and hand it to the business people and let them sort it all out. That's all I want now. But John won't do it.' And so he continued, letting rip at Klein, Lennon's political posturing and the Apple bureaucracy that wouldn't let him leave the label: 'I didn't want to bring the new album out on Apple. I phoned the others up and asked them, "Well, what about it?" They hummed and aahed over the phone but a couple of days later when I spoke to them they didn't like the idea. So I asked them, "Have you been talking to Klein?"' Legal staff at EMI and Apple spent several weeks debating the issue of whether McCartney would be allowed to release *Wild Life* without using the familiar Apple logo that symbolised everything he wanted to escape.

Lennon could no more restrain himself than McCartney. He was so outraged by McCartney's comments in the rock paper *Melody Maker* that he typed a three-page reply, headed 'Please publish, "equal time".' It was as acerbic and wounding as 'How Do You Sleep', as Lennon revealed how McCartney had told him, 'if we didn't do what you wanted, you'd sue us again, and that "Ringo and George are going to break you John" . . . Who's the guy threatening to "finish" Ringo and Maureen, who was warning me on the phone two weeks ago? Who said he'd "get us" whatever the cost? As I've said before – have you ever thought that you might <u>possibly</u> be wrong about something?' Lee Eastman was caught in the line of fire: 'You must <u>KNOW</u> we're right about Eastman; he can't control himself in <u>PUBLIC</u> – even the people he buys paintings from squirm! (Shit from the inside, baby!)' Lennon briefly managed to calm himself: 'No hard feelings to you either. I know we basically want the same . . . whenever you want to meet, all you have to do is call.' But his sarcasm won out: 'P.S. The bit that really puzzled us was asking to meet WITHOUT LINDA AND YOKO. I know you're camp! But let's not go too far! I thought you'd have understood BY NOW, that I'm JOHNANDYOKO. P.P.S. Even <u>your</u> <u>own</u> lawyers know you can't 'just sign a bit of paper' (or don't they tell you?!).'

A month earlier Lennon had asked journalist Ray Connolly to deliver a letter to McCartney in London. 'He wanted to tell Paul something without going through the lawyers,' Connolly said. 'I phoned Paul when I got home, but he had changed his number, so I dropped John's letter into his postbox. Later I phoned Paul's dad to check that

Paul had received the letter. "I think so," Jim McCartney said, "but things have got worse since then. If I were you, I'd keep well out of it."' The exchange of insults in *Melody Maker* demonstrated the breadth of the divide.

Remarkably, this very public duel provoked a truce. McCartney dared to make the first call, and the pair avoided arguing long enough to reminisce about the distant past. Within a few days Lennon sent his ex-colleague a gift* with a handwritten note: 'Happy Xmas! (war is over if you want it . . .) THE BEATLES. Dear Paul, Linda et al. This is THE DECCA AUDITION!! I found the bootleg not the tape: they were a good group fancy turning THIS down! Love John + Yoko.' Shortly after Christmas the McCartneys visited the Lennons at their Greenwich Village apartment. The two men talked reconciliation and a solution to their business differences. But a few months later Linda McCartney admitted, 'We saw John and Yoko at Christmas, and it was all, "We're going to do it" and "You'll be out by March, man", and Yoko Ono said, "To hell with the contracts." But nothing happened.'

The Lennons suddenly had more pressing issues to confront. They wanted to release an album of two impromptu performances from 1969 and 1971, under the title *Live Jam*, or perhaps *London Air & New York Wind*. But Allen Klein strongly resisted the idea. He was equally unimpressed when the Lennons started work on an album of political material in spring 1972. Klein explained why: under the terms of the contract they had signed with Capitol, the four Beatles would only be entitled to a second increase in their royalty rates if the two most recent albums they had released by autumn 1972 had each sold 500,000 copies. Previous records by the solo Beatles had easily surpassed that figure, but Klein feared that a live or political offering from the Lennons might struggle to reach the target. Lennon cared nothing for long-term financial gain – all he wanted was unconditional support from his manager – and he felt that by daring to question his artistic decisions Klein was demonstrating a fundamental lack of confidence.

His growing distrust of Klein would pale alongside another looming crisis. For all his revolutionary rhetoric, Lennon had a naive faith in the morality of the capitalist system. He had experienced censorship

---

* The record was not, as Lennon believed, the Beatles' 1962 audition for Decca Records but a collection of early BBC radio performances.

in the past, but he never imagined that by aligning himself with some of the most notorious revolutionary figures in America he might incur the wrath of the US government. The more often he cavorted with the Yippies and the Black Panther Party, the more dangerous he appeared to the already paranoid Nixon administration. They feared that dissent organised by one of the world's most influential public figures might endanger Nixon's chances of re-election that November. On 4 February 1972 Senator Strom Thurmond wrote to the US attorney general, enclosing a summary of Lennon's contacts with the revolutionary left and suggesting that the Immigration and Naturalisation Service (INS) might intervene. 'This appears to me to be an important matter,' Thurmond wrote, 'and I think it would be well for it to be considered at the highest level. As I can see, many headaches might be avoided if appropriate action is taken in time.' Lennon was only in America on a six-month visa, due to expire on 29 February, but he blithely continued to plot with his fellow radicals. He and Ono had sealed their solidarity with Rubin and Hoffman at Bank Street, in a blood pact: the four of them nicked their thumbs with a penknife and let their collective life force run together. With that gesture the Lennons pledged themselves to the revolution. After months of political disillusionment, Rubin was ecstatic: 'Something new is in the air. Somehow the arrival of John and Yoko in New York has had a mystical and practical effect that is bringing people together again.'

While Lennon relished the excitement of being a subversive, Ono retained her natural pacifism. 'I made John and myself isolated from the rest,' she insisted later, 'as our friends were trying to lash out, wanting to bomb the White House, something violent like that. I insisted that we should keep doing things in a peaceful way, because violence breeds violence.' Yet a more sinister form of isolation was creeping into their relationship. As an FBI informant noted, 'John Lennon does not give the impression he is a true revolutionist since he is constantly under the influence of narcotics.' Another detected a rift between Rubin and Lennon regarding the latter's 'excessive use of narcotics'. The Lennons were forced to travel to the US Virgin Islands in an attempt to conquer his renewed addiction to heroin. When they returned, tensions were evident in their relationship. 'If you were around them, you would see very quickly that she runs the show,' recalled

TV presenter Mike Douglas, whose programme they commandeered for a week. 'She was very rough on the staff. The kids were very young, and probably fans when they arrived, [but] probably terribly let down at some of the behaviour.' A few weeks later the couple travelled to San Francisco to undergo treatment with methadone – withdrawal from which, Lennon admitted later, 'almost killed Yoko'.

On 30 January 1972, British army paratroopers shot dead 13 Catholics on the streets of the Northern Irish city of Derry. It was the single most radicalising moment of the entire 'troubles' that afflicted the area from 1968 onwards. Lennon memorialised the tragedy in a song, 'Sunday Bloody Sunday', which preached the republican manifesto of the IRA in an affected New York accent. Much less predictable was Paul McCartney's reaction to the shootings. Two days later he took Wings into the studio to record his own political anthem, the inappropriately chirpy 'Give Ireland Back to the Irish'. 'I always used to think, God, John's crackers, doing all these political songs,' he explained. But the events in Derry slapped him in the face and demanded a response. Ironically, his song kept closer to the Lennons' peace ethic than theirs did, striking a tone of disapproval rather than rebellion. When Lennon had first written about the situation in Ireland, in a song called 'The Luck of the Irish', he had promised to donate all his earnings to civil rights activists there. If McCartney made a similar gesture, he kept it quiet. It was hard to avoid the cynical feeling that one of McCartney's motives was to show Lennon that he too had a political conscience.

From the Lennons, there was now the promise of a series of fund-raising concerts for the Irish struggle. They would begin at Madison Square Garden, echoing Harrison, and then tour Ireland itself. Friends began to scout for a suitable home there for the couple. Meanwhile, Allen Klein boasted that George Harrison was proposing to perform a charity show in London on behalf of the homeless. 'You know what's happening at Wembley?' he crowed. 'George will announce he's gonna do a concert, right? About two weeks before, Ringo will say, "Hey, I'll play too." Then John says he's gonna be there. Everyone will wanna know where Paul is. He'll think I'm trying to embarrass him. You betcha. I'm gonna roast his fucking ass.' None of these events happened, however, and by early March 1972 it was apparent that if Lennon left the USA the immigration authorities would not allow him back in. His life degenerated into a routine of INS hearings, deportation orders and appeals, sapping his radical energy.

Meanwhile, Klein's own activities flashed into the spotlight. Journalist Peter McCabe published 'Some Sour Notes from the Bangladesh Concert' in the magazine *New York*. He alleged that, far from channelling the royalties from Harrison's album to charity, Klein and ABKCO were making a profit of $1.14 on each copy. A further 25 cents was supposedly earmarked for Bob Dylan, and 50 cents to the songwriters and publishers who were also supposed to be donating their services for free. Assuming an eventual sale of three million copies, McCabe said, this meant that around $6 million would not be reaching its intended destination.

Phil Spector, who had co-produced *The Concert For Bangla Desh*, phoned the magazine to register his disapproval of McCabe's piece. Klein's reaction was more substantial: he filed a libel suit against this 'false and defamatory matter', demanding $150 million to compensate for the damage to his reputation, the distress the article had caused and the loss of sales it would provoke. He called a press conference to defend himself, and prepared a detailed breakdown of the costs and receipts of the project, which he sent to *Rolling Stone* magazine. They printed it verbatim and then queried his arithmetic. But Klein insisted that he and ABKCO hadn't taken a penny from the project; indeed, they were actually losing a dollar on each set.

The press conference descended into farce because Klein's staff made the mistake of issuing invitations to the city's underground press. Among those who accepted was A. J. Weberman, who had already led a demonstration against Capitol Records, complaining that they should be manufacturing and distributing the Bangladesh album at cost, not at a profit. He was predictably outraged by McCabe's article, and led a small party of Rock Liberation Front activists to the ABKCO office, chanting slogans such as 'You'll wonder where the money went, when Klein runs a charity event.' 'We brought along some rotten fruit,' he recalled. 'We called it our Free Food for Starving Music Executives Programme. We said, "Hey, if you guys have to steal from the people of Bangladesh, you must be a bunch of hungry motherfuckers. So what we have for you is free fucking lunch." We took all these vegetables that we got from the dumpster and threw them all over the office.' He and Spector got into a fist fight, Weberman said, 'and

Spector attacks my old lady, Ann. He likes to beat on women, you know. Wonderful fucking human being.'

When news of the demonstration reached the underground press, Weberman received an unexpected phone call. 'John and Yoko called me up,' he remembered,

and they said, 'Hey, man, bring your old lady for tea, cos Klein is ripping us off too, man.' So we went over there to Bank Street. John and Yoko were there, stark naked. And I started hanging out with them. Sometimes he would be going through cold turkey. He got deeper and deeper into junk. Lennon would sit around and tell me how much he hated McCartney, and how he'd like to punch him out. But if I ever said anything bad against [Bob] Dylan, he wanted to punch me out too, and Yoko had to restrain him.

A maverick even by the standards of Greenwich Village, Weberman had connections with dope dealers and revolutionaries, sometimes in the same skin. So too, he claimed, did Lennon: 'There was one guy who was smuggling Lebanese hash into the US. With the money he got, he'd go into gun stores and purchase weapons, and then ship the weapons back to Ireland. Lennon introduced me to this guy, who was a total fucking revolutionary from the IRA. I said to Lennon, "Man, you're pretty well connected back in England. Now I'm gonna hook you up here in the United States."' So, Weberman claimed, he hooked Lennon up with a group long suspected of funnelling money from Irish republican sympathisers in the USA to the IRA. They became the beneficiaries of Lennon's song 'The Luck of the Irish'. 'Lennon gave them this huge contribution,' Weberman says, 'and they had a big party to celebrate. They invited me – at last I was a hero! Everyone was saying, "Hey, this is Weberman, he turned Lennon on to us."'

The Irish republican movement was stoutly defended by the British underground press until February 1972, when several catering workers were killed in a bomb explosion at a barracks in Aldershot. Further killings followed, as the conflict in Northern Ireland hardened into guerrilla warfare. Thereafter, the IRA lost the sympathy of everyone in the UK but the revolutionary left. From his distant vantage point in New York, however, Lennon maintained his contacts with the organisation. 'I was over there on a speaking tour,' said Gerry O'Hare, then a prominent member of the more militant Provisional wing of the

IRA. 'A guy said to me, "Would you like to meet John Lennon?" I said, "Are you spoofing?" Two days later I went to his apartment.' He asked if the ex-Beatle would perform a benefit concert for the republican movement. 'He offered to do one in Dublin,' O'Hare said. 'He gave me the impression he was genuine. But I got the impression that if he did one in Dublin, he also wanted to do one in Belfast too, for the Protestant community. But he said he had a problem, that if he left America he might not be able to get back in.'

As Professor Jon Wiener's detailed research has demonstrated, several arms of the US government were now keeping Lennon and his comrades under surveillance, with a view to securing his deportation.* Fortunately for Lennon, they worked in competition rather than concord, ensuring that – despite strong rumours about his heroin use – they could never catch him in possession of illegal substances, even though a simple bust would have meant immediate deportation. As spring became summer, Lennon gradually eased back from active participation in the revolution. But the flow of money continued. Besides the Rock Liberation Front, Weberman and Peel were also prominent in a group called the Zippies. In June 1972 Apple issued Peel's album *The Pope Smokes Dope*, which Lennon and Ono had produced, and took out an advert in the Zippies' news-sheet *Beach Blanket Struggle*. They could probably have booked the space for $50, but instead Lennon arranged to pay the paper $50,000. 'I told him we were going to have a riot at the Republican Party convention in Miami,' Weberman explained,

and that we needed money to get buses and bring in the demonstrators. John gave us a couple of thousand dollars in cash, and the rest came from this ad. He had some idea what was going to happen – he knew there was a chance that it would turn out not to be a peaceful event, but he still gave us the money. You can't tell me that he didn't believe in violence. He helped to pay for it.

Once again the combined resources of the FBI and the INS failed to spot this evidence of subversion. But one political gesture was

* Wiener's dogged persistence secured the release of hundreds of pages of secret government documents relating to surveillance of Lennon and his friends.

impossible to ignore. In June 1972, as his lawyers were advising him to keep a low profile, Lennon issued *Some Time in New York City*, an album of radical political anthems.* The production (by Phil Spector) and vocal performances were exhilarating, but the simplistic content of the material, which sounded like a precocious child's guide to revolution, was severely damaging to Lennon's reputation. One of his staunchest supporters in the British underground dismissed the record as 'irritating, embarrassing and, finally, just plain unpleasant'. *Some Time in New York City* not only failed to match the commercial impact of McCartney's *Wild Life*, but was outsold by Starkey's *Sentimental Journey* and *Beaucoups of Blues*. The man widely regarded as the leader of the Beatles was once again their weakest commercial asset.

The record's failure was symptomatic of a wider feeling that the four Beatles were yesterday's men. It wasn't just that Lennon was the only one of the quartet to issue an album in 1972, or that two of the group (Harrison and Starkey) had effectively vanished. The outside world had been entranced by the human drama of the Beatles' split and the almost weekly sparring between Lennon and McCartney during 1971. Now the saga seemed passé; and so, in every dimension but nostalgia, did the Beatles. For fellow musicians, their influence had been inescapable during the 1960s: everyone seemed to be following the Beatles or, if they were courageous, reacting against them. Now there were new stylists in town, and nobody wanted to be caught in last year's designs. Acts who consciously maintained the Beatles' tradition, such as the Electric Light Orchestra, Badfinger and Raspberries, endured jibes about their outdated, 'retro' sound. It was as if the Beatles were the hangover from a decade that the world was already embarrassed to remember.

Lennon's battles with US immigration officials ensured that he remained newsworthy, but his former colleagues were less visible. While Lennon mixed with revolutionaries, Starkey appeared at events

---

*The set also featured the delayed *Live Jam* album. Allen Klein was forced to negotiate with EMI/Capitol for Lennon to take a reduced royalty rate on the package, in return for which the company agreed that it wouldn't count as a Beatles album in contractual terms. Klein's caution was well founded: the set failed by some distance to reach the 500,000 sales that would have triggered the royalty increase. When considering Klein's reign as manager, Lennon never gave him credit for this attention to detail.

such as Elizabeth Taylor's 40th-birthday party, where Hollywood celebrities and minor European royals welcomed him into their exclusive milieu. He released one single in 1972, 'Back off Boogaloo', the lyrics of which seemed to echo his disappointment with McCartney's recent output: 'Everything you try to do, you know it sure sounds wasted.' The title was a gift from Britain's pop phenomenon of the moment Marc Bolan, and when his band T. Rex performed at Wembley in the summer, before an audience exhibiting 'Bolanmania', it seemed appropriate that Starkey should be there to document the occasion for an Apple Films production. Reporters noted gleefully that he was able to pass through the pre-teen crowd without being recognised.

For Harrison, 1972 was a year of recuperation and retreat after the exertions of the Bangladesh benefit. But there were always meetings to determine which department of which government was now stalling the funds needed so desperately in the newly independent nation. They drained Harrison's already depleted creativity, ensuring that if he did feel inspired to write a song, it was usually tinged with despair at the failings of humanity. At home he grew increasingly estranged from his wife. When he made a rare appearance at Apple, he could seem tense and removed. Geoff Emerick was running Apple Studios at this time. 'George could be infuriating on occasions. Every now and then he would get into his Hare Krishna thing, and he'd walk around with this little bag that resembled a sling: he looked as if he'd broken his arm. You'd go up to him and ask him a question, any question: "Do you want to do your vocals now?" or something like that – and he'd start to answer you but then begin mumbling away, chanting his mantra.' Everything connected with the physical world seemed to annoy him. When EMI failed to offer an appropriate advance for his next album, he sent an angry postcard to the managing director: 'How much did EMI make from All Things Must Pass/My Sweet Lord?' He addressed the card symbolically to 'EMI Wreckords'.

Meanwhile the negotiations about the Beatles' partnership simmered expensively. But another item of business forced its way to the top of the agenda. In May the third year of Allen Klein's three-year management contract came to an end, and both sides had the option to call a halt. Harrison had become alarmed by the morass into which the Bangladesh project had fallen; Lennon felt personally betrayed by Klein's apparent distaste for his political campaigns; Starkey would do whatever the others agreed. But none of them was yet prepared to crawl back to McCartney and admit that perhaps he had been right. Neither did they wish to endure the very public humiliation of looking for a new manager. So they compromised, and agreed that because Apple was effectively dormant and consequently required very little management, they should renew Klein's contract for two or three months at a time, rather than a full year. Lennon, however, had a more sinister agenda. Beat poet Allen Ginsberg, who had recorded an album for Apple at Lennon's request in December 1971, explained: 'Lennon had realised he wanted to cut off from Klein, and he had to do it in a ruthless way, the same way that Klein worked. So he was not able to tell anybody. He just started legal proceedings secretly, and then he was ready to pull the trap when the moment came.'

Maybe Klein guessed what was happening; maybe he still had faith in his personal rapport with the three Beatles. Either way, it was now in his financial interest to find a project that would emphasise his importance to Apple, and reinforce his grip as the company's manager. After suggesting to Harrison that he should look for an offshore tax haven to safeguard his income, he focused his attention on the documentary movie that Neil Aspinall had assembled a year earlier. The film had been shelved, but Aspinall remained hopeful that one day all four of the Beatles would agree to its release. He intended to accompany it with an album of the group's greatest hits, guaranteed to sell in millions. Aspinall was aware of Klein's waning popularity among his clients, however, and also realised the financial implications of allowing the American to take credit for the project and claim a share of its earnings. To ensure Klein could not seize the film, he dismantled the master reels kept at the Apple office. Around the same time Aspinall formed his own company, Standby Films, which meant that he could retain control of the Beatles film as a personal project. Its name reflected his subservient role in the Beatles organisation: waiting until he was needed.

One problem confronting both Klein and Aspinall was McCartney's reluctance to become a museum piece. 'It's rather like an obituary to me,' he complained in May 1972. 'I don't like these old "remember when" things. I don't like talking about the old thing when inevitably anything I say I'm doing now won't match up to all the glorious things they'll show happened in the past.' He was talking on the occasion of a nostalgia trip over which he had no control: a lengthy BBC Radio series, *The Beatles Story*. The corporation secured interviews with Lennon, McCartney and Klein, but none of them was in the mood to glorify the past. 'So much emphasis is put on "Oh, the Beatles have broken up,"' Klein said. 'I don't think it was a tragedy. They haven't died. Maybe it was time they had a chance to live their own lives.' Lennon concurred. 'We were friends, and we had a function,' he said, 'but the function ended and the relationship had nothing to last on but memory, and it broke down. I know a lot of people were upset when the Beatles finished, but the circus has to come to an end. The Beatles were a monument, and had to be either changed or scrapped.' As if to acknowledge the point, Lennon, Harrison and Starkey withdrew their support from the Beatles' Fan Club, and it folded that spring – its membership reduced from a 1963 peak of 350,000 to just 11,000.

McCartney's reluctance to be judged against his past achievements reflected insecurity about his latest venture. Wings became a quintet in January, in time to record their 'Ireland' single. Briefly, McCartney could luxuriate in the kind of controversy that had been Lennon's domain, as radio stations refused to broadcast the record. In its Top 40 countdown, the BBC would only refer demurely to 'a record by Wings'. In early February McCartney fulfilled the fantasy rejected by the other Beatles in 1969, when Wings performed unannounced concerts at British universities. The novelty of seeing a Beatle in the flesh overshadowed any qualms about the group's music, which sounded under-rehearsed and inchoate. 'We all wanted to play Beatles tunes,' recalled drummer Denny Seiwell, 'but Paul wanted to start a whole new world for himself – rightly so. He wanted the world to get to know us, like they knew John and Ringo and George, but we could never be Beatles.' The closest that McCartney came to his past was a rousing finale of Little Richard's 'Long Tall Sally', which had closed the last Beatles concert in 1966.

Gradually, however, he began to build the skeleton of a new career. His decision to update the nursery rhyme 'Mary Had a Little Lamb' for his next single attracted derision from critics, but the record became an instant children's favourite. Like Starkey's attempt to confound public opinion by switching from country to electronic music, McCartney appeared to relish puncturing expectations. He continued to encourage his wife's musical ambitions, agreeing a deal with

Northern Songs that would let her composing credits stand, in return
for McCartney's agreement to make a TV special for Sir Lew Grade.
In July Wings undertook their first scheduled tour, though they avoided
major cities and concentrated on small towns in Europe. When the
press tracked them down, they found McCartney bullish. 'The Beatles
have definitely ended,' he repeated like a mantra, as if repetition would
bring acceptance. 'The man from the record company said, "Would
you play just once a year, lads?" like a sort of memorial tribute. Well,
I'm not going to get into that, because I'm not dead yet. It's no good
for me now.' His wife complained, 'We have no income, it all goes to
Apple. We are stuck, let me tell you.' 'What annoys me is the other
three and their preaching,' McCartney added. 'John goes around saying,
"Join Rock Liberation – give the people what is theirs," and he could
get us out.' But the partnership remained intact, despite Klein's claim
that Lennon, Harrison and Starkey were ready to buy out McCartney's
25 per cent share and then let ABKCO assume complete control of
the Apple empire. 'I don't really see them much,' McCartney said,
'and I don't really see why I should see them. We had a bit of trouble,
and that trouble is still on.'

Lennon could have echoed that sentiment. By late summer his anxi-
eties about Apple and the Beatles paled alongside the pressure he was
enduring from the US government. He was convinced that FBI agents
were shadowing his movements and taping his phone calls. A. J.
Weberman scoured his underground connections to secure Lennon a
telephone that couldn't be bugged. In return, the Lennons – who, after
Ono's film *Fly*, had some experience with insects – helped Weberman
procure 500 flies, which he released into the Republican Party national
headquarters. But constant meetings with lawyers and their insistence
that Lennon should do nothing to antagonise the authorities gradually
forced him and Ono away from their comrades. 'I know we haven't
got many friends,' he admitted that summer, 'but I never did have.'

During a visit to rehab in San Francisco earlier that year the Lennons
had met investigative TV reporter Geraldo Rivera, who had uncovered a scandalous history of abuse in a New York State children's
institution. In July Rivera asked Lennon if he would consider a
Harrison-style fund-raiser – which expanded to two shows at Madison
Square Garden, the same venue where Lennon had originally planned
to perform for Irish civil rights. 'Geraldo wanted to help John stay in

the USA, so he arranged this benefit concert,' recalled Steve Gebhardt, who filmed the event for the Lennons. David Peel had introduced them to a local bar band, Elephant's Memory, who had been put on retainer the previous Christmas on the assumption that they would be touring the world in 1972. Aside from the *Some Time in New York City* sessions and an occasional TV appearance, the One To One concerts on 30 August represented the sum total of their work together. Embarrassingly, tickets for the event sold far more slowly than Harrison's a year earlier, reflecting the toll that Lennon's political activity had taken on his popularity. He was reduced to recording radio ads guaranteeing a splendid time for all. When the tickets still didn't sell, he swallowed his pride and phoned Paul McCartney to see if he would join him on stage, but McCartney declined. Klein discreetly gave the remaining seats away.

This time there was no confusion about the charitable status of the concerts, and the money swiftly reached its target. Moreover, Lennon delivered a performance worthy of the occasion. 'The weird thing was turning left and right and seeing different faces,' he recalled. 'It didn't matter what I was singing – I'd see Yoko or one of the Elephants or [Jim] Keltner on the drums, and feel little flashes of, Oh, it isn't one of *them*, this is different. I've got to sing *all* the damn numbers.' If he lacked the stage polish of McCartney or the finesse of Harrison's Bangladesh big band, Lennon compensated with a quality that was his alone: passion. So intense was his focus that when he revisited the primal pain that had inspired him to write 'Cold Turkey' or 'Mother', he screamed and writhed like a man possessed, a living emblem of Arthur Janov's therapy. Yet the audience reserved its most fervent reaction for the moment when Lennon promised to 'go back, just once' and delivered a compelling rendition of the Beatles' 'Come Together'. He forgot the lyrics, but the spectacle was vivid enough to suggest that the spirit of the 1960s was still alive. The shows closed with a mass chorus of 'Give Peace a Chance', for which the crowd were given percussion instruments. After the performers left the stage, fans streamed out onto the streets of New York, still chanting, still banging their tambourines joyfully. It seemed like one last sunlit gathering of the tribes before the clouds descended and the hippie dream faded to dusk. Lennon was ecstatic, and began to talk again about the world tour he'd imagined a year before.

There were excitable suggestions that Lennon might share the bill at another Madison Square spectacular with Wings and a Harrison/Starkey big band. But the Beatles were otherwise occupied. Harrison was at Apple, recording an album with the hubristic working title of *The Magic Is Here Again*. Starkey was engaged in his most challenging and fulfilling film role, playing a version of his teddy boy past in *That'll Be the Day*. McCartney was at Abbey Road, completing the Wings double album that had been in preparation since the spring. And at the Record Plant in New York Lennon was watching his wife record her own double album of feminist songs with the bar band who were supposed to be his. 'When I decided to make a double album, their faces all became very long,' Ono complained of the Apple/ABKCO staff. 'But I decided to do it anyway, because I figured that if George Harrison can put out a triple album then I can put out a double album. Later I began to think that if George Harrison can put out a triple album, then *I* should be able to put out a triple album. But I decided to stop at 22 songs.'

That was precisely 22 songs more than Lennon had completed in recent months. The more creative Ono became, the more Lennon faltered. 'It is very difficult for two composers to be living together,' Ono said, admitting that she rose several hours earlier than her husband so that she could work undisturbed. Were they happy, she was asked? 'Not necessarily. Sometimes we're very happy, sometimes we're not. We're human. There was a negative situation at one time, like Scott and Zelda [Fitzgerald], but we overcame that because we were a bit more aware, thank God.' Lennon's awareness was coming under extreme pressure, however. On election night in November the couple attended a party at Jerry Rubin's apartment in SoHo. The revolutionaries had opted to support the Democratic Party candidate, George McGovern, who had promised to end the Vietnam War. They had gathered – Rubin, Hoffman, Allen Ginsberg and their comrades – in the expectation that righteousness would seize the day. But McGovern lost to Nixon in the biggest electoral landslide yet recorded.

When the Lennons arrived the party was soaked in despair. Lennon was drunk, artistically blocked, jealous of his wife's creativity, harassed by the US immigration authorities. Now he saw the radicals on whom he had staked his reputation, and whom he blamed for his persecution by the government, weeping for their own lost dreams. He ripped into Rubin and Hoffman, calling them 'middle-class Jews' and 'pigs'. When theatre director Judith Molina tried to calm him, he screamed at her, 'I want to cut you with a knife.' Others remember him threatening to go outside and shoot a cop. The only person who could quell his anger was Carol Realini, Rubin's room-mate. In full view of Ono, Lennon and Realini began to talk, and then kiss, before he led her into the next room. She told him that she couldn't make love while his wife was outside the door. 'We're getting divorced,' he told her. Soon Ono and the remaining guests were forced to listen to cries and groans of sexual pleasure. Then Lennon re-emerged, gestured silently at Ono and headed for the door.

This was an extreme but not isolated incident of marital discord. 'After we'd done the One To One concert film,' recalled Steve Gebhardt, 'I remember John saying to me that the days of everything being Johnandyoko – one word – were over. I was shocked.' Ono completed her record, *Approximately Infinite Universe*, which was greeted more positively than her previous releases. Lennon did his best to publicise it, writing a personal note to the Capitol Records boss asking him to throw the company's weight behind it. But in mid-January 1973 Lennon and Ono quarrelled publicly at another party. 'I wish I was back with Paul,' Lennon reportedly said. His young assistant May Pang insisted that the idea of a Lennon/McCartney reunion was 'ridiculous'. New York newspapers began to speculate that the Lennons were separating. To dispel the stories, the couple bought each other Valentine's Day cards in the Village, rightly confident that their gesture would make the gossip columns.

In March the couple flew to Los Angeles for an urgent meeting on Apple business. The company had been renewing Allen Klein's management contract regularly, but when the end-of-February deadline arrived, they asked for the notice period to be reduced to two weeks. Klein's office had compiled two double albums of the Beatles' greatest hits in preparation for Neil Aspinall's unfinished documentary film. News of the project had filtered out, and a manufacturer of bootleg records was preparing to distribute an illegal Beatles compilation to steal Apple's thunder. Also in America were George Harrison, who was collaborating with Ravi Shankar, and Richard Starkey, who was preparing to make his first album of pop material since the Beatles' break-up. The two men met amicably with Klein in New York, and then flew on to California 'We're all friends, even if we had split up,' Starkey recalled, 'so I said "Have you got any songs, boys?" and John said, "Yeah, I've got a song," so I said, "Well, come and play."'

Lennon arrived with 'I'm the Greatest', which he'd begun to write after watching *A Hard Day's Night* more than two years earlier. Then, it had sounded sullen and bitter. Retooled for Starkey, it emerged as a sardonic tribute to the Beatles. There was a reference to 'Billy Shears', the role Starkey had played on the *Sgt Pepper* album, and producer Richard Perry added sound effects of a similar vintage. 'Ringo, John, Klaus [Voormann] and myself grouped around a piano in the studio to put the finishing touches on that song,' Perry recalled.

Then someone called me out of the studio to say that George was on the phone. 'I hear there's some recording going on,' George said. 'Can I come down?' So I said to John, 'George is on the phone and wants to come down to record with us. Is it OK?' 'Hell, yes,' John said. 'Tell him to get down here right away and help me finish this bridge.' George arrived, and without saying a word he joined in on the same wavelength we were on. He played guitar and John played piano, and they complemented each other perfectly. There was the Beatles' magic unfolding right before my eyes!

Perry's excitement was forgivable: he was watching the revamped Beatles line-up that never coalesced in 1970. For Lennon, though, Voormann was clearly not a substitute for McCartney: 'The three of us were there,' he said, 'and Paul would most probably have joined in if he was around, but he wasn't.' Even without McCartney, 'I'm the Greatest' sounded like a lost gem from the *Abbey Road* sessions. 'Everyone in the room was gleaming,' Perry purred. 'It's such a universal gleam with the Beatles.' Lennon complained later that Harrison had suggested the Beatles should make that gleam a permanent feature; and one major obstacle to a reunion, desired or otherwise, was about to be removed.

Chapter 7

I love him, you know. I mean, he really has made me secure
enough. I do have money for the first time ever, really . . . He's
a great guy, highly sensitive, highly intelligent.
 John Lennon on Allen Klein, June 1971

He's a naughty boy, and he's too greedy, and he didn't do what
he said he'd do, which was manage our affairs, which are in a
worse state than when . . . well, according to the accountants,
anyway.
 John Lennon on Allen Klein, November 1973

On 2 April 1973 Allen Klein issued a statement from his office on
Broadway: 'It is not now felt in the best interests of ABKCO to put
forward a proposal for its continued management of Apple Corps and
Messrs Harrison, Lennon and Starkey. Under these circumstances,
ABKCO has terminated its efforts with respect to its possible acquisi-
tion of Apple Corps. We wish Harrison, Lennon and Starkey continued
success.' With those carefully phrased sentences Klein acknowledged
that his quest for control of the Beatles was over. Divorce was
inevitable, but it could be achieved with dignity.

 Klein had seized the initiative, suggesting that the decision was
entirely his own. His former clients disagreed. That morning John
Lennon and Yoko Ono called a press conference to announce the

formation of Nutopia, an imaginary country with no borders. As the self-appointed Nutopian ambassadors to the United Nations, they were claiming asylum in New York. It marked a last despairing effort to outwit US immigration officials and a symbolic farewell to their roles as political activists. It was significant that the official emblem of Nutopia was the white flag of surrender.

Lennon was asked whether it was true that Allen Klein was no longer his manager. 'We separated ourselves from him,' he confirmed. Why? 'Why do you think?' he snapped. 'We will go into that next time.' Later, Lennon was slightly more forthcoming:

There are many reasons why we finally gave him the push, although I don't want to go into the details of it. Let's say possibly Paul's suspicions were right, and the time was right . . . Although I haven't been particularly happy personally for quite a long time with the situation, I didn't want to make any quick moves, and I wanted to see if maybe something would work out.

This vague comment masked the truth: for several months Lennon, Harrison and Starkey had been taking legal advice about severing their ties with Klein. He had certainly caught the scent of betrayal in the wind, as he had already asked his accountants to prepare detailed profit-and-loss figures for the Beatles' companies during his reign. In late February he pleaded his case with Richard Starkey and George Harrison in New York. He warned them that the Beatles were in danger of failing to fulfil their obligations to EMI/Capitol, and so he had asked Allan Steckler, head of Apple's US division, to assemble two compilations of the Beatles' best-loved songs. Klein also reminded Starkey that the three Beatles and Apple still owed ABKCO a considerable sum in managerial commissions. Could he guarantee that ABKCO would get paid? Starkey unhesitatingly agreed that they would always live up to the terms of their agreement. But as he already knew, the agreement was doomed. Apple renewed the management contract for two more weeks, and then another two, before Klein's reign as manager of the Beatles Group of Companies ended on 31 March 1973.

Of the three Beatles who had signed the contract, Starkey had least reason to reject Klein. 'No matter what everyone says, he's fair,' he had said of the American in 1971. 'He doesn't wanna shit on anyone, really.' Klein had recognised Starkey's precarious position after the demise of the Beatles and encouraged him to pursue his acting career, even financing the Western *Blindman*, in which the drummer had a leading part.* Starkey was promised $150,000 for his role, placing him among Hollywood's higher earners. But in any division of loyalties Starkey would always favour the Beatles over an outsider, and so it proved with Klein.

As Allan Steckler recalled, Klein's tragic flaw with the Beatles was not his financial ability but his handling of tiny details:

Things would happen that seemed unimportant to Klein, but much more important to the artist. I remember having a phone conversation with Klein when Ringo came in the room. I hung up, and Ringo said, 'I wanted to talk to him, can you get him back?' So someone in the office made the call for Ringo, and was told that Klein wasn't in. Klein didn't realise that Ringo had already heard me talking to him! That kind of thing made him really pissed.

Despite the judge's damning portrayal of Klein's actions during the 1971 court case, Lennon, Harrison and Starkey had chosen to keep faith with their manager. 'He made them feel financially and artistically secure,' Steckler reckoned. So why did they decide that Klein had to go? Steckler believed he knew the answer. 'George called me and said, "We're not re-signing with Klein,"' he recalled. 'I asked him why, and he said, "The only way the Beatles can get together again is if Allen isn't there. I'm ready to do it, so is Ringo, and I think we can persuade John to go along with it. But if we're going to work with Paul, we need to get rid of Klein."'

McCartney certainly felt that Klein's departure had opened a vital channel of communication. 'The only thing that has prevented us from getting together again has been Allen Klein's contractual hold over the Beatles' name,' he commented, ignoring the personality clashes that predated Klein's arrival. Three of the four Beatles were now prepared to consider a reunion. But the fourth member quickly dampened their enthusiasm. 'The chances are practically nil,' Lennon declared. 'And imagine if they did get together' – the choice of personal pronoun was telling – 'what kind of scrutiny would they be under?

* *Blindman* also afforded Klein a cameo role, as a sharpshooter alongside Beatles aide Mal Evans.

Nothing could fit the dream people had of them. So forget it, you know, it's ludicrous!'

The dream that scared Lennon was about to reveal its financial power. Early in 1973 US national magazines such as *Penthouse* and American radio and TV stations in the ABC network ran advertisements for *The Story of the Beatles*, a multi-record set that offered a rich sampling of the Beatles' 1960s catalogue alongside the pick of their solo singles. This was not an officially sanctioned replay of the past, however, but a strictly black-market affair, prompting Allen Klein to shut it down. George Harrison, Apple and Capitol Records duly filed a joint lawsuit against the distributors of the record, alleging 'illegal pirating' of the Beatles' music. One of Klein's final acts as Apple manager was to authorise two official collections of the group's greatest hits, 1962–1966 and 1967–1970. They appeared in matching jackets, the first using the photograph from the Beatles' first album, the second opting for the near-facsimile taken in 1969 and originally intended for their *Get Back* album. The public appetite was voracious, and soon the two sets were jockeying for chart supremacy around the world.

Klein had originally intended the albums to accompany Neil Aspinall's documentary history of the Beatles and had consulted all four members about the track listing. McCartney refused to co-operate, however, while Lennon offered little of value. 'George controlled the choice of material on those albums more than any of us,' he admitted. 'They sent me lists and asked for my opinion, but I was busy at the time.' McCartney demonstrated even less interest: 'I still haven't heard them,' he said several months later. EMI/Capitol, who released the albums for Apple, were anxious to rush the records into the stores, but a series of mysterious delays meant that they didn't appear until early April, after Klein's contract had expired, removing the obligation to pay him a percentage of the profits.

Lennon and Harrison had been less careful about their dealings with Klein. They retained the same naivety about business affairs that they had displayed during the launch of Apple, imagining that they operated in some magical dimension where their actions had no consequences. It was what allowed them to maintain their friendship with Klein and simultaneously work for his overthrow – a talent for duplicity that might have brought them success in Caesar's Rome. But they were dealing with a man who enjoyed nothing more than the forensic examination of music business accounts.

As late as March 1973 Harrison was still treating ABKCO like a bank. While he was in New York the journalist Al Aronowitz came to him with a hard-luck story and an empty wallet. Harrison agreed to lend him $20,000, ostensibly from the funds of his US publishing company, although the cash actually came straight from Klein. The Aronowitz loan was merely the most recent example of the Beatles' generosity with Klein's money. By Klein's calculations, he had lent Harrison approximately $270,000 over the previous two years. Lennon's debts to his manager were equally profound. Klein claimed that Lennon had borrowed almost £50,000 since 1971. In addition, Klein had funded Lennon and Ono's fruitless quest to obtain custody of Kyoko Cox, which had involved travel between several countries. Those costs came to $34,000, alongside further loans to the Lennons' company Bag Productions totalling $48,000. Between them, Harrison and Lennon had borrowed almost $500,000, all of which was now due for repayment.

Four years after Klein was deputed to save the Beatles from bankruptcy, their corporate affairs were in chaos. The facade was impressive: the two retrospective packages were selling in vast quantities, providing a platform for imminent albums by McCartney and Harrison. But who was managing the store? Although Apple's headquarters was still ostensibly in London, Klein had been handling its affairs from New York, where ABKCO held many crucial contracts and files. Meanwhile, the four founders of Apple were still locked in an enervating legal battle about the precise status of their joint partnership, and Apple's business affairs were under the supervision of the UK official receiver. He granted the four Beatles an increase in their monthly allowance from the partnership funds in May 1973, to protect them against the rampant inflation affecting the British economy. They were now being paid a 'salary' of £3,000 apiece every month, three times more than before. But John Lennon, in particular, was in trouble, struggling to maintain a New York lifestyle while maintaining a mansion in England that he hadn't seen for nearly two years.

In late spring 1973 he and Ono negotiated the purchase of an apartment in the Dakota Building, a grandiose block on Manhattan's West Side overlooking Central Park. Their break with Klein had interrupted their cash flow, so they were forced to sell their house in Ascot,

Tittenhurst Park, to Starkey and his wife. Starkey also took over the recording facility that Lennon had built but hardly ever used. Their English home wasn't their only sacrifice. For more than a year they had been paying each of the members of Elephant's Memory $200 a month. Now Lennon told the band, 'It's costing too much bread to keep you on a retainer – and I/we have no plans to tour or anything money making.' But these savings didn't balance Lennon's books: with Klein's money now unavailable, he had to look elsewhere for personal loans.

One person retained the trust of all four Beatles. In 1967 Neil Aspinall had been asked to rescue the group from the disarray left by Brian Epstein's death. During Klein's reign he had remained on salary, keeping a discreet eye on the London office while leaving Klein's supremacy unchallenged. Now his moment had come, and all four Beatles were happy to reinstall him as Apple manager, under the supervision of the official receiver. Aspinall couldn't repair the Lennon/McCartney relationship, but he could ensure that both men were equally informed. His position was only tenable if he didn't take sides: he might once have been closer to Lennon, but now he had to maintain a diplomatic show of neutrality. And so he slipped into a routine of constant attention to the Beatles' demands which required him to be on call throughout the 16-hour transatlantic working day. It was a role that won him their undying trust and a handsome salary but took a fearful toll on his health. And trust did not always equal respect. 'You have to remember that Neil started out as their roadie,' one insider said. 'Even when he was running the company, they still regarded him as the guy who carried their amplifiers and got them sandwiches.' There could be no complaints about his commitment, however. 'He worked very hard to preserve the Beatles' legacy,' said publisher Sean O'Mahony, who often negotiated with Aspinall. 'He could be a difficult bugger, but that was his job.'

As early as mid-April 1973 lawyers and accountants began to meet regularly in New York to discuss the consequences of Klein's departure. McCartney's interests were protected by the Eastmans, but the other Beatles now needed personal representation. There would no longer be any collective management; each man picked his own adviser. Lennon chose US lawyer Harold Seider, who had previously worked for Klein and had an intimate knowledge of the contractual web. Starkey opted for Hilary Gerrard, a 40-year-old Londoner who became his personal manager and ultimately his representative on the Apple board. Harrison, meanwhile, had been introduced to Denis O'Brien, an American lawyer and banker who had previously handled Peter Sellers' affairs. In early July 1973 Harrison asked O'Brien to become his business manager. In a hint of the contractual complications to come, Harrison signed the deal on a personal basis with O'Brien, who then officially commissioned his own company, Euroatlantic Ltd, to do the work. Meanwhile, O'Brien was not paid by Harrison, but by his publishing company, Harrisongs Ltd. This arrangement depersonalised the contract between the two men and ensured that lawyers would struggle to understand its full ramifications.

Unbeknown to the Beatles, the British government was taking a keen interest in their financial affairs. The Inland Revenue was pursuing Harrison for tax from the Bangladesh film and album; as he had been warned, the proceeds from both projects were treated as his personal income, even though he donated all the money to charity. He eventually fed the government's uncharitable greed with a personal cheque for one million pounds – bitter reward for his generosity. Under the circumstances it seemed somewhat churlish that Harrison and Lennon were also under investigation by the Bank of England. There were precise rules limiting the money that British citizens could carry in and out of the country, and the bank had unearthed the loans from ABKCO, which appeared to breach UK law. For several months officials were employed to delve into the details of these loans, before deciding that although the transfers were technically illegal the sums involved were too trifling to repay any further effort.

No amount of money was too small, however, to escape the attention of those who were squabbling over the Beatles' fortunes. The four now inhabited two mutually antagonistic worlds, as pawns of the legal profession, and as flourishing artists and entertainers. Their music produced the money that paid for the businessmen, while Lennon, McCartney, Harrison and Starkey tried to pretend that none of the problems touched them or their work. Their fans had no inkling that their lives were now dominated by business and legal disputes. In retrospect, it is amazing that any of them managed to function under this pressure, let alone that two of the group were able to create their most enduring solo work.

Lennon faced additional burdens: he was still being pursued by the US immigration department, and was close to exhausting his possible grounds for appealing against deportation. 'I tried to call him,' said his friend Gail Renard, 'and I got a message back from his people, which said, "I'm in a bad way and I'm not seeing anyone."' Meanwhile, his marriage was failing. It didn't help that while he was experiencing a creative drought Yoko Ono was recording a dozen feminist songs, just six months after completing her last double album. This time Lennon kept his distance from the sessions, though he was inveigled into making a cameo appearance as a henpecked husband. 'I was just having fun,' Ono explained, 'but also I was trying to show what *we* go through, what men tell women. How do you like it when *we* say it?' In an attempt to keep pace, Lennon used Ono's band to cut his own *Mind Games* album, exploring familiar themes in conventional ways. It did nothing to alter his status as the least commercially successful Beatle. Yet he displayed no appetite for the obvious solution to his financial problems: 'The only talk about Beatle reunions comes from people at the side of the Beatles who want to put us together and make millions and millions of dollars. And I'm not interested in that, or in playing with the old team again.'

On the title track of his *Living in the Material World* album George Harrison devoted a laboured but affectionate verse to his Beatle colleagues, before pledging his allegiance to 'the spiritual sky' rather than the terrain of dollars and pounds. To reinforce his lack of interest in the objects of this earth, he diverted the proceeds to the Material World Charitable Foundation Trust, which continues to fund worthy causes to this day. Both the album and its single, 'Give Me Love', topped the US charts, repeating the success of *All Things Must Pass* two years earlier. But the prevailing tone of the record was moral disapproval, never an attractive quality in a popular entertainer.

There was no underlying message on Starkey's first pop album, simply titled *Ringo*. Besides the collaboration with Lennon and Harrison on 'I'm the Greatest', it included one hit single co-written with Harrison ('Photograph') and another featuring McCartney ('You're Sixteen') – both also reaching No. 1 in America. As Starkey explained, he was able to force McCartney's hand: 'I said, "John and George have written me a song. You're not going to be left out, are you?" So he wrote me a song. And whoever wrote the song worked on it.' The album set a precedent for Starkey's entire career: he would rely on his friends and his charm, and if both were on tap, then the results were usually appealing. The appearance of all four Beatles on his album reinforced the hope that they might soon collaborate in a more formal setting. Even Lennon was gradually warming to the idea: 'There's always a chance. As far as I can gather from talking to them all, nobody would mind doing some work together again. But if we did do something, I'm sure it wouldn't be permanent. We'd do it just for that moment.'

While Lennon, Harrison and Starkey continued to draw on the same reservoir of musicians, producers and studios, collaboration was always a possibility. Paul McCartney, however, remained defiantly in his own orbit. His band Wings had taken time to settle. EMI Records advised him not to release a proposed double album, *Red Rose Speedway*, because the material was substandard. McCartney must have been irked when Yoko Ono issued her own two-record set on Apple. The shortened version of Wings' album was little more impressive, though it did spawn one of the year's four chart-topping singles by an ex-Beatle, the sickly 'My Love'. (Lennon was the only Beatle who missed out on this achievement.) It was accompanied by an insipid TV special unrecognisable as the work of the man who had conceived *Magical Mystery Tour*. And Wings finally undertook a British tour, their deliberately brief performances convincing most critics that the band did have an artistic purpose.

Those members of Wings whose surname wasn't McCartney continued to chafe at his non-democratic working methods, and viewed the mounting speculation about a Beatles reunion with resignation. 'I don't suppose we'll be forever together,' commented guitarist Henry McCullough. 'I'm sure Paul's got more of a tie to the Beatles than to Wings.' In fact, McCullough acted first, leaving the band (with Denny Seiwell) shortly before they were due to fly to Nigeria to record another album, in August 1973. This offered McCartney the perfect excuse to abandon his group and resume his solo career. Instead, he elected to continue as the leader of a trio, assuming the roles of drummer and lead guitarist himself.

Separation was in the air during the final months of 1973. Wings' personnel crisis paled alongside the traumas confronting the other Beatles. George Harrison's marriage to Pattie Boyd had been stale for several years, and their mutual friend Eric Clapton was still encouraging Boyd to leave her husband. Boyd attempted to refresh her marriage, but felt increasingly estranged by Harrison's spirituality and cocaine use. During 1973 their house became a haven of adulterous intrigue. While Harrison holidayed with Krissie Wood, Boyd enjoyed a brief affair with Krissie's husband Ronnie. Clapton visited the house regularly, barely attempting to conceal his desperate passion for Boyd. To complete the circle of dangerous liaisons, Harrison began a relationship with Richard Starkey's wife Maureen. 'She was the last person I would have expected to stab me in the back,' Boyd recalled, 'but she did.' Boyd tried to warn Starkey, who didn't believe her until – as she wrote later – 'George, in front of everyone, proceeded to tell Ringo that he was in love with his wife. Ringo worked himself up into a terrible state and went about saying, "Nothing is real, nothing is real."' When the affair ended, the Starkeys' marriage soon collapsed. Maureen Starkey was so upset that she deliberately drove her motorcycle into a brick wall, causing such extensive facial injuries that she had to undergo plastic surgery. By February 1974 the Harrisons had also separated, and Boyd began a long and eventually traumatic relationship with Clapton.

Only the barest details of these marital upsets reached the media. It would be many years, for example, before Harrison's affair with Starkey's wife was revealed. Neither of the Beatles hinted at a rift, and time eventually repaired the wound, as it did the friendship between Clapton and Harrison. John Lennon could not escape so easily. He had chosen to portray his relationship with Yoko Ono as one of the century's great love affairs, and when it failed he had nowhere to hide. The vast majority of the public had no idea who Harrison or Starkey had married, but the single identity of Johnandyoko was burned into the global retina. By September 1973 gossip columnists were reporting that the Lennons had separated. His childhood friend Pete Shotton recalled, 'He said it was just that Yoko and he had been getting on each other's nerves, so they'd decided to take a break for a year. I asked him where Yoko was, and he said, "Oh, just screwing around somewhere."' It was generally assumed that, as the man, Lennon was the motivating force behind the break-up; only after his death did it emerge that Ono had not only expelled him from their New York apartment, but also arranged for him to seek consolation with their young assistant May Pang. Lennon wrote optimistically to Derek Taylor, 'Yoko and me are in hell, but I'm gonna change it, probably this very day,' but this was a wildly unrealistic assessment of the situation.

Journalist Chris Charlesworth met Lennon soon after his separation from Ono. 'I got the impression that he seemed to be very isolated,' he recalled, 'or rather he had chosen to isolate himself. It was almost as if he was homesick, though he would later deny that.' Lennon could have abandoned the immigration case and returned to Britain, and possibly even to McCartney, but that would have meant accepting that his relationship with Ono was over. Instead, he insisted that nothing serious was happening, that Pang was merely an aide, not a lover, and that (as he told Charlesworth) he and Yoko were 'just playing life by ear, and that includes our careers. We occasionally take a bath together and occasionally separately . . . I know people are calling from England suggesting we've split up. It's not so.'

Lennon had now broken his ties with the Beatles, banished Klein (like so many father figures in the past) and was separated from Ono, on whom he had depended for five years. His new companion was charming, beautiful – and a former employee, many years younger than him, who could not provide the psychological security that was his greatest need. For the first time since his teens he was effectively alone, forced to trust his own logic and rely on his own resources. He had no idea where to start. So he stumbled into an ill-fated project in California, recording vintage rock 'n' roll tunes under the extremely erratic guidance of Phil Spector, who facilitated Lennon's penchant for alcoholic and chemical excess, and outstripped it with his own. Outside the studio Lennon's life was now dominated by legal hearings. Even his work was being shaped by the lawyers, who had negotiated a truce in the case regarding 'Come Together' and Chuck Berry's 'You Can't Catch Me'. Rather than claiming royalties, Berry's publisher, Big Seven Music, agreed that Lennon would cut three of their songs on his oldies album.

Lennon knew that he was walking on fire. 'He didn't used to drink with Yoko,' recalled his friend Steve Gebhardt, 'maybe just an occasional glass of wine at dinner. He said, "I have a problem if I do this. It doesn't do me any good."' But now those self-imposed boundaries were erased. 'John would drink a bottle of brandy or vodka a day,' May Pang said of these troubled sessions. 'I was so naive at that time that I did not realise that John was also on heroin.' Lennon's vocal performances were certainly raucous and chaotic, such as the take of 'Just Because' that subsided into a drunken rant about the charms of his backing singers. 'I want to suck your nipples, baby,' he leered, before admitting, 'I need some relief from my obligations. A little cocaine will set me on my feet.' And all the while Spector's gargantuan arrangements matched the incoherence pouring from Lennon's mouth. Within weeks the sessions had collapsed.

Lennon's 'obligations' in 1973 were headed by a barrage of lawsuits from his former manager. On 16 June, ABKCO sued George Harrison for the money he had borrowed from Allen Klein. Two days later Lennon sent May Pang to ABKCO's office to collect dozens of master tapes for Apple releases that Klein had accumulated since 1969. Lennon and Klein corresponded amicably over the summer, Lennon signing one note, 'Love John, President, Apple Records Inc(apacitated!)'. Meanwhile, Klein fired lawsuits at Lennon and Apple: an action to recover loans of $226,000 from one of the company's US subsidiaries; another to regain $153,000 from Apple Films; a third to reclaim the money Lennon owed Klein; and a bumper bundle of no fewer than 42 suits, filed in a single action against all four of the Beatles, Yoko Ono, nine of their companies, a lawyer and a further ten John Does. Klein demanded the immediate settlement of his management commissions and expenses from 1969 onwards, which he alleged had been underpaid by more than $6 million, and a further $23 million that he claimed was due for services rendered. The final charge was that all the defendants had been involved in a conspiracy to deprive ABKCO of its rightful income, for which it was now claiming more than $10 million in punitive damages.

All these cases were filed in the Supreme Court of the State of New York, and entailed depositions, affidavits, subpoenas and all the rigmarole associated with the legal machine. Apple's lawyers began to assemble an equally vigorous defence, claiming that the personal loans had all been repaid, that the demands for management commission were either erroneous or overblown, and that in any case several of the companies named in ABKCO's suit could not be sued in America, as they did not trade there. There were countless hearings and conferences, all of which ate away at both sides' capital without any progress being made.

On 18 October 1973 a special meeting of Apple executives was held at the London offices in St James's Street, into which they'd moved earlier in the year, vacating their more expensive home at Savile Row. Two weeks later Apple opened a second front, hoping to isolate Klein in foreign territory and cut off his retreat. Besides suing the Beatles in New York, he would now have to defend himself in London. The primary case featured Klein and ABKCO as defendants, under fire from no fewer than 32 plaintiffs, including all the Beatles except McCartney, plus Ono and every imaginable member of the famous Beatles Group of Companies. Apple alleged that Klein had failed to tell Lennon, Harrison and Starkey that they needed to take independent legal advice before they signed their management deal with him, and failed to ensure that they understood the full implications of what they were signing. It was a curious line of defence, giving the impression that they were no more than children, incapable of acting in their own best interests without constant supervision. (Embarrassingly, Lennon and Harrison had signed an affidavit in February 1971 confirming that the deal *had* been fully explained to them.) Apple asked for the original management deal to be annulled, and for Klein to return much of the money he had already been paid in commissions – some of which, they said, he had calculated at a grossly excessive rate.

To enliven the proceedings, Apple also alleged that Klein had deliberately ordered extra US copies of the *Let It Be* album to be manufactured and then claimed a commission on the unsold records – although this suggestion was soon withdrawn. Apple further complained about problems with the staging of the concerts for Bangladesh, particularly regarding their charitable status; said that Klein had encouraged Lennon, Harrison and Starkey to break British law by taking too much money in and out of the country; and alleged that he had told them that they had no need to worry about their finances, with the result that their spending had outstripped their income. Finally, Apple complained that Klein had been responsible for failing to nurture the careers of other artists on the label – among them, amusingly, Yoko Ono – and for neglecting to replace them when they left the company. Short of accusing him of using the last bottle of milk and leaving the fridge door open, it was difficult to imagine any possible sins that Klein hadn't apparently committed.

Inevitably, Klein replied with another flurry of lawsuits, running to

26 counts this time, lodged by ABKCO against Apple and four subsidiary companies, plus Lennon, Harrison and Starkey. These alleged the usual underpayment of commissions and lack of reward for services rendered – ensuring that Apple and the three Beatles were now facing virtually identical charges on both sides of the Atlantic over exactly the same money.

None of the four Beatles could now go out in public without the risk of being served with a writ. Even McCartney, who had never signed with Klein, was not immune. 'Just as I was going to do a radio show interview the other day,' he recounted in December 1973,

this fellow walked up to me and said, 'Hello, Paul.' I thought, What's he want with me? Looks a bit dubious. He pushed a little bit of paper in my hand, and said, 'I don't want to embarrass you, Paul. I'm sure you know what this is all about, but I've got my job to do.' A wife and three kids, all that. So I walked on, muttering, looked at the bit of paper, and it says, 'ABKCO hereby sue you, John, George, Ringo and everything you've ever been connected with,' companies I'd never even heard of. 'Sue you all for the sum of $20 million.' That is the latest little line.

Of Apple's own lawsuit, he said, 'Of course I loved that. My God, I hope they win that one.' And he complained about the naivety with which Lennon had welcomed Klein five years earlier: 'John said, "Anyone whose record is as bad as this can't be so bad." But that was Lennonesque crap, which John occasionally did – utter foolishness.'

Behind the scenes accountants were doing their best to safeguard the Beatles' cash, with several million dollars alleged to have been moved out of US jurisdiction into bank accounts in the Channel Islands around May 1973 – proof, so ABKCO said, that the Beatles were expecting to be sued. Moved at the same time was some $1.6 million from George Harrison's US publishing company, which also travelled to the Channel Islands before being re-routed elsewhere. As Paul McCartney explained in 1973, this was another defensive ploy:

Klein made his way into George's big songwriting company, which is George's big asset. The main one was 'Something' on *Abbey Road*. That was George's great big song, George's first big effort, and everyone covered it and it was lovely and made him lots of money that he could give away,

which is his thing, you know. Well, it turns out that Klein has got himself
into that company. Not only being paid 20 per cent – there's a thought now
that he's claiming he owns the company!

The proceedings in both Britain and America trundled inexorably
through the courts, occasionally requiring one of the Beatles to make
an appearance. In May 1974 Lennon met Klein in New York for the
first time in more than a year. Had a lawyer been present, the conversation between the two men would never have gone beyond 'Good
morning.' Instead, Lennon and Klein discussed the ongoing litigation,
and Lennon admitted that he knew he owed his former manager
money, and that he was deliberately trying to strangle ABKCO in
litigation and exhaust Klein's resources. At a subsequent court
appearance Lennon was overheard telling a legal aide that he believed
Klein would soon have to drop his lawsuits because he was about to
run out of money. Klein's lawyers eagerly exploited these lapses of
judgement.

Apple and the Beatles were now providing full-time employment
for five legal firms in London and New York. Although McCartney
could console himself that he was not personally involved in most of
the litigation, he was still a member of the Beatles' partnership, and
therefore liable for 25 per cent of the expenses that the multiple court
proceedings entailed. And through it all he was being represented by
his own legal team, who were negotiating with Lennon, Harrison and
Starkey's lawyers, as part of his apparently endless crusade to dissolve
their financial union.

The deeper the legal minds delved into the Beatles' affairs, the
more anomalies and eccentricities they discovered – money being owed
to one Apple company, for example, but paid to another without
anyone in the organisation worrying or even apparently noticing.
ABKCO unearthed a fiendishly complex arrangement governing the
way in which the Beatles' records were released in the USA, which
involved the rights being shepherded through a corporate maze for
nobody's apparent gain. Meanwhile, Apple's lawyers were involved in
minute scrutiny of the corporation's earnings over the duration of
the Klein contract, and alleged that Klein had claimed commissions
that weren't due for records that were sold before he took over as
manager and on items which were not covered by the original,

1. A final glimpse of unity, during the filming of *Magical Mystery Tour* in September 1967.
Thereafter it was difficult to force the four men into the same frame, let alone expect them to smile.

2. The Lennons, Harrisons and Jenny Boyd, leaving London in search of spiritual regeneration, February 1968. Lennon couldn't dream up a convincing reason why Yoko Ono should accompany them to India.

3. Revolution in the studio, June 1968: Paul McCartney with Francie Schwartz, while Yoko Ono carries the can for disrupting the Beatles at work.

4. John Lennon with his past and future collaborators, at the *Yellow Submarine* premiere, July 1968, before Ono and McCartney realised that their roles were mutually incompatible.

5. A rare moment of harmony at Apple, 1969: Harrison soon lost patience with the Beatles' utopian dream.

6. The Beatles on their Apple rooftop, 30 January 1969: making a self-conscious show of togetherness for an invisible global audience.

7. New York swagger and Liverpudlian loyalty: Allen Klein and Neil Aspinall, the two men entrusted with running Apple.

8. The Plaintiff and his wife leaving the London High Court after launching a lawsuit against his three closest friends, February 1971.

9. Two Beatles, one widow, two sons: the Fab Five are inducted into the Rock and Roll Hall of Fame, 1988.

10. The Montagues and Capulets stage a brief ceasefire, as John Lennon posthumously enters the same institution, 1994.

11. There can be no Beatles reunion, George Harrison once declared,
'as long as John Lennon remains dead'. But desperate times provoke
desperate measures, as this March 1995 photo proves.

extremely loose, contract. Apple even suggested that Klein had established a financial system whereby he would be paid his 20 per cent management commission twice on the same earnings – once when the money arrived at Apple, and again when it had been on the corporate merry-go-round. Naturally Klein denied all these claims.

Both camps made occasional, half-hearted attempts to have the other side's litigation annulled. Ferocious attempts were made by the rival lawyers to prove that one Apple company or another was, or was not, an active concern in New York or Los Angeles. There were queries about the legality of a corporate system under which George Harrison could resign as the employee of a company that he himself ran and in which he held 99 per cent of the shares, before deciding that he did want to work for himself after all, and applying to himself for his job back.

At the moment when it seemed that the legal picture could not be less clear, more mud was applied. Klein launched two more court cases, claiming that Lennon had never paid him for his work on the Northern Songs saga five years earlier, and that ABKCO was now the rightful owner of Harrisongs Music Inc., which held the US copyright of Harrison's compositions. That case, at least, could be settled: a judge decided in June 1975 that Harrisongs Music Inc. was owned, as the musician's lawyers claimed, by Harrisongs Ltd, and hence by Harrison himself. Two other proceedings ended that year, when Lennon and Harrison quietly agreed to repay the money they had borrowed from Klein. But the bulk of the litigation rolled on, funded by the remarkable sales of the Beatles' recent compilation albums.

In late 1973 Paul McCartney endeavoured to bring the Beatles together in the same room for the first time in more than four years, hoping that they might be able to agree a collective strategy to reduce the legal burden. 'I just got my visa,' he explained.

I rang John up, and John was keen to do it. He was going to fly in today from LA to New York. Great! I was going to be here; John was going to be here. Then I rang Ringo, and Ringo couldn't figure out what we were actually going to say, outside of 'Hi there.' And he didn't want to come all the way to New York from England, he was just getting settled for Christmas.

So he was a bit down on it, that kind of blew it out. Then I called John and he said he was talking to George and George was having some kind of visa problems. So it's a bit difficult to get the four of us together. But it will happen soon.

Though McCartney denied the connection, it was surely no co-incidence that his latest album with Wings was entitled *Band on the Run*. Recorded under conditions of extreme duress in Nigeria, it was widely greeted as his most coherent work since leaving the Beatles. The device of opening and closing the album with the same melodic theme encouraged reviewers to make comparisons with *Sgt Pepper*, a trick that worked so well McCartney repeated it on several subsequent albums. Perhaps McCartney's creativity had been freed by his moral victory in the debate over Allen Klein; perhaps he simply thrived on adversity. But *Band on the Run* exhibited a frothy self-confidence that was reminiscent of the Beatles at their most productive, although its songs lacked any of the emotional grounding that Lennon and Harrison might have provided. It re-established McCartney as the most commer-cially viable of the ex-Beatles, consolidating the shift in power that had begun earlier in the year with Klein's dismissal.

The year's frantic recording activity – five solo records from the four Beatles and a batch of hit singles – raised the possibility that McCartney, Lennon, Starkey and Harrison could be accepted as legitimate artists (or entertainers) in their own right, without being compromised by the lucrative trade in Beatle nostalgia. Yet the media and public still wanted a reunion of the entire quartet. McCartney's father-in-law, Lee Eastman, was convinced that despite their differences the four Beatles shared a 'fervent hope' of a reunion. 'First,' he explained, 'they have to sever their economic interests. Then they could be friends. Then, finally, they might play together.' Other sources suggested that their legal obligations were so demanding that they would re-form to meet the costs of the litigation.

For two weeks in February 1974 lawyers congregated in New York to analyse the intricacies of the litigation between Apple and ABKCO. All four Beatles were represented, and Lennon and McCartney also made brief appearances, but negotiations broke down, according to Lee Eastman, 'because lawyers for Mr Lennon made financial demands that lawyers for the other three principals considered excessive'. As

Paul McCartney recalled, 'John came to a meeting and asked for a £1 million loan. That made us stumble! Everyone went, "Say what?!" and jaws dropped, and the meeting was cancelled.' His separation from Ono and carousing in Los Angeles had clearly taken their toll on Lennon's already precarious finances.

All this legal activity was interpreted as proof that a reunion was imminent. The British rock paper *Melody Maker* announced excitedly, BEATLES GET TOGETHER!, claiming that 'the four of them are preparing a joint statement to be issued in the next few days, revealing their plans for a new Beatles album'. Harry Nilsson, a mutual friend of all four, was named as the catalyst for the project. The *New York Times* proclaimed that Harrison, Starkey and Eric Clapton were about to tour together, an unlikely prospect given their complicated marital arrangements at the time; while Lennon and Starkey were tipped to play at a fifth-anniversary celebration of the Woodstock festival. David Geffen, president of Asylum Records and manager of acts such as Crosby, Stills, Nash and Young and Joni Mitchell, offered $30 million for a new Beatles album. And even if they refused to co-operate, there was money to be made from their name, as two entrepreneurs prepared theatrical adaptations of the *Sgt Pepper* album.

In March 1974 all four Beatles were in Los Angeles, although they contrived not to meet. Harrison was producing an album for Ravi Shankar at A&M Records, where he met a secretary named Olivia Arias. 'My first impression of George was that he was smaller than life,' she remembered. 'Very humble, normal and thoughtful. He was very focused. He had such a strong sense of self. He didn't seem to be a frivolous person, though he was, but from the first day I met him, he was working on music.' The couple soon began a relationship that would last for more than 25 years.

Lennon was also acting as a producer, for Harry Nilsson. Besides recording a dark, riotous album (*Pussy Cats*), the pair rampaged through Hollywood's chic nightlife, throwing back brandy Alexanders like nomads at an oasis. One night they visited the home of *Playboy* executive Hugh Hefner, and Lennon supposedly stubbed out his cigarette on a painting by Magritte. On another they found themselves at the Troubadour club for a performance by comedians the Smothers Brothers, and were expelled for bellowing 'I Can't Stand the Rain' during the show and tossing insults at the stars. 'I heard someone yelling about pigs,' said Tommy Smothers, who had befriended Lennon in 1969. 'It was fairly disgusting. The heckling got so bad that our show was going rapidly downhill.' Lennon threw punches at everyone who got in his way, and was subsequently sued for assault by a waitress. 'It's not the pain that hurts,' she said, 'it's finding out that one of your idols is a real asshole.' Then he went outside and attacked the young man looking after the club's parking lot. Pictures of Lennon launching himself at a photographer were telegraphed around the world. A few days later Nilsson had to restrain Lennon at the Beverly Wilshire Hotel, as he attempted to strangle May Pang because she wanted him to stop drinking.

A few weeks earlier, in February, Yoko Ono had celebrated her 41st birthday at the Dakota with friends such as Allen Ginsberg and James Taylor, but she was suffering from low blood pressure caused by anaemia, and was reported to be frail and depressed. During a brief trip to London she paid an unexpected visit to the McCartneys. 'Linda or I said to her, "Do you still love John?,"' McCartney recalled.

'Do you want to get back with him?' She said, 'Yes.' We said, 'Well, what it would take, then? I can take a message. What would I have to tell him?' And she gave me this whole thing: 'He would have to come back to New York. He can't live with me immediately. He'd have to court me, he'd have to ask me out. He'd have to send me flowers, he'll have to do it all again.' Of course, she'd sent him off with May Pang, but that wasn't the point at the time.

The balance of Lennon and Ono's relationship was shifting. As the instigator of their separation, Ono supposedly held the initiative, yet she demanded that Lennon keep in constant contact with her and phoned him incessantly. Lennon claimed to be relishing his freedom, although his self-destructive behaviour suggested otherwise. But he was back in touch with old friends such as Mick Jagger, who discovered it was easier to communicate with Lennon when he was apart from Ono. McCartney also found May Pang more welcoming than Ono had been. But ironically he now set out to reunite Lennon with his wife.

'I went there,' he recalled, 'and he was doing Pussy Cats with Nilsson and Keith Moon and Jesse Ed Davis – three beautiful, total alcohol nutters, plus John, forget it! We went round to a session and sat there for a bit.' That night at Burbank Studios Lennon and McCartney jammed together for the first time since 1969, on a ramshackle rendition of the folk tune 'Midnight Special'. Three days later the McCartneys returned to the studio, prepared to record with Lennon. 'It was a strange session,' McCartney said. 'The main thing that I recall is that someone said, "What song shall we do?" and John said, "Anything before '63. I don't know anything after '63." Anyway, it wasn't a very good session.'

McCartney wasn't exaggerating. Many years later the evidence emerged in the form of a 30-minute tape. It revealed no hint of the Beatles' magic, no rapport between the two men, merely a cocaine-driven Lennon berating and bullying the engineer before floundering through fragments of half-forgotten rock 'n' roll hits. This was the moment the world had been waiting for: the reunion that would thrill the planet and shake up a moribund music industry. And it was a fiasco. Small wonder that none of the participants mentioned the session until after Lennon's death.

After McCartney left, Lennon drifted back into his compulsive hedonism, out of habit more than pleasure. The next morning McCartney visited the house that the revellers were renting. 'I remember Harry Nilsson offering me some angel dust,' McCartney said. 'I said, "What is it?" He said, "It's elephant tranquilliser." I said, "Is it fun?" He thought for about half a minute. "No," he said. I said, "Well, you know what, I won't have any."' It was late morning, and Lennon was still in bed. 'He was a teenager again,' McCartney reflected. 'He was just being his old Liverpool self, just a wild, wild boy.' When Lennon eventually surfaced, McCartney told him that Ono was prepared to take him back and explained the conditions she had laid down. 'That's how they got back together again,' McCartney explained, although nearly a year passed in the interim and Ono later ridiculed his claim.

Lennon's conduct was arousing some concern. 'There has been much talk here in Los Angeles,' commented local reporter Chris Van Ness, 'that something is wrong with John. Many have speculated that his break-up with Yoko is the cause of his violent behaviour, but it seems to me that it must be something more pronounced than that.' Van Ness, who had witnessed the furore at the Troubadour, added, 'Now John's ego-anchors are gone. His marriage appears to be on the rocks, and his career is at its lowest ebb for ten years. Perhaps there lies the understanding for John Lennon's actions of late.' Speaking with a year's hindsight, Lennon reflected, 'With my personal life and the Apple business, the Klein business and the immigration business . . . you don't want to admit it while it's happening, that that's what's making you go barmy. You're still living every day, and you think you're going to a party, then you end up throwing up in the toilet. I just woke up in the middle of it and thought, There's something wrong here. I'd better straighten myself out.'

Hollywood was not the place to do it. For the rock aristocracy 1974 was the year of cocaine. Everyone snorted, everyone felt invincible, and nobody noticed that their music was suffering. Propelled by epic quantities of alcohol, it sent Lennon and his playmates on a switchback ride from ecstasy to despair, never allowing a moment's contemplation to interrupt the thrill. Its effects could be heard on the records made that summer – Nilsson's *Pussy Cats*, Keith Moon's *Two Sides of the Moon* and Ringo Starr's *Goodnight Vienna*, all starring the same bunch of party animals, with the perpetually juiced Starkey and Lennon at their heart, and their long-time aide Mal Evans alongside them, on the same reckless pursuit of oblivion. While *Pussy Cats* channelled these emotional extremes into music that was compelling and confessional, *Goodnight Vienna* was a curiously tame affair. It marked a significant step away from the rosy bonhomie of the *Ringo* album, anticipating a future in which Starkey would effectively vanish as a personality from his own records.

It's easy to imagine Lennon drowning in someone's pool or choking on his own vomit in the summer of 1974. Instead, he and May Pang returned to New York, where he could connect with something deeper than his stardom. They took an apartment in midtown Manhattan and welcomed visitors. For the first time in three years Lennon established contact with his son Julian, who flew over with Cynthia. Pang recognised how important this link was for father and son, and did her best to maintain it. Paul and Linda McCartney were also frequent visitors. 'We spent two or three nights together,' Lennon said, 'talking about the old days, and it was cool, seeing what each other remembered from Hamburg and Liverpool.' Other comrades from the old days reappeared in his life. 'I didn't see John that much until he separated from Yoko,' Mick Jagger recalled. 'We got really friendly again, more friendly than we'd ever been, in fact.' The two men recorded together, and Jagger let Lennon know how much more relaxed he seemed since he'd separated from his wife. Not that the separation was complete: Ono was still phoning every few hours to check what her husband was doing. For the first time though, Pang recalled, Lennon had begun to resent her constant monitoring: 'It seemed that John had made up his mind to run away from Yoko. She would telephone him, and in a rage John would say, "I'm not talking to that woman." John was rediscovering so many things – his friends, his music, his son.'

The change in Lennon's life was apparent on *Walls and Bridges*, the record he made in July and August 1974. In the studio he was focused and driven, riding the band through take after take like a pocket general. 'I just got back into music,' he explained after the sessions were over. 'As long as I'm going through something, I've got something to say. I have to bang my head on the wall and then write about how good it is to stop. Otherwise I think you die as an artist. I always have to keep moving or falling over just so something's happening to me. I've died artistically a few times. I didn't like it. As long as I'm writing songs, I know where I am.' Not since *Imagine* in 1971 had he demonstrated any genuine inspiration. Now he was able to tap into his emotions without becoming their slave. 'Bless You' was a touching farewell to Yoko Ono; 'Surprise Surprise' an equally heartfelt message of lust and love for May Pang. There were songs of ecstasy and despair plus a cameo from the Lennon of old, 'Steel and Glass', in which he subjected Allen Klein to the 'How Do You Sleep' treatment. For the first time since he left the Beatles Lennon was creating music that was not just psychotherapy or political sermonising. Like McCartney's *Band on the Run*, *Walls and Bridges* represented a reconciliation with the past: an ability to build on what each man had learned from the Beatles and reshape it for a more adult audience. Lennon would never sound so self-assured on record again.

Confident about the merits of his work, he threw himself into an exhaustive campaign of self-promotion. On radio and in print he sounded thrilled to be alive and to have experienced and survived his spectacular past. 'I'm going to be an ex-Beatle for the rest of my life,' he reflected,

so I might as well enjoy it, and I'm just getting round to being able to stand back and see what happened. A couple of years ago I might have given everybody the impression I hated it all, but that was then. I was talking when I was straight out of therapy and I'd been mentally stripped bare and I just wanted to shoot my mouth off to clear it all away. Now it's different . . . I can see the Beatles from a new point of view. Can't remember much of what happened, little bits here and there, and I've started taking an interest in what went on while I was in that fish tank. It must have been incredible.

Lennon revealed that he had begun to collect Beatles memorabilia with the same enthusiasm that he had once devoted to denying his past. 'Why not? It's history, man, history!' In mid-September he asked May Pang to represent him at the first Beatlefest celebration at the Hotel Commodore in New York. Neil Aspinall at Apple supplied a film of the group's 1965 concert at Shea Stadium, while thousands of fans milled around the memorabilia stalls and greeted 'celebrity' speakers such as concert promoter Sid Bernstein. All four Beatles had donated instruments for a charity auction. As journalist Joel Siegel discovered to his amazement, the crowd was awash with 'fourteen- and fifteen-year-old faces, faces that hadn't started kindergarten when the Beatles invaded America, faces that hadn't even begun to flesh out into adulthood when the Beatles last played together'. They could barely remember a time when there had been Beatles in action. For these teenagers, the lure was nostalgia for a golden age that they had been told was brighter and more meaningful than the present day. Some had been attracted by the success of McCartney and Wings, but most simply wanted to be transported back to 1964, when Beatlemania was young.

May Pang arrived home with a bundle of bootleg records and – at the suggestion of reporter Chris Charlesworth – a set of photographs of the group taken by their friend Jürgen Vollmer in the early 1960s. Lennon quizzed her. Who were these kids? What did they want? Who did they think he was? 'I think it's great,' he commented a few days later. 'Smells a bit of Rudolph Valentino, but they must be the people who buy the repackages, because some of them are only 14 or 16. I mean, it's good for business, isn't it? It goes to the family. And if we ever did anything together, there they are, waiting. It's nice to know.' It suited him to deny the possibility of a reunion: 'No! What for? We did it all.' But increasingly his mind turned to the rapport he'd shared with the only men who understood what he'd been through. 'Together we would sound exactly the same,' he admitted, 'only better, because we're all better now.'

During the *Walls and Bridges* sessions Lennon had tried to forget the deal that his lawyers had cut with Big Seven Music over the 'Come Together' plagiarism case. The album he had begun with Phil Spector was still unfinished, and the music publishers were threatening to renew their legal action. To calm them, Lennon promised that he would complete the Spector project, if necessary without the errant producer, who had vanished with the tapes, leaving Lennon to pay the studio bills. In October 1974, as *Walls and Bridges* climbed the charts and its single 'Whatever Gets You Thru the Night' headed for No. 1, he pulled a band into the studio, overdubbed the best of the Spector tracks and polished off a slick set of cover versions in less than a week.

Over the fade of 'Just Because', the song that had been a vehicle for his psychological disintegration a year earlier, Lennon now delivered greetings to his friends and family in England, including his fellow Beatles – only to remove their names before the record was released. But the track included another significant message, as Lennon explained: 'You hear me saying, "And so we say farewell from Record Plant East" . . . Something flashed through my mind as I said it, am I really saying farewell to the business?'

The business was not ready to wave him – or the Beatles – goodbye. Entrepreneurs still dreamed of the millions to be made from the quartet's name. Promoter Bill Sargent emerged in June 1974 with the extravagant vision of a concert that would not only reunite the Beatles, but also tempt Bob Dylan and the Rolling Stones onto the same bill, with a stadium crowd to share the experience and four million more watching via worldwide closed-circuit TV. He offered the Beatles a guaranteed cheque for $10 million – not quite enough to meet Allen Klein's demands – as an advance against ticket sales. The plan was enough of a novelty for the Beatles to consider it; subsequent proposals would be dismissed out of hand. It was McCartney who delivered the death blow to Sargent's scheme, and none of the others tried to persuade him otherwise.

One of the *Sgt Pepper* stage shows reached Broadway in November 1974, and Lennon attended the premiere with May Pang. The musical left him amused rather than annoyed, but George Harrison had a more visceral reaction in London, walking out of Willy Russell's play *John, Paul, George, Ringo . . . and Bert*. Its centrepiece was a surprise Beatles reunion, abandoned when news reached the media. The drama was seen through the eyes of Bert, an imaginary ex-member of the group who represented Everyman. Derek Taylor attended the opening with Harrison, and recalled that the musician had found it uncomfortable to watch 'himself' on stage. Meanwhile McCartney complained that Russell laid the blame for the Beatles' break-up on his shoulders, and refused to allow his old adversary from the NEMS era, Robert Stigwood, to produce a film version. Convinced that a Beatles-related movie had commercial potential, Stigwood turned his attention to *Sgt Pepper* and commissioned a script loosely based around the album which would not feature the group as characters and hence wouldn't require their approval.

The consequences of fame continued to haunt the Beatles. With Apple now merely an agency for collecting money and lawsuits, and the company's last artists released from their contracts, no trace remained of the utopian ideal that Lennon and McCartney had preached in 1968. Yet the other two members of the quartet now chose to launch miniature replicas of the original Apple design. In September 1974 George Harrison announced the formation of Dark Horse Records, a vehicle for talent new (a pop duo named Splinter, who enjoyed immediate success) and old (Ravi Shankar). Harrison announced his intention of joining the label himself, once his contract with EMI had expired in January 1976. Meanwhile, Richard Starkey formed Ring O' Records – a name coined by Lennon. The company's ethos sounded eerily familiar: 'I thought, we'll form a label. No one will have to beg.' Soon, however, Starkey discovered something he should already have known: 'I ended up being in the boardroom too much, being bored. Business! Musicians, we're creative, we're not businessmen.'

While Starkey's venture was little more than a plaything, Dark Horse shaped up to become a more significant force in the music business. To consolidate its identity, Harrison recorded an album of the same name. More surprisingly, he announced a lengthy concert tour of North America, starting on 2 November 1974. Unfortunately, his record was still unfinished when rehearsals began, and by the time of the final sessions his voice was 'dark hoarse', as critics soon noted.

Harrison's enthusiasm for the venture began to fade at the opening press conference, where he was besieged with questions about a Beatles reunion. It didn't take long for his patience to crack as badly as his voice. Soon he was admitting, 'The biggest break in my career was getting into the Beatles in 1963. In retrospect, the biggest break since then was getting out of them.' He added determinedly, 'People are afraid of change. You can't live in the past.' But you can talk about it, endlessly, and the reporters continued to prod the same wound. Eventually the scar tissue gave way, and Harrison's true feelings erupted: 'It's all a fantasy, putting the Beatles back together. If we ever do that, it's because everybody is broke.' Then he focused on one of his colleagues: 'I'd rather have Willie Weeks [from his 1974 band] on bass than Paul McCartney . . . Having played with other musicians, I don't think the Beatles were that good . . . Paul is a fine bass player, but he's a bit overpowering at times. I'd join a band with John Lennon any day, but I couldn't join a band with Paul. That's not personal, but from a musical point of view.' As Starkey noted a few days later, 'How can we get together if George won't play with Paul?' Having survived vitriolic press criticism from Lennon, McCartney took Harrison's comments on the chin. 'I think the others are great. I'd always stick up for them. I don't agree with George. I don't think the Beatles weren't any good. I think they were *great*.'

Harrison's comments aroused the same sense of shock as Lennon's earlier admission, 'I don't believe in Beatles.' The furore heightened the already formidable pressure on the guitarist to justify himself. Sadly, his *Dark Horse* album had the same ragged quality as Harry Nilsson's *Pussy Cats* but little of the psychological drama. 'After I split up from Pattie,' Harrison admitted later, 'I went on a bit of a bender to make up for all the years I'd been married. I wasn't ready to join AA or anything – I don't think I was that far gone – but I could put back a bottle of brandy occasionally, plus all the other naughty things that fly around. I just went on a binge until it got to the point where I had no voice and almost no body at times.' That was exactly how the record sounded, with 'Simply Shady' offering the clearest portrait of an artist in distress. His seasonal single 'Ding Dong' was so banal that few people noticed the accompanying video, in which he mockingly donned his Beatles suits from 1963 and 1967, before posing naked apart from a strategically placed guitar and a pair of Himalayan boots.

As with Richard Starkey's *Goodnight Vienna*, sales of *Dark Horse* owed more to habit than enthusiasm, and it soon faded from the charts. It didn't help that Harrison's early concerts received disapproving reviews.

After the first-night audience in Vancouver became restless while Ravi Shankar's musicians were playing, Harrison told them that he was prepared to die for Indian music, but not for rock 'n' roll. The ravaged condition of his voice was impossible to disguise, and when he ventured into his back catalogue, he altered lyrics that were almost regarded as holy writ. The key line of John Lennon's 1965 song 'In My Life' now ran, 'In my life, I love God more.' Another Beatles classic became 'While My Guitar Gently Smiles', and he cheapened his most famous composition by singing, 'Something in the way she moves it.' The whole exercise was tinged with typically sly humour – 'Bring your lawyers and I'll bring Klein', he quipped on 'Sue Me Sue You Blues' – but the audiences had come to relive the past, not satirise it. 'They wanted a Beatle tour,' Harrison believed. As keyboardist Billy Preston recalled, 'George didn't want to do "Something" at all. I knew he was gonna have to do it. So he started rebelling against it by doing it in a different way.' After the Vancouver show Harrison complained, 'Why do they want to see if there is a Beatle George? I don't say I'm Beatle George. The image of my choice is not Beatle George. If they want to do that they can go and see Wings. Why live in the past? Whether you like me or not, this is what I am. I didn't force you or anybody at gunpoint to come to see me. And I don't care if nobody comes to see me, nobody ever buys another record of me. I don't give a shit, it doesn't matter to me.' And there were still 44 shows to go.

Asked later what he had gained from the tour, he replied, 'I learned that I should make sure that I have plenty of rest.' Despite the sense of purpose he experienced when the band kicked in and the music took over, he felt increasingly estranged from his fans. One night he watched after the show as the crew 'were bulldozing all the rubble left by the audience. There were mountains of empty bottles of gin and bourbon and tequila and brassieres and shoes and coats and trash. I mean, it was unbelievable. I'd go on out there, and you'd just get stoned, there was so much reefer going about. And I just thought, Do I actually have anything in common with these people?'

Four weeks in, when Harrison had reached Atlanta, attention was distracted from his failing voice by events in New York City. Lennon had promised that in the unlikely event his latest single reached No. 1, he would join Elton John onstage at Madison Square Garden. His surprise appearance on 28 November 1974 comprised just three songs

– two of them, it was noted, taken from the Beatles' catalogue, including 'I Saw Her Standing There', written 'by an old estranged fiancé of mine called Paul'. Elton John was arguably pop's hottest property, but he was happy to be upstaged by his hero. 'Even [Lennon] was overwhelmed,' a critic reported. 'You could see it. He tried to continue chewing his gum in regular jaw patterns, and he pulled funny faces, even lounged against the piano in an attitude of mock-relaxation – but that deafening cry, a vocal anthem for old heroes, as you might say, and him the biggest hero of them all, had him swallowing hard.' As Lennon recalled, 'They were all screaming like Beatlemania.' Backstage, he was visited by Yoko Ono, and according to the myth they constructed in his final months, 'We got together that night.' But in fact he went home with May Pang, with whom he was planning to buy a house in the New York suburbs.

In mid-December Lennon and Pang met Harrison and his new companion Olivia Arias at the Plaza Hotel in New York, before attending Harrison's show the following night. They agreed that when the tour reached Madison Square Garden that weekend, Lennon would make another cameo appearance alongside his former bandmate. '[George] was pretty weird,' Lennon recalled, 'because he was in the middle of that tour, and we hadn't communicated for a while. I was a bit nervous about going on stage, but I agreed to because it would have been mean of me not to go on with George after I'd gone on with Elton.'

First they had to take care of business. After more than three years of negotiations, and cripplingly large lawyers' bills, the representatives of the four Beatles had finally concocted a separation document that would mark the formal dissolution of their legal partnership and allow the official receiver to divide up the royalties accrued since spring 1971. As Harrison, McCartney and Lennon were all in New York, it was arranged that they should sign in each other's presence on the morning of Harrison's first concert in the city. 'We had all arrived for the big dissolution meeting in the Plaza Hotel,' McCartney recalled. 'There were green baize tables with millions of documents laid out for us to sign . . . and John wouldn't show up! He wouldn't come from across the park! George got on the phone and yelled, "Take those fucking shades off and come over here, you!" John still wouldn't come over. He had a balloon delivered with a sign saying, "Listen to this balloon." It was all quite far out.'

'I didn't sign it because my astrologer told me it wasn't the right day,' Lennon explained. 'The numbers weren't right, the planets weren't right, and John wasn't coming,' Linda McCartney sneered. 'Had we known there was some guy flipping cards on his bed to help him make his decision, we would all have gone over there. George blew his top, but it didn't change anything.' As Lennon recalled, 'Somehow or other I was informed that I needn't bother to go to George's show. I was quite relieved in the end, because there wasn't any time for rehearsal and I didn't want it to be a case of just John jumping up and playing a few chords.' So Lennon stayed home, and his son Julian, who was visiting for the Christmas holidays, went in his place. The following day peace was restored, and Lennon met McCartney at Lee Eastman's law office. Then the McCartneys left town, and Lennon attended the final show of Harrison's tour. Backstage, he and May Pang talked amicably with Harrison, Ono and Neil Aspinall, who had flown over for the signing ritual.

A week later Lennon and Pang took his son to Disneyworld. 'I think [Julian] likes Paul better than me,' he admitted afterwards. 'I have the funny feeling he wishes Paul was his dad. But he's got me.' Father and son took a ride on the monorail that crosses the park. 'We went on what must have been the most crowded day of the year,' he recalled. 'I was sitting along with everyone else, not being recognised, and I heard someone with his back to me say that George Harrison was there today. The guy was leaning on me, and he'd heard that a Beatle was there somewhere. He couldn't see the wood for the trees.' Lennon was carrying the Beatles' legal documents with him, and May Pang took photos of the moment when he signed. It amused him to think that the saga that had begun nearly twenty years earlier, and that had carried him and his comrades around the world, should end in the cartoon splendour of a theme park. Lennon, McCartney, Harrison and Starkey were no longer the Beatles: they were no longer tied together by name or by law. They were free to become whatever Beatles could become, perhaps even free from their past.

Chapter 8

I am an artist, and that's what I want to be. Let me make the
music!
    John Lennon, February 1975

The Beatles' thirteen-year partnership was formally dissolved in the
London High Court on 9 January 1975. The lawyers could step aside,
and the accountants could take their place. Four years of earnings
had to be calculated, divided and safeguarded from the greedy hands
of the taxman. A dividing line was drawn: royalties from everything
they had released, together or alone, before October 1974 were divided
equally between them. For records issued after that date – including
the latest albums by Lennon, Harrison and Starkey – each Beatle only
took home the money he had earned.

The four men were still bound together as the joint owners of
Apple Corps Ltd, which now entered sedate middle age, with its
recording studio closing in May 1975 and all pretence abandoned that
it was still an active record company. Most of its staff were given
notice; only Neil Aspinall and his accountants remained. It now suited
the Beatles to pretend that the idealistic Apple of 1968 had never
existed. 'What people don't realise,' Starkey said, 'is that Apple was
never really much more than an extension of [EMI label] Parlophone.'
In that sentence he wrote off the legacy of the 1960s counterculture,
the hope that the Beatles could overturn the commercial model of

the music industry and the dream of enabling artists to reach the public without tangling with businessmen.

Not that the Beatles had ever achieved that dream. A month later Lennon said hopefully, 'After I deal with this last batch of lawsuits, I ain't gonna have any more. I don't know how they happen. One minute you're talking to someone, the next minute they're suing you.' He discounted the instinctive greed of the business community and his own equally innate naivety. At heart Lennon still believed that if he wanted something to happen, it would happen, and there would be no consequences. After twelve years swimming in the waters of fame, he was still surprised to find himself getting wet.

His almost preternatural talent for stepping from disaster to catastrophe was demonstrated by the sorry saga of his *Rock 'n' Roll* album. The entire saga was pockmarked with good intentions. In 1969 Lennon had been asked to pen a campaign song for radical activist Timothy Leary. Instead, he took the idea and the title, and turned it into his last major contribution to the Beatles, 'Come Together'. Its lyrical spark was a couplet by Chuck Berry, which Lennon borrowed quite consciously, considering it an artistic homage in the tradition of Yoko Ono's Fluxus group rather than an act of theft. But music publishers find it easier to calculate money than gestures, and Lennon was sued for plagiarism. There followed the chaos of the Phil Spector project, Lennon's failure to include three Big Seven Music songs on *Walls and Bridges*, and the hurried sessions in October 1974 with which he appeared to have fulfilled his obligations.

Despite his history of throwing himself into the arms of saviours and being disappointed when they let him slip to the floor, Lennon continued to assume that anyone whose company he enjoyed was automatically a friend. Had Allen Klein been on hand, Lennon would never have slipped into his latest quagmire; Klein knew a villain when he saw one. But when Lennon encountered Morris Levy, who now owned Big Seven Music, he was entranced. Like many Britons brought up on American thrillers, he had a soft spot for anyone who reminded him of Jimmy Cagney or Edward G. Robinson. Levy fitted the bill: he was a classic music business gangster, with a history of exploiting young talent and ensuring that copyrights always ended up in his pocket. He had great stories of Tin Pan Alley and the Brill Building, and Lennon was a sucker for anybody who could spin a tale. When

Lennon and Levy met to discuss the settlement of the Big Seven case, the musician was thrilled to be in the presence of a character rather than a bureaucrat.

So it was inevitable that when Levy offered Lennon the use of his farm in upstate New York as a rehearsal studio for his *Rock 'n' Roll* sessions, Lennon would accept; and when Levy said that the best way of selling records in the mid-1970s was via TV advertising and mail order, Lennon agreed to give it a try. He never thought of alerting EMI or Apple; after all, he wasn't a contract lawyer. He simply handed Levy a rough cut of the *Rock 'n' Roll* album as proof that he had satisfied the Big Seven deal, and then waited for nothing to happen. But Levy took Lennon at his word and worried about the legalities later. As far as he was concerned, Lennon wanted him to promote his new album on TV, so he set about the task as if it was still 1955, and Lennon was simply another two-bit kid with a song who thought that royalties lived in English castles.

By late January Levy had thrown together a garish album package and booked TV time. His error was telling Allen Klein what he was doing. Klein was still suing, and being sued by, Lennon; but business and friendship were separate in his mind, and he asked Lennon if he knew about the advertising campaign that Levy was planning. Only then did Lennon tell his record company that he might possibly have handed over his forthcoming album to one of the industry's most notorious outlaws. In Britain it would have been easy to close down Levy's outlets, but in the USA it took time, and meanwhile Levy was able to begin marketing the record, which he retitled *Roots*. Capitol immediately sent out a cease-and-desist order, and accelerated the schedule for their official release by several weeks, with the result that *Rock 'n' Roll* appeared without the extensive liner notes that Lennon had written. Ironically, his text included a wry summary of the album's tortuous gestation: 'The behind the scenes story on this long unwinding will be revealed by a congressional committee to investigate psychodrama in the music business, but only after a period of grateful silence.' And that period was what Lennon now resolved to observe. Finally realising that every time he signed a contract, he opened himself up to litigation, he resolved to free himself from his contractual ties and see what happened next.

The comparison with McCartney was revealing. In sacking the only man who understood the full financial ramifications of his career, Lennon had exposed himself to fate. McCartney, on the other hand, had married into the gods. Like Klein, his father-in-law Lee Eastman was an expert in making money out of music. As early as 1971 he encouraged McCartney to invest his income in something substantial. Already wearied by the Apple saga, McCartney was unwilling to embark on another business adventure, but Eastman suggested that he could combine his passion and his financial interests by investing in music publishing. 'Whose music do you like?' he asked his son-in-law, and returned a few days later to tell McCartney that Buddy Holly's catalogue of songs – the inspiration for the earliest Lennon/McCartney compositions – was for sale. This was the birth of a formidable publishing empire, which would see MPL (McCartney Productions Limited) Music become a major player in one of the few sectors of the entertainment business that would never go out of fashion. The Eastmans expanded MPL's catalogue with great shrewdness, creating a reservoir of Broadway and Tin Pan Alley standards, material which had already proven its staying power and would continue to generate income long after most solo albums by ex-Beatles had been forgotten.* Best of all, MPL Music owed nothing to Apple or the other Beatles, and it was guaranteed to provide for McCartney's children and grandchildren. For a family man, nothing could be more attractive.

Yet one thing still eluded him. 'I know that Paul was desperate to write with John again,' Linda McCartney remembered in 1984. 'The sad thing is that John and Paul both had problems, and they loved each other, and boy, could they have helped each other! If they had only communicated! It frustrates me no end, because I was just some chick from New York when I walked into all of that. God, if I'd known what I know now . . . All I could do was sit there, watching them play these games.'

In January 1975 the McCartneys and Wings, rebuilt as a quintet after the traumas of 1973, travelled to New Orleans. The city had a rich heritage of black music, which McCartney was keen to access. Once he was settled, he phoned John Lennon in New York. Lennon had already agreed to work with David Bowie in California, and for the

---

* Ironically, it was McCartney who collected the publishing royalties from Lennon's cover of 'Peggy Sue' on the *Rock 'n' Roll* album. Another song, 'Bring It On Home to Me', benefited Allen Klein. 'I don't care who gets the money,' Lennon said bravely.

first time he was prepared to contemplate a reunion with McCartney. Singer Art Garfunkel had recently worked with Paul Simon for the first time in six years. Lennon invited Garfunkel to dinner and told him, 'I'm getting calls from *my* Paul. And he wants to know if I'm available for the recording. What should I do?' Garfunkel told him, 'John, I would do it – put all personality aside and go with the fun of the [musical] blend. Make music with somebody you have made a sound with. A great pleasure is the thing to stick with.'

Lennon asked May Pang a similar question: 'What would you think if I started writing with Paul again?' As she recalled, 'My mouth fell open and I said, "Are you kidding? I think it would be terrific."' When Lennon wrote to former Apple press officer Derek Taylor, he told him in his inimitable approximation of typewritten English, 'Bowies cutting 'universe' (Let It Beatle). Am a gonna be there (by reqest of courset). Then possibley down to New Orleons to see the McCartknees.'

It was the perfect moment. Their business quarrels were settled, Lennon had shown himself a master of contemporary soul styles on *Walls and Bridges*, and McCartney was recording in a haven of rhythm and blues. Moreover, McCartney realised that he was not at a creative peak. 'I reckon I've made some bum records in the last couple of years,' he had admitted a few weeks earlier. 'I like them, and they're all OK, but the things I've been through in the last few years aren't very conducive to inspiration.' At the same time he reckoned that Lennon's *Walls and Bridges* had been 'great, but he can do better . . . I heard [the Beatles] "I Am the Walrus" today, for instance, and that's what I mean.' Both men had recently proved themselves superior craftsmen, but together they might rekindle the spark that had fired the Beatles.

There was still resentment on both sides. A few months before, Lennon and Richard Starkey had taped radio commercials for each other's albums, the kind of co-operative gesture that Lennon would never have considered with McCartney or Harrison. Between takes, the two men had talked about McCartney's recent success. 'Does Paul know who you are, Ringo?' Lennon asked sarcastically, before quipping that he would 'swap two Pauls for a George'.

Yet the affection between the two men was genuine, as long as nobody mentioned Apple or Allen Klein. So was Lennon's willingness to consider revisiting the Beatles catalogue. 'I've lost all that negativity

about the past,' he conceded. 'I'd be as happy as Larry to do "Help!".
I've just changed completely in two years. I'd do "Hey Jude" and the
whole damn show.'

A key factor in the rapprochement between Lennon and McCartney
was the fact that the McCartneys had no history of tension with May
Pang. Johnandyoko had the power to make McCartney feel insignificant; John and May were simply an old friend and his attractive young
partner. But the past was about to claim a stake in the future. Lennon
and Pang had now been together for 18 months, and planned to buy
a cottage in Montauk on Long Island in early February, but Ono still
rang Lennon constantly. As Pang recalled, Ono phoned Lennon at the
end of January and 'told him she had a method to help him stop
smoking, and that he should come over to the Dakota. I told him I
didn't like him going over there, and he said, "Stop it!". He was yelling
at me, "What's your problem? I'll be home by dinner; we'll go have
a late dinner, and then we'll make plans to go to New Orleans and
see Paul and Linda."'

In Lennon's account, 'I was just going to visit [Yoko]. I visited her
many times before. And I just walked in and thought, I live here, this
is my home. Here is Yoko, and here is me.' Elsewhere he said simply,
'It fell in place again. It was like I never left.' Ono's recollection, shortly
after her husband's death, was more realistic: 'We sat trembling in
each other's presence, not talking and sometimes crying the first times
we were together again.' Lennon said, 'I feel like I went to get a coffee
and a newspaper somewhere, and it took a year.'

When he returned that night, Pang said, 'He was a different person
about Paul. It wasn't the same. He was saying, "Oh, you know when
Paul and Linda used to visit us? Well, I couldn't stand it." Obviously
something had happened on the other side of Central Park.' Within
a day or two he had moved back into the Dakota. 'I was so numb,'
Pang recalled. 'He told me Yoko would still allow me to see him. But
it didn't make any sense to me. I kept asking him, "What about our
love?" We were just about to buy a house together, but he just shrugged
and said, "It'll be all right."' Johnandyoko was reborn, and there was
no trip to New Orleans. Lennon, it seemed, had to choose between
Ono and McCartney: he couldn't have both.

Two weeks later Lennon claimed to be ecstatic. 'This is no disrespect
to anybody else I was having relationships with, but I feel like I was

running around without my head on.' He told another reporter, 'I don't wanna put May down. She is a nice girl. But she knew what the scene was.' He said that he had 'sort of filled in' with Pang, 'so as not to be alone at night'. Ono, by contrast, could never be dismissed as a 'nice girl'. Even Pang realised that 'Yoko dominated John just as he had been dominated by his Aunt Mimi when he grew up.' She came to understand that 'John felt guilty because he was having so much freedom.' He needed the boundaries that his relationship to Ono would provide. Lennon was still the boy who had lost his parents and who believed he could only function if somebody else was in control.

By 1980, when Lennon gave his final interviews, his 18-month separation from Ono was described as 'a lost weekend', a period of emotional anguish and creative bankruptcy between two great romantic eras. This revision of history discounted the artistic worth of *Walls and Bridges*. It asked people to believe that Lennon was more himself in the years ahead, when he produced nothing, than when he was making two coherent albums in the space of a few weeks. And it prolonged the myth that the most productive relationship of Lennon's life was not with Paul McCartney but with Yoko Ono.

What happened at the Dakota in January 1975? Various biographers have suggested that Ono might have drugged Lennon or hypnotised him, or used her esoteric knowledge of witchcraft. But these far-fetched rumours underestimate the power of Lennon's psychological drives. More intriguing, in retrospect, is Ono's rationale. Did she choose this moment for a reunion because the numbers were right, or was she afraid that she might lose him forever if he reunited with McCartney? Whose dependence was greater: Lennon's on the woman he called mother, or Ono's on the man who had brought her global recognition? One thing is certain: Lennon and McCartney would have worked together in February 1975 if Lennon had not returned to the Dakota, and history – theirs and ours – might have been very different.

The reunion of Lennon and Ono could have triggered another propulsive era of artistic and political collaborations, but the times had changed and the energy had dissipated. Briefly Lennon threw himself into publicising his *Rock 'n' Roll* album, letting it be known that he was not blocking a collaboration with the other Beatles. But, he admitted, 'I no longer have the dream of wanting to be the record company . . . the record business is filled with lawsuits and immigration is just one lawsuit. I would like to live life without litigation.' Morris Levy filed a $73 million lawsuit against him within weeks of his return to the Dakota, and the case would linger for another year before Lennon finally emerged victorious.

'I meself have decided to be or not to be for a coupla years,' Lennon wrote to Derek Taylor that spring. 'Boredom set in . . . how many back beats are there? I ask meself.' In March Ono discovered that she was pregnant. 'I was with them when Yoko had her pregnancy confirmed,' said EMI executive Bob Mercer. 'They were absolutely ecstatic about it and John turned to me and said, 'Well, that shelves the work for some time now.' He just said that his own feelings were that he didn't want to have his signature on any pieces of paper. He'd had enough of contracts.' In April Lennon ended a four-year legal battle with Sir Lew Grade and ATV by appearing on a TV tribute to the entrepreneur, accompanied by a band wearing two-faced masks to reflect his genuine feelings. The following month he made a fleeting appearance at a charity radiothon in Philadelphia. Informed that 98 per cent of the American public wanted the Beatles to re-form, he quipped, 'I'd like to meet the 2 per cent.' As the summer passed, and Ono's pregnancy continued without serious incident, he told a friend, 'I am currently going through one of my 18-month or so retreats – à la Primal Therapy.' He said that Yoko's condition 'happens to coincide with my natural and instinctive hibernations. At the ripe old age of 34 I find myself going back to the age-old question, What the hell is going on? Why are we here? Followed closely by, Am I doing what I really want to do . . . or simply doing what I'm supposed to do?!?!'

During his process of self-discovery he made strenuous efforts to connect with his family in Britain – cousins, half-sisters, his son. But with the birth of his child imminent he chose to shut the door again. 'As time went by and John's calls ceased,' recalled his sister Julia Baird, 'we found it impossible to reach him. Every time I tried, I got Yoko . . . She seemed to me to be monitoring his life and equally he seemed to be allowing it. "John is asleep. You don't understand his life. No, I can't wake him up." . . . Whether or not John ever knew that I was still trying to make contact, I will never know.' That summer Lennon channelled his creativity into writing a book, telling Derek Taylor, '[I] don't feel like dealing with assholes.' He added that Linda McCartney was constantly suggesting that he and Paul should work together, but 'I can't really see it myself.'

In October 1975 several events conspired to shape the years ahead. Lennon issued a compilation of his solo singles to complete his recording contract with EMI/Capitol. 'Make me an offer,' Lennon told Derek Taylor when he was asked about the prospect of signing with Warners, but when Taylor did, Lennon didn't reply. He was equally curt with EMI, when executive Len Wood tried to persuade him to renew his contract: 'Yes, it was a high old time we all had in the 60s . . . but not judging by your "offer" (I could think of a better word for it). Corporate vision, even after all these years, never ceases to amaze me! I am enjoying my family, and uncommitted freedom.' The US Court of Appeals overturned the government's order for his deportation, stating that his 'four-year battle to remain in our country is testimony to his faith in the American dream'. Two days later, and seven years after the couple's first miscarriage, the Lennons' son Sean was born. 'We might get over there early next year,' Lennon told his sister in England, but he would never return to his homeland again. Aside from a brief recording session with Richard Starkey the following year, Lennon abandoned music, art and any connection with the Beatles.

More by inebriated accident than design, Richard Starkey had taken a similar decision. He divorced his wife and set up home in Monaco and California with American actress Nancy Andrews – one of a series of relationships with younger women that filled the rest of the decade. His closest friends were alcoholics – Keith Moon, Harry Nilsson, Monty Python member Graham Chapman – and he prided himself on being able to match them, drink for drink. 'Someone said, "We weren't musicians dabbling in drugs and alcohol; now we were junkies dabbling in music,"' he recalled. 'I was sliding down. I wasn't taking enough interest.' One day he shaved his head completely, even his eyebrows, in a desperate search for novelty. Freed from EMI in January 1976, he signed a new deal that required him to deliver an unfeasible seven albums in five years, but the record label backed out after four increasingly mediocre efforts. Chapman and his collaborator, Douglas Adams, attempted to find Starkey a purpose, crafting the skeleton of a TV sitcom for him. 'It was to be a science fiction comedy,' Adams recalled.

'It involved a bloke called Ringo Starr who worked in an office as a walking chauffeur – he carried the bosses around on his back – until one day a flying saucer landed, bearing a robot which gave Ringo the power to travel through time and space, do flower arranging and destroy the universe by waving his hand. That's as far as we got.' Instead, Starkey starred in an impeccably uncreative US television special, inevitably titled *Ringo*, narrated a children's album and waited for death or oblivion to deliver him. Lennon noted to a friend that nothing could be done to save him.

George Harrison had charted a more positive path into the future. Shortly after completing his traumatic US tour, he met the Monty Python team of comedians, and recognised that he had found a boys' club to replace the Beatles. As early as January 1975 Michael Palin wrote in his diary, 'He wants to be involved in some kind of way with us in the States. He said he has so many ideas to talk about, but I was a little wary, especially when he said he envisaged a Harrison–Pythons road show with us doing really extraordinary things throughout the show, such as swinging out over the audience on wires.' Visiting Harrison's mansion later in the year, Palin lamented, 'One can't escape the feeling of George somehow cut off from everyday life by the wealth that's come his way' and found the ex-Beatle anxious 'that we should stay the night, play snooker on his Olympic-size snooker table, drink and generally enjoy ourselves'. Harrison found that the Pythons' defiantly English humour exactly matched his own. In December 1975 he happily satirised his image on Eric Idle's TV show *Rutland Weekend Television*, in contrast with the world-weary atmosphere of his final Apple/EMI album, *Extra Texture*. Though the record betrayed traces of comedy – in place of the standard Apple logo, Harrison used a chewed-up apple core – its portentous and moralising tone won few admirers, continuing his steady slide out of public affection.

Harrison could rightfully have complained that his old schoolfriend Paul McCartney had cornered the market in moralising. Completing his sessions in New Orleans without Lennon, McCartney issued a public scolding to his former colleagues of the kind that had infuriated them in 1969. 'I really ought to talk to those boys,' he said patronisingly, '[and] tell them the facts of life. I thought we were finished with all those immature things – religious kicks, drug kicks, chasing birds – that was good when we were kids, but it's no good now.' His reference to religion might have been intended to rile the increasingly devout Harrison. A few months later McCartney made amends, insisting,

George is so straight. He's so straight and so ordinary and so real. And he happens to believe in God . . . There's nothing freaky about George at all . . . John's supposed to be a loony according to some people, and I know he isn't. If you ask me, the Beatles are very sane, but they're cheeky with it. With the Beatles, our great in-joke was always that whenever we'd split up, we'd do a Wembley concert, and John was going to do this big thing, like 'Fuck the Queen.' We were really going to blow it. It was a beautiful dream.

In late May 1975 McCartney and Wings issued *Venus and Mars*, another collection of exquisitely produced but lightweight pop, which dominated the airwaves as the Beatles had done a decade earlier. Three months later Wings opened a tour that would eventually – once McCartney's visa problems, caused by a series of drug busts, were solved – take them around the world. At the first show, in Southampton, McCartney was so nervous that the show started several minutes early. After a couple of songs someone shouted at him, 'What about John Lennon?' McCartney stared back for a few seconds and said dryly, 'What *about* John Lennon?' But the key moment came when he played the unmistakable opening chords of the Beatles' 'Lady Madonna'. It was the first time he had performed one of the group's songs in public for nine years. 'We were keen for Wings to get an identity of its own,' he recalled, 'and not rely on the Beatles. By then you could look at them just as songs, not as statements, and not as an admission of failure. By then it was clear that we'd proved our point.'

McCartney was still wrestling with the comparison between the two bands. A few months earlier he had commissioned veteran sci-fi author Isaac Asimov to write a screenplay. 'He had the basic idea for the fantasy, which involved two sets of musical groups,' Asimov recalled, 'a real one, and a group of extraterrestrial imposters. The real one would be in pursuit of the imposters and would eventually defeat them, despite the fact that the latter had supernormal powers.' Beyond that framework, McCartney offered Asimov nothing more than 'a snatch of dialogue describing the moment when the group realised they were being victimised by imposters'. Asimov set to work and produced a screenplay that he called 'suspenseful, realistic and moving'. But McCartney rejected it. As Asimov recalled, 'He went back to his one scrap of dialogue out of which he apparently couldn't move.' It's tempting to imagine that the project collapsed because McCartney knew subconsciously that he was aligned with the losing side.

While George Harrison and Richard Starkey were directing their money towards offshore havens and Swiss banks, McCartney was creating a business empire in the heart of London. A mass of companies was now run out of the same small office, including McCartney Pictures, McCartney Publishing, MPL Pictures, MPL Music, MPL Productions and their parent, MPL Communications. Besides offering ample opportunity for offsetting income against expenses, this complex structure symbolised his independence from the corporations that had controlled the Beatles for more than a decade.

On 26 January 1976 the Beatles' recording contract with EMI Records expired. The following day George Harrison joined his Dark Horse label, under the wing of A&M Records. Richard Starkey's deal with Polydor (for Europe and the UK) and Atlantic (for North America) followed in March – not a moment too soon, as he had financial worries and had been forced to borrow large sums against future royalties. McCartney agreed to remain with EMI, albeit with a renegotiated contract that offered him a substantially higher royalty. According to Lennon, McCartney was also promised increased payments on the Beatles' catalogue – but only if he succeeded in reuniting the group and bringing them to EMI. Meanwhile Lennon opted to remain out of contract, telling friends that he had some 'beautiful songs' but no desire to release them.

Another link with the past was severed that month. Since the break-up of the Beatles their road manager Mal Evans – who shared none of his colleague Neil Aspinall's financial acumen – had struggled to cope with the collapse of the dream that had carried him through the 1960s. Initially he provided tea and sympathy for Lennon, Harrison and Starkey's early solo projects. But as their work rate slowed and they became scattered across the globe, Evans had no obvious role in their lives. He left his family in England and attempted to become a record producer in Los Angeles, but he was unable to control the drinking buddies working on Keith Moon's solo album, and he was thrown off the project. Instead he found a ghostwriter for his auto-biography – as Lennon quipped, 'Should be a laugh . . . "Tues: 1965: Got up, loaded van"' – and appeared as a guest speaker at a Beatlefest celebration.

On 4 January 1976 he phoned his former Apple colleague Ken Mansfield, who thought he sounded upset. 'Nothing is wrong,' Evans told him. 'Paul and I just worked out some problems, and he is going to give me credit for some of the things I wrote with him.' It had long been an open secret within the Beatles' circle that Evans had contributed some lines to the *Sgt Pepper* album; indeed, Lennon had been hurt by McCartney's willingness to ask Evans for suggestions rather than him. But Evans didn't live long enough to sign that agreement. Later that day Los Angeles police arrived at his apartment after his girlfriend told them he was waving a gun around and seemed out of control. When the officers challenged him, he refused to drop the gun – effectively committing what has become known as 'suicide by cop'. 'Mal was a big lovable bear of a roadie,' McCartney recalled. 'He'd go over the top occasionally, but we all knew him and never had any problems. Had I been there I would have been able to say, "Mal, don't be silly." In fact, any of his friends could have talked him out of it without any sweat.' Instead, Evans died instantly.

Evans had been a friend, a servant, a confidant and (alongside Aspinall) one of two men who had shared the Beatles' daily lives. Lennon wept uncontrollably when he heard the news; Evans had been one of the few people who had welcomed Yoko Ono into the Beatles' milieu, and Lennon never forgot his generosity. Tragedy soon ebbed into farce, however: after Evans was cremated, his ashes went missing. His friend Harry Nilsson recalled, 'Neil Aspinall called from Apple and kept saying, "Where's Mal?" I said, "I sent him." And he said, "Well, we can't find him. He's not here and his mother's downstairs and his wife Lil is here and they're all crying. What am I supposed to tell them?" Finally a few days later I got a call from somebody and they said they found him. I asked where, and they said, "In the dead letter office."'

He died at a time when it seemed possible that the Beatles might, after all, be requiring the services of a road manager. Once their EMI deal expired, they were barraged with ever more outlandish financial offers for a reunion. Promoter Bill Sargent promised the quartet

$50 million for a single show. They could play solo, he stipulated, but must perform together for a minimum of 20 minutes. In return, Sargent would retain full commercial rights around the world, a clause that the Beatles' advisers would never have tolerated. When the group's approval wasn't forthcoming, he doubled his offer, to no avail. Meanwhile, the boss of Electro-Harmonix electricals, one Mike Mathews, seized his moment in the spotlight, offering £3 million in cash for a one-off Beatles concert, plus a share in the profits of closed-circuit broadcast that would raise their income to around £30 million. By the summer writer Kathleen Tynan was proposing a benefit concert for Vietnamese children, which the Beatles could headline. 'How about a cup of tea together?' Harrison said sarcastically. 'Get these four people and just put them in a room to have tea. Satellite it around the world at $20 each just to watch it, and we could make a fortune.' Like Henry Kissinger's Nobel Peace Prize, this illustrated the moment when reality made satire irrelevant: millions of Beatles fans would happily have paid to study these four men who had not shared a room since 1969.

The most persistent advocate of a reunion was Sid Bernstein. In September 1976 he ran a full-page ad in major US newspapers, pleading with the Beatles to unite for 'a one-off charity concert'. Today the world 'seems so hopelessly divided', he wrote; 'more than ever, we need a symbol of hope for the future . . . Let the world smile for one day.' In the 1960s parents had brought their disabled children to the Beatles' dressing room, as if the laying-on of hands might cure them. Now the group was expected to bring about the spiritual renewal of the entire planet. 'I wrote to him and said, "Look, that was then,"' Harrison complained. 'The Beatles can't save the world. We'll be lucky if we can save ourselves.' Yet the sheer weight of Bernstein's figures overshadowed any attempt at logic. He calculated that a concert broadcast around the world on TV and issued subsequently on film and album might generate $230 million. The Beatles might like to donate 20 per cent of their earnings, he suggested. He would take 10 per cent for his trouble, but would give three quarters of that to charity, ensuring that he would still walk away with almost $6 million.

When news of Bernstein's offer broke, comedian Eric Idle rang Harrison. 'He didn't know about it,' Idle reported. 'He said, "Fucking hell."' McCartney's response was equally concise: 'You can't reheat a soufflé.' Lennon remained enigmatically silent. Starkey had an album to sell, entitled *Ringo's Rotogravure*, with lukewarm contributions from Lennon and McCartney, so he was left with the burden of framing an official response. 'I think Sid is trying to get his name in the papers,' he said. 'I don't care about Sid Bernstein; I'm promoting my record. Next week someone's gonna come in with $500 million.' When the questioner persisted, Starkey snapped, 'Look, we've just spent ten minutes talking about this guy who writes to a newspaper.' His final word on the subject: 'We didn't start doing it for money, and we ain't going to end it that way.'

Only one offer came close to provoking a reunion, and it was the least lucrative. On the US TV comedy show *Saturday Night Live* producer Lorne Michaels ridiculed the furore by offering the Beatles $3,000 if they performed together on the show. When that didn't work, he threw in an extra $250 and overnight accommodation. In April 1976 the McCartneys paid one of their periodic visits to the Lennons at the Dakota, and watched Michaels' show. Lennon suggested they take a cab downtown to the studio and surprise Michaels, before he and McCartney decided they couldn't be bothered. Several months later Harrison had his own album to sell, and he agreed to guest-star on *Saturday Night Live* with Paul Simon. The opening skit showed him bargaining with Michaels, who was explaining patiently that he could only collect the full $3,000 if he brought all the other Beatles with him. Lennon's ego would never have allowed him to satirise himself on TV, while McCartney would have ruined the sketch by hamming it up. Harrison played it deadpan, another sign that he was now prepared to play the public role of the comic Beatle.

It was Harrison who encouraged his friends Eric Idle and Neil Innes to create their own Beatles reunion in the satirical form of the Rutles. The so-called Pre-Fab Four debuted on *Saturday Night Live* in October 1976 with a delicious parody of the Beatlemania era, a song entitled 'I Must Be in Love'. 'It wouldn't have happened without George,' commented Innes, who was the Rutles' songwriter and also played the Lennonesque Ron Nasty. 'He was the one thinking it would be great if somebody made fun of all this. Which is why he helped the Rutles . . . he was a fan. He thought the spirit of the Beatles had been passed on to Python. He once said that the Beatles, the Pythons and the Rutles should all get together for one big concert.'

Idle obtained the finance to make a Rutles movie, which developed into *All You Need Is Cash*, a wicked pastiche of Neil Aspinall's long-buried visual biography of the Beatles. 'It's a perfect thing for parody, the Beatles,' Harrison admitted. 'Eric chose the right Beatle for the project,' declared their mutual friend Derek Taylor. 'I cannot see Paul or John leaving well so alone – though Ringo, I think, could have fitted in very comfortably.' But Starkey was adrift in alcoholism, leaving Harrison to parody Derek Taylor in a cameo role (as Eric Manchester), preaching the Rutle Corps gospel as Taylor had done for Apple a decade earlier. Some of Idle's script was joyously childish, and some extremely pointed: there was a foreign Rutle wife who wore Nazi uniforms, a terrifying New York manager called Ron Decline and a wide-eyed balladeer addicted to the creation of sentimental cliché. Innes's music was precisely observed and brilliantly conceived; indeed, it evoked the spirit of the Beatles so accurately that the owners of Northern Songs, ATV, sued for plagiarism, and an inevitable legal battle ensued. Innes lost his songwriting royalties, and Lennon/McCartney now have to be credited as co-writers of such delicious nonsense as 'Cheese and Onions' and 'Piggy in the Middle'. 'George occasionally attempts to get the rights back for me,' Innes revealed in 1996. 'But it's not high up on anyone's agenda. I've stopped sulking about it. It's water under the bridge.' Harrison admitted his own rationale for supporting the project: 'I loved the Rutles because, for the Beatles, the [idea of] the Beatles is just tiresome. It needs to be deflated a bit, and I loved the idea of the Rutles taking that burden off us in a way. Everything can be seen as comedy, and the Fab Four are no exception to that.'

The Rutles' musical tribute was timely. After several years when it was anathema for new artists to admit being inspired by the Beatles, suddenly there was nothing more commercially acceptable than echoes of the past. ELO, led by Beatles fanatic Jeff Lynne, provided the most blatant homage to their sound, winning applause from John Lennon and rivalling Wings' ubiquity on Top 40 radio. A new wave of punk and power-pop artists was emerging, many of whom betrayed a Beatles influence, from the 1963 stylings of the Jam and the Pleasers (who took their name from the Beatles' first album), to the more frenetic sound of the Ramones, whose name was borrowed from a pseudonym once used by Paul McCartney. The Clash might have promised 'no

Elvis, no Beatles or Rolling Stones in 1977', but there was a familiar lilt to their ragged vocal harmonies and melodies.

Some artists were less subtle about their inspiration. In 1976 a pirate radio promoter named Rohan O'Rahilly, who had once collaborated with the Lennons on the launch of a 'Peace Ship', announced the most important musical event of the era: the arrival of 'The New Beatles'. Even before the lawyers had reached for their writs, O'Rahilly renamed his protégés Loving Awareness, with a message to the old Beatles: they should either heal mankind by reuniting or stand aside and bless their successors. So eager were the British public to believe in musical reincarnation that rumours soon spread that Loving Awareness were none other than Lennon and his chums in disguise.

To prove that you can fool the public as long as they wish to be fooled, four Canadian musicians pulled a similar stunt. Klaatu took their name from a 1950s sci-fi movie – also referenced by Starkey on the cover of his 1974 album *Goodnight Vienna*. None of the musicians was named or pictured on their debut album, which sounded like the work of people who had exhaustively studied *Sgt Pepper*. Therefore, with a giant leap of faith, Klaatu must be the Beatles in disguise. The final 'proof' was that their record appeared on Capitol, the label that had released the Beatles' American hits. By the time Klaatu's more mundane identities were revealed, their album had sold more than 500,000 copies.

EMI/Capitol had a more direct route to the profits of Beatlemania. In March 1976 all 22 of the group's original hits were reissued in Britain, alongside the first appearance on a UK single of 'Yesterday'. Next, EMI delved into the vaults to discover if there was any previously unheard material that could be released. They began to assemble a double-album entitled *Rock 'n' Roll Music*, and briefly toyed with unveiling some of the lacklustre oldies that the group had recorded during their January 1969 sessions. Fortunately, artistic discretion prevailed over greed, and the album simply repackaged familiar material. EMI mounted an extravagant publicity campaign, and the set climbed to No. 2 on the US charts. Other retrospectives appeared in the years ahead, including *Love Songs*, *Rarities*, *Beatles Ballads* and *Reel Music*.

Richard Starkey voiced the group's misgivings. 'I'd like some power over whoever at EMI is putting out these lousy Beatles compilations,' he complained.

They can do what they like with all our old stuff, they know that. It's theirs. But Christ, man, I was *there*. I played on those records, and you know how much trouble we used to go to, just getting the running order right? And those album covers! John rang them up and asked them if he could draw one . . . he told me he was told to piss off. All of us looked at the cover and could hardly bear to see it. It was terrible.

EMI replied that they had attempted to contact Lennon, but that he had failed to reply in time. As a sign of the rising tension between the group and their original record company, battle was rejoined over the royalties from the *Let It Be* album. The warring parties would soon reserve a regular berth in the London High Court.

Soon nostalgia was everywhere. Publisher Sean O'Mahony, who had issued the official magazine *The Beatles Book* between 1963 and 1969, began to reissue all the original copies on a schedule that expired in 1982, allowing him to substitute a brand-new Beatles publication at the moment when EMI were celebrating the group's 20th anniversary. *The Beatles Book* continued to run until 2001, mocking Paul McCartney's original comment to the publisher: 'What will you find to write about us every month?'

Certain members of the Beatles were particularly averse to this obsession with the past. When journalist David Wigg planned to issue an album of his late 1960s interviews with the group, Starkey and Harrison attempted to halt the project despite the fact that there was nothing illegal or demeaning about it. They failed, merely stirring up sufficient publicity to carry the package into the UK charts.

John Lennon found that the simplest way of avoiding the past was to remove himself from the present. Aside from an occasional appearance in public, pushing his son's buggy around Manhattan or shopping in Tokyo's deluxe stores, he remained absent and silent. When journalist Roy Carr encountered him at the Americana Hotel, Lennon said that he was concentrating on giving his son Sean the kind of childhood he hadn't enjoyed himself. Another reporter, Chris Charlesworth, asked Lennon for an interview and received a postcard in return: 'No comment was the stern reply! Am invisible.'

When McCartney visited in April 1976 Lennon told him that his sole ambition was to write a classic novel. McCartney explained the touring schedule that faced him over the next few months and Lennon said, 'Sooner you than me.' In one of his final interviews Lennon claimed that he had become so tired of McCartney turning up on his doorstep clutching a guitar that he asked him to phone ahead first. 'This isn't the 1950s, you know.' But as their mutual friend Derek Taylor wrote,

It wasn't like that at all . . . John was very funny about the extraordinary McCartney panache, cheek, impudence that enabled Paul to pass doorman, cops, fans, almost anyone in the world except Japanese customs officers without let or hindrance. "I dunno how he does it," John marvelled, "the cheeky get; but he's the only one who can get in here without anyone being able to do anything about it. Elton can't get away with it, nor can Bowie or Mick – and if it was me going to see Paul, I'd definitely be stopped." So I don't buy all that stuff about Paul barging in on The Great One's peace of mind.

Yet friction remained. As McCartney noted later, the key was not to mention their business difficulties, which could still catapult them into open conflict. 'I happened to be on my way to the Caribbean, passing through New York,' he recalled of a conversation in spring 1977, 'so I rang John up. But there was so much suspicion, even though I came bearing the olive branch. I said, "Hey, I'd really like to see you." He said, "What for? What do you really want?" It was very difficult.' Twenty years after their first meeting McCartney could still be intimidated by the man he'd imagined as his closest friend. 'He had a great line for me. He said, "You're all pizza and fairy tales." He'd become sort of Americanised by then, so the best insult I could think of to say was, "Oh, fuck off, Kojak," and slam the phone down,' knowing that as usual he had just lost the argument.

No problems affected Lennon's relationship with Richard Starkey: the two men saw each other as often as they wanted, usually once or twice every year. For George Harrison though 'There was a lot of alienation between us and him. Well, there was alienation amongst all of us. Suddenly we're all grown up and we've all got these other wives. That didn't exactly help. All the wives at that time really drove wedges between us.' He was not referring to his own wives, or to Starkey's. Harrison did occasionally visit Lennon at the Dakota, and 'always got an overpowering feeling from him. Almost a feeling that he wanted to say much more than he could, or than he did. You could see it in his eyes. But it was difficult.' That adjective disguised the identity of the obstacle, as far as Harrison was concerned. 'It was almost like he was crying out to tell me certain things, or to renew things, relationships,' he continued, 'but he wasn't able to, because of the situation he was in.'

Other friends were more explicit about Lennon's 'situation'. As May Pang said, 'I still remember vividly the day John moved out. Mick Jagger had rung up looking for him. I remember his reaction when I told him John had gone back to Yoko. There was a long pause, and then Mick said, "I guess I've lost a friend."' In an Ono-approved anthology of tributes to Lennon, Jagger reiterated the charge: 'When he went back to Yoko, he went into hibernation. He was living close to where I was living in New York City, but I was probably considered one of the "bad influences", so I was never allowed to see him after that.'

Lennon's friend Pete Shotton, who'd known him since they were five, offered a disturbing portrait of the artist in retreat. He left a message at the Dakota to say he was in town, and Lennon invited him over. 'He said first of all he'd had to ring his numerologist, to ask if it was OK to see me,' Shotton recalled. 'I said, "You had to ask permission to see me?" He sort of flushed up, like a child.' That evening Shotton found his friend 'warm, funny and at peace with himself and the world. It was the real John Lennon, the one I always knew was there.' But two days later, when Shotton called again,

In the background I could hear Yoko shouting something, and John saying, 'Look, Yoko, he's fucking coming over and that's it.' John didn't realise I could hear all this. I thought, Fuck, here we go again. Yoko is just the same about me. Then I thought, What the hell? I'll go anyway. When I got there, all three of us went out for dinner, to the same Japanese restaurant. But the atmosphere was totally different. They were both uptight. They hardly spoke to each other, or to me. John looked pale and drawn, not as fit or healthy as he'd looked three days earlier. We didn't talk about the old days or personal things this time. Just about the occult and mysticism.

Every couple has its tensions, but Shotton's account chimes not only with the sensationalist tomes published in the wake of Lennon's death, notably John Green's *Dakota Days*, a pseudonymous astrologist's view of the Lennons' marriage, but also with the faintly eerie reports from Cynthia Lennon in 1968 and May Pang in 1975. All three represented Lennon's past; all three reported their friend, husband or lover seeming somehow different, and removed. Was there a darker message that Lennon was attempting to communicate to George Harrison than a simple 'Leave me alone'?

Lennon promised to attend a New York concert by Paul McCartney and Wings in May 1976, and possibly appear on stage. Inevitably, he didn't turn up. McCartney had solved his visa problems and was free to perform in North America for the first time in a decade. 'Everything we did was in the shadow of the Beatles,' McCartney admitted later. 'So we did everything with quite a lot of paranoia. You look at 1976 – we have this big, big tour, and at first everyone wants to know, Is this gonna be a Beatles reunion? Even in our most successful year they were taking our success off us. But the great thing was that three weeks into the tour it was suddenly, Who cares? This is a great band. We did this thing that we set out to do. And we needn't have worried.'

McCartney had drilled Wings into a formidably tight touring unit, light on spontaneity – for the rest of his career he relied on well-rehearsed stage patter – but delivering a spectacle that rivalled any of his mid-1970s contemporaries. By late June, when the tour climaxed in California, he could boast that Wings had established itself beyond any comparisons with the past. Two singles from their hastily assembled album *Wings at the Speed of Sound* had topped the US charts; so did the LP. But *Speed of Sound* was a distinctly patchier effort than its two predecessors, not least because McCartney had attempted a more democratic distribution of songs among the five members, with decidedly mixed results. In a sour 1984 interview his bandmate Denny Laine complained, 'Paul and Linda smoked a fantastic amount [of cannabis] by anybody's standards. They smoked joints the way ordinary people smoke cigarettes. That's why Paul's albums take him ages and ages to make. He just cannot be decisive about anything. It is very frustrating for people to work with him, because he changes his mind so often.' In particular, Laine highlighted the delayed release of the films documenting Wings' triumphant tour: *Wings Over the World* wasn't premiered until 1979, and *Rockshow* the following year. But McCartney did manage to complete a triple-album anthology of live recordings, *Wings Over*

America, for Christmas 1976. Five songs from the Beatles era were included, and for all of them, the original 'Lennon/McCartney' songwriting credit was altered to read 'McCartney/Lennon'. There was no objection from Lennon.

The most reclusive of the Beatles was forced into public that summer, at a formal hearing to mark his victory against the US immigration department. He was now free to travel without the fear of being barred from returning to America. His first destination was widely expected to be England, but instead he flew to Hong Kong, apparently at the suggestion of Ono's numerologist. There he fell into the company of David Bowie and Iggy Pop, and enjoyed a brief weekend of rock star hedonism, before returning home obediently on the flight Ono had reserved for him. In New York Lennon and Ono rarely socialised, beyond occasional dinners with actor Peter Boyle and his journalist partner Loraine Alterman (Lennon was best man at their 1977 wedding). Their most regular visitor was a former DJ named Elliot Mintz,* who had interviewed the couple in 1973 and become particularly close to Ono. He became the Lennons' spokesman and travel companion, though as another friend of Lennon's, record producer Jack Douglas, noted, 'It was so weird, because John never had a good word for Elliot. In the studio, if Elliot was coming, John was like, "Ugh."' But Mintz offered the attractive quality of not representing Lennon's past or threatening to question his withdrawal from the world. Softly spoken, obsequious but strong-willed, Mintz soon became the Lennons' loyal buffer against media intrusion.

George Harrison also recognised the attractions of withdrawal. He made an anonymous appearance on stage with the Monty Python troupe in New York 'looking tired and ill', as Michael Palin recalled. A vacation in the Virgin Islands failed to restore him, and he was diagnosed as suffering from hepatitis. The collapse of his marriage and the criticisms levelled at his touring and recording activities had encouraged him to take refuge in alcohol and drugs, and now his body was calling a halt. The illness was a decisive moment in his life. Secure in his new relationship with Olivia Arias, he decided that happiness and health were more important than stardom. He was still a Beatle, with

---

* Mintz's career path, from radical DJ on 1960s underground radio to apologist for celebrities such as Paris Hilton, is a paradigm of the surreal metamorphosis of pop culture over the past 40 years.

the psychology and self-importance that entailed. But he no longer courted the life of a celebrity.

One consequence of his illness was that he failed to deliver his first album to A&M by the due date, 26 July 1976. This forced the cancellation of a major world tour and doomed his Dark Horse Records label. A new legal team had taken over at A&M and discovered that their predecessors had separated Harrison's contract from the rest of the Dark Horse roster: if Harrison's other signings failed to make a profit, A&M couldn't reclaim their losses from the ex-Beatle's royalties. 'What happened was that they realised they had not made themselves such a good deal,' Harrison explained as the relationship unravelled.

They found that the only legal grounds they had [against me] was that I had had hepatitis, so my album was two months delayed. And so they picked on that legal point and said, 'OK, we'll get him on that.' I arrived in LA with the album under my arm, all happy, and I was given this letter saying, 'Give us back the million dollars,' which was an advance, 'and give us the album, and when you give us the album, you don't get the million back.' I turned down a deal from Capitol/EMI that was of more value than what I took with A&M. But I took that because of the relationship we were supposedly going to have – which it turned out we never did have.

So Harrison returned the advance and cancelled the A&M deal. 'We backed the truck up to our office and filled it with our stuff,' he recalled. Warner Brothers was happy to offer Harrison what he wanted, but their commitment to Dark Horse's other artists was merely symbolic, and he was soon the only viable performer on the label.

The album, *Thirty-Three-and-a-Third*, was more tuneful and lighter in spirit than its predecessors. It contained a sly satire about the 'My Sweet Lord' plagiarism suit, which promised, 'This song has nothing Bright about it.' The timing was ironic: just before 'This Song' appeared as a single, a New York court ruled on the case of Bright Tunes vs Harrisongs. It decided that when Harrison wrote 'My Sweet Lord' in 1969, he had been guilty of 'subconscious plagiarism' of Bright's song 'He's So Fine'. A second set of hearings was scheduled to calculate Harrison's liability for damages. 'It's very difficult to just start writing after you've been through that,' he admitted. 'When I put the radio on, every tune I hear sounds like something else.'

The earnings power of 'My Sweet Lord' was boosted by the release of *The Best of George Harrison*, a Capitol/EMI album deliberately scheduled to coincide with his new record. Both Lennon (*Shaved Fish*) and Starkey (*Blast From Your Past*) had been under contract to EMI when their anthologies were released, so a degree of co-operation between artist and corporation had been involved. But Harrison had no such leverage. To his embarrassment, EMI decided that his solo catalogue was not strong enough to command a compilation album, so they filled half of the record with Beatles material. 'I don't see why they did that,' Harrison said, interpreting the decision as a personal slight and ensuring that he would remain a staunch opponent of EMI in the litigation with Apple that lay ahead.

Another enduring legal battle was nearing its denouement, as the London High Court set a January 1977 date for hearing the case brought by three of the Beatles and Apple against Allen Klein and ABKCO. At stake were the infamous management contracts from 1969/70 and millions of pounds in commissions that had either been paid in error (Apple's case) or grossly underpaid (according to ABKCO). The verdict would not be binding on the reverse litigation that was being brought on the other side of the Atlantic, but it was difficult to imagine that the US actions would not be influenced by the judge's decision in London.

To add an extra frisson to the dispute, Allen Klein had made a mischievous intervention in the 'My Sweet Lord' saga. Having acted as Harrison's adviser during the early years of the plagiarism case, he now emerged as the new owner of Bright Tunes, buying it for $587,000 on the assumption that the company would soon be worth much more. The judge in the case estimated that Bright's share of the income from 'My Sweet Lord' could exceed $1.5 million, but Harrison's lawyers challenged Klein's right to switch sides midway through the litigation, and any hope of a quick resolution was lost.

Meanwhile, Harrison, Lennon and Klein were set to face each other in the High Court. 'Paul doesn't have to go,' Harrison explained, 'because he didn't do the deal, and Ringo has got out of it because he's got a tax year out of Britain. So it's John, Yoko and I versus Klein. It's for huge figures, but it's completely like a game.' The prospect filled him with dread: 'It's going to be awful if it does come to court, a fiasco and

a nightmare, because it's going to be open to the public and the press
. . . It's very strange. I've got to put my body there, and I'll be sitting
in it, but really I'll be somewhere else.' The alternative to this process
of mental withdrawal was grim: 'People commit suicide in that sort of
situation, and I've decided I'm not going to be a rock casualty.'

Lennon faced an equally forbidding ordeal. When he had imagined
returning to Britain, he had envisaged a scene of triumph mixed with
sweet nostalgia. Instead, he would be dragged home by the legal system
to face the humiliation of his financial affairs, his private life and every
facet of his relationship with Allen Klein undergoing intense public
scrutiny. Like Harrison, Lennon had chosen to withdraw rather than
expose himself to the world. Both men now had to consider whether
any sum of money could compensate for their loss of privacy.

They agreed to trust their cause to an unlikely saviour: Yoko Ono.
'Somebody has to take care of business,' Lennon explained, 'and there's
no way I can do it. I don't have that talent. So she had to do it. She
has the talent to do it . . . We decided not to have an outside party.
We had to look after our own stuff and face that reality.' Over the
weekend of 8–9 January 1977 Ono and Allen Klein negotiated at the
Plaza Hotel in New York. On Monday morning Lennon, Ono and
Klein assembled at the hotel to make a formal announcement: all the
cases involving Apple and ABKCO were now at an end. Apple would
pay Klein $5,009,200 as total and final payment of any outstanding
management commissions; and with that, Klein's involvement with the
Beatles ceased. Lennon signed a document confirming the settlement
in front of a photographer, while Klein graciously praised 'the tireless
efforts and Kissinger-like negotiating brilliance of Yoko Ono Lennon'.
There would be no embarrassing pursuit of the Lennons through a
London airport lounge, no court appearance and no return to Britain.

Klein's money came from the collective Apple pot earned by the
four Beatles up to September 1974. Not everyone thought it was such
a wonderful deal. 'It's true she settled with Klein for $5 million,' said
Linda McCartney later. 'But it wasn't her money, really. Each Beatle
gave a share, Paul included, and he never wanted that man as manager
in the first place. Five or six million! When you think that they were
pulling bloody [tarot] cards to see what they would do! If only we
had known what they were doing.' But as a joint owner of Apple, still
in a minority of three to one, McCartney had no option but to accept

the settlement, pay the money and claim the moral victory. Later he could enjoy the glow of vindication when Klein was put on trial in New York for tax evasion. The first trial in 1977 resulted in a hung jury; a second was held in May 1979. It was alleged that Klein had accepted 'substantial cash payments' for copies of Apple albums that were intended to be given away for promotional purposes but not reported that money to the Internal Revenue Service. Klein's colleague Pete Bennett testified against him, and he was found guilty of not declaring his full income in 1970 to the IRS but not guilty of two further charges. Inevitably the appeals process was invoked, but Klein began a two-month jail sentence in July 1980.

'I feel sorry for him now,' McCartney said magnanimously while the trial was under way. 'I was caught in his net once, and that panicked me. I really wanted to do everything to get him. I was contemplating going to where he lives and walking outside his house with placards. I was really that crazy at the time. I would have done anything to get out of it, but it all turned out OK.' Harrison separated his affection for Klein from his dismay at the consequences of their business relationship. But Lennon, Klein's first and most ardent supporter, was less compassionate, refusing to acknowledge the profound empathy he had once shared with his manager.

Having proved her worth during the negotiations with Klein, Ono became Lennon's primary representative at Apple board meetings. There she sparred with Lee Eastman, Denis O'Brien and Hilary Gerrard, each championing the cause of his Beatle patron. Meanwhile the four protagonists maintained a wary distance from each other. Yet their unwillingness to act as Beatles did nothing to restrain the industry that had grown up in their name. In 1977 two vintage live recordings – neither authorised by the group – competed for attention. *Live at the Hollywood Bowl* was collated from tapes of concerts in 1964 and 1965, edited and remixed by George Martin. 'It's not very good,' Harrison said dismissively, 'it's just a bootleg.' 'We never wanted it out,' Paul McCartney admitted.

But after we'd split with Capitol Records, they acquired the rights to all that material and didn't bother asking us any more about what should be released. We never used to like the tapes of those two concerts, because we always thought all the songs were played much too fast. We also thought it was all out of tune. But nowadays we can't even say if we like the cover artwork or not, it's got nothing to do with us. All those old Beatles repackages smell a bit like a rip-off to me.

Although McCartney could not prevent the *Hollywood Bowl* tapes from being released by the company to which he was still signed, Apple felt more optimistic about halting the second project. In December 1962 a fellow Merseybeat musician, Ted 'Kingsize' Taylor, had recorded the Beatles at the Star-Club in Hamburg. He offered his tapes to the group's manager Brian Epstein for a paltry sum, but Epstein wasn't interested. Nine years passed before Taylor collaborated with another key figure from the group's early career, ex-manager Allan Williams, who recognised a commercial opportunity. The tapes had all the clarity of an alarm clock buried in sand, but they captured the group on the cusp of fame, at the last moment when spontaneity still governed their live performances and they had no reputation to lose.

In August 1973 Williams met Harrison and Starkey at Apple. He played the tapes and offered them to the Beatles for £5,000. The musicians declined, though Harrison tempered the refusal by slipping a present for Williams' wife into his hand: sixteen uncut rubies, which he'd been given by a member of the Krishna community. Undeterred, Williams joined forces with businessman Paul Murphy, who arranged for the tapes to be remixed into a state that was nearly listenable. At Easter 1977 the tiny independent label Lingasong announced that it would be releasing a double album from the tapes.

Only then did Apple act. On 1 April 1977, one week before the Star-Club album was released, Apple's lawyers served a writ demanding that it should be withdrawn. In reply, Ted Taylor testified that at least one of the Beatles had given him permission to make the tape. That would have counted for nothing had Apple examined the recording logically and recognised the obvious clues that it post-dated the signing of the Beatles' June 1962 contract with EMI. An expert witness was available in the shape of John Lennon, who supplied a detailed letter about the album, noting perceptively, 'The sleeve note, apart from being inaccurate, seems to have been written with a court case in mind.' He added a handwritten postscript: 'THIS IS A FUCKING FAKE!' But by then Apple had already lost its case. The High Court judge not only accepted Taylor's story but pointedly criticised Apple's tardiness in launching the action. The Star-Club album duly appeared, to the enormous benefit of Beatles scholars but to no great commercial effect: it failed to enter the Top 100 chart in the USA or UK, while *Live at the Hollywood Bowl* reached No. 1 in Britain and No. 2 in America. Paul McCartney sounded less concerned by Lingasong's package than by EMI's: 'On a personal level it's quite nice to have a memory of those days. On a business level it was all very weird. Nevertheless, I don't think it does any harm.' But while the *Hollywood Bowl* album soon vanished from the Beatles' catalogue and was never issued on CD, the Star-Club tapes were repackaged endlessly over the next 20 years.

Through the late 1970s exploitation of the Beatles' name supported a healthy if rarely attractive industry. 'They're like leeches or crows, feeding off the Beatles,' George Harrison complained. A Broadway musical called *Beatlemania* featured imitators reproducing the group's hits, while Robert Stigwood proceeded with his cinematic interpretation of the *Sgt Pepper* album. Some of the most successful pop stars of the age, including the Bee Gees and Peter Frampton, were recruited to form Sgt Pepper's band, who – according to the movie's *Official Scrapbook* – become 'entangled in an even more villainous web of greed and meanness spun by an international syndicate with the motto of "We Hate Love, We Hate Joy, We Love Money"'. The scenario must have sounded uncannily like real life to the Beatles, who would have greeted these comments by Bee Gees singer Robin Gibb with some amusement: 'There is no such thing as the Beatles now. They don't exist as a band and never performed *Sgt Pepper* live in any case. When ours comes out, it will be, in effect, as if theirs never existed.' As Harrison lamented, 'We didn't have any control over that.' But referring to all the unauthorised productions that were under way, he added, 'I don't really think they're supposed to do that, and in fact we've just got together a group of people to go and sue them all.' In September 1979 Apple duly filed a lawsuit against the producers of *Beatlemania*, who had franchised their musical around America; but it didn't prevent a London presentation from opening three weeks later.

Like water dripping through plaster, the flow was irregular but infuriating. Film-maker Steven Spielberg produced *I Wanna Hold Your Hand*, a teen drama hinged around a 1964 Beatles concert. Impresario Dick Clark invested in a television movie, *The Birth of the Beatles*, for which he recruited the group's former drummer Pete Best as consultant. 'People think we're giving all these producers permission to do it,' Harrison complained, 'and that we're making money out of it, but we don't make a nickel.' He added forbiddingly, 'There's not much more we can be sued for, but we can sue a lot of other people.'

One immediate target was John Lennon's first wife, Cynthia. In June 1978 she published a mild, bittersweet memoir, *A Twist of Lennon*. The juiciest portions were serialised in the reliably exploitative *News of the World*. Lennon was incensed and issued an injunction to prevent further publication, claiming libel. His ex-wife's defence was simple: she had told the truth. That might be so, Lennon's lawyers replied, but the articles had invaded his privacy – a claim breathtaking in its hypocrisy, given Lennon and Ono's willingness to turn their private lives into art. The presiding judge, Lord Denning, agreed: 'I cannot see that either of these two parties has had much regard for the sanctity of marriage. It is as plain as it can be that the relationship of these parties has ceased to be a private affair.' Publication proceeded, without any serious damage to Lennon's reputation.

'We've been nostalgia since 1967,' George Harrison contended as he released a self-titled album that was arguably his most consistent work. To reinforce his view, he resurrected a lost Beatles song from 1968, "Not Guilty", in which he had wryly expressed his desire not to 'upset the Apple-cart'. It gently satirised the global obsession with the past, and specifically the era that the Beatles allegedly epitomised. 'It's like Britain has always been hung up about the Second World War,' he said. 'The Beatles were in and out of people's lives in a flash, and yet they're still there 15 years later . . . They've got lots and lots of songs they can play forever. But what do they want? Blood? They want us all to die like Elvis Presley?' Harrison noted, 'Every year we were Beatling was like 20 years . . . We were just four relatively sane people in the middle of madness. People used us as an excuse to trip out . . . That's why they want the Beatles to go on, so they can get all silly again. But they don't have consideration for our well-being.' In any case Harrison still refused to consider the possibility of ever working with Paul McCartney again. 'Paul was very pushy . . . so in that respect it would be very difficult to ever play with him. But we're cool as far as being pals goes.'

In one area Harrison squarely represented public opinion: he wanted to know what Lennon was doing. 'I myself would be interested to know whether John still writes tunes and puts them on a cassette or does he just forget all about music and not touch the guitar.' Only after Lennon's death did it emerge that during the late 1970s he regularly attempted to compose songs but rarely managed to complete them. 'I know John was desperate to write,' Linda McCartney commented in 1984. 'Desperate. People thought, Well, he's taking care of Sean, he's a house-husband, and all that, but he wasn't happy. He couldn't write, and it drove him crazy. And Paul could have helped him – easily.' But the two men were rarely in contact, and whenever they did talk it usually decayed into a petty argument about their legal ties.

Authorised and unauthorised accounts of Lennon's life in the late 1970s vary so widely that both are unbelievable. In 1980 he claimed that he had spent the five years since his son's birth as a full-time carer and part-time baker, exhibiting his fresh loaves with the same pride that he had once devoted to his music. A mysterious open letter from the Lennons, printed as a paid advertisement in several newspapers in May 1979, reinforced the message that the couple were undergoing spiritual and artistic renewal. Yet so-called insiders – his personal assistant and Ono's astrologist and tarot reader – recounted a different narrative: Lennon was embittered, drug-ridden, despairing, lethargic, violent, sometimes suicidal, requiring constant nasal massage to counteract years of cocaine abuse. In an audio diary that he kept sporadically in 1979 Lennon lashed out at his contemporaries, including 'the mighty McCartney', with a degree of venom that hinted at acute envy.* Yet the anger could shift abruptly into a deadening depression: he no longer listened to new music, he admitted; 'There doesn't seem any point now.' He lamented the nagging insistence of his sex drive and then confessed to fantasies about sucking his mother's breasts. At

---

* Lennon wrote diary entries throughout his final years, and the manuscripts – removed from Ono's apartment after her husband's death but later returned to her – have been seen by at least two biographers, Geoffrey Giuliano and Robert Rosen. Neither dared to quote from the text, instead coyly paraphrasing Lennon's accounts of his sexual fantasies (he was apparently perturbed by an erotic dream in which George Harrison had performed fellatio on him) and depression. From the sketchy accounts that have been published, Lennon appeared to turn to his diary in times of crisis, thereby giving an unbalanced account of his daily life.

least once he flirted with suicide, an experience that later inspired a song, 'You Saved My Soul'. His saviour was Ono, who also 'rescued' him from a brief infatuation with a television evangelist. Whatever was happening in the Dakota between their annual visits to Japan, Lennon sounded anything but fulfilled, creatively, psychologically or sexually. Even at his most positive, he could only describe himself as 'the same but different . . . it's been a long haul'.

After his death Yoko Ono claimed that around 1978 the couple had planned an autobiographical Broadway musical, inevitably titled *The Ballad of John and Yoko*. In a book of Lennon's posthumous writings she included an essay of that name, purportedly intended for the theatre programme. It was the most sustained piece of prose writing that Lennon ever attempted, in a literary voice as direct and acerbic as his 1970 *Plastic Ono Band* album. It ridiculed his fellow Beatles, 'Paul, George and It's Only Ringo'; satirised his adventures in radical politics; and delivered a damning verdict on his career: 'The lesson for me is clear. I've already "lost" one family to produce what? *Sgt Pepper*? I am blessed with a second chance. Being a Beatle nearly cost me my life, and certainly cost me a great deal of my health . . . I will not make the same mistake twice in one lifetime . . . If I never "produce" anything more for public consumption than "silence", so be it.' It is impossible to reconcile the valedictory tone of these remarks with a man celebrating his own life. More likely these were diary entries never intended for public consumption; the work of an artist who could no longer communicate anything apart from the rejection of his own past.

Occasionally Lennon attempted to revive his creativity: he visited artist Andy Warhol's studio in late 1979, intending to produce screen prints in the master's style. But it was a rare venture outside the Dakota. As one of their neighbours noted, 'When the Lennons go out, they go to Japan.' 'I enjoyed being the foreigner,' Lennon said of his visits to Ono's homeland. Otherwise they were effectively invisible. They were not short of places to hide. Ono had become a canny speculator in real estate, and the Lennons owned several farms in Delaware County, a beachside residence on Long Island and a holiday home in Florida. Their stake in the Dakota Building increased to six apartments, offering not only residential space and office facilities, but also storage for the exotic fruits of Ono's passion for ancient Egyptian artefacts and that most essential of Upper West Side accoutrements, a world-class collection of fur coats. Lennon's famous line, 'imagine no possessions', grew increasingly ironic.

In April 1979 he felt guilty enough about his elder son to invite him for a vacation in Florida. Julian was approaching his 17th birthday and was in awe of his father, but Lennon barely knew how to talk to him and was prone to violent surges of anger. 'Julian was constantly on tenterhooks,' his mother reported, 'sensing that an eruption was coming and retreating to his room in the hope of avoiding it.' One minute they might be relaxing like a real family; the next, Lennon would be screaming at one of his sons*, and a staff member would escort them away. 'One incident in particular did him lasting damage,' Cynthia Lennon explained. 'Julian giggled [and] John turned on him and screamed, "I can't stand the way you fucking laugh! Never let me hear your fucking horrible laugh again." He continued with a tirade of abuse until Julian fled once again to his room in tears. It was monstrously cruel, and has affected him ever since.' It was the last time father and son were together.

More tender care was lavished elsewhere. While Ono worked extended office hours, Lennon scribbled lists for his staff, specifying his choice of cat food and sugar-free snacks. Helpless as a child, he demanded help with fixing the hi-fi and banging nails in his bedroom wall, and asked his assistant for new albums by McCartney and David Bowie, and a biography of evangelist Billy Graham. 'Remind Y.O. her teeth will be needed in later life (i.e. Dentist's must be visited),' he wrote in one note, presumably afraid to raise the subject himself.

Lennon had succeeded in removing himself from the media. Ono's financial manoeuvres generated an occasional paragraph – she donated $1,000 to buy flak jackets for New York police, for instance, and sold a prize Holstein cow for the record price of $265,000. Occasionally there would be a wistful rumour that he was about to record an album, but more significant was his decision to dissolve the companies that had handled his avant-garde activities earlier in the decade. Gallery owner John Dunbar had introduced him to the London underground and to Ono, but when Dunbar unexpectedly visited Lennon in spring

---

* As an adult, Sean Lennon recalled that his father had once shouted so loudly in his ear that he required medical treatment.

1980 'Yoko explained that they'd been going through a period of seeing no one, that John had been like that for about a year, and going anywhere or seeing anyone seemed like a great effort.' So estranged was Lennon from the world around him that he failed to notice when Ono slipped into a period of heroin use. 'I made a mistake,' she admitted later, 'but I'm proud that I conquered it.' Meanwhile, Lennon was writing desultory letters to his relatives in England, telling his cousin, 'I'm 40 next. I hope life begins – i.e. I'd like a little less "trouble" and more – what? I don't know.'

'How Does a Beatle Live?' Maureen Cleave had asked in the article that sparked the 'bigger than Jesus' fiasco. The question still stood. While Lennon chose isolation, Richard Starkey found another refuge: alcohol. Despite nearly dying in a 1979 attack of peritonitis that required the removal of several feet of intestines, he maintained a resolutely excessive lifestyle. By day he slept or sunbathed, 'and then evenings, all you can do is eat and gamble . . . I like to play blackjack and a little roulette.' Rooted in the shallow earth of Monte Carlo, Starkey inhabited the most vacuous brand of celebrity hedonism. 'I worked hard enough to become a playboy,' he explained defensively. 'And I am a jet-setter. Whatever anyone thinks, and whoever puts it down, I am on planes half the year.' Like many alcoholics, he felt as if he carried the sun on his shoulders: 'Wherever I go, it's a swinging place, man. It's a crazy kind of world.' Unable to hold down a record contract, he regarded work as a distraction and the past as a trap. 'I, personally, don't want us to get together,' he said when asked the inevitable question about a reunion. 'Or they can get together, but I'm not getting together.'

In May 1979, however, Starkey, McCartney and Harrison made music for the first time since January 1970 – drunken, shambolic music, but together nonetheless. The occasion was the wedding celebration for Eric Clapton and Pattie Boyd. Clapton recalled, 'John later phoned me to say that he would have been there too if he had known about it,' but no one thought to invite him. 'It's lucky nobody made a tape,' said McCartney's Wings colleague Denny Laine. 'The music was terrible, absolute rubbish.' Clapton complained that it was impossible to stop Laine's then-wife, Jo Jo, from hogging the limelight. But between the cocktails and the showboaters the three Beatles and assorted friends stumbled through such familiar material as 'Get Back',

'Sgt Pepper' and 'Lawdy Miss Clawdy'. 'I feel that I want to do one like that again,' said Starkey afterwards, 'with just the four of us, once Sean Lennon is five and John starts playing again.'

George Harrison's wedding to Olivia Arias the previous year had been a much quieter affair, following a month after the birth of their son Dhani. 'He's one of the few morally good people that rock 'n' roll has produced,' said his friend Eric Idle. 'He's extremely generous, and he backs and supports all sorts of people that you'll never, ever hear of.' A typically selfless gesture was his agreement to fund the film *Monty Python's Life of Brian*. 'George had been thinking about setting up a film company,' recalled director Terry Jones, 'so he talked to Denis O'Brien, his manager.' The pair formed HandMade Films, under the control of O'Brien's Euroatlantic company. 'George paid for the whole thing; he mortgaged his house and raised the money,' Idle said. 'He paid for it because he wanted to see it. The most anybody's ever paid for a cinema ticket in history.' The film was a box-office success, ensuring that the Harrisons were not evicted from their home, though the musician did receive letters from American Christians threatening they would never listen to his music again. The Pythons never forgot the risk that Harrison and O'Brien had taken. 'No wonder they were nervous,' Jones noted.

Richard Starkey's advisers had arranged a route for his income that involved investment companies in London, the Virgin Islands and the Bahamas – the Caribbean offering copious tax havens. O'Brien appeared to be another financial wizard. When he took over the management of the Python troupe, he dazzled the comedians by talking of 'the bizarre journey that some of our earnings will make, via Holland, Panama and Switzerland', as Michael Palin noted at the time. 'Denis speaks of all this with the zeal of a fiendishly clever scientist who cannot help but be light years ahead of governments and bureaucracy and officialdom . . . When we re-emerge, we have all become accomplices in something most of us don't understand.' George Harrison's business interests enjoyed equally exotic locations, with production companies based in Switzerland and the Cayman Islands. The complex corporate map also involved such recherché companies as the Swiss-based Glenbrook Securities Corporation and Harrison's own Clog Holdings, officially resident in another Caribbean hideaway, the Netherlands Antilles. Harrison trusted O'Brien implicitly; as Palin recounted, 'dependable Denis' was introducing all his clients to a 'wonderland of vastly increased wealth'.

There were other methods of wealth creation available to the ex-Beatles, especially Paul McCartney, the one member of the group who retained a work ethic that bordered on the obsessive. In 1978 his solo contract with EMI/Capitol expired. After a bidding war, the Eastmans secured him a lavish set of deals that involved his signing to Columbia Records for North America with a contract that involved the transfer of one of Columbia's richest publishing catalogues to MPL. The deal allowed McCartney to record for another label under one specific circumstance: a reunion of the Beatles.

Elsewhere in the world, McCartney remained with EMI. As a reward, the company agreed the 'McCartney override', a slight but significant amendment to the Beatles' royalty structure. The group's existing deal – based on a long-standing verbal agreement between the quartet – ensured that their earnings were split into four equal portions. The McCartney override, which operated from 1 January 1979, destroyed that agreement.

His bonus apparently ensured him an additional royalty believed to be about 2 per cent. As a comparison, the four Beatles shared a 2.5 per cent royalty on the *Please Please Me* album; 5 per cent on *With the Beatles*, *A Hard Day's Night* and *Beatles For Sale*; and 15 per cent on all their albums after that, although all these figures were based on 90 per cent of the gross income, to allow for the proverbial 'breakages'. If this estimation of the override were correct, Lennon, Harrison and Starkey would each receive 3.45 pence from each pound earned by *Sgt. Pepper*, against McCartney's 5.45 pence. The difference would be more dramatic on *Please Please Me*: three of the Beatles would earn just 0.56 pence apiece, while McCartney's take was 2.56 pence, almost five times as much. The arrangement remained a secret – guarded most carefully of all from Lennon, Harrison and Starkey. It represented a major triumph for the negotiating skills of McCartney's family financiers but a departure from the mutual trust that had once fired the band. McCartney, however, could have retorted that all trust had vanished when his fellow Beatles signed with Allen Klein. There was a solid case for arguing that he was merely compensating himself for the $5 million deal with Klein that Ono had secured two years earlier.

EMI certainly had no qualms about favouring McCartney, the only

Beatle who demonstrated loyalty to the company. In late 1977 he had released 'Mull of Kintyre', a Scottish folk ballad that became the best-selling single in UK history, supplanting the Beatles' 'I Want to Hold Your Hand' and 'She Loves You'. Two years later the publishers of the *Guinness Book of Records* awarded him a unique rhodium disc to commemorate his stature as the most successful musician of all time. The quality of his output remained erratic, and so did his ability to maintain a stable band – the Wings line-up that toured the UK in 1979 was the sixth in eight years – but his commercial instincts were undimmed.

His final live appearance of the decade was a London concert to raise money for the suffering people of Kampuchea. Three months earlier United Nations secretary general Kurt Waldheim had begged the Beatles to reunite for the related cause of the Vietnamese boat children. The *New York Post* exclaimed, 'The Beatles Are Back! Exclusive: Fab 4 Reunited For Big UN Concert In NY'. Other newspapers suggested that three of the Beatles had agreed to take part, and that only Lennon was reluctant. The speculation continued in London, where there was general disappointment that McCartney was only joined by the assorted stars who had performed at his 'Rockestra' sessions the previous year – none of them a fellow member of the Beatles.

The following month Wings prepared for their first tour of Japan. Two days before his departure, McCartney is alleged to have phoned the Dakota and told Ono that he wanted to offer Lennon 'some dynamite weed'. As usual, Ono kept him at bay. At Tokyo airport customs officials found the 'weed', barely concealed in McCartney's baggage. His fellow band members had been told 'to keep our pockets clean and to have no telltale signs' of drug use, as guitarist Steve Holly recalled. Either McCartney believed he was too famous to be searched, or subliminally he wanted to sabotage the tour – which turned out to be Wings' bathetic swansong. He was held in jail for six days, under threat of a decade's imprisonment, before being deported without charge. Some chroniclers have suggested that the Lennons tipped off the Japanese police because they didn't want McCartney to stay in their favourite hotel suite; others that Ono interceded on McCartney's behalf with the Japanese authorities. Both stories rely on a ludicrously far-fetched notion of Ono's power. In any case, McCartney confirmed that both Harrison and Lennon had sent messages of support, though Starkey didn't, explaining, 'I didn't even have his phone number.'

With Wings sidelined, McCartney issued a lacklustre solo album, donning his 1963 stage costume for a promotional video, as Harrison had done four years earlier. When, inevitably, he was quizzed about the reclusive Lennon, he said, 'The last time I asked John to write a song with me, for old time's sake, he said he was too rich to bother.' It was widely reported that Lennon was keen to sell his 25 per cent stake in Apple, abandon his multiple properties and sail around the world on a yacht called *Isis*. Instead, he set out on another numerologically approved journey, to the apartheid citadel of South Africa, from where he contacted his old flame May Pang. A decade earlier he had campaigned for political freedom; now he was happy to vacation in a country built on racial discrimination. A month later he sailed to Bermuda, where he was joined by his son Sean and his assistant Fred Seaman, who brought portable recording equipment, and Lennon began to assemble the songs for his first album in five years. Seaman alleged later that Yoko Ono was about to tell Lennon that she wanted a divorce, but changed her mind – perhaps because she glimpsed the possibility of a return to the limelight via her husband's new project. Jack Douglas, chosen as the album's producer, recalled Ono telling him, 'I'm going to have a few songs on it, and John doesn't know yet.' A few days later Lennon sent Douglas a demo tape of his new material, with a note that read, 'I think it's kind of the same old shit,' and a spoken message that the songs could always be given to Starkey if they weren't up to scratch.

Although Lennon claimed that the album had come to him in an intense flurry of inspiration, that description only applied to one song, the poignant ballad 'Woman'. The rest betrayed years of agonised patchwork, reshaping melodic and lyrical fragments until Lennon could finally bear to present them to the world. 'He wasn't sure if he could do it,' Douglas recalled. 'He was very, very insecure about this stuff. He didn't think he had it any more. He thought he was too old. He just couldn't write. He couldn't sing. He couldn't play. Nothing.'

His feeling of emptiness, his fear that his life had been meaningless, was enhanced when he read *I Me Mine*, a leather-bound anthology of George Harrison's lyrics accompanied by a brief and decidedly spotty memoir. Lennon complained that Harrison had omitted him from his life story, but neither McCartney nor the Beatles made more than cameo appearances in the text. 'George's not disowning the Beatles,' explained his ghostwriter, Derek Taylor, 'but it was a long time ago and actually a short part of his life.' It was hard enough, Taylor recalled, to persuade Harrison to mention his first wife, Pattie Boyd, let alone acknowledge an era that he wanted to forget.

When he entered the recording studio in August 1980 to record the aptly titled *Double Fantasy*, Lennon was embarrassed to discover that 'Woman' sounded like an old Beatles tune, 'because I'm still feeling that I'm supposed to be macho, Butch Cassidy or something, tough Lennon with the leather jacket and swearing and all that'. Little of that attitude translated to his new music, which was dominated by love songs for Ono, confessions of marital guilt (one with the marvellously self-abasing title 'Forgive Me My Little Flower Princess'), with just one revelatory lyric ('Watching the Wheels'), in which he mustered an unapologetic defence of his five-year seclusion.

Lennon's insecurity was almost instinctive, though the persona he offered to his fellow musicians was confident and commanding. But there were limits to his power. Two compelling performances with the band Cheap Trick were vetoed by Ono, who – ignorant of the group's commercial profile – complained, 'Why should they get a free ride on John's coat-tails?' As Jack Douglas explained, 'John loved [the tracks], but he was not one to argue with Mother. Plus he was trying to get laid at that time, and he was having a hard time, so John wasn't going to argue with her.'

Douglas claimed that 'very rarely did I ever have [the Lennons] in the room at the same time. It just didn't work. John always wanted to get into Yoko's stuff and she could not bear it. There was already too much competition between those two.' Ono was definitely present, however, on the day Paul McCartney phoned the studio, asking to speak to Lennon. Instead, he reached Ono, who told him that Lennon could not be disturbed. 'John was looking to get hooked up with Paul, to do some writing,' Douglas said later. 'I can't speak for Yoko. Maybe she thought it'd be a distraction. I don't think it would have been.' One more opportunity for a Lennon/McCartney reunion had passed.

The couple allowed reporters from *Playboy* magazine – its ethos at odds with their feminist stance – to shadow them during the sessions. Then they ruined *Playboy*'s exclusive by talking to *Newsweek*, who published the Lennons' first interview in five years. Ono confirmed that they were planning to shed their shares in Apple; Lennon spoke eloquently about how his retreat from fame had enabled him to regain touch with his inner self, beyond the Beatle image. In 1970 his *Rolling Stone* interview had complemented his *Plastic Ono Band* album. Ten years on, his rhetoric outstripped *Double Fantasy*. Where his music sounded hesitant and forced, his conversation was vivid, witty and focused. And once again he used the press to denigrate his former colleagues and their music, and to promote the image of his choice: a loving husband and father who had a clear vision of his own humanity and the pitfalls of celebrity, and who had been seized by a gloriously uncontrollable spasm of creativity.

In mid-September 1980 Lennon and Ono agreed to sign with Geffen Records. Lennon told David Geffen that he didn't care about his own success; this was Ono's moment to shine. And most critics agreed, reckoning her contributions more contemporary (and hence relevant) than her husband's. Charles Shaar Murray, who had recorded with Lennon in 1971, noted that 'all the most interesting material on *Double Fantasy* is Yoko's . . . I wish that Lennon had kept his big happy mouth shut until he had something to say that was even vaguely relevant to those of us not married to Yoko Ono.' But Lennon's fans were simply delighted that *Double Fantasy* existed, and it was soon selling in respectable, if not incendiary, style.

The album was presented to executives at Geffen's distributor, Warner Brothers, in late September. That afternoon Lennon's old friend Derek Taylor arrived at Warners with the master tapes of a George Harrison album, *Somewhere in England*. 'Later I found that John's album had been much the better received,' Taylor recalled. Warners president Mo Ostin told him, 'If George wants a million-seller, it's not on here. It's not current, and it won't sell.' Ostin invoked a clause in Harrison's contract whereby Warners could reject a maximum of four songs, and asked for changes. 'If that's what they want, they can have it,' Harrison told Taylor, and he returned to the studio in November with four new songs, including an assault on the short-sightedness of record executives entitled 'Blood From a Clone'.

First another project had to be completed. That summer Richard Starkey had approached his three former colleagues for assistance in making a record. McCartney was the first to agree, supervising a series of sessions in July. Four months later Starkey visited Harrison's home studio before flying to New York with his girlfriend, actor Barbara Bach, for dinner with the Lennons. It was the night after Thanksgiving, and the two couples celebrated in style. Lennon promised to work with Starkey in January, and handed over a tape of several new songs. 'He was really up,' Starkey recalled.

That morning Paul McCartney had appeared on TV's *Good Morning America*. He was asked why Lennon seemed, in his *Newsweek* interview, to resent him. 'I don't know,' McCartney replied. 'I actually keep a bit quiet now because anything I say he gets a bit resentful. It's a weird one. I don't quite know why he thinks like that. I really just shut up these days.' If there was an edge to McCartney's voice, it was because he was feeling jilted. According to Jack Douglas, McCartney and Lennon had agreed to collaborate on material for Starkey to record. 'There was a writing session that was cancelled by a third party,' Douglas claimed. '[John] was waiting for Paul to show up. He was told that Paul did not show. Paul was told John was too busy.' At least McCartney could relish his memory of their final phone call: 'It was just a very happy conversation about his family, my family . . . I remember he said, "Oh God, I'm like Aunt Mimi, padding round here in me dressing gown . . . This housewife wants a career!"'

The next day Lennon visited Apple's New York lawyers, who were preparing a court case against the producers of *Beatlemania*. He swore an affidavit, which included the startling statement: 'I and the three other former Beatles have plans to stage a reunion concert, to be recorded, filmed and marketed around the world.' The claim was obviously designed to reinforce the case against the imitation Beatles by suggesting that their activities might impinge on the authentic version of the group. But it amounted to little less than perjury as there was no definite plan for a reunion. One of Lennon's staff attempted to contact McCartney at MPL to ask him to support the deposition, but without success.*

---

* There was a strange addendum to Lennon's affidavit: that week the New York Parks Department was approached by an unknown organisation asking if it would be possible for the city to prepare a feasibility study for a Beatles reunion concert in Central Park. The details are lost in time; all that remains is this tantalising fragment of a rumour, which might have been nothing more than an attempt to justify Lennon's sworn testimony.

Between 5 and 8 December Lennon and Ono undertook a second wave of promotional interviews for their album, taking in the BBC, RKO Radio and *Rolling Stone* magazine. He talked excitedly to Jack Douglas about his plans to return to Britain after New Year as part of a world tour, and admitted that he was looking forward to re-arranging Beatles standards such as 'She Loves You' and 'I Want to Hold Your Hand'. On 6 December he phoned his Aunt Mimi to tell her he was coming home.

Two days later Lennon rose early after a late-night session with Douglas working on Ono's eerie rock-disco track 'Walking on Thin Ice'. He ate breakfast around the corner from the Dakota and had a haircut, while Ono phoned journalist Ray Connolly in London to invite him to interview Lennon the following day. His cheeks rash-raw after a clumsy shave, Lennon posed for a photo session with Annie Leibovitz, looking skeletally thin but controlled and intense. 'This is the way we used to wear our hair,' he said proudly of his 1950s hoodlum cut, 'but it takes a lot of keeping up.' He undertook a lengthy radio interview, dismissing the spirit of the 1960s with an intensity that suggested a man high on adrenaline or more artificial stimulants. Then he signed a copy of *Double Fantasy* for a chubby, strangely reticent fan in the entrance to the Dakota and rode downtown in a limousine with Ono to the Record Plant studio.

'We were really celebrating, the three of us,' Douglas recalled a few days later. 'Everything was going right at that point.' In retrospect, however, he confessed to a more chilling memory of Lennon's final session: 'There were some strange things said in the control room. I don't want to talk about it. I erased the tape because it was a real painful tape.' To this day he refuses to discuss the subject further, leaving boundless scope for speculation about what he heard – Lennon predicting his imminent death, perhaps? There have been rumours that Lennon was seriously ill; that his pale, tightly etched features owed less to a careful dietary regime than to the onset of cancer or an equally brutal disease. Douglas's enigmatic comments lend an enduring sense of mystery to the final hours of Lennon's life.

When David Geffen arrived around 9 p.m. that night, he found no hint of doom: 'When I walked in, John was smiling and jumping around, dancing. He said, "Wait'll you hear Yoko's record. It's a smash!"' Geffen suggested they have dinner the following night, though they didn't need to decide yet where they were going. 'He said, "Yeah, that's right,"' Geffen recalled. 'And we said goodbye.'

'They wanted to get something to eat,' Douglas recalled. 'John was going to head over to the Stage Deli and get some sandwiches, and then go home. Normally I rode home with them, but I had another project to do. The last thing John said to me was, "See you tomorrow morning, bright and early" . . . I saw him with his new leather jacket that he'd gotten at the Gap a few weeks earlier, which he loved, and just this big smile on his face.'

Lennon and Ono walked outside to the limousine, and during the journey they talked briefly about where they could get some food. They arrived home at 10.54 p.m. EST; six minutes later and the entrance to the Dakota would have been locked against intruders. Their driver could have taken them inside the safety of the courtyard, but Lennon asked him to stop at the kerb. He got out of the car first, and strode towards the entrance, clutching cassettes of Ono's song. As he neared the cubicle where the night guard was sitting, a voice called from the shadows: 'Mr Lennon?' Then there was only a barrage of noise that echoed through his head. He stumbled forward a few paces, out of the instinct to survive, and fell to the ground. A torrent of blood, fragments of bone and fleshy tissues surged in his chest and was propelled out of his mouth, and oozed from the wounds torn in his torso and neck. His face was grotesquely squashed against the floor. There was a gurgle, which might have been a word lost in the ebb of his life force, and slowly his body rolled onto its side, having served its final purpose. Then the scene reels away, as if in horror, to a world from which John Lennon would always be absent.

Chapter 9

It doesn't matter how many times we deny the reunion stories,
it'll still go on. Even if there's only one of us left, they'll say he's
getting it together with himself.
Richard Starkey, 1981

'We had talked about living until we were 80,' Yoko Ono told a reporter
two days afterwards. 'We even drew up lists of all the things we could
do together for all those years.' 'Three or four days after it happened,'
recalled Jack Douglas, 'Yoko and I went back into the studio and put
together some collages with John's voice and music. We did that for
two nights. That seemed to provide some kind of therapy or release.'
By then the body had been cremated and the ashes returned to the
Dakota. The final picture of John Lennon was obtained by the *National
Enquirer*: his body lay on the mortuary slab, showing obvious signs of
the autopsy knife. 'I kept telling my staff, who were hiding razors and
newspapers from me, to show me everything,' Ono revealed later. 'I
saw the death photo. John looked peaceful, like in the back of the
Imagine cover.' But rumours persist that the autopsy was filmed and
that mortuary attendants posed for grotesque pictures with the corpse.

Since the death of John F. Kennedy speculation has been the coda
to American assassination. Conspiracy theorists soon found the hand of
the FBI or CIA in Lennon's murder, his killer acting under sophisticated mind control like Sirhan Sirhan, who shot Robert Kennedy in

1968, or a hapless patsy like Lee Harvey Oswald. Paranoia hinted that the newly elected President Reagan must have ordered the hit, to prevent Lennon from leading a renaissance of the counterculture. But Lennon's final interviews lent more weight to the killer's own story, that he had shot his hero because he felt betrayed by the former Beatle's materialistic lifestyle.

After more than a decade of public ridicule, Ono was now portrayed as the grieving widow. 'For ten years I was the devil,' she noted wryly. 'Now I'm an angel. Did the world have to lose John for people to change their opinion of me? It's unreal. If it brought John back, I'd rather be hated.' She pleaded with Lennon's fans to control their grief after hearing that two had committed suicide. She organised a global vigil in her husband's memory. She solicited charitable donations, to be handled by the couple's Spirit Foundation. She said that people should not be afraid to profit from Lennon's name by selling magazines or posters, but that they should not exploit him or his followers. She penned a message to her husband, reproduced inside a tribute issue of *Rolling Stone* magazine: 'I love you I miss you You're with god I'll do what I said "Yoko hold on" I'll make sure I promise xx'. And a month after his death she asked fans not to harbour thoughts of revenge: 'The only "revenge" that would mean anything to us is to turn the society around in time, to one that is based on love and trust as John felt it could be.'

Double Fantasy went to No. 1 all over the world, as Lennon had hoped it would. So did singles new and old. The McCartneys visited Ono at the Dakota. 'We all cried so hard,' McCartney recalled. Lennon's elder son, Julian, announced his intention to live with Ono. 'Yoko was in a terrible state,' he revealed. 'She breaks down when she goes places she went with Dad, or if a programme comes on that they watched together.'

Shortly after Lennon's death his long-time friend Bill Harry paid tribute: 'So many dreams were killed with him, so many potential rock masterpieces lost forever, all speculation about a Beatles reunion finally laid to rest.' By early February 1981 the speculation had undergone a miraculous resurrection. Paul McCartney flew to Montserrat, where Beatles producer George Martin had installed a state-of-the-art studio, to begin work on a solo album. The studio manager revealed that McCartney was planning to record with both Harrison and Starkey;

'John Lennon may well have been on the album as well if he had still been alive.' A guest at the sessions was the Beatles' long-time friend rockabilly pioneer Carl Perkins. He played McCartney a song he had just written, entitled 'My Old Friend'. 'After I finished,' he recalled,

Paul was crying, tears were rolling down his pretty cheeks, and Linda said, 'Carl, thank you so much.' I said, 'Linda, I'm sorry, I didn't mean to make you cry.' She said, 'But he's crying, and he needed to. He hasn't been able to really break down since that happened to John.' And she put her arm around me and said, 'But how did you know?' I said, 'Know what?' She said, 'There's two people in the world that know what John Lennon said to Paul, the last thing he said to him. But now there's three, and one of them's you, you know it.' I said, 'Girl, you're freaking me out! I don't know what you're talking about!' She said that the last words that John Lennon said to Paul in the hallway of the Dakota building were, he patted him on the shoulder and said, 'Think about me every now and then, old friend.'

And that, with minor alterations, was the chorus line of Perkins' song. 'McCartney really feels that Lennon sent me that song, he really does.'

Later, Perkins played the song to George Harrison. 'Well, Paul has told me,' Harrison said, 'John will come back, there'll be another thing that'll hit you some day.' The three ex-Beatles were now in more frequent contact than at any time since 1969. 'We were constantly talking to each other but saying nothing,' Starkey said of the aftermath of Lennon's death. 'We were just phoning up to check everyone was OK. "Hi, George." "Hi, Ringo." "Well, well, well." "Oh dear, oh dear, oh dear." There was nothing you could really say at the beginning. We were just stunned.'

Music was their most eloquent form of communication. There was no reunion on Montserrat, although Starkey did participate in McCartney's sessions. Harrison took a song he had originally offered to Starkey, entitled 'All Those Years Ago', and wrote new lyrics pertaining to Lennon. He invited the McCartneys and Denny Laine to add background vocals, and George Martin to supervise the session. Starkey wasn't present, although his drumming appeared on the track. 'All Those Years Ago' was banal and inappropriately jaunty, but the fact that it featured all three Beatles ensured it was seen as their official tribute to their fallen colleague. Meanwhile, McCartney channelled his impossible feelings into another song, 'Here Today'. 'Paul is a complex guy,' Denny Laine commented later. 'He is the best person I have met in all my life at hiding his innermost feelings.' His lyrics, with their imaginary characters and cartoon situations, often reinforced Laine's judgement. But 'Here Today' came from a different place. It was self-conscious, perhaps because McCartney wasn't used to expressing his emotions so clearly. But his sincerity was unmistakable, as he told Lennon what he could never have said to his face: I love you.

Around this time McCartney had several 'strange conversations' with Beatles biographer Hunter Davies. He kept going back to his relationship with Lennon, like a child picking at a scab: 'John and I were really army buddies. That's what it was like, really. I realise now we never got to the bottom of each other's souls. We didn't know the truth. Some fathers turn out to hate their sons. You never know.' Each sentence needed to be deciphered like a gnostic text. Maybe, McCartney told himself, he and Lennon had never been as close as he had imagined. Then he turned the argument on its head: now Lennon was his surrogate father, and 'Some fathers turn out to hate their sons.' The only certainty was that Lennon was gone and he remained. The rest? 'You never know.' As he admitted in his first formal interview after the murder, 'I thought it all. I went through it all.' But it became no clearer or less painful; there could be no resolution without the one thing he could not have: validation from his old friend.

Time passed, and the world continued. Yoko Ono issued the single that represented Lennon's final work, and 'Walking on Thin Ice' suggested that he had glimpsed a way of moving into the future rather than relying on echoes of the past. In June 1981 she released *Season of Glass*, a chillingly fragile album haunted by the tragedy. 'Eighty per cent of my power and personality is being an artist,' she explained later, 'and I had to live. I had to survive. I would have gone crazy or become very ill if I didn't do that.' One song, 'No No No', tackled her grief via the language of sexual dysfunction; the track opened with a flurry of gunshots and a heart-rending scream. Where Harrison was glib and McCartney sentimental, Ono had the courage to be real. Attention focused on the cover, which pictured the blood-spattered glasses Lennon was wearing when he was shot. 'People are offended,' she admitted. 'Well, there was a dead body, you know. I wanted the whole world to be reminded of what happened. If people can't take the picture of glasses because they're bloody, I'm sorry but I'm not sorry. John had to stomach a whole lot more. His whole body was bloody. There was lots of blood all over the floor. That's the reality.' But her exploration of darkness ended there. Subsequent albums showed a surprising talent for experimental pop, and remained resolutely positive in a conscious attempt to maintain Lennon's credo that 'all you need is love' to 'imagine'. 'It's a blessing,' she would say relentlessly of everything that happened, offering a benediction to Lennon or some unnamed deity.

Beyond grief, there was always business. *Sunday Times* journalist Philip Norman had been working on a Beatles biography for three years, but benefited from his timing: the boldly titled *Shout! The True Story of the Beatles* appeared to great acclaim in March 1981. 'John Lennon was the Beatles,' Norman declared on US breakfast TV, thereby winning an invitation to tea from Ono; McCartney must have seen the broadcast, as he held an otherwise unfathomable grudge against the book. Jack Douglas wasn't invited to the Dakota, however. The producer of *Double Fantasy* contacted Ono, wondering when he would receive his royalties, and 'I got a nasty letter. Almost like, "Fuck you, you're not getting anything." All kinds of nasty business went down after that. All I could ever think of was that I knew too much. She suspected that everyone who knew a lot was gonna write a book. But I made enough in the royalties, and she really lost a good friend.'

The Beatles' empire continued to keep the legal profession afloat. In February 1981 a court in New York awarded Bright Tunes – owned by Allen Klein – $587,000 as compensation for the damage caused to their copyright by 'My Sweet Lord'. The sum was exactly what Klein had paid to purchase the company, the judge clearly feeling it would be immoral for Harrison's ex-manager to profit from the deal. 'It's a total joke,' Harrison said. The saga finally ended in 1990 with copyright of both 'My Sweet Lord' and 'He's So Fine' awarded to Harrison in Britain and North America, and to Klein elsewhere.

Yet this apparently endless case would be outstripped by another legal marathon. In 1978 Apple managing director Neil Aspinall learned that a young computer company in California was using the Apple name and a fruity logo. He filed a suit claiming infringement of the Beatles' copyright. The two companies eventually agreed that Apple

Computers would only use its name and logo on computing products, and it would never stray into the music business. Indeed, Apple Computers founder Steve Jobs admitted that he had chosen Apple as his company's name because it reminded him of his musical heroes. And here the case rested until it rose zombie-like later in the decade.

There was no shortage of opportunities to make money. Albert Goldman, who had appalled fans of Elvis Presley with a biography that accentuated the star's failings and frailties, signed a $1 million deal for a book about Lennon. Scurrilous 'revelations' were offered by Ono's tarot card reader, Lennon's assistant at the Dakota and assorted survivors from the NEMS and Apple payrolls. Those who couldn't muster a book depended on a magazine or newspaper exposé, such as the 'exclusives' credited to Wings guitarist Denny Laine. 'He wrote two articles,' retorted Linda McCartney. 'One said I led Paul around totally, the other that Paul totally dominated me. I thought Denny came off badly.'

Laine's disaffection with McCartney probably stemmed from the decision, formally announced in May 1981, to disband Wings. Laine insisted that he'd quit before he was sacked. 'Paul is doing other things, that's all,' said McCartney's press spokesman Tony Brainsby. As the group's drummer Steve Holly recalled, 'I picked up the *Evening Standard* and read that Wings had broken up. I rang Paul up and said, "What's this?" and he replied, "Well, I'd been meaning to tell you."' We just picked the wrong people,' Linda McCartney said ungraciously of Wings' multiple incarnations. '[Paul] needed the band to work with, but he had to carry almost all the weight. None of the Wings were good enough to play with him. They were good, but not great.' Years later McCartney admitted, 'To me there was always a feeling of letdown, because the Beatles had been so big that anything I did had to compare directly with them.'

Working as a solo artist hereafter, McCartney no longer needed to display even the faintest hint of democracy. Every musician was for hire and could be replaced. The one person who had the power to challenge him was George Martin, whom he courageously chose to produce three early 1980s albums. Martin laid down his terms, rejecting most of the songs McCartney auditioned for him. As a gesture of rebellion, the musician revived one of the rejects. 'He thought it was worthwhile,' Martin recalled, 'and he was hammering himself into the ground. I went in and said, "Paul, it's not working." He said, "Why isn't it working?" looking at me accusingly. "Because the song's not good enough." He looked at me and there was a kind of stand-off; and then he said, "Do you think I don't know?"' Eventually McCartney chose to work with producers who would be more wary about questioning his judgement.

Richard Starkey wielded less power than his former colleague. When he delivered his first album after Lennon's death, it was turned down despite cameos from Harrison and McCartney. Only after much revision was the playful *Stop and Smell the Roses* released in late summer 1981, to minimal sales and critical disdain. Nor was Starkey able to escape entirely unscathed from the legal cavalcade. In April 1981 his ex-girlfriend Nancy Andrews filed a suit against him in the LA Superior Court, claiming more than $5 million as her share of his earnings during their relationship. The trigger was the news that Starkey was planning to marry Barbara Bach. He had been wary of television since a disastrous chat show appearance in 1979, when his alcohol-soaked performance endangered a lifetime of goodwill. But he and Bach were under contract to promote their feeble film comedy *Caveman*, and TV allowed the couple to publicise their most valuable asset – their celebrity. It also exposed Starkey to public scrutiny of his reaction to Lennon's death – visibly shaken on *The Barbara Walters Special*, grimly fatalistic on *Donahue*, almost tearful on *Good Morning America*. 'He'd like to smile,' he told one audience, before looking up and addressing his old friend: 'How are you doing, Johnny?' More often, he leaned on an actor's repertoire of tricks to avoid displaying the depth of his emotion, employing gallows humour, gulping down his tears or biting his lips to distract him from his pain.

Lennon's absence clouded the wedding of Richard Starkey and Barbara Bach on 27 April 1981. The three Beatles and their wives posed for their first joint portrait since 1969, suggesting that if Lennon had lived the ceremony might have achieved the reunion that Sid Bernstein and the United Nations could not. The press claimed to have witnessed 'the days of Beatlemania all over again on a small scale', as a few hundred fans 'screamed and shouted and one even fainted'. To his delight, Harrison's arrival at the register office was scarcely noticed, so seldom had he been seen in recent years. An array of instruments was delivered to the reception at Rags, a celebrity haunt in Mayfair, in case the Beatles wished to perform together. 'Paul played the piano and Ringo was playing the spoons,' said photographer Terry O'Neill. 'It was fabulous.' *Life* magazine printed a photograph of McCartney behind the piano, Harrison sporting a guitar and Starkey – suitably enough – armed with a champagne bucket. Yoko Ono was not invited to the party. 'They felt intimidated about inviting me, because it was really not the right time to encounter people being happy,' she observed. 'But it would have been nice to have been told about it.'

A fiendishly complex etiquette now surrounded Ono's role as Lennon's widow. EMI Records was exploring the possibility of plucking unreleased Beatles material from its archive but had a 'gentleman's agreement' with the group not to release anything without their approval. 'Yoko Ono doesn't enter into this, because it's strictly an artistic decision and she's not a Beatle,' said a company spokesman. But after her husband's death she chose not to sell the family portion of Apple and appointed herself the guardian of his artistic heritage – and effectively a voting member of the Beatles. Moreover, she and McCartney were now the joint curators of the Lennon/McCartney songwriting empire. 'I had so many responsibilities,' she recalled. 'There was so much I had to do as Yoko Ono Lennon, that I forgot about being Yoko Ono.'

Still doubting the depth of his relationship with Lennon, McCartney needed to deal with Ono on some level of intimacy. He often telephoned after the murder, and then kept phoning, until eventually Ono asked him why he was so keen to keep in touch. 'I think I've misunderstood you,' McCartney admitted. 'Don't do me any favours,' Ono retorted. 'I don't want any charity.' A few weeks later he tried again. 'Look, I'm real nervous about making this phone call,' he began. 'You're nervous?' Ono replied. 'You're kidding! I'm more nervous than you!' That broke the ice, and in April 1982 the McCartneys, the Eastmans and the Ono-Lennons met in New York at Le Cirque.

Under discussion was the vexed issue of the Northern Songs catalogue. Sir Lew Grade, whose ATV corporation had bought the publishing rights to Lennon/McCartney's songs in 1969, was nearing retirement, and had offered to sell Northern back to McCartney for £20 million. 'I gulped, thinking, Oh my God, I wrote them for nothing! Your own children are going to be sold back to you at a price,' McCartney recalled. By his account, he offered Ono the chance to be part of the deal, and she claimed that she could call in some favours and get the price reduced to £5 million. She later disputed this story, but either way Grade was soon ousted during a boardroom tussle, and the opportunity was lost.

Ono's bereavement had won her an unprecedented level of public support. Gradually, however, sympathetic profiles began to be balanced by more negative reporting – much of it provoked by her 18-year-old stepson Julian Lennon. Having elected to move to New York, he returned home in October 1981, admitting, 'Yoko's OK, but she doesn't mean anything more to me than the fact that she was married to my father.' He naively seemed to relish publicity, and was soon complaining about the meagre stipend (£150 per week) he received from the Lennon estate. Once again Ono was portrayed as a witch-like figure: 'Dad was always totally under her influence. She is a very strong person. She has a lot of power. She is a bit scary too.' Ono herself sent out contradictory signals, asking, 'I don't intend to spend the rest of my life alone, but could I bring another man into all this?' as she gestured at the pictures of Lennon that filled the Dakota, while being seen arm in arm with antique dealer Sam Havadtoy, her close companion for nearly two decades. More damaging were the revelations of tarot card reader John Green, the first of the Dakota insiders to break ranks. He claimed that the Lennons' sex life had been perfunctory, and that Ono regarded contact with her husband 'as an assault on her person. When this happened, John would go out to whorehouses' or, so Green alleged, grope other women in front of Ono, in the hope she might find it erotic. True or not, each tabloid revelation widened the chasm between two irreconcilable legends, each kept alive by the media: the romantic ballad of John and Yoko, and the *noir* portrait of a couple in distress.

Similar stories were being printed about Starkey: less than a year after his marriage, there were reports of explosive quarrels in Caribbean hotels and a relationship that 'could crash-land at any time'. Twelve months earlier the same exploitative newspapers had alleged that the McCartney marriage was on the verge of disintegration; only Harrison remained immune from this forced exposure.* Yet behind the walls

---

* Not entirely immune. A collection of pseudonymous reminiscences by Hollywood prostitutes, *You'll Never Make Love In This Town Again* by Robin, Liza, Linda and Tiffany (Pan Books, London, 1996), contained a lurid account of Harrison being serviced by 'Liza' while strumming happily on his ukulele. In the cover blurb, Harrison's name was bracketed with the likes of Jack Nicholson and Warren Beatty as one of 'Hollywood's users and abusers'.

of his Henley-on-Thames mansion the most secretive of the Beatles was confronting his own demons. 'George was always worried that somebody would try to kill him,' revealed Colin Harris, who had worked for Harrison since 1975. 'He kept himself hidden and was even afraid to go for a walk in the garden. There was a time – a few years after Lennon was shot – when he wouldn't go out. We didn't see him for three months. He brought in security men and they patrolled the grounds day and night. One went everywhere with George.' His sister Louise concurred: 'George was finding fame very intrusive. But that was a family trait, in a way; we all preferred it when it was peaceful.' So complete was Harrison's withdrawal that when he issued his 1982 album *Gone Troppo* he refused to publicise it, effectively sabotaging the agreeable but low-key record's commercial chances.

McCartney was too conscientious a trouper to neglect the PR machine. In early 1982 he delicately tested the waters of self-publicity for *Tug of War*, an adult pop album that was his most successful venture since the height of Wings' popularity. Like a penitent, he submitted to public displays of his grief, weeping gently while listening to Lennon's 'Beautiful Boy' on the BBC's *Desert Island Discs* and appearing uncharacteristically numb during interviews. Earlier media encounters had barely grazed the surface, but now he seemed to welcome the pressure, as if it would assuage some obscure sense of guilt. 'I would've liked to have seen [Lennon] the day before [his death],' he admitted, 'and just straightened everything out. There was a lot left unsaid.' Compulsive truth-telling now replaced the spinning of myths: 'People like a loser, people like to feel there is something wrong with you. Now, with someone like me, I cover up what's wrong . . . I'd like to be a whole lot looser.' The tragedy seemed to have had only one cathartic result: 'A thing like that, it's very final – end of an era. It really wrapped up the Beatle thing for me.' He confirmed, 'One of the things we'd been consciously aware of with the Beatles was to leave them laughing, and we thought we'd done that, you know. We didn't want to come back as decrepit old rockers.'

The commercial potency of the Beatles was illustrated once again in 1982. Anniversary festivals had once been the domain of the royal family, designed to celebrate the silver or golden jubilee of a monarch's reign. But now the baby-boomer generation had seized control of the media, it was determined that nobody should forget its tumultuous rise to power. The twentieth anniversary of the Beatles' emergence spawned a documentary film, copious press coverage and a comprehensive reissue campaign which carried 'Love Me Do' into the British Top 10.

McCartney now embarked on a project that was intended to acknowledge his glorious past and to extend it. Cinema was a medium that he was desperate to conquer, not least because George Harrison's HandMade Films was emerging as a major player in the British film industry. As his abortive collaboration with Isaac Asimov had shown, McCartney was determined to mythologise his own stardom. Although he had been dubious about the merits of Willy Russell's dramatic representation of the Beatles, he asked the playwright to prepare a script in the late 1970s – the proviso being that it had to revolve around Wings' *Band on the Run* album. Once again McCartney was dissatisfied with the results, so he tried again, with the dramatist Tom Stoppard. But none of these collaborations produced the results that McCartney had anticipated, so he decided that he had no alternative but to write his own script.

As a master of musical spontaneity and melodic invention, McCartney had every reason to trust his talent. Recognising his limitations had never been one of his strengths though, and accepting negative feedback from his peers was also a challenge. The result was *Give My Regards to Broad Street*, one of the most disastrous episodes in British film history. Written by and starring McCartney, it was the story of a much-loved superstar who finds himself under threat from a mysterious businessman when the tapes for his new album go missing. With dialogue so flat it wouldn't have disturbed a spirit level, and a plot built around the storyteller's creakiest cliché ('It was all a dream'), *Broad Street* was weighted against success. McCartney's wooden performance as a man of the people compounded the misery. Despite one academic's subsequent claim that the film was an unconscious re-enactment of his 'psychosexual matrimony' with John Lennon, the most benign interpretation was that McCartney was attempting to convey the trauma he had experienced during Allen Klein's reign at Apple. ('What I'd like to know is, how did we get involved with that Roth character?' the screen McCartney asks.) But the film's portrait of the music business was laughably unrealistic, robbing the narrative of any drama or purpose.

Equally pointless was McCartney's decision to re-record several Beatles songs for the film's soundtrack. Richard Starkey, who played a cameo role in the movie, refused to participate in the remakes, apparently telling McCartney, 'I've already played on them once. Why would I want to do it again?'

There were compensations from the project – the soundtrack included a worldwide hit single – but his devotion to the film apparently put a strain on his marriage, to the point where he was forced to deny that the relationship was 'on the rocks'. It was a frustrating period for McCartney: his *Pipes of Peace* album was markedly less successful than its predecessor, and he was said to have been furious when his joyless collaboration with Michael Jackson 'Say Say Say' failed to top the British charts. His staff were now required to sign pledges of secrecy, but even so tales emerged of his temper tantrums when his wishes weren't obeyed. Such behaviour merely proved that he was human, not a saint, but it didn't gel with the image of an ageless, happy-go-lucky charmer.

McCartney could content himself perhaps with the announcement in late 1983 that he was now officially the richest entertainer in the world. Journalist Laurence Shames, the author of a 1980 *Esquire* article about Lennon's wealth that had apparently influenced Mark Chapman to murder his hero, noted pointedly, 'The mistake most people make is to still regard the Beatles as the young, boyish stars of fond memory. In fact, they are middle-aged men who have had lots of money for a long time, and have become conservative about it.'

George Harrison used his money as a form of insulation against the madness of the world. Besides his mansion in Henley, the guitarist now owned a sizeable spread in a remote corner of Australia, plus a beach-front residence in Nhiki, on the Hawaiian island of Maui. But his pleasure in this last paradise was tainted by the discovery that right of way allowed ramblers access to the shoreline border of his property, within view of his house. In August 1983 he launched a court battle to restrict public access, claiming that he was 'being raped by these people' and that 'privacy is the single most important thing in my life'. Ironically, the case – which was only settled in 2001 – merely robbed Harrison of more privacy, as legal documents revealed that the property was actually owned not by the musician but by obscure corporations that could be traced back to Denis O'Brien's web of

Euroatlantic companies. In the glorious tradition of Beatle-related litigation, Harrison's quest for secrecy spiralled into epic legal battles that seemed to envelop the entire population of Hawaii. By the time he had won the right to privacy in 2001, he was too ill to visit the island – the dictionary definition of a Pyrrhic victory.

Harrison's prospering film business still allowed him the luxury of such protracted engagements with the legal profession. Richard Starkey had no such reliable source of earnings; nor did his sparse songwriting catalogue generate much income. By 1983 he was reduced to narrating a banal radio history of his own career, *Ringo's Yellow Submarine*. His most recent album, the unpretentious *Old Wave*, had been rejected by both UK and US record companies, and eventually surfaced only in Germany and Canada. His career mined new depths with his portrayal of a bisexual fashion designer in the TV movie *Princess Daisy*.

Facing the ignominy of life as a professional nostalgist, living off the 'promotion fees' he was granted by Apple and the other Beatles, Starkey would have welcomed a lucrative Beatles project – for example, Neil Aspinall's documentary film *The Long and Winding Road*, which was once again under consideration. 'You'll never get them all to agree to anything,' noted Lee Eastman wryly, and he was right: at a summit meeting in July 1983 Harrison vetoed any further progress on the film.

Five months later, on 1 December 1983, the surviving Beatles and Yoko Ono endured an eight-hour legal conference at the Dorchester Hotel in London. During the preparation of a lawsuit against EMI alleging underpayment of royalties, Starkey, Harrison and Ono had discovered the existence of the McCartney override, guaranteeing their colleague a higher return from the group's record sales than they were receiving. Harrison alleged – quite wrongly – that McCartney had deliberately prevented his colleagues from sharing this increase in revenues; he was reminded that McCartney had been negotiating his own solo contract, not a Beatles deal. But McCartney was prepared to offer a compromise: he would help the others achieve the same royalty rate he was receiving, if they each agreed to give him a substantial cash payment in recompense for his co-operation. Thus united, they would be in a more powerful position to extract money from EMI.

Starkey, Harrison and Ono agreed, but the meeting soon descended into petty squabbles. Weary of hearing the same circular arguments and convinced that all their problems ultimately stemmed from the

Allen Klein contracts that he had never authorised, McCartney's patience finally snapped. Either the group came to a collective arrangement, he threatened, or he would use his veto and effectively capsize Apple. 'What about the tax?' the others asked, aware that the British government would claim almost everything if Apple were liquidated. McCartney replied that he didn't care: he'd rather lose the money than go through any more meetings like this. 'I don't need this grief,' he told his colleagues. Starkey pleaded with McCartney not to take away the promotion fees on which his financial survival depended. Eventually, the three Beatles and Ono managed to negotiate a ceasefire, McCartney promised Starkey another year's worth of support, and the weary participants left the hotel. 'Are the Beatles getting back together?' a reporter shouted at Starkey. 'Don't be daft,' was his blunt reply.

While the surviving Beatles battled over their legacy, John Lennon returned from the grave. A medium claimed to have conducted an interview with Lennon's spirit in which he revealed (in a bizarre approximation of a Scouse accent) that he was enjoying a series of unearthly affairs with dead film stars, was intending to 'materialise on television when the world is ready for it', and had just written a new song: 'You won't have a say, you won't lose your head / When at last it's your day, you're gonna be dead.' Cynics noted that death seemed to have had an adverse affect on Lennon's skills as a wordsmith.

In the absence of a reunion, physical or ghostly, EMI Records – unaware that the Beatles had them under financial surveillance – were anxious to find novel ways of exploiting the group's catalogue. In July 1983 the company opened Abbey Road's Studio 2, where most of their records had been made, to the public. Fans were treated to an audio-visual presentation that featured tantalising extracts from the group's session tapes, in professional quality. The three ex-Beatles were invited to private screenings – Harrison preferring to go alone rather than join McCartney and Starkey – and professed themselves impressed by EMI's archive work.

The company now hoped that the group might look more kindly on the release of a 'new' album of Beatles offcuts. Cassette tapes of a collection entitled *Sessions* were circulated among senior EMI executives, bearing the secretive label 'Abbey Road Project'. Release was scheduled for Christmas 1984, preceded by a single, 'Leave My Kitten Alone'. Unfortunately, this coincided with Apple's decision to sue EMI/Capitol. The group's chief US legal representative, Leonard Marks, explained, 'We have filed complaints which charge these record companies with, among other things, breach of contract and fraud, and have sought compensatory and punitive damages totalling on the order of $100 million.'

The Beatles were expert at pretending that legal action did not concern them, but this case was too serious to allow any co-operation with EMI. McCartney and Harrison filed affidavits declaring that 'they felt the quality of the work on the *Sessions* material was not up to their standards, and that's why they didn't approve the release of it in the first place'. Unfortunately for both parties, at least one Abbey Road Project cassette fell into the wrong hands, and within months bootleg release of the *Sessions* album was available on the black market, followed by several volumes of *Ultra-Rare Trax* releases containing further gems from EMI's supposedly impregnable archive.

No sooner were the Beatles united in one legal action than they were divided in another. The result was what one tabloid subeditor dubbed an AMAZING BEATLES BUST-UP. In February 1985 Harrison, Starkey and Ono filed a $8.6 million writ against McCartney in the New York Supreme Court, on the basis that he was 'earning a preferential royalty from Beatles records to the others, as an incentive for him to re-sign with Capitol as a solo artist'. EMI spokesman Bob O'Neill conceded that the allegation was correct, but that the money came from the company's share of the profits and didn't affect the sums earned by the other Beatles.

The Beatles had now reverted to the three-against-one split of the early 1970s, and once again McCartney was exposed as the apparent culprit. He resisted the option of spilling the group's financial secrets in public, held his tongue, and instead abandoned the legal dispute between Apple and EMI, believing that it would cost more than it could possibly gain. His opponents reacted by raising the stakes, claiming not only financial compensation but demanding EMI give up any rights to the Beatles' recordings. That would have had catastrophic repercussions for the company, affecting its short-term share price and its profits for decades ahead, so it was not surprising that in March 1986 a compromise was agreed. Under the terms of the deal the Beatles would receive £2.8 million in lieu of underpaid royalties, plus the freedom to delve further into EMI's overseas accounts. The musicians were now hyper-sensitive to the company's every move, and further litigation was inevitable. As Linda McCartney quipped, 'All I know is, with all the advisers and lawyers and parasites, we're putting a lot of kids through prep school and buying a lot of swimming pools.'

One kid who could afford his own pool was Julian Lennon. In late 1984 he issued an attractively crafted debut album, *Valotte*, which sold more than a million copies and spawned two Top 10 US singles. Record producer Phil Ramone, who handled the project, glimpsed the spirit of redemption at work: 'This freaky guy shoots your dad, and no matter which way you look at it, you can't recover him. But you can say, "Maybe there's a legacy here. Maybe there's something I'm supposed to do that I feel comfortable with." And use it – use it in the proper sense.' Press and public seized on the family resemblance between father and son, and before long there was speculation that the Beatles would re-form with Julian replacing John. Valiantly attempting to retain his individuality, Julian Lennon still felt compelled to end his live performances with a brace of songs from his father's repertoire, 'Stand By Me' and 'Day Tripper'. He must have wondered how much of the applause was being evoked by his name rather than his music.

Speculation about a cross-generational reunion of the Beatles was revived in July 1985, when the Live Aid concerts were staged to raise funds for the starving people of Ethiopia. McCartney was named as the headline act for the British event at Wembley Stadium, and like Harrison fourteen years earlier he was prepared to consider a Beatles reunion for a worthy cause. He recalled later that Live Aid's organiser Bob Geldof had pleaded with Harrison and Starkey to take part, 'but they declined. I don't know why.' Harrison's memory was rather different.

I was away at the time, and I got back to England the day before, or two days before, the concert. When I arrived at Heathrow airport, the press said, 'Are you doing the concert, George?' I said I didn't know anything about it. Then I read something in the papers saying, 'The Beatles are getting together.' There were a few phone calls. I think Bob Geldof phoned my office and asked if I would like to sing 'Let It Be' with Paul. But that was literally the day before the concert. And I don't know . . . well, I was jet-lagged for a start. I saw that they had everybody in the world in on this concert, and I didn't see that it would make that much difference if I wasn't.

His explanation was strangely reminiscent of McCartney's in 1971. 'You know, I have a problem, I must admit, when people try to get the Beatles together. They're still suggesting it, even though John is dead. At the time of Live Aid I didn't particularly want to go back into some situation that looked like the past. I don't want to be set up, put in a situation where I'm tricked into being in the Beatles again. If I'm going to be in them, I'd like to know up front.' So the Beatles were represented at Live Aid by McCartney (with malfunctioning microphone) and Elvis Costello, whose set consisted of 'an old Liverpool folk song' called 'All You Need Is Love'.

A similar situation arose three months later, when Carl Perkins invited all three Beatles to participate in a London TV special. Harrison and Starkey eagerly accepted, but McCartney prevaricated and then declined. He offered to make amends by filming an insert for the special, but as Perkins told him, 'Paul, it will look like it was put in there.' Officially, he was on vacation during the filming, but backstage there was speculation that he did not feel comfortable about sharing a stage with his two ex-colleagues when they were still in legal dispute. He missed out on a night of nostalgia and genuine affection for one of the creators of rock 'n' roll, who had succeeded in enticing Harrison into his first live appearance for more than a decade. Wearing a suit and a haircut that might have been teleported from the mid-1950s, Harrison reeled off favourites from the Perkins catalogue with a swagger that suggested he had spent months preparing in front of his bathroom mirror. The TV special captured the essence of the show, although it didn't reflect Starkey's increasingly disruptive behaviour as his nightly ration of alcohol took hold.

The show offered Harrison the chance to escape from an era of solitude and morose introspection. Friends reported that he often showed signs of obsession with perceived slights from the Beatles era – complaints about the way he'd been treated by McCartney or the press, misgivings about the money he'd lost in business deals and unnecessary litigation. Now he slowly began to imagine a return to public life. 'I think in some ways he is just recovering from being a Beatle,' reckoned his friend Michael Palin. 'I think he's deciding now that he can't live locked away all the time.' In an ironic restaging of his past, Harrison found himself hosting a press conference for the singer Madonna in London a few months later. She was starring in the ill-fated HandMade Films production *Shanghai Surprise*, to which Harrison contributed his first new material for several years. He displayed a wry humour and an intelligent distance from the madness of the proceedings, as if he had handed down the torment of his fame to the next generation.

The same qualities were evident in his contributions to *Fifty Years Adrift*, the autobiography of his friend and former employee Derek Taylor. A cornucopia of personal and Beatles anecdotes and memorabilia, including reproductions of letters and postcards from the group, Taylor's book was as warm, witty and wise as its author, and a worthy successor to *As Time Goes By*, penned in the aftermath of his departure from Apple in 1970. Sadly, *Fifty Years Adrift* only appeared in an extraordinarily expensive (albeit exquisitely bound) edition of just 2,000 copies. Taylor had no qualms about Harrison's reaction to his text – the two men embarked on a promotional tour together in Australia – but anticipated a more ambivalent welcome from the other Beatles. 'My turn for some stick will come,' he admitted, 'and from a surprising quarter (or half), no doubt.'

Taylor's work represented the most elegant response to the ongoing challenge of how to make money from the Beatles. Equally justified though more prosaic was *Beatle*, the first in a succession of memoirs by the group's one-time drummer Pete Best. As Beatles memorabilia began to be sold at the world's most prestigious auction houses, Paul McCartney and Yoko Ono began to build rival collections. McCartney was the first to venture into the market, buying back the letter he had sent to *Melody Maker* about a possible reunion in 1970. As his archive expanded, he leased a subterranean storeroom in central London, hinting that he might one day open a Beatles museum.

One essential collector's item eluded him, however. In the early 1980s McCartney had briefly collaborated with soul singer Michael Jackson, now the biggest-selling artist of the era. Adopting an avuncular role, McCartney advised Jackson to invest his vast earnings in music publishing, as he had done a decade earlier. 'As a joke,' he recounted, '[Jackson] looked at me and said, "I'm going to buy your songs one day." And I just said, "Great, good joke."' But in August 1985 his manager told him that Jackson had indeed bought the Northern Songs catalogue of Lennon/McCartney songs, pre-empting McCartney's attempts to lodge another joint bid with Ono. 'I haven't spoken to him since,' McCartney said 'I think he thinks it's just business. I think it's slightly dodgy to do things like that – to be someone's friend, and then to buy the rug they're standing on.' His mood wasn't improved by the obvious rapport between Jackson and Ono, who let her nine-year-old son Sean play with the inveterately childlike singer. 'Paul probably suspects there was some sort of alliance between Michael and me,' she reflected later, 'but there wasn't. I do think it's good that Michael bought the catalogue, because he's an artist rather than an ordinary businessman.' The fact that McCartney might also consider himself an artist clearly escaped her.

Even before Jackson took control of Northern Songs, Lennon/McCartney compositions had begun to appear on television commercials, Lincoln-Mercury selling their cars with 'Help!' and Schweppes' Spanish subsidiary choosing 'She Loves You'. 'There seems to be some consternation among Beatles fans if Beatles music is used in commercials,' a spokesman for ATV said, as computer company Hewlett-Packard paid £50,000 for the rights to a re-recorded version of 'We Can Work It Out'. So far, none of the advertisements had used the original recordings, but on 27 March 1987 the Beatles' performance of 'Revolution' appeared on an advertisement for Nike. In response, McCartney, Harrison and Starkey were reunited in law as they launched another court case. EMI/Capitol called the suit 'totally groundless', not least because the advert had been approved by a director of Apple: Yoko Ono. She claimed that McCartney had been the first to agree to the ad: 'Paul's office had called me and said that they had no problem with it; and I thought that if they didn't, I wouldn't either. I think it's a good thing that John's song could be used in that way, so that a younger audience who hadn't heard it could.' But McCartney rejected any commercial endorsements: 'The Beatles never did any of that. We were offered everything. We were offered Disney, Coca-Cola, the hugest deals in Christendom and beyond. And we never took them, because we thought, Nah, kind of cheapens it.'

Yet the Beatles weren't afraid to market themselves as a commodity. They were aware that they had lost millions through their manager Brian Epstein's naivety in the 1960s, and this time they were prepared. In May 1986 they signed a merchandising deal with Determined Productions Inc., who handled the image rights for Snoopy and Betty Boop. In effect the Fab Four had become little more than cartoon characters themselves, branded on T-shirts, calendars and posters. A month later Ono agreed a similar arrangement for her late husband's artwork. 'It was John's wish shortly before he died to stage an exhibition of his works,' said Lynne Clifford, who headed Ono's Bag One company. 'Yoko has made a silent promise to John's fans to keep him in their hearts by releasing the drawings.' Dozens of images were published, in books, on greetings cards and as limited-edition prints – many of them 'colorised' under Ono's supervision to make them more commercially attractive. The same ethos produced a documentary film, *Imagine: John Lennon*, which erased all unpleasantness from its subject's life. 'The John Lennon I knew was not in that movie,' said his friend Steve Gebhardt. 'You can't excise John's use of certain substances out of his life and expect to tell his story.'

Other reincarnations were better received. Many of Lennon's half-finished recordings from 1980 were issued on the 1984 album *Milk & Honey*, while subsequent records were devoted to out-takes from 1973/4, and the One To One concert. Yoko Ono's most generous gesture, however, was her decision to open the Lennon vaults to the radio network Westwood One, as the basis of a long-running, sometimes infuriating but often rewarding series entitled *The Lost Lennon Tapes*.

The Beatles' willingness to consider marketing opportunities did not extend to EMI. In 1986 the record company agreed a co-promotion with the brewers Whitbread, whereby purchasers of Heineken beer could buy a Beatles tape. 'I personally don't want to be on a beer can, or any other kind of can,' Richard Starkey complained, as Apple fired off yet another lawsuit. The Whitbread cassette was hastily withdrawn and the case added to the bulging pot of Apple–EMI litigation. Amidst this turmoil EMI began to release the Beatles' albums on compact disc in February 1987. They sold in huge quantities but inevitably provoked a court case. Ono, Harrison, Starkey and Apple sued EMI/Capitol for $40 million in July, alleging that the company had unnecessarily delayed the release of the CDs, and were underpaying them royalties on the sales.

Under the circumstances it was not surprising that McCartney was the only representative of the Beatles at a celebratory party on 1 June 1987 to mark the 20th anniversary of *Sgt Pepper* and the album's long-awaited appearance on CD. This was, quite blatantly, an Event. EMI proclaimed *Pepper* 'the most important record ever issued on compact disc' and 'the Beatles' first great album', something with which the group might not have agreed. In 1967 a simple advert in the pop papers had sufficed to announce the album's arrival. Twenty years on there was a multimedia promotional circus which involved a TV documentary and tie-in book, the latter ably assembled by Derek Taylor, and generous coverage in newspapers that would not have deigned to acknowledge the original release.

Later that week the Prince of Wales invited all three Beatles to participate in charity concerts for his Prince's Trust. McCartney had appeared a year earlier, reprising three Beatles-era songs in ebullient style alongside an array of celebrities 'by royal appointment'. The 1987 events followed a similar pattern, with stars old and new offering a tame facsimile of rock's rebellious spirit in front of an over-exuberant crowd. The fear of unpredictability that was apparent when the Beatles first appeared before a royal audience in 1963 had gone. But there was still nervousness: this would be George Harrison's first major concert appearance since 1974. Richard Starkey agreed to accompany him for a timely revival of his *Sgt Pepper* showcase 'With a Little Help From My Friends'. But McCartney was absent, openly admitting that he was retaliating for his former colleagues' non-appearance at Live Aid. 'It was all too convenient for me to pop up,' he said, suggesting that some inconvenience on their part might be required before he would agree to appear alongside Harrison and Starkey. But he conceded, 'You never know, the Beatles might feel like getting back together. But we'd do it very privately . . . If things loosen up, we might play together again. I'm in no hurry, but I'd like it. They're good guys, you know. I like them.'

McCartney now seemed increasingly preoccupied with how history would perceive his role in the Beatles. Since his death Lennon had effectively been canonised as an apostle of peace; exposés of his less attractive behaviour had scarcely tarnished his reputation. McCartney suffered by comparison: he was inconveniently alive and fallible. He could not be blamed for wanting to defend himself when he read repeated claims that the Beatles had been built entirely on Lennon's genius, with the others mere craftsmen in his shadow.

On his lacklustre 1986 album *Press to Play* McCartney made a deliberate attempt to rekindle the spontaneous spirit behind Beatles tracks such as 'I Am the Walrus'. The results were embarrassingly self-conscious, but they did allow McCartney to introduce a theme that would become little short of an obsession. He raised the subject gently: 'The funny thing is, there was a time when I was the avant-garde one in the Beatles . . . I was trying to get everyone in the group to be sort of farther out, and do this far-out album . . . I was the one who introduced John, originally, to a lot of that stuff.' For too many years he had been caricatured as the 'straight' Beatle (not least by Lennon), alongside the freewheeling, daredevil brilliance of his song-writing partner. The evidence supported him: he had been the insti-gator of the Beatles' forays into experimental music and the early champion of the psychedelic underground. But he had always lacked Lennon's casual genius for transforming novelty into enduring art; he was too much of a populist to throw himself into anything as confronta-tional as Lennon's late-1960s exploits with Ono. Moreover, the further he pursued this theme, the more graceless he appeared.

Another Beatle was turning gracelessness into a vocation. Bloated with alcohol, Richard Starkey had stumbled into an ill-fated project with veteran R & B/country producer Chips Moman, to which George Harrison had also agreed to contribute. Meanwhile Harrison had recruited his own catalyst, Jeff Lynne. Besides fashioning Beatle-inspired records with ELO, Lynne had become a trusted midwife for vintage acts who wanted to deliver something appropriate for the late 1980s. Harrison was reluctant to embrace modernity, but Lynne enabled him to remain true to his creative instincts within a contemporary context. So relaxed was Harrison that he was even comfortable offering a sly pastiche of *Sgt Pepper* on 'When We Was Fab'. An accompanying video featured Harrison and Starkey in Beatle garb plus – so Harrison suggested during a drunken radio appearance – McCartney in disguise. 'George wanted me to be in it,' McCartney revealed later, 'but I wasn't available. So I suggested he put someone else in a walrus costume and tell everyone that it was me. We don't lay many false trails, but the walrus has always been one of them.'

Ten days before Harrison's *Cloud Nine* album was released, the three Beatles gathered at McCartney's London residence. 'He'll always be my friend,' said Harrison of Starkey, while he was prepared to admit that the icy surface of his relationship with McCartney was gradually melting.

Yeah, Paul and I are friends now. There was a period when we weren't very friendly . . . but all that past stuff is buried, and everybody's cool. I also think he's changed. I think that although it mightn't have been a good experience for Paul, that the *Give My Regards to Broad Street* experience made him better. I think maybe it's good sometimes to have something that doesn't succeed like you would hope, in order to bring you back down a little bit and make you a better person. He's been much more humble and pleasant, at least to me, during the past few years.

Though many of its charms soon dated, *Cloud Nine* was received more favourably than any Harrison album since *All Things Must Pass*. In mid-January 1988 a computerised revival of an early 1960s R & B tune called 'Got My Mind Set on You' became his first US No. 1 single since 1973. Harrison even agreed to publicise his work for the first time in almost a decade. For one interviewer he showed off an unheralded talent for forgery, scribbling perfect facsimiles of all four Beatles autographs. 'We'll see that one in Sotheby's next year,' he quipped.

The week after his single topped the charts, the Beatles were due to be inducted into the Rock and Roll Hall of Fame – not so much an honour as an excuse for hip millionaires to don tuxedos and celebrate their own success. The three Beatles, plus Lennon's widow and sons, were invited to accept the award. With Harrison and McCartney reconciled, Starkey happy to drink with them both and Ono keen to celebrate her late husband's achievements, it seemed inevitable that the gala occasion would provide the closest possible approximation to a reunion – and might even see the three musicians joining the jam session that would provide the evening's finale.

'It didn't mean anything to me until I got there,' Harrison admitted later. 'It was just some idea that someone had.' But a friend advised him to go, telling him, 'It's history, and you'll enjoy it.' That afternoon, however, McCartney sent a terse message to the organisers: 'I was keen to go and pick up my award, but after twenty years, the Beatles still have some business differences, which I hoped would be settled by now. Unfortunately, they haven't been, so I would feel a complete hypocrite waving and smiling with them at a fake reunion.' It was the action of a petulant child who had suddenly found himself in a situation that he could not control. He portrayed himself as the victim, and came across as the villain – exactly the same mistake he had made in 1970. Eighteen years had passed, but McCartney seemed to have learned nothing about the art of personal relations.

His refusal generated worldwide headlines, though it was soon overshadowed by the bizarre behaviour of Beach Boys vocalist Mike Love, who chose to attack the entire rock aristocracy for not being as hard-working as he was. In McCartney's absence, five people took the stage to represent the Beatles. 'There seem to be more of us than there used to be,' Starkey said wryly. Yoko Ono was gifted a moral victory over McCartney: 'John would certainly have been here,' she claimed. Harrison could have gloated or complained, but he chose to accept the award with dignity and humour. 'I don't have much to say,' he began, 'because I'm the quiet Beatle. It's unfortunate Paul's not here, because he was the one with the speech in his pocket. We all know why John can't be here. I'm sure he would be. It's hard, really, to stand here supposedly representing the Beatles. But' – he glanced across the stage – 'it's all that's left, I'm afraid. But we all loved him so much, and we all love Paul so much.' He added later, '[Paul] was just trying to use that situation for some personal motive. But we've gone past the squabbles now.'

That was an optimistic judgement. While McCartney retreated into silence, Harrison continued to land jabs on his undefended target. Two months after the Hall of Fame ceremony, he revealed, 'Paul has suggested that maybe he and me should write something again. I mean, it's pretty funny, really. I've only been there about thirty years in Paul's life, and now he wants to write with me.' But he conceded, 'Maybe it would be quite interesting.' During a live TV show he was asked about McCartney's plan to record several Lennon songs as a tribute to his friend. 'Maybe it's because he ran out of good ones of his own,' he said. When his interviewer looked shocked, he continued, 'It's true!' As the years passed, his rhetoric hardened. When McCartney's name was mentioned in November 1989, he said, 'We don't have a relationship.' He let a long silence hang in the air. 'I think of him as a good friend, really, but a friend I don't have that much in common with any more. You wish the other person well, but life has taken you to other places. To friendlier climes.'

And why would Harrison care about McCartney when he was collaborating with the most influential songwriter in rock history? 'He wanted to be in a band,' said musician Tom Petty. 'But he wanted to avoid all those pitfalls that a band has. He didn't want it to be so overtly serious that it became a chore.' Asked by Warner Brothers to record a new song for a single, he recruited a bunch of friends: Petty, Jeff Lynne, Roy Orbison and his long-time hero Bob Dylan. Together, they became the Traveling Wilburys, one of those rare agglomerations of star performers that actually matched its potential. 'It was about as much fun as you can legally have,' Petty said of the sessions for their debut album. 'Everyone was so up. I think everyone was grooving on the fact that the whole thing didn't lay on any one person's shoulders.' But, Petty conceded, 'George was our leader and our manager.'

Twenty years earlier Harrison had dreamed of joining a collaborative, fully democratic unit like Bob Dylan's former backing crew The Band. Now his wish was fulfilled. 'We wanted it to be something that warmed the heart,' Petty explained, and their album – apparently effortless, spontaneous, mischievous and instantly attractive – did exactly that. McCartney raised a dissenting voice: 'I don't really see the point,' he said later, admitting, 'I'm not really in with a crowd like that.' But he was out of sync with the widespread sense of joy that the Wilburys engendered – only tarnished by the death of Roy Orbison soon after their album was released. There was a second album in 1990, rougher and less tuneful than the first, and, as Petty recalled, 'There was always a lot of talk about the Wilburys doing a performance. You know, George often talked about it. Especially when we'd have a few drinks he'd get very keen on the idea. And then the next day he'd not be so keen on it.'

Faced with the choice between a partnership of equals and the renewal of a relationship that had no history of equality, Harrison's decision was easy. In November 1989 McCartney again raised the possibility of collaborating with his younger colleague. Harrison's response was rapid, and curt: there could be no reunion of the Beatles, he stated, 'as long as John Lennon remains dead'.

Chapter 10

We are the only ones who know each other. We knew what it was like. They are the only two that don't look at me like I'm a Beatle. They look at me like I'm a Ringo, and I look at him like he's a Paul or a George.

Richard Starkey, 1992

When Albert Goldman published his 600-page biography *The Lives of John Lennon* in August 1988, Paul McCartney was outraged. 'Boycott this book,' he told Lennon's fans. 'It's disgusting that someone like Goldman can make up any bunch of lies he sees fit, and can be allowed to republish them without fear of repudiation.' 'He ought to be ashamed of himself,' Goldman replied. 'The generation of the sixties were scathing in their criticism of everybody. Now, suddenly, they've become very prissy and moralistic when someone says something they don't want to hear about themselves. They can dish it out, but they sure can't take it.'

Goldman portrayed Lennon as mummy-fixated, drug-riddled, instinctively violent, psychologically flawed, a bully who might have been responsible for the death of his friend Stuart Sutcliffe, a closet homosexual and the assaulter of his baby son. Even at his most affectionate – and Goldman claimed above all to have been an admirer of Lennon's work – the writer employed terms such as 'genetic brain damage', 'violence' of 'an epileptic character', 'extreme passivity', 'gullible', 'very intimidating' and 'threatening'.

The Lives of John Lennon was lousy with errors of fact and interpretation, speculative in the extreme, ill-willed and awash with snobbery. Yet Goldman pinpointed Lennon's almost clinical need for domination by a strong woman; the dark ambiguity of a man of peace being governed by violence, either vented or repressed; the unmistakable decline in his work after he left England in 1971; and the instinctive need to believe in a force greater than himself, which led him from guru to guru, each obsession spilling into disillusionment and creative despair.

Ironically, the book – a global best-seller, which nevertheless vanished from history after Goldman's death in 1994 – provided a cause around which Ono and McCartney could unite. Their rapprochement was aided by the efforts of their lawyers to settle the lawsuits that divided them. After motions were granted and denied, appeals heard and overturned, all the parties in their various disputes finally realised that extravagant legal costs were threatening to outstrip their potential earnings. The most obstinate of their disagreements concerned the McCartney override and the associated wrangles over EMI's royalty payments. After more than a year of discussions, Apple, the Beatles and EMI were finally ready to settle. The documents were officially signed on 7 November 1989, and the terms were kept secret, though EMI would no longer be able to proceed with Beatles projects without the express approval of Apple and its four owners. 'The settlement was about ten feet thick,' Harrison complained. 'I don't think anybody but the lawyers read it. It's a good feeling to be done with it. The funny thing is, most of the people who were involved with the reason that lawsuit came about aren't even in the companies any more. So the people at Capitol and EMI had to take on the karma of their predecessors, and I'm sure that they're relieved too.'

Under the agreement all four Beatles would now benefit from the improved terms that had been enjoyed by McCartney. But as Harrison noted, 'It doesn't wash away the politics of it. Some of the original causes can't go away, in my mind. Because there are certain things that never should have happened in the first place. If I stab you in the back and you happen to get to the hospital and don't die . . . you may not want to see me in case I do it again.'

During the final year of negotiations Richard Starkey's life was transformed. His alcoholism had spiralled out of control in the late summer of 1988. 'Years I've lost, absolute years,' he recalled. 'I've no idea what happened. I lived in a blackout. I don't know how I'd get to bed every night. We didn't know. That's how crazy it gets.' By early September he was drinking and snorting cocaine to violent excess. Finally, Starkey and Barbara Bach realised that they needed help, and booked themselves into an Arizona rehab clinic. 'Heading for the detox centre,' he confessed, 'I was as drunk as a skunk. But after the detox I felt things had to change. I didn't know it then, but I can survive without alcohol and drugs.' After six weeks the couple flew home to England, determined to live without the stimulants that had protected them from reality. 'I get bewildered and frightened,' Starkey admitted. 'If I live day to day, I usually have a great day. If I start living in the future or the past, it gets silly.' As one observer noted, 'He is resentful of the past, frightened of the future.' 'God watches out for me,' Starkey said, 'and he laughs when I make plans.'

Yet plans were his chief defence against his illness. In July 1989 Ringo Starr's All-Starr Band began their first tour. Like the Traveling Wilburys, Starkey's was a gathering of veterans, but unlike Harrison's project, his band was rooted firmly in the past. There was scepticism when the initial line-up was announced, as it featured some notorious excessives, such as Rick Danko of The Band and Billy Preston. But Starkey resisted all temptations, and his self-esteem grew as he discovered the affection with which he was still regarded, by musicians and fans alike. The All-Starr Band became his regular touring vehicle for the next two decades, its line-up gradually declining in quality but its purpose – keeping its star out of trouble – steadfast. The consistency on which the band was built could be irksome for its members, though, as Todd Rundgren recalled: 'Maybe on a good night I was only bored half the time, while on a bad night it was all the time. They only knew a couple of my songs, so I had to play the same damned song every night. But there's a karmic aspect to it. I wouldn't be in the music business if it weren't for the Beatles, so when Ringo Starr calls, you have to answer!'

One casualty of Starkey's reformed lifestyle was the album on which he had been working with Chips Moman. 'He wanted to put it on hold,' Moman complained. 'That didn't seem fair because I'd been working for months on this album and put a lot of my money into it. I'm not as rich as Ringo! It went on for months. Finally I said,

"Ringo, I'm gonna put this album out. It's taken me a year to get you on the phone. Send me your picture. If not, I'll just have an artist draw one." Now, I wasn't really about to do that, but I had to draw matters to a head.' Lawyers were summoned, and everyone else ended up out of pocket: Starkey paid Moman compensation, which according to Moman amounted to less than his studio costs. All that remained of the album was a pile of tape boxes in Moman's barn which he was legally barred from playing to anyone.

The guardian of Starkey's new career was his business manager Hilary Gerrard. The son of a European émigré to London who adopted the surname after finding himself in Gerrard Street, he is perhaps the most enigmatic character in the entire Beatles' story, and has rarely been photographed. Charming or abrupt as the occasion requires, his manner has been compared to an East End cabbie, albeit with the discreet ponytail and ear stud of a music business maverick. It was Gerrard who supervised the formation of Widgeon Investments in 1989, to handle the money that would accrue from Starkey's adventures in sobriety and send it on vacation to the Caribbean. This was a time of corporate consolidation. Through the 1980s Paul McCartney had launched a series of British companies using his trademarked juggler logo, each handling a specific interest in his creative and business portfolio. Now his empire expanded again, with the formation of companies such as McCartney Enterprises and MPL Tours. After a decade in which his appearances had been restricted to charity events and his nerve profoundly shaken by Lennon's murder, McCartney was ready to return to the road.

He had last toured in 1979, with Wings and a repertoire that touched only gently on the Beatles. Now, at last, he was prepared to acknowledge his lifetime's work. Buoyed by the reception for his inventive *Flowers in the Dirt* album, he fashioned a schedule that would eventually involve 87 concerts around the globe across the course of six months, in venues ranging from a 5,000-seat arena in Norway to a world-record stadium crowd of 184,000 in Brazil. Few, if any, of his peers could have conceived such an ambitious project or fulfilled it with such panache. His lack of spontaneity was apparent – even his ad-libbed introductions were carefully scripted – and sometimes his voice displayed signs of weariness and age. But any misgivings were outweighed by the sheer daring of the enterprise, which involved a set of 30 songs or more, equally divided between his solo career and his Beatles catalogue. McCartney supervised everything with his customary attention to detail, from the film presentation that preceded him on stage to the arrangements of such unexpected delights as the closing medley from *Abbey Road*, delivered with stunning fidelity to the original record. The tour virtually defied criticism, and it established McCartney as arguably the most popular touring attraction in the world.

Facing a press conference in every city, McCartney inevitably annoyed the ever-sensitive George Harrison. A casual admission that he would be interested in working with Harrison brought a swift and sarcastic response. As the tour ended, Harrison was still muttering discontentedly, 'He's left it a bit late, is all I can say to that. I'm entrenched with Bob Dylan, Tom Petty and Jeff Lynne, and I don't see any reason to go back to an old situation.' So McCartney was forced to defend himself once more: 'George has taken the liberty of answering that question with shocking regularity for you media guys. He's had a field day getting publicity from his negative responses. So obviously it's never going to happen, no matter what I think.'

Beneath this machismo, a healthier line of communication had been opened. The Beatles' wives had been blamed unfairly for provoking the group's demise 20 years earlier. Now they became a means of reconciliation. When the organisation Parents For Safe Food was launched in 1989, Barbara Bach and Olivia Harrison became active campaigners, and the loyal Derek Taylor wrote the campaign's handbook. A few months later Olivia Harrison enlisted Bach, Yoko Ono and Linda McCartney to raise money for starving Romanian orphans. The Traveling Wilburys contributed a single to the cause, and a charity album followed featuring both Harrison and Starkey.

Other well-intentioned projects proved more divisive. Early in 1989 Cynthia Lennon was approached by promoter Sid Bernstein, who wanted to stage a charity concert to mark John Lennon's 50th birthday in October 1990. Cynthia lent her support, and secured the tentative involvement of Michael Jackson, Ravi Shankar and Paul McCartney. Later that year Cynthia attended a concert by her son Julian Lennon at which his half-brother Sean made an emotional cameo appearance. Backstage, Lennon's two wives discussed Bernstein's plan. Cynthia Lennon returned home believing that Ono would co-operate, only to hear that Ono had withdrawn her approval and was planning her own anniversary event.

On 5 May 1990 Ono staged her tribute to her late husband in Liverpool. The attendance was disappointing, and an occasion that was intended to generate a vast sum for Ono's newly incorporated charity, the Spirit Foundation UK, collapsed into financial controversy. Meanwhile, Bernstein continued to dream, his next fantasy involving a Beatles reunion with Julian Lennon at the Brandenburg Gate in Berlin. As United Nations adviser Hans Janitchek said, 'The significant thing is to bring the Beatles together. If they played "Happy Days Are Here Again" at the Berlin Wall, wouldn't that be terrific?' Twenty years after their dissolution, the Beatles were still carrying the weight of the world's expectations.

Maintaining a safe distance, McCartney and Starkey contributed videotaped performances to Ono's concert – Starkey revisiting the Beatles' 'I Call Your Name' with gusto, and McCartney offering a banal medley of the songs from the group's first single. But Harrison refused to participate. 'I don't think John would like it, and I don't want to keep dabbling in the past either. Personally, I've made a pact with myself not to get involved in anything to do with ex-Beatles. The Beatles ceased to exist in 1969. They meant whatever they meant to various people across the world, and it was fun at the time, but it has affected the rest of our lives. Let sleeping dogs lie.'

Some dogs were reluctant to snooze. Having secured an under-taking that Apple Computers would never become involved with the music business, Neil Aspinall and Apple's lawyers discovered in late 1988 that the American firm was planning to add a sound chip to its computers which could produce melodic content. On 29 October the Apple vs Apple dispute reached Court 53 of the London High Court, starting a hearing that ran for 116 days, plus ten days more at the London Court of Appeal and another at the European Court in Brussels. The two sides had gathered evidence from dozens of witnesses prepared to testify either that nobody could confuse Apple Computers with the Beatles, or that Apple Corps was a world-famous company whose trademark was being abused by an American upstart.

It was now fifteen years since Apple Corps had last actively func-tioned as a record company, and it was a moot point whether its name and logo were more associated with the Beatles or with pioneering computer technology. But suddenly Apple Corps announced a global relaunch. Now it was once again a record label, and to show how seriously it took its responsibilities it launched a salvo of court actions in a bewildering variety of directions. It won a High Court injunction against EMI, who had been preparing to release the 1973 compilations by the Beatles (1962–1966 and 1967–1970) on CD without securing the necessary approval. Apple also targeted Sony, which via a complex series of sub-licensing deals had emerged – as much to its own surprise as anyone else's – with a CD of the Beatles' legally contentious Star-Club recordings from 1962. The record was swiftly withdrawn. But the Beatles' most ambitious move was effectively to sue themselves, in a move worthy of the satirical genius of Eric Idle's Rutles film. Apple had approved the release of a video documentary about the Beatles' 1964 arrival in America entitled *The First US Visit*. The UK rights were licensed to Richard Branson's Virgin company; but Apple then served Virgin with a writ to cancel the release – for motives that only became clear when the *Anthology* project was announced a few weeks later.

On 11 October 1991, just as it threatened to become the longest hearing in British legal history, the battle between the rival Apples came to an unexpected halt when the two sides announced that they had reached a settlement. The long-suffering Mr Justice Ferris noted wryly, 'I do not know whether my surprise at this development at this stage outweighs my relief at not having to write a definitive judgement.' The terms of the agreement were believed to include a payment from Apple Computers of some $29 million and a pledge not to stray into music again. It seemed a comprehensive victory for Apple Corps, and it was surely a strange coincidence that its rebirth as a record company was forgotten soon after the lawsuit was won.

The Apple empire was now secure for the final decade of the century, with Neil Aspinall still controlling its activities with an eye for detail and a tenacious refusal to give ground to any opponent. The company's ethos now represented the polar opposite of its original philosophy – unless, that is, one remembered that Apple was originally envisaged as a method of creative tax reduction. Each Beatle was still represented by a director on the board, which comprised Yoko Ono Lennon, John Eastman (replacing his father Lee, who died later that year aged 81), Denis O'Brien and Hilary Gerrard. The same personnel controlled all the other surviving Beatle companies: Apple Electronics Ltd, Apple Management Ltd, Apple Publicity Ltd (all three effectively extinct), Subafilms Ltd, Apple Publishing Ltd, Python Music Ltd and the mother of them all, The Beatles Ltd. And each Beatle/director combination could boast his/her individual corporate maze to keep the accountants occupied.

Nobody's maze was more circuitous than George Harrison's. The 'money-go-round' (to borrow a phrase from Ray Davies) invented by Denis O'Brien had already scared the Monty Python troupe. Michael Palin remembered O'Brien showing them 'a blackboard, with all these various companies here, there and everywhere, and it was very good, real state-of-the-art tax avoidance, mentioning lots of countries in the world and various names of people there who would run our affairs in the Bahamas or the Caymans or Panama'. For a while each of the comedians was too embarrassed to admit that he didn't understand O'Brien's explanation; when they realised that they were all equally bamboozled, they decided not to sign up for this financial mystery tour. 'I'd observed him quite a lot,' said Eric Idle, 'and I also knew George really, really well, and I said, "You know, you want to be very careful. There's something going on."'

Harrison felt he had every reason to trust O'Brien, who had appeared as his saviour in the aftermath of his relationship with Allen Klein and had masterminded his stunningly successful venture into the British film industry. 'When we got rid of Allen Klein,' he said in 1988, 'I was 15 years behind with my taxes, and Denis helped me sort out that mess.' HandMade Films' initial success – including hits such as *The Long Good Friday* and *A Private Function* – suggested that business acumen, instinct and luck were working in their favour. But that streak ended with *Shanghai Surprise*, the Madonna vehicle that cost HandMade £10 million and took less than half that at the box office. Subsequent HandMade releases, such as *The Raggedy Rawney*, were even less successful; and the nadir was *Checking Out*, a comedy that grossed less than 3 per cent of its costs. For any independent film company these figures were ruinous, and in 1991 production was abruptly halted on all HandMade's projects. Harrison attempted to sever his ties with the industry, faxing the London office staff to tell them they were fired and announcing that he no longer wished to be involved with the company.

Even a Beatle, however, could not dispose of his business obligations so swiftly. O'Brien repaired the public damage that Harrison had caused, and the company stumbled on. But history was about to be replayed. In 1972 Lennon and Harrison had ordered a clandestine investigation of Allen Klein's business affairs. Now Harrison was forced into the same manoeuvre, knowing that the stakes were enormous. At risk, ultimately, was his Friar Park mansion and his quarter interest in Apple and the Beatles. HandMade had offered him a journey out of the past. Now only a return to the past could safeguard his financial future.*

In 1990 Neil Aspinall had advised Yoko Ono and the three Beatles to reconsider the idea of producing an official documentary about their career. Harrison was dismissive, but the others remained open to negotiation. While Harrison grappled with potential disaster and Starkey battled to keep his addictions at bay, McCartney seemed secure and fulfilled. Ono was moved by his decision, during a Liverpool concert that June, to celebrate Lennon's memory by performing three of his best-known songs, 'Strawberry Fields Forever', 'Help!' and 'Give Peace a Chance'.† Despite his success as a live performer, however, McCartney had always found it difficult to communicate in public. His stage patter was wooden and often embarrassing, and after a brief period of unthinking honesty provoked by Lennon's death, he had returned to his standard interview technique of hiding his discomfort in familiar anecdotes. After former tabloid journalist Geoff Baker became his press spokesman, it did McCartney few favours when he told journalists that the album *Off the Ground* was 'the best thing Paul's done since the *White Album*', when it so blatantly wasn't. McCartney was at his most impressive when he wasn't trying so hard to impress – filming an episode of the *MTV Unplugged* series, for example, on which he revisited songs such as 'And I Love Her' with a delicacy that

---

* Harrison's mood darkened considerably during this period. On one drunken occasion he ended up in the office of Warner Brothers Records promotion head Bill Fowler. Spotting a framed photograph of Fowler with Lennon and Ono taken two days before Lennon's death and clearly a prized artefact, he reached for a marker pen and defaced it with speech bubbles and humorous, sometimes sexist comments. To his credit, he phoned the next day to apologise.

† The sequence featured in his DVD documentary *From Rio to Liverpool*, although it was accompanied by McCartney claiming that he had written a sizeable proportion of 'Help!', a song that Lennon had always proudly asserted as entirely his own work.

was all too rarely found in his performances. Even then, McCartney could not be entirely spontaneous. In one of the most endearing moments of the programme an attempt at 'We Can Work It Out' ground to a halt after a few bars. 'This is so informal that we'll start again,' McCartney said. What the audience didn't realise was that the mistake had been carefully planned. As an aside, *MTV Unplugged* marked the debut of Stella McCartney's fashion career; the 18-year-old received a wardrobe credit on the show.

The McCartney family widened its horizons in 1991, with Paul venturing into classical composition and Linda launching an enormously successful range of vegetarian foods. Their contentment was sharply at odds with Harrison's financial insecurity. With Handmade Films in disarray, he needed cash, and by autumn 1991 he had agreed to let Aspinall assemble a documentary crew. Inevitably, it was McCartney who announced the news, and Harrison who immediately dampened any illusions about a Beatles reunion. 'No, it can't be possible,' he insisted in late November, 'because the Beatles don't exist, especially now as John Lennon isn't alive. It just comes every time Paul needs some publicity, he announces to the press that the Beatles are coming together again, but that's all. I wouldn't pay too much attention to that.'

He was speaking in Tokyo at the start of his first concert tour in 17 years. 'I had to do something when I gave up smoking,' Harrison quipped, discounting his business problems. As in 1974, the constant enquiries about the Beatles irritated him. 'The press conference set the tone for the whole thing,' reflected Eric Clapton, who supported Harrison on the Japanese tour. 'They were asking him inappropriate questions and he went on the defensive and stayed that way.' In retrospect, Clapton viewed the tour as a last chance to tug Harrison out of the lethargy that had begun to envelop him. 'I only wish I could have been more help,' he said in his autobiography. 'It was a fine show, well rehearsed with great songs and tremendous musicianship, but I knew his heart wasn't in it. He didn't really seem to like playing live, so it did nothing for him, except maybe he saw how much he was loved, both by his fans and by us.' None of that affected the monetary significance of the tour, which comprised twelve sell-out shows in large arenas and spawned a double album. There was talk of taking the show to America, but Harrison's discomfort made that impossible.

He did agree to play one more show, however, on 6 April 1992, his first full-length British concert since 1969. It was another fund-raiser, not for HandMade Films but for the newly formed Natural Law Party. This mysterious organisation had put up several hundred candidates for the UK general election three days later. Their goal was ambitious: 'to create a disease-free, crime-free, pollution-free society – Heaven on Earth' based on the principles of Transcendental Meditation espoused by the Maharishi Mahesh Yogi. Harrison, not previously noted for any political allegiance, promised, 'I will vote for the Natural Law Party because I want a total change and not just a choice between left and right . . . I believe this party offers the only option to get out of our problems and create the beautiful nation we would all like to have.'

Welcome though the concert was, many regarded Harrison's support for the NLP as evidence of his total isolation from real life. The party did little to aid its cause with an election broadcast that demonstrated the joys of 'yogic flying' and asked the populace to imagine a future in which the entire British nation could defy the laws of gravity. Yet Harrison's enthusiasm was undimmed by public cynicism. A few days before his concert he phoned Paul McCartney, 'giggling', from Los Angeles. 'I've been up all night, and you may think this is a bit silly, but Maharishi would like you, me and Ringo to stand as Members of Parliament for Liverpool. We'll win! It'll be great!' McCartney politely declined.

Fortunately, Harrison's Albert Hall show was a celebration of his music not his political philosophy. Eighteen months earlier he had attacked McCartney for staging 'a Beatles tour. He's decided to be the Beatles. I'm not interested: for me, it's the past.' Now he opened his show with the Beatles' 'I Want to Tell You', sending a shiver down the spine of everyone who imagined how the group might have sounded in 1966 if they had only bothered to rehearse. He seemed genuinely moved by the audience response. 'I'm always paranoid about whether people like me,' he admitted from the stage. 'You never know.'

The night was triumphant, with cameo appearances from Starkey and Harrison's son Dhani; the election less so, as only one in every 250 people voted for the NLP. Even the adrenaline rush of the gig quickly dissipated. 'I really enjoyed playing,' Harrison admitted a few weeks later. 'But I have a conflict: I don't particularly want to play to audiences. It's unhealthy to be the star.' He was happy to accept the trappings of his stardom, the freedom, the vintage guitars and the mansion; but when he looked back at the Beatles he could only think, 'What a waste of time! The potential danger of forgetting what the purpose is supposed to be in life and just getting caught up in this big tangle and creating more and more karma. I wouldn't want to do it again.'

Yet that was exactly what he had just agreed to do. In January 1992 a film crew began work in an anonymous-looking office in west London. In May Apple was ready to announce that *The Long and Winding Road* – the Beatles' official history of their own lives – was under construction, and that the three surviving musicians had agreed to work together. 'We went through the stages of the three of us saying hello in different situations, in restaurants and offices,' Starkey explained later, 'then we started working separately and then we started doing a bit together, and then of course it ends up with us recording together.' Initially their contribution was limited to scouring their private film archives for rare footage; soon they agreed to be interviewed for the project by the unthreatening figure of musician Jools Holland. 'None of the guys saw what the others had said,' explained producer Bob Smeaton. 'We did interview the three of them together, but I preferred to speak to them individually, because they're a lot more honest. They became protective of each other.'

One major problem facing Smeaton, Aspinall and director Chips Chipperfield was the missing Beatle. The crew had access to hours of Lennon interviews and were adamant that they didn't want Yoko Ono to act as a surrogate for her late husband. 'We didn't want her talking about John when she hadn't been around,' Smeaton recalled. 'But we said, "The guys are obviously going to talk about you. Do you want to be on screen?" But we wouldn't let her see what they had said about her. She had to make a decision there and then. And she said no.' She retained the same power of veto as the three Beatles, but her absence from the screen offered McCartney, Harrison and Starkey a sense of psychological freedom.

By agreeing to participate in Apple's documentary, the surviving Beatles were, consciously or not, sacrificing some of their carefully guarded privacy. But Harrison could no longer afford isolation. By late 1992 he had been advised that he was on the verge of bankruptcy, as HandMade's debts ate into his capital. It transpired that for years Harrison's wealth had been cross-collateralised to finance HandMade's features: in effect he was liable for 100 per cent of the company's losses, but only 50 per cent of its profits. 'To have someone sit at your table with your family every night and then betray your trust is one of the worst experiences imaginable,' he commented later. After almost 20 years O'Brien was removed as Harrison's manager and a director of Apple in early 1993 – Harrison assuming the latter role himself.

Two years of investigation followed before Harrison, his Harrisongs company and HandMade Films collectively filed suit against O'Brien in January 1995. Harrison's claim alone amounted to $25 million. In 1988 O'Brien had described his client as 'an absolutely extraordinary individual . . . I'd do anything for that guy.' Now Harrison alleged in his legal complaint that O'Brien had been 'a faithless and fraudulent manager' whose intention was 'to get a "free ride" at Harrison's expense' and 'to aggrandise himself personally, professionally and socially'. As one commentator noted, the allegations were effectively 'an 18-page insult'. When Harrison had split from Klein, the musician had retained a grudging affection for his former manager. This time the breach was total. Twelve months later the Los Angeles Superior Court issued a summary judgement that O'Brien was responsible for half of HandMade's debts, and that he therefore owed Harrison $11.6 million. 'It's a help, but I didn't actually get any money,' the musician commented. 'We've got to follow him to the ends of the earth, getting the case registered in every different area where he could have any assets. It's one thing winning, but actually getting the money is another thing.' Meanwhile, HandMade was sold to the Paragon Entertainment group for a reported £5 million.

The saga took its toll on Harrison's goodwill and health, and forced him into the unwelcome role of nostalgic Beatle. His colleagues were enjoying somewhat better fortune. In the mid-1980s Starkey had narrated a series of children's films, *Thomas the Tank Engine*, for British TV. His reward was an 8 per cent stake in the production company, which paid enormous dividends when the series was reworked as *Shining Time Station* for US consumption, with Starkey's lugubrious voice at its heart. He was locked into a healthy marriage and regular touring routine, had resumed his recording career, and appeared to have found the stability he had lacked since the demise of the Beatles. McCartney's situation was even rosier. In December 1992 he signed a new recording deal with EMI/Capitol, ambitiously described as a lifetime agreement that could net him as much as $100 million.

On 10 December McCartney and Harrison met in California. The following day McCartney announced, 'We're getting together, you know, for this [documentary] – it's bringing us together. And there's a chance we might write a little bit of music for it.' It was the kind of statement that he'd been making for years – every time he had an album to promote, Harrison would have said. But this time there was no sarcastic response from Harrison; merely silence. He insisted only that the project must not be named after McCartney's song 'The Long and Winding Road'. And so *The Beatles Anthology* was born, comprising a TV series of six or eight or ten episodes (the scope seemed limitless), a set of videotapes and possibly, just possibly, some new music from the surviving group members – some instrumental backgrounds, McCartney suggested, rather than a fully fledged studio reunion.

Once he had promoted his inconsistent *Off the Ground* album, suggesting as usual, 'John's spirit was in the studio with us,' McCartney embarked on his New World Tour. Like its predecessor, this was a gargantuan affair that leaned heavily on his heritage. Every show opened with a film dominated by footage from the Beatle era, although none of it post-dated the arrival of Yoko Ono. When the tour reached London in September 1993 Harrison attended one of the shows. 'He came back afterwards,' McCartney recalled, 'and criticised the gig in a sort of professional way. "A bit too long," George reckoned. Well, fuck you. And the old feelings came up. But George is a great guy. Even with old friends, this shit happens.'

The two men did agree on one subject: they weren't happy about delving too deeply into the Beatles' archive of unreleased recordings. Their producer George Martin was sent to investigate the possibilities and emerged unimpressed. 'I've listened to all the tapes,' he declared in March 1993. 'There are one or two interesting variations, but otherwise it's all junk. Couldn't possibly release it!' Then the financial potential of a series of archive releases was explained to Martin and the Beatles. Within a few months Martin had agreed to assemble three double CDs of unissued material, by which time the vaults of junk had magically become a treasure trove.

The Beatles Anthology was now proceeding on several fronts: the film team in Chiswick editing the archive footage and the new interviews with the Beatles; George Martin at Abbey Road preparing an alternative musical history of the group; and Derek Taylor at Apple gathering quotations old and new for a Beatles autobiography. Only one piece remained elusive: the music that McCartney, Harrison and Starkey had agreed to record together.

On New Year's Day 1994 Paul McCartney placed a call to Yoko Ono. 'She was a little surprised,' he admitted,

but we got chatting. I rang her a few more times after that, we got quite friendly, and this idea came up. I said, 'Look, the three of us were thinking of doing a little instrumental for the film, just to get together.' But as the thought of the three of us actually sitting down in a studio started to get nearer and nearer, I got cold feet about it. I thought, does the world need a three-quarter Beatle record. But what if *John* was on, the three of us *and* John, like a real new record? I talked to Yoko about that and she said she had these three tracks.

On 19 January McCartney and Ono attended the Rock and Roll Hall of Fame dinner, where McCartney had agreed to induct Lennon – on the understanding that he would be honoured himself the following year.* He read an open letter to his late friend, recounting familiar anecdotes, and shared a magnificently awkward hug with Ono – she throwing her head back in mock-ecstasy, he leaning in tentatively as if he was about to embrace a crocodile. After the ceremony Ono handed over a bundle of tapes containing Lennon's home recordings of several songs, most of which had been aired on the *Lost Lennon Tapes* radio series. 'We know we can't do anything better than the Beatles,' McCartney said modestly, 'but for old time's sake, we thought it would be nice to give it a whirl.'

That was the story that went around the world: the Beatles were reuniting, and McCartney had made it happen. But Ono soon let slip

---

* In fact, McCartney had to wait until 1999, when he was accompanied by his daughter Stella wearing a T-shirt with the message 'About fucking time'.

that she had first been approached by George Harrison and Neil Aspinall in 1991, relegating McCartney to the role of messenger: 'It was all settled before then. I just used that occasion to hand over the tapes to Paul.' Whereupon McCartney revised his narrative, now claiming to have suggested the concept to Ono earlier still. 'I checked it out with Sean,' he said, 'because I didn't want him to have a problem with it. He said, "Well, it'll be weird hearing a dead guy on lead vocal. But give it a try." I said to them both, if it doesn't work out, you can veto it. When I told George and Ringo I'd agreed to that, they were going, "What? What if *we* love it?" It didn't come to that, luckily.' Ono admitted that she had initially been dubious about the project: 'I remember how John always said there could be no reunion of the Beatles because, if they got together again, the world would be so disappointed to see four rusty old men. I also felt that those tracks were private. It was like a kind of physical hurt to me to think of someone taking them and messing with them.' It was perhaps not the most diplomatic way to describe the other Beatles' input, but Ono concluded, 'The Beatles have become a very important power to many people. I felt that for me to stand in the way of that reunion would be wrong. So I decided to go with the flow. And after all the Beatles were John's group. He was the band leader and the one who coined the Beatles' name.' She had lost none of her flair for annoying McCartney while appearing to act with grace and dignity. The origin of the Beatles' name – always ascribed humorously by Lennon to 'a vision' of a man on a 'flaming pie' – would cause a rift during the final edit of the *Anthology* documentary. According to McCartney, Ono insisted that Lennon's account was literally true, not a joke, and wouldn't hear otherwise. The argument inspired the title track of McCartney's 1997 album *Flaming Pie*, which tapped into the Beatles' spirit more successfully than anything he'd composed in years.

There was much excitement at the news of Lennon's posthumous involvement in the reunion. But the Beatles themselves were more ambivalent. An initial recording session scheduled the week before McCartney collected the tapes from Ono was cancelled when Starkey chose to go skiing instead. There followed negotiations over the choice of producer and venue. 'I told them I wasn't too happy with putting them together with the dead John,' George Martin recalled. 'I might have done it if they had asked me, but they didn't ask me.' McCartney believed that Martin had withdrawn from the running by confessing that he was losing his hearing – though that begged the question of why he was being allowed to compile the *Anthology* albums. Harrison effectively issued an ultimatum: either they hired Jeff Lynne as producer or he wasn't taking part; and Starkey backed him. McCartney was concerned that Lynne would automatically favour Harrison's views over his own, but he reluctantly agreed, and the Beatles gathered at McCartney's Sussex studio on 11 February, for what was originally intended as a week of sessions. In the event, the reunion was extended for a second week, allowing the group to come close to completing one song ('Free as a Bird') and tinker with two others ('Grow Old With Me' and 'Now and Then').

McCartney kept a private diary of the sessions, so he could document this moment of personal history. The initial sessions were said to have been tense, particularly between Harrison and McCartney. 'There have been a lot of bad feelings,' Starkey conceded. 'We've been in and out of favour with each other for the last twenty years. But this project brought us together. Once we get the bullshit behind us, we all end up doing what we do best, which is making music. The crap went out the window, and we had a lot of fun.'

'Free as a Bird' was identified as the most promising of Lennon's songs – not least because it was clearly unfinished, and therefore allowed for creative input from the other Beatles. 'I actually originally heard it as a big, orchestral, Forties Gershwin thing,' McCartney revealed later, 'but it didn't turn out like that. In the end we decided to do it very simply.' While he and Starkey said they felt tearful when they heard Lennon's voice through the studio speakers, Harrison maintained a sense of distance: 'Maybe I'm peculiar, but to me he isn't dead.' But he admitted, 'I miss him in the context of the band, because he wouldn't take any shit, and I think that aspect's missing. In some ways I feel that I'm trying to make up for that aspect of John, because I don't like to take much shit either.' Identifying the source of 'shit' did not require a DNA test. In return, McCartney tried to prevent Harrison from playing his trademark slide guitar on the track. 'I thought, Oh, it's "My Sweet Lord" again,' he admitted, before conceding that Harrison's solo was 'a blinder'. Yet despite their mutual misgivings, the two men were able to pool their strengths rather than their weaknesses, disguising the dirge-like quality of Lennon's performance. Their almost instinctual blend of talents was exemplified by the layers of harmony vocals, which gave the track a distinctively Beatlesque flavour. As Starkey crowed, 'It really sounds like a Beatles track. I think you could say they could have made this in 1967. It was weird for me, and I'm *on* it! When I was listening to it, it was like a light going on in my head – "It's them!"'

Despite efforts to maintain secrecy, news of the sessions broke in the press within two days and was immediately inflated. The *Mail on Sunday* claimed that the three Beatles had agreed to perform in New York's Central Park with Julian Lennon, earning £20 million apiece; its daily sister paper added to the confusion, asserting that the group would perform 'In Spite of All the Danger', a 1958 composition that was actually the earliest recording exhumed from the archives by George Martin. In expectation that the Beatles would be unable to resist the lure of live performance, festival organisers clamoured for their services. Apple received an offer of £2.5 million for a two-hour Beatles set from the organisers of a concert on the Isle of Wight, while the promoters of Woodstock 94 also lodged a bid. Neither offer was acknowledged, let alone considered.

The Beatles kept their distance from each other after the February sessions. Only in May did they meet again, watching early rushes of the documentary and adjourning to a vegetarian restaurant, where they were spotted again with their wives a month later. June 22, 1994 found the three men back at McCartney's studio, but work on a second Lennon composition, 'Now and Then', ceased almost immediately. 'It was one day – one afternoon, really – messing with it,' Jeff Lynne recalled. 'It was a very sweet song, and I wished we could have finished it.' 'It didn't have a very good title,' McCartney conceded, 'but it had a beautiful verse and it had John singing it. But George didn't want to do it.' McCartney was left with the consolation that he had been able to hear Lennon's voice through his studio headphones as if it was still 1967. 'It was like he was in the next room.' McCartney beamed. 'Fuck, I'm singing harmony with John! It's like an impossible dream.'

As an apology for having sabotaged the session, Harrison invited his colleagues to his home the following day, accompanied by a film crew. They briefly debated re-recording 'Let It Be' (one Beatle vetoed that idea) before settling, just as they had in 1969, for the safety of reviving less controversial material. While cameras rolled, the three-man

Beatles flirted with their pre-fame repertoire – vintage rock 'n' roll standards, primitive Lennon/McCartney originals and even their debut single, 'Love Me Do'. Through it all Starkey kept perfect time with a broad smile on his face, as if he'd just arrived home after an epic voyage; McCartney whooped and vamped like a schoolboy on a sugar rush; and Harrison did his best to suggest that although his body was present, his spirit was on a much higher plane. In the garden a more self-conscious McCartney and Harrison swapped songs on their ukuleles, before calling time on their first fully documented reunion performance since 1970. Then they resumed their habit of non-communication – to the extent that when McCartney suffered a car accident in November 1994 he received anxious phone calls from Starkey and Ono, but not from Harrison.

If the youngest Beatle was preoccupied by the lawsuit against his former manager, Starkey faced the tragedy of the death of his first wife, Maureen Cox, from cancer on 30 December. 'They always loved each other,' a friend recalled. Starkey joined their children and Cox's second husband at her bedside as she died. McCartney was so touched that he penned the poignant 'Little Willow' for her bereaved children. Another former Beatle wife, Cynthia Lennon, returned to the media in happier circumstances.

This German record label faxed us at home, wanting to know about Julian's career. It's not the first time that's happened, but I'm his mother, not his manager, so why do they come to me? My partner faxed them back, saying jokingly that 'Julian isn't available but his mother is.' Then they got straight back in touch: 'We're really interested. Can she sing?'

She could, though that didn't make her revival of the 1968 Apple Records hit 'Those Were the Days' anything more than a novelty.

One year after their first reunion the Beatles had completed just one of the three songs they had planned to record. In early February 1995 they returned to McCartney's studio to work on Lennon's 'Real Love'. Harrison complained that the tape was 'this bad copy, and it had this tambourine that was out of time and real loud'. Lynne was forced to spend days cleaning, editing and improving the track before the Beatles could begin work. Bizarrely, none of them realised that a far superior performance of the song had already been released in the

1988 documentary film *Imagine: John Lennon*. 'I don't like it as much as "Free as a Bird",' McCartney admitted later. But he refused to criticise Lennon and was affronted when Harrison did. 'He was saying to me, "I sort of felt John was going off a little bit towards the end of his writing [career],"' McCartney noted. 'I personally found that a little presumptuous.'

Further sessions were held in March and May, but they ended in failure, with Harrison observing, 'It's just like being back in the Beatles.' That was not intended as a compliment. After years of sparring, Harrison and McCartney had attempted to write together, sketching out a song with the unpromising title 'All For Love'. When the two men launched into a vehement argument, an engineer stepped in to support McCartney, who told him to keep out of it. 'He's still a Beatle, you know,' he said, pointing at Harrison. 'George had some business problems,' McCartney said later, 'and it didn't do a lot for his moods over the last couple of years. He's not been that easy to get on with.'

The three Beatles found it easier to socialise together than to work. 'When Ringo said, "I've done my bit," and left me and George to do it,' McCartney remembered, 'we had a little bit more tension.' Yet when Apple's in-house photographer Tommy Hanley took some spontaneous photos of the trio in March 1995 they looked relaxed and playful.

If the Beatles' reunion was a surprise, McCartney's decision to record with Yoko Ono beggared belief. She and her son visited England in March 1995 and taped an experimental soundscape entitled 'Hiroshima Sky Is Always Blue' with the entire McCartney clan. This was her sonic territory, not his, but like his collaboration with poet Allen Ginsberg around the same time it allowed McCartney to restate his credentials as the Beatles' true champion of the avant-garde. A few weeks later he unveiled an anarchic US radio show entitled *Oobu Joobu* in honour of Alfred Jarry's absurdist 1896 drama *Ubu Roi*. 'The most refreshing thing about Paul is that he's completely and utterly unpredictable,' said his producer Eddy Pumer. 'There are no rules, no formats, no restrictions. There were no scripts; it was entirely improvised.' Lennon and Ono would have been proud of it; Harrison derisive. Indeed, Harrison's major creative decisions of the summer were negative. He was said to have rejected the idea of issuing a ten-video boxed set of the full-length *Anthology* because the number was 'karmically wrong'. He also vetoed the inclusion of the McCartney-inspired sound experiment 'Carnival of Light' from 1967 on any of the *Anthology* releases, repeating his oft-heard claim, 'Avant-garde is French for bullshit.'

There were now two priorities for Apple: selling the TV rights to the *Anthology* documentary around the world and securing the approval of Ono and the three Beatles for a final cut. Ono complained that, in the rough edit, 'there was so much Paul and very little John. They said, "No, no, equal time." So I got an engineer to time it and it was one to four. Then the Apple people said, "Oh, really? We didn't notice that." I only found out because I used a stopwatch to check.'

The man with the ultimate responsibility for ensuring that the Beatles were happy with the *Anthology* was, still, Neil Aspinall. 'He's been in the Beatles since 1961,' said the documentary's producer Bob Smeaton. 'He was in the Beatles when the Beatles weren't the Beatles any more. Every day Neil lives the Beatles. He's hard. He shouts a lot. He's very abrasive. We've had tremendous rows. He wants to get it right.' Derek Taylor, now re-installed as Apple's press agent, said that Aspinall 'has these voices in his head, and their whims and fantasies are constantly with him. When he rings around, it has to be done with some method and subtlety. He doesn't want Paul ringing George, and saying, "Neil has been doing this or that." He wants them all in the loop.' As Aspinall himself noted, 'The point about this place is that everybody knows where the buck stops.' For his services, his company Standby Films received between £400,000 and £500,000 per year.

Ono, Harrison and McCartney assumed responsibility for their own decisions. McCartney, said one observer, could be 'an imperious employer, making it uncomfortably plain to his key staff that he has bought them 24 hours a day'. 'He'll never admit that he's wrong,' one insider said. 'You can't criticise anything he's done; you just have to go along with it, and hope it works.' By comparison, Ono was happy to delegate much of the work involved in the Lennon Estate, freeing her to resume her art career. Harrison maintained the smallest staff of the three, centring his business interests around a handful of trusted aides. 'He's charming to the people who work for him,' one revealed. 'He'll bring you a cup of tea, and talk to you rather than shout at you.'

The most mysterious of the four support networks was Starkey's. It revolved around the secretive Hilary Gerrard, plus an unshakeably loyal secretary who could dispatch unwelcome enquiries with the rigour of Miss Jean Brodie, and fiendishly expensive lawyers in London and Los Angeles. The most vulnerable of the quartet to commercial vagaries, Starkey was always open to offers that the others would have rejected with contempt – TV advertisements for cars, for instance, or a Pizza Hut commercial in which he joked about 'getting the boys back together' and ended up with three of the Monkees instead.

The financial potential of the *Anthology* project had been demonstrated by the 1994 release of *Live at the BBC*, a collection of early-1960s radio performances by the group. It sold 100,000 copies in America on its day of release, and immediately topped the British charts, demonstrating the continued potency of the Beatles' name and ensuring keen bidding for the television rights to the *Anthology*. In May 1995 the US TV network ABC announced that it would screen the five-hour history of the Beatles over two nights in November, and would also be granted the world premiere of their first new recording since 1970. In Britain the ITV network offered more than £5 million for a six-part version of the same material. There was only one stipulation: ITV would not be allowed to seek sponsorship from anyone involved in selling alcohol, tobacco or meat, by order of the Beatles.

Not for the first time it now suited both Apple and EMI/Capitol to abandon all their outstanding litigation. Lawyers worked feverishly to secure a final and binding agreement – for eternity, it was hoped – before the unveiling of the *Anthology*. They succeeded, but only just: all the interested parties, including the three Beatles and Yoko Ono, only put their names to an epic heads of agreement document the size of a telephone directory on 17 November, two days before the first *Anthology* show was premiered. The deal halted all the global disputes about the Beatles' royalties, ensured a sizeable (£2 million was the figure quoted) payment to each Beatle, and secured a substantially larger sum for Apple's corporate coffers.

There was a strict embargo on 'Free as a Bird', chosen as the long-awaited Beatles reunion single. It was broken only once – by George Harrison, who attended the Australian Formula 1 Grand Prix in Melbourne a week before the release date, and played the song to commemorate the victory by his friend Damon Hill. Everyone else had to wait until 19 November, when 48 million Americans witnessed the first two-hour segment of *Anthology*, and endured a nervous 60-second countdown before 'Free as a Bird' was given its premiere. As the final chords died away, the BBC was allowed to broadcast the song for the first time in Britain, at 4 a.m. Later that morning the world's media assembled at London's Savoy Hotel, expecting to see the three Beatles. Instead, they were greeted by the familiar but less glamorous faces of George Martin, Derek Taylor, Neil Aspinall and Jeff Lynne. Asked where the Beatles were, Taylor replied urbanely, 'They are all at home, everywhere else but here.'

The Beatle industry proceeded apace: the TV programmes (with sharply decreasing viewing figures for each episode), the single (poorly received by critics but avidly devoured by fans) and the first of three double-CD sets offering previously unheard recordings. What did it all amount to? 'Free as a Bird' evoked a poignant wave of nostalgia, especially when Harrison and McCartney's voices soared behind Lennon's, but ultimately it was nothing more than a sophisticated pastiche of what the Beatles had been, attractively finished with the thinnest of veneers. The *Anthology* TV series was equally comforting, but skilfully evaded the issues that had divided the group, from the sacking of Pete Best in 1962 to the agonising corrosion of 1969. A celebration of the Beatles rather than a truthful self-portrait, it struck exactly the right note of nostalgia, without endangering the group's delicate internal framework. Ironically, it was the least controversial of the Beatles' offerings – a collection of early music entitled *Anthology 1* – that cut the deepest. Its artwork, an apparently haphazard collage of Beatles imagery prepared by their old friend Klaus Voormann, utilised a familiar 1962 portrait of the group, but with Best's likeness torn away to reveal a picture of Starkey beneath. The gesture was both witty and cruel, although Best finally did receive adequate compensation for his role in the fairy tale and his performances on the album, negotiating a payout rumoured to be around £1 million.

'Me and George Harrison are talking about the next album being called *Scraping the Bottom of the Barrel*,' McCartney joked as this first package was released. 'And George Martin reckons if we put anything out after this, it'll have to be issued with a government health warning.'

Industry pundits noted that EMI/Capitol seemed to be staking their financial health on the power of the Beatles to rescue them after a meagre year. Capitol believed that co-operation with Apple was vital; in return, the group was expected to deliver a succession of lucrative archive projects, including a collection of the demo recordings they had taped after their return from India in 1968 and an enhanced revamp of the *Let It Be* album and film. Although 'Free as a Bird' and *Anthology 1* did not sell in quite the spectacular fashion that the company had anticipated, they did ease the Beatles' return to the airwaves. For several years their songs had won poor approval ratings on US oldies stations, but now they could be broadcast without listeners reaching for the dial.

The surge of publicity and excitement survived into the spring, when *Anthology 2* topped the British charts. While its predecessor had focused on the group's early career, this set concentrated on what was arguably the Beatles' most fertile period, from 1965 to 1967. But many aficionados were dubious about the artificially created rarities assembled by George Martin from a variety of out-takes and rough mixes. Issued at the same time was the second reunion single, 'Real Love'. Fans relished the snippets of reunion footage that were featured in the video, but there was a widespread feeling that the track lacked even the confected magic of 'Free as a Bird', and it was not playlisted by the BBC's pop network, Radio 1. This decision was queried in Parliament by publicity-hungry politicians, but there was no surge of popular outrage.

McCartney made a final attempt to persuade Harrison to join him in creating a third 'new' track for *Anthology 3*, but without avail. Even without this bonus, the set was arguably the most satisfying of the three retrospectives. It was released in October 1996, and promoted as 'The final chapter in the story of the greatest band there ever was . . . or ever will be'. Within days of its release, Apple issued an official statement with funereal grandeur better suited to the death of a monarch. 'The end has finally arrived,' it said. 'The Beatles are no more. The official word is that Paul McCartney, George Harrison and Ringo Starr will never play together again as a group, and they have decided that there will be no more singles issued from their back catalogue.'

The chief architect of the announcement was, of course, George

Harrison. The *Anthology* had solved his financial problems; the Beatles had answered the prayers of the world; and now the world could leave the Beatles alone. But the world could not forget the Beatles that easily, and neither, it seemed, could they.

Finale

People still haven't gotten over the Beatles yet.
  Sean Lennon, 1998

I should be more modest, but I don't care now. The Beatles is over. It's a body of work. I can now stand back and say, 'That was great.'
  Paul McCartney, 2006

It was a conundrum that would have taxed the wits of any messiah. What if the Second Coming wasn't enough?

Those who had watched the constantly surprising drama of the Beatles unfold were deflated when the stars walked off stage because they were no longer enjoying the performance. People who loved the Beatles' music had experienced a sense of the possible, a dream of companionship, unity and love. After the split, they still had the music and the memories, but the glow of nostalgia couldn't match the gleam with which the Beatles had floodlit the past.

If there was something painful about life without the Beatles – and there was, even the Beatles knew it – then it surely followed that only a reunion could ease the pain. In 1964 sick and disabled children had been wheeled to the group's dressing room, as if their holy presence could effect a cure. After the group broke up, everyday miracles were no longer enough: now the Beatles had the responsibility of carrying the ideals of the 1960s, tangled and battered though they were, into a future that had a very different vision of utopia.

Within the collective belief that the Beatles could transform reality and recreate the past, expectations were divided. There were those who wanted to be delivered back to the real or imaginary paradise of 1967. Others had more modest ambitions: they simply desired some momentary distraction from a life that had never quite matched the dreams of the 1960s. Built into both fantasies was the desire that the Beatles should carry their listeners to some other place, spiritual, political or merely emotional. Each person's vision of what a Beatles reunion might bring was subtly different; what never varied was the weight of hope and the crushing certainty of disappointment.

After the *Anthology* the world had to accept that the Beatles *had* reformed – and nothing had changed. Reality took the place of illusion. In 1980 John Lennon had insisted that the group could never be responsible for anyone else's happiness. It took 15 years, and the reunion that he insisted was impossible, for the world to realise that he had been right.

Second time around, there was no global sense of grief when the Beatles split. Indeed, the decision was scarcely noticed. If anything, there was collective embarrassment that so much hope had been placed on this incomplete, fallible and slightly ill-fitting group of men. The long-anticipated reunion records, 'Free as a Bird' and 'Real Love', slipped quietly out of memory, as if they had never been, nor ever should have been.

In any case the institution was being undermined by age and fate, as if the effort required to bring it together was now taking its toll. Cancer spread callously through the Beatles' community – no hollow metaphor, but a grim alignment of chance. Its first victim was Maureen Cox, in December 1994. The next was Linda McCartney, who unexpectedly burst into tears at an awards ceremony in 1995 and told her husband that without him she wouldn't be able to carry on. That December the reason for her distress became clear: she had been diagnosed with breast cancer. There followed the ritual of surgery, containment and fear, all too familiar yet jarringly new to everyone who endures it. There were occasional bulletins, all of them optimistic; sometimes she would appear in public, smiling as her daughter Stella launched her career as a fashion designer, or beaming confidently alongside her husband at a premiere.

The following year Derek Taylor – recovering alcoholic, long-term smoker, champion of the jazz cigarette – underwent major surgery for cancer of the oesophagus. He retained his stoic, cynical idealism. 'They tell me I can't smoke dope any more,' he told me with a characteristic twinkle of the eye, 'so I'm just going to have to eat it instead.' He died on 7 September 1997, robbing George Harrison of a loyal friend, Apple of its spokesman and talisman, and the world of a humane and witty soul who had epitomised the ideals of the 1960s social revolution.

Two months before Taylor died Harrison discovered a sizeable lump on the side of his neck. Geoff Baker, the McCartney aide who succeeded Taylor as Apple PR man, insisted that Harrison 'doesn't think he has cancer and is totally cool about it'. Talking himself deeper into trouble, he claimed, 'There's been no cancer scare,' and, 'I'm not a lump person.' Neither, it can be imagined, was Harrison, but the lump had to be surgically removed and examined, and was shown to be malignant. 'I'm not going to die on you folks yet,' Harrison said in June 1998. 'I am very lucky because it didn't go anywhere – all it was, was a little red mark on my neck.' He blamed cigarettes and claimed to be fully recovered. But by then he was aware of what might lie ahead, having attended the funeral of another cancer victim, his friend and hero Carl Perkins, in January;* and more recently a memorial service in London for Linda McCartney, who had died on 17 April 1998.

Her death was shrouded in confusion in which Geoff Baker played a part. It was announced on 19 April as if it had just occurred. Baker said she had died in Santa Barbara, California, but local authorities launched an investigation and discovered that no death certificate had been filed. 'There is an inference that there is something to be hidden,' said a spokesman for the coroner's office. 'It does present the possibility of an assisted suicide or some other sinister-type thing going on.' It transpired that she had actually died at a previously secret McCartney ranch in Arizona. 'It was a decoy,' Baker confessed. 'It was nothing to do with the McCartneys. It was my decision. I said she had

---

* Coincidentally, Apple inaugurated its own charity on the day Perkins died. Its work has never been publicised, but one beneficiary was a cancer hospital in Manchester.

died in Santa Barbara because if I had said where she died it would have been overrun straight away, and they needed time because of their grief to come back in private. I am just trying to keep this family together.' But his statement simply raised more questions, as the McCartneys had already returned to England by the time the announcement was made. What should have been reported as an agonising family tragedy had become a story about media manipulation instead.

There had been a recognisable shift in Linda McCartney's public reputation during her final decade: her skills as a mother (evident in the no-nonsense worldliness of her children) had long been acknowledged, and she had won widespread support for her campaigns against animal cruelty and in favour of vegetarianism. When she died, one reporter managed a final twist of the knife: 'The [Beatles'] demise was often attributed to her supposed ambition to record with Sir Paul herself,' wrote Mark Henderson in a cruel case of mistaken identity. But one of Britain's most conservative newspapers dubbed her a 'crusading vegetarian whose successful marriage defied all the doubters'. Her husband penned a tribute of heartbreaking honesty, to which the *Daily Mirror* responded, 'Nothing Paul McCartney wrote before was as beautiful and moving as the tribute to his late wife Linda.'

As his friend George Martin noted later that year, McCartney was sent headlong with grief. 'He is managing, but only just,' Martin revealed. 'It's a tough time for him. He's so alone now.' His wife's illness had shadowed him through 1997 and a succession of events that should have been celebrations. On New Year's Day it was announced that he had been awarded a knighthood. He claimed that his fellow Beatles now addressed him as 'Your Holiness', but that sounded like the invention of a PR man. Thirty-two years after the Beatles' MBE awards had sparked widespread controversy, this honour was eagerly anticipated and warmly welcomed. In April 1997 Sir Paul McCartney debuted his *Flaming Pie* album – his most exhilarating work in recent memory, which he attributed to the desire to create something that would match up to the Beatles' legacy. Almost as a matter of habit, he promoted the record by suggesting that the Beatles might yet reassemble to complete the third song they had left unfinished two years earlier, and at the same time he revealed the difficulties he had recently experienced in communicating with Harrison. In October he and his wife watched the unveiling of Stella McCartney's first collection. The following month he attended the *Q* magazine awards ceremony, pointedly walking out when his old nemesis Phil Spector made a speech. And then, as his wife's health declined, the widow of his former best friend chose to revive a family feud that seemed destined to outlive them both.

An apparent truce between the Lennons and McCartneys had endured for two years but collapsed when Ono commented on the respective merits of the two Beatles. 'I know Paul thinks he was leading them,' she said, insisting that the Beatles' real leader was Lennon. 'The way John led the band was very high level, on some kind of magical level. Not on a daily level, like Paul said, 'Oh, I was the one who told them all to come and do it. I made the phone calls.' John didn't make the phone calls. John was not on that level of a leader. He was on a level of a spiritual leader. He was the visionary, and that's why the Beatles happened.' She added, 'Paul's put in the position of being Salieri to Mozart' – a craftsman forced to compete with a genius, in other words. After which Ono can hardly have been surprised that she was not invited to the memorial services staged for Linda McCartney in London and New York. But she did post her own tribute: 'Linda and I did not meet up and have coffee and muffins in a corner café, or anything like that. But we communicated. We communicated in deeds more than in words. When she was strong, I felt strong.' And Ono also seemed to gain strength from Paul McCartney's weakness, as if the pair shared an eerie symbiosis. McCartney might have insisted in 1995, 'There are those who think John was the Beatles; that is not true and he would be the first to tell you that.' But he was permanently at risk of sounding churlish and oversensitive, while the same rules did not apply to Ono, who was widely expected to be unreasonable and only evoked surprise if she appeared (as she often did) considerate and modest.

McCartney intended to set history straight, but his efforts were understandably impeded by his wife's worsening health. In October 1997 his friend Barry Miles published *Many Years From Now*, an authorised biography of McCartney centred around their mutual adventures in the alternative London of the mid-1960s. The book was the apotheosis of the theme that McCartney had introduced a full decade earlier: he was the original avant-garde Beatle. Here was all the evidence to prove the point, but presented in such a defensive way that it begged criticism from those who felt that he ought to let history run its course and the facts speak for themselves.

The process of revisionism continued in 2000 with the belated publication of *The Beatles Anthology*, an epic oral history of the group that would have appeared years earlier had its original editor Derek Taylor not been stricken with cancer. The difference was that here McCartney's views were often contradicted by his colleagues; while *Many Years From Now* was, quite rightly, the unchallenged verdict of one very opinionated participant. The person with the strongest claim to feeling diminished by McCartney's book was George Harrison, whose contribution to the Beatles was consistently underplayed. Yet the time for Harrison and McCartney to fight had passed.

As he recovered from his cancer treatment, Harrison distanced himself from his past and the industry it had created. 'In my heart I still am on a mountain in India somewhere,' he said when required to do some Beatle business, 'and that suits me . . . It's hard to think of leaving the privacy and quiet of the happy life I have.' As his wife Olivia recalled later, 'When I met him, his ambition was to have no ambition. And I think he achieved that. For the last five years he felt like that, actually.'

Yet still the industry claimed him back. In March 1998 he intervened to prevent the Beatles from forming a business relationship with Volkswagen – the gimmick was that they would receive $10 million for sanctioning a branded Beetle model. It was VW's second attempt at enticing the group, who had already rejected $5 million to author-ise the manufacture of a White Album car. 'Unless we do something about it, every Beatles song is going to end up advertising bras and pork pies,' Harrison complained, and the deal was quietly abandoned.

Two months later he unexpectedly appeared at the London High Court as the official representative of the Beatles. 'I got the short straw and was the one who had to go to court for Apple,' he explained, grumpily shoving a press photographer. The case was triggered by Apple's belated attempt to regain control of the Star-Club tapes made in 1962 and first released in 1977. Since then the 1988 Copyright Act had been passed, and Apple's lawyers could demonstrate that the tapes were recorded when the group was under contract to EMI (Apple's partner in this action). Looking like a teddy-boy-turned-college-professor, Harrison gave a virtuoso performance in the witness box, delivering a rare history lesson in vintage Beatle lore while never hiding his contempt for the entire subject. 'Unlike the experts who wallow in Beatle trivia,' he explained, 'I spend a lot of time getting the junk out of my mind through meditation, so I don't know or remember – I don't *want* to know or remember – every last detail, cos it was trivial pursuit.' Countering the testimony of the man who'd originally made the tape, Ted Taylor, he described it as 'the crummiest recording ever made in our name' and said, 'One drunken person recording another bunch of drunks does not constitute a business deal.' Impressed by his testimony, the judge ruled that the tape should be returned to Apple – though it was safe to assume that most interested parties had already purchased a copy during the previous 21 years. Harrison continued to wage a private war on those who wished to take financial advantage of his name. He took a particular dislike to the sales of Beatles memorabilia held regularly in prestigious auction houses in London and New York. On one notable occasion a fan's scrapbook was sold, which included items collected from the Harrison family home in 1963, including corners of toasted bread left uneaten by the guitarist. 'That's total bullshit,' Harrison retorted. 'I ate all my toast. I never left any. The madness is the people selling it, and the people actually buying it.' In June 1999 he attended the private party for a charity auction of guitars from the collection of Eric Clapton. Harrison arrived late, clutching a tiny kids' guitar which he proudly placed alongside Clapton's valuable Fenders and Gibsons. But he exuded an aura of discontent that acted as a force field around him for the rest of the evening.

Harrison's obsession with privacy had long seemed like a fetish, but the events of December 1999 demonstrated that paranoia is sometimes justified. On the 23rd a young woman named Cristin Keleher broke into his home in Maui, the residence which he had been seeking to protect from outside gaze for nearly two decades. The Harrisons weren't present, so having triggered the alarm system Keleher tucked into a frozen pizza and waited for the inevitable police response. On the 30th she appeared in court and was sentenced to four months' imprisonment; it transpired that she had been stalking the Harrisons for several years.

As she answered the charge of trespassing, Harrison lay in a Henley hospital, undergoing emergency surgery. Around 3.30 that morning he had been woken at his Friar Park mansion by the sound of breaking glass. 'There were security cameras by the main gates and the back entrance,' his gardener Colin Harris explained, 'but in some parts of the grounds the fence was falling down. Anybody could wander in, and doors to the mansion were often left wide open in daytime. Security should have been a lot stricter. I knew someday somebody would get in there.'

Harrison ventured downstairs to investigate, wearing only pyjama bottoms, while his wife rang for help. There he was confronted by Mick Abram ('Mad Mick' to the British tabloids), a mentally disturbed young man who attacked him with a long kitchen knife. In an attempt to calm himself and Abram, Harrison began chanting the Hare Krishna Mantra – which Abram interpreted as the tongue of the devil, spurring him to further violence. As the blade slid repeatedly into Harrison's bony chest, he admitted, 'I thought I was dying. I vividly remember a deliberate thrust of a knife and I could feel the blood entering my mouth and hear my breath exhaling from the wound.' His life was saved by the courageous intervention of his wife, who brought down a weighty lamp on Abram's head, knocking him out. 'I was terrified,' she remembered, 'but it is one of those things that you just do in a heightened sense of awareness so that you can never really forget any of it. It was a freaky thing.'

The seriousness of the incident was deliberately underplayed by the Harrison family. He was quoted as saying of Abram, 'He wasn't a burglar and he certainly wasn't auditioning for the Traveling Wilburys.' But like Ronald Reagan's celebrated quips after the attempt on his life in 1981, the remark was designed to suggest that Harrison had scarcely been touched by the assault. The reality was much less pleasant. As Rolling Stones drummer Charlie Watts explained,

I spoke to Ringo about a month after it happened and he told me exactly what went on, and it was horrific. George was stabbed about 40 times. It happened outside his bedroom on the landing. He would have been dead if he'd been lying in bed, he wouldn't have been able to fight. The papers did say that one wound punctured his lung, but a lot of the others were just as horrific. The man was slashing him everywhere. George's wife hit him again and again on the head with this brass lamp, but he just wouldn't stop. There was blood everywhere.

Surgeons were forced to remove part of Harrison's lung, and his wounds left him scarred and breathless. More damaging still was the psychological impact. When he returned home, he sat in his kitchen with Eric Clapton, turning over and over again the precise details of the attack. 'George was still very disturbed,' Clapton recalled, 'and didn't seem to know where to go with his life. I could only use my own predicament with addiction as a reference, encouraging the potential use of some kind of support system.' 'It changed him,' one of his closest aides recalled. 'We all felt that. And we were sure that's why the cancer came back. He'd been looking so well, but after the attack he didn't have the strength left to fight.'

Through 2000 Harrison rested, worked sporadically on material for a new album and supervised the reissue of *All Things Must Pass*. It included a revised arrangement of 'My Sweet Lord', carefully omitting all the elements that had made the original record so commercial. It was a typically wilful gesture, infuriating yet strangely admirable, like the man himself. There were rumours that the Harrisons might abandon Friar Park, though their home in Maui was still the subject of litigation. More surreal was the suggestion that Neil Aspinall might retire as managing director of Apple and that Harrison might take his place – a bizarre option for a celebrity recluse to consider.

There was, it soon became apparent, no time for change and precious little time for life. In March 2001 Harrison underwent surgery to remove a tumour from his lung. The following month he came under the care of the Oncology Institute of Southern Switzerland while staying in a lakeside home by the Italian border. He met Paul McCartney briefly in Milan a few weeks later, but otherwise lived as privately as he had always wished, albeit with the knowledge that his illness was outpacing him.

If John Lennon's murder had provided the starkest possible exhibition of the perils of celebrity, Harrison's final months were, in their way, an equally cruel reminder. It was a savage irony that this most reluctant of public figures should be exploited, not once but twice, by those who cared less for his humanity than his fame. He issued a statement in early July 2001, claiming that he was 'feeling fine' and apologising for any concern felt by fans. But two weeks later Beatles producer George Martin was widely quoted as delivering a virtual death sentence: 'He is an indomitable spirit but he knows that he is going to die soon, and he is accepting this.' When this appeared in print, the appalled Martin rang Harrison to apologise and deny ever making the remark. And he was right: his actual words were, 'He's been rescued many times . . . I guess he's hoping he's going to be rescued again. And I think he will. But he knows perfectly well there's a chance he may not be.' This story was then twisted by a succession of editors into something more sensational. Harrison insisted that he was 'active and feeling very well', but the original story was what people remembered, even after Richard Starkey had visited his friend and announced that Harrison was 'fine'.

At the start of October Harrison entered a recording studio for the last time, to tape a song entitled 'Horse to Water' with Jools Holland's band. 'He hadn't been well earlier in the year,' Holland admitted, 'but he seemed much, much better. He seemed strong, and his voice was really strong. He'll continue to improve.' Yet Harrison's lyrics had the dull ring of an Old Testament prophet confronting the apostasy of his nation from his deathbed. There was a verse about 'a friend of mine in so much misery', in which it was difficult not to recognise the haunted face of the bereaved Paul McCartney; another about an alcoholic; a third about a 'preacher' who 'warned me against Satan', the inference being that none of these apparent heroes had been able to find peace. When the song was copyrighted, Harrison assigned it to a new company: RIP Ltd 2001. It was a final stroke of black humour.

Within two weeks of that session Harrison's health had sharply declined. Aware that his struggle was entering its final weeks, he resigned as a director of Harrisongs, yielding his place to his wife, who soon succeeded her husband on the Apple board as well. The cancer had followed a familiar path, from his lungs to his brain; he was agonisingly thin and suffering hallucinations from his weighty intake of painkillers. He crossed the Atlantic for the final time, to try experimental radiation treatment at the pioneering clinic of the Staten Island University Hospital. Within a few days he was visited by McCartney. The two men, friends for more than 45 years but so often divided by the aftermath of their fame, spent their final hours together reminiscing about their shared past. 'We were laughing and joking, just like nothing was going on. I was impressed by his strength,' McCartney recalled later.

A team was focusing high-density doses of radiation on Harrison's brain tumour in an effort to win him a few extra months of life, but according to an indictment filed several years later one medic was overcome by the lure of Harrison's fame. Olivia Harrison alleged in 2004 that the medic drove his children to the house that the Harrisons had rented, 'where [George] was bedridden and in great discomfort'. There the medic made Harrison listen while his son played the guitar, and then asked him to autograph the instrument for the boy. The frail musician refused: 'I do not even know if I know how to spell my name any more,' he said. The medic allegedly told him, 'Come on, you can do this,' placed a pen in Harrison's hand and helped him scrawl his name on the guitar.

Harrison abandoned the treatment and flew to Los Angeles for a more conventional course of radiotherapy. During the flight Harrison was so weak that he nearly died, but he clung to life for another two weeks. On 28 November, however, it was obvious that he was close to death, and his old friend Ravi Shankar flew to Los Angeles to visit him. Shankar's daughter Anoushka recalled, '[George] had a look that I'd never really seen before, so full of love and peace. He wasn't able to say anything with his lips, but his eyes were saying it. That house was just so full of love.'

The following day George Harrison died at 1.30 p.m., in the presence of his wife, his son and fellow devotees of Krishna. 'George aspired to leave his body in a conscious manner, and that was a goal of his life,' his wife recalled. His friend Mukanda Goswami said simply, 'He was a very spiritual person, who was unafraid to die.' He passed from this world with the scent of incense in his nostrils, while his friends chanted the praises of Krishna. His body was covered with a yellow silk blanket, and sprinkled with rose petals and holy water. The official cause of death was less poetic: 'metastatic non-small cell lung cancer' accompanied by 'head and neck squamous cell carcinoma'.

There was none of the shock that had accompanied Lennon's death 21 years earlier; just a profound sense of regret that this complex and determined man had died at the age of 58. His son Dhani captured Harrison's spiritual nature: 'There was no urgency for him. Occasionally he'd get motivated, but not because he felt like he was going to die. He never sat and felt sorry for himself. He had no fears or worries left when he died.' He would be missed, said Richard Starkey, for his humour and his generosity of spirit. Paul McCartney, who still remembered how a single misplaced word had haunted him when Lennon died, pronounced careful but heartfelt tribute: 'I am devastated and very very sad. He was a lovely guy and a very brave man, and he had a wonderful sense of humour. He is really just my baby brother.'

Harrison's body was cremated, and his family took his ashes to Varanasi in India, where the holy waters of the Ganges, the Yamuna and Saraswati meet. Olivia Harrison delivered a suitably spiritual requiem: 'We are deeply touched by the outpouring of love and compassion from people around the world. The profound beauty of the moment of George's passing – of his awakening from this dream – was no surprise to those of us who knew how he longed to be with God. In that pursuit, he was relentless.'

In a bizarre repeat of the aftermath of Linda McCartney's death, the media noticed a discrepancy on Harrison's death certificate – creating a five-day mystery that was solved when the real location of his death, a house in the Hollywood Hills that had been leased to Paul McCartney, was revealed. (The certificate listed Harrison's home as being in Lugano, Switzerland, presumably for tax purposes.) By January 2002 'My Sweet Lord' was the best-selling single in Britain, and Olivia Harrison was preparing a lawsuit against a member of her extended family, whom she accused of stealing her husband's possessions and selling them the day after George's death. In July she held a private commemoration of her husband's life at Friar Park, attended by McCartney, Starkey and George Martin. And on 29 November 2002 – 'one year to the day', as the posters said – she organised the Concert For George at the Royal Albert Hall, at which many of his closest friends paid musical homage. Dhani Harrison, looking eerily like a reincarnation of his father circa 1963, remained on stage throughout. As Eric Clapton admitted, George Harrison would probably have said something like, 'Thanks very much, but I don't really want this.' He would, Clapton added wryly, 'try to queer the pitch a bit . . . He could be very contrary.' But the Harrison that was celebrated was the spiritual seeker, the master of subtle melodic shifts and deeply personal lyricism. Both of the surviving Beatles were there. Starkey almost upstaged the event: 'I loved George; George loved me,' he declared confidently. By contrast, McCartney appeared uncertain, almost embarrassed – perhaps intimidated to be in the company of Harrison's closest allies. Anxious not to appear to be seeking the limelight, he performed with uncharacteristic restraint, though his emotion was clear to see. But it wasn't hard to imagine Harrison's cynicism as McCartney led the band into a soulful rendition of 'All Things Must Pass' – one of the songs that the other Beatles had refused to take seriously in January 1969.

Moving as the occasion was, the concert could only hint at the breadth of Harrison's character. 'George was the funniest man I knew,' his widow declared. 'When he died, it was like, Oh, no, the party's over.' With sly humour that her husband would have relished, she recalled, 'He didn't put up with any crabbiness, other than his own.' In the years to come she and Dhani would oversee the repackaging of Harrison's albums, and Dhani would launch his own musical career, besides taking on the much-needed role of providing Apple with a link to the 21st century audience. 'My job description is being enthusiastic,' the 30-year-old said in 2009.

No such obvious role was open to Richard Starkey. Alcohol and drugs had clouded his life in a comforting haze for two decades after the demise of the Beatles; then the effort to maintain sobriety and the habit of work filled his time. 'I've finally become everyone I used to hate!' he joked to a friend in 1990. But there was a darker subtext. Once the Beatles had re-formed, to his great delight, and disbanded again; once his second or third album crafted with skill and without stimulants had been released and widely ignored by the public; once a proposed supergroup with Willie Nelson and Merle Haggard had failed to materialise; once he had launched a new record label (Pumkinhead Records) without any noticeable impact; once the fifth or sixth incarnation of his All-Starr Band had filled the same halls as its predecessor, what was left? 'Living sober was difficult,' he recalled, 'I had to start again.' But starting was no longer the problem; the challenge was to fill his life with something that was as much fun as partying and as exciting as being in the Beatles, and there were few things that were both legal and sober enough to qualify.

In public Starkey was still the lovable joker with the maudlin face; it's hard to imagine any of the other Beatles being easy-going enough to discuss the group's relative penis sizes, as he did on Howard Stern's show in 1998. His humour was natural and unforced: seemingly without effort he exuded charm and self-respect. But sometimes a sourer side of his personality became visible. It was there when he dismissed yet one more enquiry about the Beatles with a sullen refusal to talk about anything except his new album, which he must have known would be forgotten in weeks; and likewise when he told a newspaper in 2005, 'I have this thing about England, that they don't really love me enough. That's just how I feel. It's not a fact, it's just a feeling.' Increasingly he carried that defensiveness with him, to the point where it became part of his psyche. In 2005, when McCartney performed 'Sgt Pepper' at the Live 8 concert with U2, Starkey complained, 'I was never asked to do it. He didn't ask me. It's too late now. It's very disappointing.' The same spirit seemed to inspire his plan to make a documentary that would set the public straight about who he really was. In his heart he was still the child who had suffered when his friends were having fun, and who had spent several years confined in hospitals. No matter that the child now lived in Monte Carlo, with additional homes in Los Angeles, Colorado, London and, just for good measure, the traditional rock star mansion (17th century, of course) in Surrey.

In 2008 his persona began to attract public criticism for the first time. He was offered the opportunity to act as the mascot, effectively, of his hometown's reign as European City of Culture. 'We never let Liverpool down,' he told the local paper, and the same message inspired the title track of his *Liverpool 8* album. Banal though it was, reducing his history to humourless doggerel, 'Liverpool 8' allowed him more TV exposure than he'd been given in years. But his once well-attuned aerial for the public mood was failing him. On a TV chat show he announced that there was nothing about Liverpool that he missed – a mild enough comment but still considered undiplomatic from the mouth of the city's unofficial cultural ambassador and enough to trigger a backlash from Liverpudlians. Two weeks later he walked off the US TV show *Live With Regis and Kelly* after being asked to perform an abridged version of 'Liverpool 8'. More bad press resulted. Record company officials let slip that they were puzzled by the frequency with which Starkey muttered the phrase 'peace and love'; one counted twenty obsessive repetitions during a one-hour business meeting. His unkind fate was that he was now more newsworthy for his minor lapses of judgement than for his talent and charm.

He was scarcely the only celebrity who felt exploited by being asked for signatures that would appear within hours on the auction site eBay.

But when his patience snapped, he was unwise enough to advertise the fact on his website. In November 2008 he posted a 40-second video message that aroused global derision. Speaking into a camera so close that he seemed to be inside a box, Starkey lectured his fans in a strangely monotonous voice, 'warning' them 'with peace and love' that he was too busy to sign any more autographs. As he repeated his catchphrase for the fifth time in this brief clip, it was difficult not to wonder whether he was undergoing some kind of psychological distress. Paul McCartney supported his friend, saying that Starkey was simply 'speaking his mind'. The following year the two men performed several songs together in Las Vegas, eliciting cries of 'Beatles reunion' from the press. It was Starkey's natural turf. As producer Don Was noted, his most enduring legacy wasn't his fame, but his musicianship: 'He had a completely different approach to rock 'n' roll drumming that has influenced everybody who came after him in a major way.'

In the wake of Linda McCartney's death in April 1998 at the age of just 56, Paul McCartney's all too visible grief demonstrated that fame was no defence against sadness. He was bereaved in a world that expected its heroes to suffer in public, and he fulfilled that role, and his private duty, in exemplary fashion – leading two poignant memorial services and then completing an album of his wife's music. He made a disguised return to public life that October, to promote his second collaboration with producer Youth under the name of the Fireman – a ruse that allowed him to explore uncharacteristic musical dimensions. An album of rock 'n' roll standards in Linda's memory, an exhibition of paintings, an orchestral album and *A Garland For Linda*, a performance of classical pieces, completed an 18-month cycle of remembrance. By December 1999 nobody questioned the propriety of staging a much-hyped performance at the replica Cavern Club in Liverpool.

McCartney was annoyed in March 1999 when he was romantically (and wrongly) linked with a textile designer. Two months later he attended an awards ceremony and was introduced to Heather Mills – a one-time glamour model who had lost a leg in a collision with a police motorcycle and had since become an outspoken charity campaigner. By November the British press were speculating that McCartney and Mills were lovers, and in January 2000 he was formally introduced to friends as her boyfriend. In March McCartney confirmed publicly, 'We are an item.' He told a reporter that he still spoke to his late wife, and that she approved of his new partner. Meanwhile, Mills' carefully erected public face began to crumble: as early as June 2000 press headlines read, I HAD TO TELL PAUL I WAS ACCUSED OF BEING A HOOKER.

McCartney proposed to Mills in July 2001. Nearly a year later hotel staff overheard a passionate argument at a Florida hotel. 'I don't want to marry you,' McCartney is alleged to have said, before flinging her engagement ring out of the window. The following month the pair were married at Castle Leslie in Ireland. Their daughter Beatrice was born in October 2003, though leading British tabloid newspapers confidently announced that she was 'a boy'.* But in late April 2006, two months after the couple visited Canada to protest against seal hunting, they announced that their marriage was over: 'Having tried exceptionally hard to make our relationship work given the daily pressures surrounding us, it is with sadness that we have decided to go our separate ways.' The Beatles family gathered round: Olivia Harrison and Barbara Bach took McCartney's daughters Stella and Mary out for lunch in London; Yoko Ono pleaded for the press to allow the McCartneys some privacy.

When McCartney and Jane Asher ended their engagement in 1968 there was a brief flurry of excitement in the press, and then the subject was discreetly dropped. The public had no knowledge of his affair with Francie Schwartz until she published her account in Rolling Stone magazine several years later. No investigative reporters were detailed to pry into the previous life and loves of Linda Eastman – or, for that matter, the more universally mistrusted Yoko Ono.

Thirty years on, the media focused relentless attention on McCartney and Mills. Both had calculated that they could channel this prurient interest to their own benefit; celebrity was not just their past but the product they were selling. Neither imagined that they might not be able to control the circus. Mills had embellished her personal history with the same recklessness with which the media promoted its modern heroes. McCartney had employed PR man Geoff Baker, and many before him, to shape reality. But both McCartney and Mills

---

* The Daily Mirror's story was traced back to a joke by McCartney's brother Michael, teasing the newspaper for its obsessive interest in the couple.

suffered from a cardinal sin in the ruthless arena of 21st-century fame: naivety. They trusted that they would always be loved; that McCartney, as a national icon, was impervious to criticism; that Mills, as a tragic victim, was beyond reproach. Their downfall was not emotional or psychological – there are millions of divorces every decade in Britain alone – it was tactical, and they were quickly given a stern lesson in the cruelty of the global media machine.

There was an initial buzz of excitement and sympathy when the couple met, and the bereaved superstar was comforted by the courageous victim. But slowly the mood changed. Mills was barely older than McCartney's children, and the media exploited every possible rift between them. She was described as a gold-digger, targeting McCartney for his fathomless wealth; he was portrayed as a foolish old man, beguiled by the attractions of a woman young enough to be his daughter. Since he had been deserted by John Lennon 30 years earlier, his survival had centred on his relationship with Linda Eastman, his public image and his music. Now two of those struts had collapsed, and the third was made almost irrelevant by the petty drama of his private life. In 2003 he released *Chaos and Creation in the Backyard*, one of the most effective solo albums in his catalogue, but it was quickly buried beneath the debris of his marriage.

When the pair separated, Mills accused McCartney of unleashing a witch-hunt against her and responded with a string of ever more shocking tales of degradation and abuse. By October 2006, for example, it was being claimed that McCartney had stabbed Mills with a broken glass, attacked her in a drunken rage, assaulted her when she was pregnant, mocked her disability and refused to let her breast-feed their daughter, telling Mills, 'They are *my* breasts.' McCartney maintained a dignified silence and let journalists find their own methods of puncturing Mills' reputation. As the stories grew more outlandish, however, it was inevitable that some of the dirt would tarnish his image. It was but a short step, after all, from the Mills camp's claims about McCartney's alleged bad behaviour to the unsubstantiated rumours about his sexual preferences that were the subject of amused speculation in media circles. No matter how ridiculous the accusations – and most of them were laughable – McCartney was damned if he answered them and equally damned if he didn't. Years of careful handling of the media were erased as it became possible to allege almost anything about one of Britain's most famous celebrities, in the knowledge that he would be unable to respond.

It was difficult not to feel that Mills had been naive in the way she had handled herself, her marriage and her past. Yet even if the cruellest tabloid allegations were true, there was something shocking in the way that she became the repository for every ill-concealed impulse of hatred against women – not least from other women, many of whom seemed to relish her transformation into a global scapegoat, like the crowds who gathered to watch mediaeval witch burnings. Mocked, battered, belittled, hated, Mills had little option but to retire into the self-justification that was her least attractive public face, and thereby toss more wood onto the pyre.

The denouement was a divorce hearing held behind closed doors in February 2008. A month later Mills arrived at the High Court to hear the judge award her an estimated £16.5 million from McCartney's billion-dollar fortune. After throwing a glass of water over her ex-husband's lawyer, she pleaded for the full judgement not to be made public, but it was too late to argue for privacy. Inevitably, the press focused on the judge's verdict that Mills was 'a less than impressive witness' who had been 'not just inconsistent and inaccurate but also less than candid'. But for McCartney it was a hollow victory. Throughout his career he had carefully satisfied the demand for knowledge about elements of his private life while retaining strict barriers around the rest, thereby allowing himself the sanity of existing – to some degree, at least – beyond the view of the world. Now everything was laid bare, as if he'd been photographed naked by a paparazzo: the homes in Beverly Hills, Long Island, Somerset, Essex and Merseyside; the £32 million collection of 'artefacts'; the £36 million pension pot; even the security arrangements at his various residences.

The saga took a savage toll. Throughout his courtship, marriage and divorce McCartney had worked, as he always will. He'd staged massively successful world tours; organised the Concert For New York City after the 9/11 disaster; made records, issued DVDs, published a children's book, exhibited paintings, raised money for charity and offered his familiar thumbs-up to a million photographers and fans. Yet through it all the world was more interested in whether he had really demanded that his estranged wife return three bottles of cleaning fluid to his home, or whether he was so addicted to marijuana that he could barely function without it. After decades of youthfulness, he suddenly aged faster than his years, and took steps to repair the damage which merely accentuated the changes. Like a fading Hollywood star, his face was a strange combination of youth and age, his hair a shade removed from nature's palette, his skin both tight and sagging. When he publicised Liverpool's Year of Culture in December 2007 he was wearing an almost bouffant approximation of his 1963 Beatle cut and appeared slightly dazed. In interviews his voice sounded restricted and slightly strangled. A month later it was reported that a 'spokesman' had confirmed that McCartney had recently undergone an operation for a coronary angioplasty, to improve his blood circulation; then McCartney countered that the supposedly official tales were 'completely untrue'. For a man who was reported to be facing a major health crisis, he was certainly energetic: during 2007 and 2008 he was linked by the overexcited media with a dazzling list of women, among them Rosanna Arquette, Sabrina Guinness, Renee Zellweger, Christie Brinkley, Natasha Marsh, Elle Macpherson, Lulu, Tanya Larrigan and Nancy Shevell, who became his regular companion. Understandably, he remained silent about his relationship with Shevell, though that didn't prevent others talking. But as a woman who was not only dignified but rich, she was perceived as a suitable candidate for McCartney's affections.

After Linda McCartney's death there was a partial truce in the battle of wills with Yoko Ono. 'It's normal in any business relationship,' Ono explained in 2000. 'Sometimes he gets upset, and sometimes I get upset. I'm not as vocal as he is in the world about it, but I do get upset. Also, I'm sure that in the case of Paul there's that feeling that I'm the woman who took away his partner – it's like a divorce.' But the two parties continued to squabble over their joint legacy. In late 2002 McCartney prepared his fifth live album in twelve years, *Back in the US* – its title deliberately evoking the Beatles, just as his previous release, *Paul Is Live!*, had done.* He chose to repeat what he had done on *Wings Over America* more than 25 years earlier, and credit the Lennon/McCartney songs – *his* songs – to McCartney/Lennon.

Ono chose to be violently offended by this effectively meaningless

---

* Besides its *Abbey Road* cover photograph, the title referred to the 'Paul is dead' media hype of 1969.

gesture; a spokesman called it 'absolutely inappropriate'. (The spokesman clearly hadn't seen copies of the earliest Beatles records, which were indeed credited to 'McCartney/Lennon'.) If her response was designed to rile McCartney, it succeeded, as he reacted like a disgruntled adolescent. 'Why do I care?' he asked himself rhetorically. 'I don't know. I've given up. I'm not going to bother with it. It's very unseemly for me to care, because John's not here and it's like walking on a dead man's grave. I was talking about him as if he were here, and he's not.' His sense of injustice was reasonable: after all, why should Lennon pass into history as the primary composer of 'Yesterday' and 'Hey Jude' when they were entirely McCartney's work? 'It's actually just a very little request,' he said, 'and it makes me look stupid.' Starkey agreed with the latter sentiment: 'I think the way he did it was underhanded,' he said of McCartney's gentle rewriting of history. 'He's wanted to do it for years. I thought he should have done it officially with Yoko.' But that was based on the unlikely assumption that Ono would ever allow the change.

In a more charitable mood Ono revealed keen insight into those who were left behind by Lennon's death – not just McCartney, but Cynthia and Julian Lennon as well. 'This is like a drama,' she said in 2005. 'Each person has something to be totally miserable about, because of the way they were put into this play. I have incredible sympathy for each of them.' Yet she had a way of expressing solidarity that could still pierce the heart: 'My perspective is that it is probably very hard to be Paul McCartney. There's a certain kind of insecurity that famous people have. And he has more than other people because he's more famous, probably.' McCartney paid constant tribute to his fallen companions during his 21st-century live shows, performing 'Something' in honour of Harrison and 'Here Today' for Lennon. But at an intimate in-store show in California 27 years after Lennon's death his persona cracked open wide, to reveal the pained, abandoned man within. In front of no more than 200 people McCartney gently began a solo rendition of 'Here Today', the letter he'd never had the chance to send to his best friend. As he acknowledged Lennon's absence, his voice faltered and broke as he choked back tears. It was a moment of naked reality almost unmatched in his career, a gesture of love and pain, and a wound that could never be healed.

Like McCartney, Ono channelled her emotions into constant activity.

Much of her work was sensitive, and generous to Lennon's fans; some was more selfish. It seemed churlish, for instance, when she reworked Lennon's promotional videos from the period when the pair were separated. Songs written during his relationship with May Pang were now accompanied by footage of Lennon and Ono as if those magical lovers had never been parted. Even more regrettable was her treatment of Lennon's *Walls and Bridges* album, a true artefact of the Pang era. Reissued in 2005, the disc now bore artwork that merged Lennon and Ono's faces. If reversing a songwriting credit was 'absolutely inappropriate', what was reversing an artist's intentions?

Some detected foul play at work in 1998 when the release of Julian Lennon's *Photograph Smile* coincided, to the exact day, with Sean Lennon's flimsy debut album. 'Julian was devastated,' his mother recalled. 'He knew it couldn't be a coincidence that he and his brother had been pitted against each other so blatantly.' Sean had hip associates (Sonic Youth, the Beastie Boys) and garnered critical acclaim; Julian sounded like Paul McCartney in his melodic prime, but was distinctly unfashionable, and his album suffered by that unbalanced comparison. He did not issue another record for the next decade, feeling that the industry was stacked against him; while his step-brother continuing to attract media attention. It didn't hurt that Sean Lennon had developed McCartney's knack for attracting press controversy to sell a record – alleging that his father used to beat him, for example, or had been killed by a US government hit man.

Ono knew what she was doing when she bracketed Lennon's oldest son with McCartney in her roll-call of victims. Lennon was commemorated when Liverpool's airport was renamed in his honour; McCartney had the knighthood but not the civic recognition. At the Q Awards in 2005 Ono carved another wound in McCartney's reputation: 'John would say to me, "They always cover Paul's songs, they never cover mine." I said to him, "You're a good songwriter, it's not June-with-spoon that you write."' Friends said that McCartney dreaded what would happen if Ono – one of life's natural survivors – outlived him.

'It's the kind of a challenge that a warrior likes,' Ono said of her responsibility as Lennon's executor. 'I would really like to see his work is properly communicated.' But the nature of that communication became increasingly controversial. In an astute article in 1995 rock critic Paul Du Noyer wrote,

You have to wonder if this is what the future will look like: all our yester-days, digitally magicked into the soundtrack of all our tomorrows. Music will never grow old – not because it is timeless, but because it will get cosmetic surgery whenever the market is ready to buy it all over again. And a company like Apple Records, which I used to imagine as the custodian of a legacy, becomes instead an incubator for endlessly refined Beatles material, perhaps in media we haven't even dreamed of.

It was an uncannily accurate vision.

As early as May 1997 Richard Starkey was promising digitally enhanced editions of the *Yellow Submarine* and *Let It Be* films, plus CD releases of the un-Spectorised *Get Back* album and EMI's *Live at the Hollywood Bowl* concoction. The first of those projects emerged in 1999, when Apple authorised the DVD release of *Yellow Submarine* alongside a 'new' Beatles album, *Yellow Submarine Songtrack* – nothing more than a compilation of the songs featured in the film. But the marketing campaign did allow Apple to license a new range of *Yellow Submarine* collectables – a Pepperland globe, baseballs, T-shirts, boxer shorts, even a lava lamp, all embellished with the images of your favourite cartoon pop stars. 'I don't think it will add any more [to the legend],' George Harrison said. 'It just keeps what is already there going, it just keeps it ticking over. But all of that really had nothing to do with us. It was like we were just put there as playthings for the rest of the world.'

The least commercially minded of all the Beatles, it was Harrison who conceived the project that would occupy Apple for the first years of the new century. He had become close friends with Guy Laliberte, owner of the Cirque du Soleil franchise. He suggested that the Cirque should design one of their spectacular fusions of circus, dance and music around the Beatles' catalogue. 'In typical Apple fashion, it began with a lot of discussion,' said Giles Martin, son of the newly knighted Sir George. His father was recruited to supervise the musical content of the show, which slowly began to take shape in the years after Harrison's death. 'I knew I was the only one who could do it with any degree of credence,' Sir George said. His son added, 'Apple wanted this to be the best show it could be, and Neil [Aspinall] made it clear that they didn't want to do anything where they sanctioned other people singing Beatles songs.'

Cirque du Soleil's show, entitled *Love*, debuted with a gala premiere at the Mirage, Las Vegas in June 2006, attended by two Beatles and two Beatle widows*. It promised to capture 'the spirit and passion behind the most beloved rock group of all time . . . underscored by aerial performance, extreme sports and urban, freestyle dance'. To accompany the astonishing visuals, Martin *père et fils* created a collage of Beatles music influenced (as Giles Martin admitted) by *The Grey Album*, an underground mash-up of samples from the Beatles' White Album and hip-hop tracks by Jay-Z.† The Martins began by preparing a 15-minute demonstration of what their techniques could create. 'Ringo thought it was fantastic,' Sir George said, 'and he said to me, "George, you can do anything you like as far as I'm concerned." Paul said, "Yeah, really great, but you know you can be more adventurous." I thought, Blimey, I thought we had been pretty adventurous anyway, but he gave us carte blanche to do even more. Olivia [Harrison] liked it, she didn't make any comments. Yoko liked it, but said she was a little concerned that what we had done with John's work wasn't quite right.' Although Sir George Martin was ostensibly in charge of the project, hearing problems restricted his involvement, and the *Love* album (issued in November 2006) was effectively compiled by Giles Martin and engineers at EMI. Paul McCartney said, 'The album puts the Beatles back together again, because suddenly there's John and George with me and Ringo. It's kind of magical.' The record briefly caught the global imagination but was as ephemeral as confectionary, melting to leave an unpleasant, chemical aftertaste.

Love was far from being the only 21st-century fantasy built around the Beatles. The TV channel VH1 screened *Two of Us*, a fictional recreation of a meeting between Lennon and McCartney in 1976. It was made by Michael Lindsay-Hogg, who had last featured in the saga as the director of the *Let It Be* film. Broadway briefly hosted *Lennon*, an Ono-approved musical that was greeted as a theatrical catastrophe. More entertaining than either was the 'discovery' in 2003 of a Beatles reunion tape supposedly made in Los Angeles in 1976. A memorabilia dealer claimed to have the only recording of this

---

* The same quartet gave a dull 'reunion' interview to TV host Larry King.
† Apple and EMI prevented *The Grey Album* from being released commercially, but thousands of copies were distributed via file-sharing sites.

hitherto undocumented session. He listed the songs that the Beatles had recorded, the titles of which were so banal that they dampened any sense of excitement: 'Happy Feeling', 'Back Home', 'Rockin' Once Again', 'People of the Third World' and 'Little Girl'. Needless to say, there was no reunion; yet it was testament to the Beatles' endless power to command publicity that such stories were widely reported as news.

In the absence of any new tapes, EMI and Apple concentrated on the old. In 2000 they released 1 (known to insiders for months beforehand as Project X). 'The Beatles are still saving the industry's ass,' one retailer noted as this compilation of hit singles sold 18 million copies around the world. Inevitably, this success prompted rumours that the Beatles would re-form for a world tour, until the extent of Harrison's illness was revealed.

The industry could continue just as well without him. By 2002 McCartney was boosting the imminent arrival of a DVD transfer of the Let It Be film and a fuller and more accurate representation of the January 1969 sessions than Phil Spector had achieved. Let It Be . . . Naked – an album but, significantly, no film – duly appeared in November 2003. Lacking either the historical accuracy of the original Get Back album from 1969 or the production finesse of Spector's edition, it was accurately described by the New York Times as 'Let It Be with a fig leaf' – a pointless and faintly insulting product, widely ignored by the public. When 2003 passed without the appearance of the long-anticipated DVD, there were rumours that McCartney and Starkey were blocking its release because it showed the Beatles in a bad light. The story wasn't true, but it was easy to believe when the financial potency of the Beatles' brand clearly outweighed the interests of their fans or their creative legacy.

Perhaps inevitably, the most satisfied consumer of the Beatles in the 21st century was the legal profession. In September 2003 Neil Aspinall's Apple Corps launched its third and, they hoped, final assault on its American near-namesake. Far from distancing themselves from the music business, as they had promised in their previous settlement, Apple Computers had launched the iTunes system of music downloads and the pioneering MP3 player, the iPod. Apple was now synonymous in the public mind with music – but not the Beatles' music, as Apple Corps refused to make its wares available for download. By 2003 it was hard to find anyone under the age of 40 who even knew that the

Beatles owned a company named Apple, so total was the computer firm's domination of the marketplace.

The early skirmishes took on a familiar pattern. Apple Corps functioned as a record company again by reissuing the CDs it had prepared during the previous court battle, and Apple Computers continued to astonish the world with its technological innovations. Analysts predicted a truce, whereby Computers would be forced to pay Corps a royalty on all their music-related activities, and the Beatles' music would then appear on iTunes. Apple boss Steve Jobs complained, 'We can't reach an agreement, and the courts could drag on for years . . . The whole thing is unfortunate, because we love the Beatles.' For Apple Corps, Geoff Baker commented, 'We have no plans at the moment to go online.' The inference was plain: what did the timeless Beatles care for such a fly-by-night novelty as the digital download?

The first battle ended in victory for the Beatles, who won the right for the case to be heard in Britain. By September 2004 informed insiders were predicting that Computers would gracefully admit defeat and deliver the largest compensation payment in legal history. Eighteen months later the case finally reached the High Court. Neil Aspinall played the digital ingénu: 'I am computer illiterate,' he testified. 'I don't even know how to turn one on.' Confronted with the information that the Beatles' own website used Apple Computers software, he pleaded ignorance. Apple Computers' QC said poetically that 'even a moron in a hurry' could tell that his clients were not trying to masquerade as the Beatles – but that was hardly the point, as the issue at stake was the agreement the two sides had made a decade earlier.

Informed observers universally expected Apple Corps to win the case. But when Mr Justice Mann delivered his verdict on 8 May 2006, he first rejected many of the arguments put forward by Apple Computers and then awarded them victory, on the grounds that they were not using their apple logo on the music they were selling – because it did not exist as a physical object. Many commentators sympathised with Neil Aspinall's stunned response: 'With great respect to the trial judge, we consider he has reached the wrong conclusion.' Aspinall immediately launched appeal proceedings.

The two sides achieved an out-of-court settlement in February 2007, but the terms of the ceasefire were startling: Apple Corps agreed to cede ownership of all the Apple trademarks to Apple Computers, who in return would license the relevant names back to the Beatles' company. Forty years after it was founded and launched as an alternative to the capitalist system, Apple Corps now only existed by permission of a corporation – which, it could be argued, had kept closer to the Beatles' original philosophy than the group had done themselves.

One more problem remained. For several years EMI and Apple had – once again – been involved in litigation about royalty payments and ownership of copyrights, fighting the same tired battles that they had been waging for nearly 30 years. But within a month of the Apple vs Apple settlement, it was announced that the Apple vs EMI contest was also ending out of court, with undisclosed consequences. It was perhaps telling that Paul McCartney had chosen to end his contract with EMI – which had endured unbroken in the UK since 1962 – and look for album-by-album deals elsewhere. Now it seemed that all the pieces were in place: the two Apples, EMI and the music. Since the departure of Allen Klein in 1973 Neil Aspinall had been fighting the Beatles' cause in courts around the world. Now all the existing legislation had been concluded, and it was time for Aspinall to reap the commercial benefits.

Instead, the unthinkable happened. On 4 April 2007 Apple Corps issued a brief statement about

the departure of Neil Aspinall, who had been with John, Paul, George and Ringo for a spectacular forty-plus years, during which he played an indispensable role for the four. He was there since the inception of the band in Liverpool and has meant so much to the Beatles' family for all these years and still does. However, he has decided to move on. Apple as a whole, and each member of the company, wishes him great success in whatever endeavour he chooses to pursue in the future.

It read like corporate gloss, disguising a forced departure. There was no suggestion that Aspinall had been sacked, but there were strong whispers that he had been placed in a position where he felt unable to continue.

Perhaps he had merely chosen to rest at the age of 65, after a lifetime in the Beatles' service. Paul McCartney insisted, 'Neil was great.

Neil was our mate for a long, long time, and nobody could replace Neil, because he was so special, he still is, he's a great guy, but he'd been wanting to retire for quite a while.' That explanation was too simple for the conspiracy-minded. It was suggested that one or more of the Beatles (or their widows) had grown impatient at the delay in making the group's music available for digital download. A team of independent accountants was said to have been employed to calculate exactly how much money Apple could have made if he had been more open to technological innovation. In his defence, Aspinall could legitimately have claimed that he was only acting as the servant of his masters, and that they employed him to say no. Others wondered whether Aspinall might have viewed the settlement with Apple Computers as a disaster, and chosen to fall on his sword like a disgraced Roman general.

Another widely believed theory was that Aspinall had come under extreme pressure from the Beatles' other representatives to squeeze maximum return from the group's name. This seemed to be supported by comments from former Apple press officer Geoff Baker, who had been sacked by McCartney for 'unstable' behaviour.* 'I fear for the integrity of the Beatles' legacy without Neil,' Baker said. This scenario envisaged a world in which their image and music would be licensed to anyone who had money in their fist, regardless of artistic or commercial consequences.

Aspinall's place as director and company secretary of Apple Corps, and CEO of its subsidiaries Apple Charity (UK) Ltd and Apple Washington was taken by Jeff Jones, a former executive at Sony Records. There he had supervised the restoration of the Miles Davis archive, a project which had won almost universal applause. Beatles fans noted his pedigree and looked forward to all the heritage CDs and DVDs that they assumed Aspinall had been hiding from the world. Less heralded was the rise of a chartered accountant, Garth Tweedale, who had helped Harrison to sort out the HandMade Films debacle and now assumed many of Aspinall's financial responsibilities within

---

* Baker replied, 'If I'm unstable, maybe that's because somebody had driven me to that.' But by March 2006 Baker was telling the press that he was actually sacked for his cocaine addiction: PAUL FIRING ME KEPT ME ALIVE was one headline. A year later Baker was back in the PR game, selling a new band while 'confessing', FOR 15 YEARS I LIED FOR MACCA. And in 2009 he was once again to be seen in McCartney's company.

the Beatles Group of Companies. Meanwhile, day-to-day activities continued to be monitored by Aspinall's loyal second-in-command Jonathan Clyde, another Harrison protégé.

In 2007 McCartney promised that the Beatles' catalogue would soon be available for digital download from iTunes, but almost inevitably, legal and financial arguments took precedence. EMI and the Beatles' company continued to battle over the precise percentages that each party would receive. Once again, technological developments had superseded an apparently 'final' settlement between the two sides. As each month passed without the conflict being resolved, huge potential earnings were squandered. Shadowing the dispute was the knowledge that, under current legislation in Britain and Europe, the Beatles' recordings would slip out of copyright between 2012 and 2020, leaving them prey to unfettered exploitation.

The news in May 2009 that the entire Beatles catalogue would shortly be reissued in remastered form appeared to signal a momentous truce. Engineers at EMI had spent years preparing revitalised editions of all their original UK albums, plus the *Past Masters* collections of stray singles and rarities. For the first time, both mono and stereo mixes would be available on CD, to the delight of diehards.

The catalogue was released on September 9, 2009, preceded by a global media campaign that even exceeded the hype devoted to the *Anthology* 14 years earlier. Amidst the sea of celebratory documentaries (including an airbrushed retrospective from Apple) and excited headlines about the return of Beatlemania, it was difficult to retain a sense of perspective. Yet despite the undoubted sonic benefits of the remastering process, the reissues were anything but a gift to fans, who were only able to purchase the much-vaunted mono mixes in an exorbitantly priced box set. Worldwide sales were impressive, however, ensuring that for one week at least, the Beatles once again reigned supreme in global sales charts.

The CDs were scheduled alongside a major announcement from Apple Computers. A few hours before the PR event in California, Britain's Sky News network claimed that Yoko Ono had told them the Beatles' music was about to become available via iTunes. No sooner had the story spanned the globe, however, than it was withdrawn from Sky's website – erased from history, it was alleged, by mysterious forces 'from above'. Had Ono boobed, and ruined Apple's grand announcement?

Did the Beatles really have the power to rewrite the news agenda? Or had Sky themselves been misled? Nobody would comment; and Apple Computers' PR launch turned out to be entirely Beatles-free. So another year ended, with no Beatles music available for download – except via dozens of fly-by-night sites offering illegal digital access to the music. Lawyers scurried to shut them down, but it was like trying to contain a tidal wave with a sieve.

Perhaps the most intriguing aspect of the reissue campaign was that it coincided with the release of a Beatle-branded edition of the computer game *Rock Band*. The project represented the triumph of youth – in the form of Dhani Harrison – over the natural conservatism of Apple. He had succeeded in persuading the Apple board that the *Rock Band* project would not only be extraordinarily lucrative, but would also consolidate the Beatles' reputation amongst those too young to remember Lennon's death, let alone the first flush of Beatlemania.

There was a tragic aftermath to the coup within the Apple boardroom. Neil Aspinall had talked happily to friends about working on his autobiography, but soon after his departure from Apple he discovered that he was seriously ill. On 24 March 2008 he died at the Memorial Sloan-Kettering Cancer Center in New York. One of his final visitors was Paul McCartney, who was reported to have paid for his treatment. Two weeks later Aspinall's funeral service was held close to his home in Twickenham. Neither of the surviving Beatles attended: Stella and James McCartney represented their father; Barbara Bach stood in for Richard Starkey. Aspinall's one-time adversary, Allen Klein, outlived him by little more than a year, dying in July 2009.

With Aspinall's death, the final link between the Beatles and the tight-knit organisation that had guided them through the 1960s was severed. Sir George Martin was enjoying well-earned retirement. The other men who had safeguarded the Beatles and their legacy Brian Epstein, Neil Aspinall, Derek Taylor – were gone. In their place were chartered accountants, entertainment and copyright lawyers, management consultants, wives, children and the prospect of the ever-present, apparently indestructible Yoko Ono guiding the Beatles deep into the 21st century.

McCartney, Starkey, Ono and Olivia Harrison now controlled a financial empire so complex that it boggled the imagination. Every year their lawyers and accountants advised them to form new companies, to cross-collateralise their tax burden, to shift their source of revenue from one jurisdiction to the next, all in the interests of empire-building and careful guardianship of their wealth. But occasionally someone would remember that the Beatles had once been a pop group, glowing with joy, lust and animal excitement, who had imagined in the late 1960s that they could remake the world in their own image. Now the dream was over, as John Lennon had predicted, and money could still not guarantee them satisfaction or love. Meanwhile Lennon himself had been canonised as a prophet of peace, his song 'Imagine' accepted as a secular hymn, his image wielded by politicians and charities as a symbol of untarnished idealism. All trace of the Lennon who recklessly pursued his freedom from the Beatles in 1969, and recognised salvation in the form of Allen Klein and heroin, had effectively been erased.

Given a second chance, the Beatles might have plotted a different course out of the Beatles and into their separate lives. Instead, their history is tinged with regret and recrimination. As Derek Taylor noted more than twenty years ago, 'Nothing should have ended that way, should it?' Yet while the story of the Beatles is doomed to end in anti-climax, their music inhabits another, more enduring realm. It survives as the vivid symbol of a golden past, an immediate trigger of nostalgic joy even for those too young to qualify for nostalgia. It breathes youth, hope and possibility, though we know that its creators proved, after all, to be merely mortal, not the protagonists of fairy tale or myth.

The music needs no mythology: it is both timeless and a staggeringly accurate document of the age from which it came. It is more magical than Magic Alex, more powerful than Allen Klein or the Eastmans, more acerbic than Lennon's wit, more refreshing than McCartney's charm, more solid than Starkey's backbeat, more spiritual than Harrison's psyche; greater, ultimately, than the men who created it or the empire they built around it. The soul of the Beatles turned out to reside not in the boardroom of Apple Corps or the bank accounts of four multimillionaires, but in the instinctive, natural grace of their songs. Their collective genius created something that not even money could destroy.

Acknowledgements

I discovered the Beatles around my sixth birthday, in 1963, when the unforgettable refrain of 'She Loves You' permeated every section of British society. I remained sufficiently interested in late 1964 to buy the *New Musical Express*, discover that the group were about to issue 'I Feel Fine', and improvise my own ditty of the same title into my father's tape recorder. This rendition was accompanied by atonal chords from my Beatles toy guitar, fashioned from brittle yellow plastic. Not surprisingly, Lennon and McCartney's tune was more polished than mine, and their instruments and voices more robust.

I rediscovered the group in 1970, just in time to learn that they had split up, when my cousin Christopher accompanied me to a double-bill of *Let It Be* and *Yellow Submarine*. A few weeks later, my father offered to mend a colleague's gramophone, and I discovered that *With The Beatles* had been left on the turntable. To test my father's handiwork, I played the album several dozen times before the machine and the record were returned.

My love affair – no exaggeration – blossomed on 28 December 1970, when I watched (as did John Lennon) the British TV premiere of *A Hard Day's Night*. Thereafter my passion for contemporary music was exceeded by my obsession with the Beatles. My first live concert featured Paul McCartney and Wings at the Southampton Gaumont; Christmas and birthday money was reserved for second-hand copies of *Live Peace In Toronto* and *The Concert For Bangla Desh*; I exhumed long-forgotten sheet music from junkshops in Bournemouth, learned to play guitar with the aid of my cousin Geoff's Beatles songbooks, and uncritically relished everything from *John Lennon Plastic Ono Band* to 'Mary Had a Little Lamb'.

In 1980, I joined the staff of the magazine *Record Collector*, to discover that the publisher was also reissuing the original editions of *The Beatles Book* magazine every month. I contributed articles to both publications for the next twenty-one years, accumulating more knowledge about the group than was healthy. Gradually I was able to separate my fan from my critic, remaining endlessly fascinated by the surreal world of the Beatles, whilst retaining journalistic objectivity towards their musical output and often careless personal lives. Encounters with many of their closest associates heightened both tendencies.

As a small child, my favourite Beatle was George, for no reason I can remember. As a teenager and beyond, I was John's; his death was – then – the most shocking and devastating moment of my life. In recent years, I have developed an almost romantic affection for George Harrison's songwriting, and often remain entranced by Paul McCartney's effortless skills. I would take *Ram* to my proverbial desert island, probably accompanied by National Lampoon's incisive parody of John Lennon, 'Magical Misery Tour'. I rarely play the Beatles' records these days, as every note is indelibly imprinted on my memory. But when I do, I am instantly transported to a more innocent time, for myself and us all.

Although this book was ostensibly researched over the course of one intensive year, it leans on forty years as a fan and collector, and thirty as a professional writer and author. During those three decades, I have seen three of the Beatles perform in venues large and small; enjoyed a brief encounter with George Harrison; and restrained myself from inflicting small-talk on Paul McCartney, not wanting to disturb his afternoon. The voices of all four Beatles are heavily represented in this book: as its narrative is, in part, a chronicle of how they have reacted in public and private to the events that peppered their lives, I have preferred to rely on their contemporary accounts, rather than well-rehearsed anecdotes about the distant past. In addition, I have been fortunate enough to encounter many of the key players in this story, in a variety of locations and circumstances. Among them were . . .

Yoko Ono, occasionally in London, and memorably in an executive suite at the Hyde Park Hotel. Just as she was telling me that she would now have to face the world alone without John, there was an ill-timed male cough from her bathroom. She looked embarrassedly in that direction, and changed the subject. She also chain-smoked the first half-inch of an entire pack of filter-tips during our longest encounter, and was infallibly charming throughout.

Derek Taylor, at Apple and various corporate Beatle events, by telephone and letter, and most enjoyably over a very long lunch in the Crypt of St Martin-in-the-Fields church in central London, where his droll wit was nearly drowned by the constant clatter of cutlery on steel trolleys. A mutual regard for Derek has sealed any number of music business friendships over the years. I'm not ashamed to say that I loved the man and his writing.

Neil Aspinall, tight-lipped, devilishly ironic, gruff and yet strangely warm, despite himself, at Apple.

Sir George Martin, inevitably dapper and exquisitely polite at the Café Royal.

Sean O'Mahony, five days a week for twenty years in our West London office, and often since. As ever, I'm indebted to him for the chance to write for a living; if he hadn't hired me in 1980, I would never have been able to write this book – or indeed any of the others.

Tony Barrow, endlessly cheerful and accommodating during maybe a hundred phone calls since 1980.

Tony Bramwell, by phone and in person in London and the far South-West, displaying the humour that ensured he remained a Beatle confidant.

Allan Steckler, an invaluable last-minute discovery on the US East Coast, with an intimate grasp on the Apple/ABKCO relationship.

Alexis Mardas, charming, debonair and persuasive, over several days in Athens and on a Greek island. His full account of the Apple Studios debacle stretched to almost two hours. Later, he clicked open a file on his computer to reveal John Lennon singing an otherwise undocumented song in his honour.

The late Alistair Taylor and the late and delightful Ray Coleman at gatherings of Beatle 'celebrities' in Liverpool.

May Pang likewise, but fortunately still with us.

Cynthia Lennon plugging her debut single in a London boutique hotel – slightly embarrassed to be famous, but as warm and welcoming as one could possibly hope.

James Taylor in a Scottish hotel complex, gently passionate and worldly wise.

David Peel, bellowing down a phone line from NYC as if he was exposing the Pope's dope habits in Washington Square Park.

A.J. Weberman (and his pug, Puddles) in a park alongside the East River in Manhattan. The dog was eager to tackle every other canine regardless of size, while A.J. offered a seamless flow of Dylanology, radical political gossip and astonishingly vivid memories of the Lennons in revolutionary mode.

Louise Harrison, open and warm from middle America, still betraying the trace of her brother's Scouse accent, and concerned about how posterity might remember him if current trends continue.

Steve Gebhardt in the London apartment of my late friend John Platt, opening a reservoir of memories from a career of radical film-making.

Allen Ginsberg, only a few months from death, yellowed by liver cancer but still a peerless coiner of images and an inveterate enthusiast for life, poetry and music.

Michael McCartney, in a London taxi and by phone in Liverpool, endlessly championing his own artistic independence in the shadow of his brother's stardom. 'Why don't you ask Our Kid?' he says, when the questioning about Paul gets too personal.

Chris Charlesworth, on too many occasions to recall, in London: always helpful, always good company.

Barbara Orbison, keeper of the Wilburys' flame, aristocratic and generous in a lavish London hotel suite.

Bob Whittaker, destined to be remembered as the creator of the Beatles' 'butcher' sleeve, which is scant reward for his artistry and ambition as a photographer; in London.

Terry O'Neill, celebrity photographer, on the phone somewhere I can't remember.

Elvis Costello in his Dublin rehearsal studio. Ask him a question, and all you have to do is remember to turn the tape over 45 minutes later.

Neil Innes, graciously trying to pretend that he was enjoying the PR duties for the Rutles' reunion in the Virgin Records office.

Leon Russell, bearded snowy-white like a counterculture Santa Claus, behind inch-thick shades in his Nashville home studio, flanked by walls of African masks.

Gail Renard in London, reflecting on her unique role in the Lennons' Toronto bed-in.

Two McCartney aides, by telephone: the charming Eddy Pumer, after producing the radio series *Oobu Joobu*; and the late Tony Brainsby, unfailingly cheerful over many years as McCartney's press spokesman.

For snapshots of the solo Beatles at work and play: Rosanne Cash, superb company in a New York diner; Linda Gail Lewis at home in Wales, with all the Killer's panache; the guru-like Don Was lounging in a Notting Hill hotel; Levon Helm down the line from one more roadhouse with The Band; Graham Nash in person and via digitally reconstituted vocal transmission, always willing to please; Stephen Stills at the Dorchester Hotel in London, his deafness colliding with my incipient deafness to comic effect; Astrid Kirchherr, winning and charming in Germany; Jürgen Vollmer from a film set somewhere in America; Carl Perkins, smoking up a storm in a London hotel a few months after his apparent recovery from throat cancer; Paddy Maloney of the Chieftains, warmly welcoming at the offices of BMG Records; Todd Rundgren, compellingly witty and intelligent in two London hotels of varying majesty, equating to the varying state of his career; Twiggy (and her felines), generous with tea and biscuits in her West London mansion-block; Willie Nelson, serene and smiling like the Buddha on a tour bus in Cambridge, and backstage in London, where I interrupted a surreal encounter between the doyen of the American outlaws and Peter O'Toole; Ray Connolly, general confidant of Lennon and McCartney; and Barry Miles, unpicking the counter-culture with enviable recall at the Groucho Club.

Various members of the staff of EMI Records, Apple Corps, MPL, Harrisongs and ABKCO have been knowingly and unknowingly helpful down the years, but did not knowingly participate in the making of this book. Sadly, 'Mr Allen Klein does not give interviews', for reasons that became obvious when his death was announced in 2009.

Several key confidants of the Beatles and their business advisers provided vital information and insights, but asked that their anonymity should be maintained, a duty I am happy to fulfil.

I have met various Beatle-related figures down the years in non-Beatle settings – among them Jane Asher, Mary McCartney, Sean Lennon and Jody (son of Allen) Klein, all of whom were very friendly, no doubt because we weren't discussing the Beatles. Interesting though those encounters were, they provided no material for this book – except that I was sufficiently impressed by Mary McCartney's worldly but unpretentious demeanour in her late teens to interpret it as a strong recommendation of her parents' child-rearing skills.

Over the thirty years in which I have been writing about the Beatles, a number of colleagues, friends and acquaintances have (like it or not) found themselves discussing our mutual interest in the group, among them Keith Altham, Keith Badman, Stuart Batsford, Mark Blake, Alan Clayson, Andy Davis, Daryl Easlea, Mike Grant, Ian Gray, Helen Hall, Sarah Hodgson, Spencer Leigh, Mark Lewisohn, Pete Nash, Andy Neill, Mark Paytress, the late John Platt, John Reed, Rachel Reilly, Tim Riley, Ken Sharp, Paul Trynka, Carey Wallace, Michael Watts and Katherine Williams. Of those, Pete Nash deserves special thanks on this occasion for his generosity and good humour, and has earned a plug for his website (www.britishbeatlesfanclub.co.uk). Apologies to anyone I've missed.

Other friends have been unfailingly loyal during the writing of this book and its predecessors: Johnny Rogan, Clinton Heylin, Debbie Cassell, Andrew Sclanders and the late Sean Body, creator of Helter Skelter Publishing and the much missed Helter Skelter bookstore, now much missed himself by all those who knew him. Thanks also to the other members of the Doggett family, Pat, Paul, RoseAnne, Anna and Alick; to my fellow travellers and tutors on the Foundation Degree course at ACE; and to Veronica Williams. Apologies to other Green Party activists for not insisting that this book was printed on recycled paper.

As ever, much appreciation is due to my rigorous and tireless agent, Rupert Heath. Thanks also to Will Sulkin, Jörg Hensgen, Kay Peddle and Hugh Davis at the Bodley Head, Frances Macmillan at Vintage and Stephen Parker in Design; and to the staff of the National Archives at Kew, the British Library, the University of London Library, the New York Public Library, and the Library of Congress.

My father-in-law, Rear-Admiral Bob Baylis CB OBE ADC RN, died a few days after this manuscript was completed. Most popular culture since the demise of Noël Coward left him cold, often with good reason. But he was a constant champion of my work, which was a welcome surprise, and his indefatigable wit and peerless skills as a raconteur were legendary to all those who encountered him. He was one of a kind, and it is a privilege to have known him.

His daughter, Rachel Baylis, has made me happier than I have ever known; and for that, and her endless support, love, wisdom and humour, I shall always be grateful. Without her, I could not have made it this far. I love you, my darling. Much love too to our daughters, Catrin and Becca Mascall, who eased the creation of this book by being away at university when it was written, to the great risk of the innocent citizens of London and Paris; and to Fred, startled by everything, but still a hardened killer of baby blackbirds.

Peter Doggett
Hampshire
July 2009

Notes

Prologue

Page 1 'She was in Los Angeles': author interview. **Page 2** 'We got some phone calls': Donahue (TV), 1981; 'Cyn, John's been shot': Lennon, *John*, p. 7; 'My first thought': author interview. **Page 3** 'I blurted out': author interview; 'I drove into the driveway': Fields, *Linda McCartney*, p. 214. **Page 4** 'It was just too crazy': *Playboy*, Apr. 1984; 'I can't remember': *Music Express*, Mar. 1982; 'He started wondering': Fields, op. cit., p. 215; 'Not a good way to start the day': *Goldmine*, 12 Nov. 1993; 'We heard the news': *Playboy*, Apr. 1984; 'I called Ray': *Goldmine*, 18 Feb. 1994. **Page 5** 'I did a day's work': *Playboy*, Apr. 1984; 'It was a strange day': author interview; 'We got there and fell': *Goldmine*, 12 Nov. 1993; 'decided I wanted to be': Davies, *Quarrymen*, p. 152; 'white as a sheet': Kooper, *Backstage Passes*, p. 232; 'I came back here': *Daily Mirror*, 12 Aug. 1981; 'We were put straight through': Lennon, *John*, p. 10. **Page 6** 'She was crying': *Daily Star*, 10 Dec. 1980; 'It was almost as if she sensed': *Music Express*, Mar. 1982; 'The consolation for me': *Record Hunter*, Nov. 1992; 'shocked, dreadfully upset': Taylor, *Fifty Years Adrift*, p. 522; 'After all we went through': ibid., p. 523; 'George phoned me': author interview. **Page 7** 'You had to say hello': Donahue (TV), 1981; 'I had just finished': *Playboy*, Apr. 1984; 'all those people': *Rolling Stone* 512, 1987. **Page 8** 'I did a lot of weeping': Miles, *Many Years From Now*, p. 594; 'Ringo never brought up': Mansfield, *The White Book*, p. 205; 'It is not difficult to imagine': *Daily Mirror*, 10 Dec. 1980. **Page 12** 'a hero, who reached out': *Daily Mirror*, 10 Dec. 1980; 'both represented': *The Times*, 10 Dec. 1980.

Chapter 1

Page 16 'The Beatles were such profoundly': author interview; 'about to fade away': *Guardian*, 8 Oct. 1963. **Page 17** 'the crystallisation of the dreams': *Observer*, 24 Jun. 1970. **Page 18** 'Paul would do that': author interview. **Page 19** 'Epstein asked the Beatles': author interview; 'What could we do?': Badman, *Off The Record*, p. 259; 'exclusive white': Jones, *Black Music*, p. 205; 'we were all going to live': Taylor, *Fifty Years Adrift*, p. 302. **Page 20** 'I'm not worried about the political': Davies, *The Beatles* [1968], p. 315; 'I was horrified': author interview. **Page 20** 'I suppose the main motivation': Miles, *Many Years From Now*, p. 378; 'It seemed strange to me': Beatles, *Anthology*, p. 255. **Page 21** 'the awakening and the realisation': ibid., p. 180. **Page 21** 'They called him the quiet Beatle': author interview. **Page 22** 'Wow! Fantastic!': Beatles, op. cit. p.233. **Page 22**

'As kids, we were always': author interview. **Page 23** 'after what had happened': Beatles, op. cit. p. 242, 'I went through a terrible': *Fusion*, 26 Feb. 1970; large, heavily panelled': Evans, *Beatles Literary Anthology*, pp. 160–3; 'I feel I want to be them all': *Look*, 13 Dec. 1966. **Page 24** 'This is the most beautiful apple': *International Times*, 14–27 Nov. 1966. **Page 25** 'Miss Ono turned out': *The Times*, 11 Mar. 1967; 'Men have an unusual talent': *International Times* 17 [1967]; 'the genius who arrived': Taylor, *Fifty Years Adrift*, p. 302. **Page 26** 'I suggested to the boys': Evans, op. cit., p. 256. **Page 28** 'remained the least challenged': Taylor, op. cit., p. 329; 'We weren't being stupid': Miles, op. cit., p. 443. **Page 29** 'When society accepts it': Maharishi, *Bhagavad-Gita*, p. 19; 'There was a collective': Beatles, op. cit., p. 262; 'the first crack': Taylor, op. cit., p. 318; 'no one could possible replace': Miles, *Beatles Diary*, p. 277. **Page 30** 'he didn't believe in us': Granados, *Those Were the Days*, p. 11; 'I said to them, foolishly': *Mojo*, Oct. 1996; 'Neil was indivisible': author interview; 'we didn't have a single': *Mojo*, Oct. 1996. **Page 31** 'We had a meeting': speech at Beatlefest, 1975; 'I was a wild 1960s': author interview; 'The film is about': *Guardian*, 27 Dec. 1967. **Page 32** 'John used to say': Miles, *Many Years From Now*, p. 595; 'Paul was always courageous': author interview; 'Paul wanted to work': author interview. **Page 33** 'I always idolised him': *Rolling Stone* 512, 1987; 'He was older': *Playboy*, Apr. 1984. **Page 33** 'George actually once got': Miles, *Many Years From Now*, p. 420. **Page 34** 'After taking acid together': Beatles, op. cit., p. 180; 'wondered what was going to happen': Miles, *Many Years From Now*, p. 428; 'the greater plan': *Record Mirror*, 23 Mar. 1968; 'I was completely out of control': author interview. **Page 35** 'You've been pretty obnoxious': Taylor, op. cit., p. 326; 'I was still an employee': author interview; 'To tell you the truth': Miles, *Many Years From Now*, p. 429; 'I had very little to do': Beatles, op. cit., p. 287; 'The Beatles weren't together': author interview. **Page 36** 'If you're a singer': *International Times*, 31 May–13 Jun., 1968; 'It was a good idea to help': author interview; 'Instead of trying to amass'. *Evening Standard*, 24 Feb. 1968; 'to go on their knees': *The Tonight Show* (TV), 1968. **Page 37** 'a mad, bad week': Taylor, op. cit., p. 327; 'Basically it was chaos': Beatles, op. cit., pp. 287, 290; 'The weirdness was not controlled': author interview. **Page 38** 'I wrote 600 songs': taped performance; 'I spent years trying': *Fusion*, 20 Feb. 1970; 'I'm Jesus Christ': Davies, *Quarrymen*, p. 125; 'I've never been frightened': author interview; 'The Beatles were, and probably': author interview. **Page 39** 'She has a tendency': *Playboy*, Jan. 1981; 'The English people were very kind': *Mojo Special Edition*, 2000. **Page 40** 'I didn't find a lot of sympathy': author interview; 'I was such a snob': *Mojo Special Edition*, 2000. **Page 41** 'This is it': Davies, op. cit., p. 127. **Page 42** 'I can understand how they felt': *Mojo Special Edition*, 2000; 'beside him in the chair': Lennon, *John*, p. 299. **Page 43** 'It brought out the child': Davies, op. cit., p. 128; 'because the message': taped performance; 'They always had a very healthy': author interview. **Page 44** 'It was essential for me': Miles, *Many Years From Now*, p. 467; 'Ringo would rather have quit': Schwartz, *Body Count*, p. 88; 'I remember being very freaked out': *Inner-View* radio show, 1976; 'It was fairly off-putting': Beatles, op. cit., p.310. **Page 45** 'She was soon treating me': Davies, op. cit., p. 128; 'We said, The Beatles': Miles, *Many Years From Now*, p. 492; 'Paul has been very nice': Unterberger, *The Unreleased Beatles*, p. 201; 'Suddenly we were together': Peebles, *The Lennon Tapes*, p. 16; 'she didn't really like us': Beatles, op. cit., p. 310; 'Unfortunately her possessiveness': Davies, op. cit., p. 128; 'It was like we were': Beatles, op. cit., p. 310; 'If I go to the bathroom': *Mojo Special Edition*, 2000. **Page 46** 'I was just trying to sit there': *Newsweek*, 23 Oct. 1995; 'I'm a composer': *Mojo Special Edition*, 2000; 'You must understand that she communicates': *Goldmine*, 19 Oct. 1990. **Page 47** 'We could recognise': *Playboy*, Apr. 1984; 'I didn't know about all': Peebles, op. cit., p. 17; 'We were trying to take photographs': author interview. **Page 48** 'Paul was absolutely devastated': Taylor, *With the Beatles*, p. 217–18; 'He was petulant': Schwartz, op. cit., pp. 82–3; 'When John came over': ibid. **Page 49** 'That was the moment': Fields, *Linda McCartney*, pp. 103–4; 'I don't think I ever hated': Taylor, *Fifty Years Adrift*, p. 347; 'There were only a few of us': author interview; 'are confident and cheerful': 'Hey Jude' press release. **Page 50** 'All of us were dissatisfied': tape of conversation; 'firmly united one for all': 'Hey Jude' press release.

Chapter 2

Page 51 'Our main business is entertainment': Taylor, *Fifty Years Adrift*, p. 345; 'I can't talk': tape of conversation. **Page 52** 'If any of our dreams': author interview; 'There is no profit motive': *Oz* 14, 1968; 'Everyone had their own autonomy': author interview; 'film flop': *Guardian*, 7 Aug. 1968. **Page 53** 'It seemed quite possible': Evans, *Beatles Literary Anthology*, p. 257; 'Nobody at Apple': author interview; 'I remember going': author interview; 'I wanted Apple to run': Miles, *Many Years From Now*, p. 479; 'like I was in an Alice': ibid., pp. 479–80. **Page 54** 'I was getting fed up': Beatles, *Anthology*, p. 302; 'I don't like it': Dilello, *The Longest Cocktail Party*, p. 63; 'I was very broad-minded': author interview; 'gave me long lectures': *New Musical Express*, 7 Jun. 1969. **Page 55** 'All of us thought': tape of conversation; 'They got involved with each other': Beatles, op. cit., p. 302; 'There's nothing to talk about': Lennon, *John*, p. 306. **Page 56** 'You had a very strong heartbeat': taped performance; 'George says it was me': Cadogan, *Revolutionary Artist*, p. 89; 'Unfortunately he was drifting away': *Rolling Stone* 482, 1986; 'Don't cry, I'm a cunt': Schwartz, *Body Count*, p. 89. **Page 57** 'the Park Avenue groupie': *People*, 21 Apr. 1975. **Page 58** 'She adored her father': Fields, *Linda McCartney*, p. 85; 'She was always flirtatious': Boyd, *Wonderful Today*, p. 58; 'Often this office': *Disc*, 11 Jan. 1969; 'I don't dig under-estimating': tape of conversation. **Pages 59–60** tape of conversations. **Page 60** 'George would start to': Boyd, op. cit., p. 122. **Page 61** 'started jamming violently': Beatles, op. cit., p. 314; 'the box George is in': tape of conversation; 'I think that if George': tape of conversation; 'It was unbearable to me': Taylor, *Fifty Years Adrift*, p. 364; 'What we need': tape of conversation; 'George in the presence of us all': court testimony, 1971; 'Yoko was doing all the talking': tape of conversation. **Page 62** 'It's a festering wound': tape of conversation; 'Showbiz people': tape of conversation; 'John had escalated to heroin': Miles, op. cit., p. 535; 'Brian Epstein, I knew': Taylor, op. cit., p. 364; 'Up yer': ibid., photo insert [k]; 'the biggest disaster of all time': ibid., p. 358. **Page 63** 'We haven't got half the money': *Disc*, 18 Jan. 1969; 'I think Billy Preston': author interview; 'It's bad enough with four': tape of conversation; 'You had a sense': *Rolling Stone*, 4 Jun. 1987. **Page 64** 'It was not insignificant': Taylor, *As Time Goes By*, p. 211; 'Klein is essential': author interview. **Page 65** 'a rough little scorpion': Spitz, *The Beatles*, p. 817; 'fast-talking, dirty-mouthed': Brown, *The Love You Make*, p. 247; 'short and fat': Gould, *Can't Buy Me Love*, p. 545; 'He had all the charm': Taylor, *With the Beatles*, p. 242; 'small tubby man': Norman, *The Beatles*, p. 360; 'Wait and see': *Melody Maker*, 12 Apr. 1969. **Page 66** 'Allen Klein could be': author interview; 'I brought him to Apple': author interview. **Page 67** 'I was driving a bridge': *Playboy*, Nov. 1971; 'He was in his early thirties': Oldham, *2Stoned*, p. 205; 'Andrew liked having me': ibid., p. 161; 'He started out representing': ibid., p.396. **Page 68** 'Klein was virtually unbeatable': Mansfield, *The White Book*, p. 111; 'Everyone knew that Klein': author interview; 'Yoko said that when she': *Playboy*, Nov. 1971. **Page 69** 'We met with Allen Klein': Beatles, op. cit., p. 324; 'Eastman wasn't a polo-neck': author interview. **Page 70** 'Apart from the fact': court testimony, 1971; 'This was the first time': court testimony, 1971; 'John Eastman gave me': court testimony, 1971; 'No allegation was made': court testimony, 1971. **Page 71** 'It was agreed by all four Beatles': court testimony, 1971; 'launched an attack': court testimony, 1971; 'New York business expert': *The Times*, 4 Feb. 1969; 'a stepped-up campaign': *Billboard*, 22 Feb. 1969. **Page 72** 'We co-operated with Klein': McCabe, *Apple to the Core*, p. 148; 'I ripped off those documents': ibid.; 'propriety of the negotiations': ibid., p. 124. **Page 73** 'He was saying to me': speech at Beatlefest, 1975; 'a hard-faced star-chaser': Taylor, *With the Beatles*, pp. 233, 238; 'You can't know how hard': Fields, op. cit., p. 123. **Page 74** 'four days shopping': *The Times*, 22 Apr. 1969; 'I don't miss being a Beatle': *New Musical Express*, 29 Mar. 1969; 'will give several public shows': *New Musical Express*, 5 Apr. 1969; 'It would be indelicate': ibid. **Page 75** 'We've got to a point': *Disc*, 5 Apr. 1969; 'They are my shares': Miles, *Beatles Diary*, p. 338. **Page 76** 'I had many meetings': court testimony, 1971; 'He wrapped it up': *Observer*, 6 Apr. 1969; 'a liar, a self-publicist': Taylor, *As Time Goes By*, pp. 159–60. **Page 77** 'I didn't mind not being': Beatles, op. cit., p. 333; 'Yoko used to sit in'. *Record Hunter*, Nov. 1992; 'Businessmen play the game': press conference, 28 Apr. 1969; 'I'm not going to be fucked': McCabe, op. cit., p. 152; 'This was like playing Monopoly': *Mojo*, Oct. 1996. **Page 78** 'I won't do business': McCabe, op. cit., p. 148; 'launched into an emotional tirade': court testimony, 1971; 'Will you please stop insulting': court testimony, 1971; 'John flew into a rage': Spitz, *The Beatles*, p. 822. **Page 79** 'Dear Mr Eastman': Christie's sale catalogue, London, May 2005; 'I was pleased to think': author interview. **Page 80** 'to the other members of the band': *Mojo*, Oct. 1996; 'I got lost in the Beatles': radio interview, 5 May 1969; 'Paul came racing out': *Mojo*, Oct. 1996; 'John was really angry': ibid. **Page 81** 'On a bad day': author interview; 'if you are one of the Beatles': author interview; 'When I think of going': author interview. **Page 82** 'Klein was a terrible idea': author interview; 'a cheerful cove': author interview with Derek Taylor; 'Not one of them took my call': Taylor, *With the Beatles*, pp. 244–5. **Page 83** 'I was not prepared to accept': court testimony, 1971. **Page 85** 'It was like a divorce': author interview. **Page 85** 'It became clear to me': court testimony, 1971; 'I said, he'll take 15 per cent': Miles, *Many Years From Now*, p. 548; 'Paul's making trouble': court testimony, 1971. **Page 86** 'Allen Klein had achieved': author interview.

Chapter 3

Page 87 'Why will people underestimate': *Melody Maker*, 19 Jul. 1969. **Page 88** 'He has refused to become': Cunliffe, *American Literature Since 1900*, p. 361. **Page 89** 'For hours, they would do nothing': author interview. **Page 90** 'We believe violent change': *International Times*, 27 Feb.–13 Mar. 1970; 'People's Park amounted': Gitlin, *The Sixties*, p. 355; 'I don't believe there is any cause': tape of phone call; 'firming up his newfound status': Christgau, *Any Old Way You Choose It*, p. 99. **Page 91** 'an establishment form': *International Free Press*, 1 Nov. 1969; 'be able to conjure up': *International Times*, 29 Aug. 1969; 'If Lennon raped a 10-year-old': *Guardian*, 14 Aug. 1969. **Page 92** 'The first thing in my life': *International Times*, 29 Aug. 1969. **Page 93** 'Paul called me': *Mojo*, Oct. 1996. **Page 94** 'to make for each one': *Record Retailer*, 16 Jul. 1969; 'They had a year to consider it': *Record Retailer*, 9 Aug. 1969; 'Just to be singing': *International Times*, 29 Aug. 1969. **Page 96** 'So far as I am concerned': court testimony, 1971; 'Jaws dropping, we all watched': Emerick, *Here, There & Everywhere*, pp. 279–80; 'not the ideal way': *Record Hunter*, Nov. 1992. **Page 97** 'which it could never have been': Sheff, *Last Interview*, p. 202; 'I was muttering, Hurry up': radio interview, 1969; 'People like myself': author interview. **Page 98** 'The problem is that two': *Melody Maker*, 20 Sep. 1969; 'They tended to be very demanding': author interview. **Page 99** 'Dear John': McCabe, *Apple to the Core*, p. 148; 'insisted that Paul should have': court testimony, 1971. **Page 100** 'It was raining': Clapton, *Eric Clapton*, p. 125; 'John threw up': *Mojo*, May 1997; 'John stood in the dressing room': *Disc*, 1 Nov. 1969; 'People were surprised': author interview. **Page 101** 'I was completely wrapped': *Rolling Stone*, 4 Jun. 1987; 'Eastman is representing': court testimony, 1971. **Page 102** 'Klein takes EMI': Taylor, *As Time Goes By*, p. 147; 'I did Capitol a great favour': McCabe, op. cit., pp. 149–50; 'Everyone was in a very cheerful': court testimony, 1971; 'We started talking about the future': *Rolling Stone* 512, 1987. **Page 103** 'I think you're daft': *Playboy*, Apr. 1984; 'in a bit of a daze': Miles, *Many Years From Now*, p. 561; 'You could see it coming': *Goldmine*, 29 Jul. 1988; 'Everybody had tried to leave': Beatles, *Anthology*, p. 348; 'It was a relief': ibid. **Page 104** 'As anyone will tell you': *Goldmine*, 29 Jul. 1988; 'I write for the Beatles': *Fusion*, 20 Feb. 1970; 'The break-up came': *Goldmine*, 29 Jul. 1988. **Page 105** 'I sat in the garden': Beatles, op. cit., p. 348; 'Ringo was just uptight': Emerick, op. cit., p. 311. **Page 106** 'To me, listening to Abbey Road': *Disc*, 11 Oct.1969; 'I was at Apple': author interview; 'we're going to get an equal': *New Musical Express*, 1 Nov. 1969. **Page 107** 'I'm sorry but I'm just not like them': *Record Mirror*, 5 Nov. 1969; 'The Beatle thing is over': *Life*, 7 Nov. 1969; 'Beatles on the brink of splitting': *New Musical Express*, 25 Nov. 1969. **Page 108** 'For about three or four months': Beatles, op. cit., p. 349; 'I think all of us': court testimony, 1971; 'The Beatles can go on appealing': *Melody Maker*, 6 Dec. 1969; 'Well, I don't understand it': court testimony, 1971. **Page 109** 'Allen Klein is coming over': court testimony, 1971; 'They were all enthusiastic': court testimony, 1971. **Page 110** 'It was mutually decided': *Disc*, 6 Dec. 1969; 'The Beatles have lost interest': *Guardian*, 1 Dec. 1969; 'I didn't think that the pop world': author interview; 'When we're not working': *24 Hours* (TV), 1969. **Page 111** 'and suggested that I should': Clapton, *Eric Clapton*, p. 129; 'said something about my not': court testimony, 1971; 'really marvellous': *Melody Maker*, 6 Dec. 1969. **Page 112** 'the only one who doesn't': *Disc*, 27 Dec. 1969.

Chapter 4

Page 114 'You mustn't pretend': *Melody Maker*, 31 Jul. 1971; 'We put every lawyer's kid': *Mojo*, Oct. 1996. **Page 115** 'I said to Phil': Beatles, *Anthology*, p. 350; 'I started thinking': ibid., p. 349. **Page 116** 'He became increasingly obsessive': Boyd, *Wonderful Today*, p. 155; 'As if the pleasures': ibid., p. 162. **Page 117** 'I didn't want to chant': ibid., p. 163; 'It was rather like throwing': *Friends*, 15 May 1970; 'We want nothing to do': *International Times* 76, 1970; 'Our latest idea': press release, March 1970. **Page 118** 'Michael was a persuasive guy': author interview; 'You have stolen the rhythms': Humphry, *False Messiah*, p. 90; 'It was such an ugly meeting': author interview. **Page 119** 'Believe it or not': *International Times* 74, 1970; '[John] read it': *Rolling Stone*, 18 Feb. 1971; 'I believe that the only way': Janov, *The Primal Scream*; 'Just as neurosis results': ibid.; 'John had about as much pain': *Mojo Special Edition*, 2000. **Page 120** 'We've got unity through diversity': *New Musical Express*, 14 Mar. 1970. **Page 121** 'and discussed with them': court testimony, 1971; 'Dear Paul': reprinted in Beatles, op. cit., p. 351. **Page 122** 'I didn't think it fair': *Melody Maker*, 31 Jul. 1971; 'I really got angry': court testimony, 1971; 'Paul's was just an ego game': court testimony, 1971; 'I'm very emotional': *Melody Maker*, 31 Jul. 1971. **Page 123** 'Phil had a style': author interview; 'If there is anything': court testimony, 1971; 'We all said yes': *Melody Maker*, 7 Aug. 1971; 'I like what Phil did': Beatles, op. cit., p. 323; 'I personally thought': ibid.; 'He always wanted to work': Wenner, *Lennon Remembers*, pp. 101–2; 'When I got the finished record': *Mojo*, May 2003. **Page 124** 'I was going through': Miles, *Many Years From Now*, p. 570; 'I can't deal with the press': *Playboy*, Apr. 1984; 'Will Paul and Linda': press release, 1970. **Page 126** 'I received one': author interview; 'This is just not true': *The Times*, 10 Apr. 1970; 'I phoned John': author interview. **Page 127** 'John had made it clear': *Playboy*, Apr. 1984; 'a good PR man': Wenner, op. cit., p. 32; 'The way it came out': *Music Express*, Mar. 1982. **Page 127** 'It was going to be an insert': *Playboy*, Apr. 1984; 'I figured it was about time': ibid.; 'It was a nasty little period': *Rolling Stone* 512, 1987; 'I think John thought': *Rolling Stone* 482, 1986. **Page 128** 'Paul told me he was devastated': author interview; 'Nowhere does he actually': *Melody Maker*, 18 Apr. 1970; 'Spring is here': Taylor, *Fifty Years Adrift*, p. 392. **Page 129** 'The wording was no clearer': ibid.; 'They do not want to split up': Badman, *After the Break-Up*, p. 4; 'I like Paul': ibid.; 'On the face of it': *Melody Maker*, 18 Apr. 1970; 'I was happy to hear': *Disc*, 18 Apr. 1970; 'I had so much in me': Miles, op. cit. pp. 570–1. **Page 131** 'Dear Sir': *Guardian*, 12 Jan. 2002; 'No one asked me': *Evening Standard*, 21 Apr. 1970. **Page 132** 'I sent a telegram': court testimony, 1971; 'I've sent Klein a letter': *Evening Standard*, 21 Apr. 1970. **Page 133** 'came on like Attila the Hun': *Rolling Stone*, 11 Jun. 1970; 'We all have to sacrifice': Sandercombe, *The Beatles Press Reports*, pp. 302–4. **Page 134** 'There was a point': ibid.; 'I get on well with Ringo': ibid.; 'Really it was his idea': ibid. **Page 135** 'that's only a personal problem': ibid.; 'The reality is that he's outvoted': ibid.; 'Everyone is trying to do': radio interview, May 1970; 'I've no idea if the Beatles': radio interview, May 1970; 'It was murderous': *Time*, 1976; 'It was just the feeling': *Playboy*,

Apr. 1984. **Page 136** 'Eventually I went and said': Miles, op. cit., pp. 570–1; 'replied with a photograph': court testimony, 1971; 'Dear Mailbag': *Melody Maker*, 29 Aug. 1970. **Page 137** 'a cheapskate epitaph': *New Musical Express*, 9 May 1970. **Page 138** 'pseudo *cinéma-vérité*': *Billboard*, 23 May 1970. **Page 139** 'Apple was an astonishing place': author interview; 'We were working for people': author interview; 'Since the break-up of the Beatles': *Evening Standard*, 4 Aug. 1970. **Page 140** 'What I really wanted to do': *Melody Maker*, 7 Aug. 1971. **Page 141** 'Even before I started': Evans, *Beatles Literary Anthology*, p. 345. **Page 142** 'the self-referential nature': Leng, *The Music of George Harrison*, p. 60. **Page 143** 'He said, Could you send': *Mojo Special Edition*, 2000; 'wanted to put an ad': ibid. **Page 144** 'Janov was an idiot': *Spin, c.* 1990; 'Phil! John is ready': *Billboard*, 3 Oct. 1970; 'suddenly we'd be in the middle': Starr, *Postcards from the Boys*, p. 49; 'Ringo was very sad': *Mojo Special Edition*, 2000.

Chapter 5

Page 146 '[The Beatles] are not children': court testimony, 1971; 'America is where it's at': Wenner, *Lennon Remembers*, pp. 144–5. **Page 147** 'Linda didn't have much to do': *Melody Maker*, 29 May 1971; 'an extravaganza of piety': *Rolling Stone*, 7 Jan. 1971. **Page 148** 'I wonder how happy George is': radio interview; 'not the kind of person': Wenner, ibid., p. 135; 'I said, Look, George': Miles, *Many Years From Now*, pp. 570–1. **Page 149** 'Come Together!': *Disc*, 12 Dec. 1970; 'The Beatles are said to be closer': *New Musical Express*, 12 Dec. 1970; 'Paul would have forfeited his right': McCabe, *For the Record*, p. 46. **Page 150** 'That was a pity': author interview. **Page 151** 'We spent an evening together': *Goldmine*, 12 Nov. 1993; 'We took H': Wenner, op. cit., p. 16; 'We got fed up with being sidemen': ibid, p. 23; 'I presumed I would just': ibid., p. 37; 'The dream's over': ibid., p. 11. **Page 152** 'Fuck you all!': ibid., p. 138; 'It's just like divorce': *Rolling Stone* 512, 1987; 'I'm glad I never answered': ibid. **Page 153** 'He'd been doing a lot of preaching': *Playboy*, Apr. 1984. **Page 154** 'I have been driven': Giuliano, *Revolver*, pp. 206ff; 'We've split': Badman, *After the Break-Up*, p. 19; 'It doesn't accomplish anything': ibid., p. 21; 'I just could not believe it': court testimony, 1971; 'I still cannot understand': court testimony, 1971. **Page 155** 'I didn't tell anybody': McCabe, op. cit., p. 51; 'is a man of bad commercial': court testimony, 1971. **Page 156** 'I wish to make it clear': *Rolling Stone*, 18 Feb. 1971; 'obviously not enhanced': court testimony, 1971. **Page 157** 'We were having meetings': McCabe, op. cit., p. 51; 'George goes through that': ibid.; 'I realised it was make or break': Miles, op. cit., p. 577; 'Paul's idea of being different': radio interview, Oct. 1969; 'in a brown turtle-neck sweater': Miles, op. cit., p. 578. **Page 158** 'He inherited a situation': court testimony, 1971; 'Klein told me': court testimony, 1971; 'From time to time': court testimony, 1971. **Page 159** 'Since Paul agreed': court testimony, 1971; 'This is why my clients': court testimony, 1971. **Page 160** 'a record manufacturer': court testimony, 1971; 'No one is getting': court testimony, 1971. **Page 161** 'I'll get it for nothing': court testimony, 1971; 'One only has to look': court testimony, 1971; 'You know why John is angry': court testimony, 1971; 'If I could have my piece': court testimony, 1971. **Page 162** 'Mr McCartney, through his counsel': court testimony, 1971; 'Having regard to his record': court testimony, 1971. **Page 163** 'The Beatles have long since': court testimony, 1971; 'I recently read that I was supposed': *Club Sandwich*, winter 1994. **Page 164** 'We see more of each other': radio interview, Mar. 1971; 'All summer long in Scotland': *Life*, Apr. 1971; 'I ignored John's interview': ibid. **Page 165** 'Of course we aren't just': ibid; 'My clients now consider': court testimony, 1971; 'I can only express': court testimony, 1971; 'My friend Johnny Eastman': McCabe, *Apple to the Core*, pp. 150–1. **Page 166** 'That was a bit strange': *Melody Maker*, 31 Jul. 1971; 'Paul's probably cost us': *New Musical Express*, 31 Jul. 1971. **Page 168** 'Fucking hell, it was awful': *New Musical Express*, 7 Aug. 1971; 'They thought the whole album': *Playboy*, Apr. 1984. **Page 169** 'I always got angry': *Crawdaddy*, Nov. 1973; 'I remember when he was writing': Peebles, *The Lennon Tapes*, pp. 44–5; 'I remember Ringo': Miles, op. cit., pp. 585–6; 'John would forgive himself': author interview; 'I used my resentment': Peebles, op. cit., p. 44; 'It's quite obvious': Miles, op. cit., pp. 585–6. **Page 170** 'It was just a bit': *Mojo*, Jul. 2001; 'I'm talking about myself: *Crawdaddy*, Nov. 1973; 'I don't have any grudge': *Club Sandwich*, winter 1994; 'I have to say the most hurtful': ibid.; 'I think he was a sod': Miles, op. cit., p. 587; 'This is so prejudiced': Sotheby's auction catalogue, London, 1986. **Page 171** 'We keep having laughs': *Melody Maker*, 24 Jul. 1971.

Chapter 6

Page 172 'Imagine how we've flowered': *New Musical Express*, 7 Aug. 1971; 'I don't think Linda': *Melody Maker*, 4 Sep. 1971. **Page 173** 'George lacked confidence': author interview; 'He didn't finish any': author interview. **Page 174** 'Everyone wanted to play': author interview; 'Klein called a press conference': *Melody Maker*, 20 Nov. 1971; 'I told George about a week': McCabe, *For the Record*, p. 32; 'There's no telling George': ibid., p. 52. **Page 175** 'Are there ever times': press conference, 27 Jul. 1971; 'I never wanted them': *Parkinson* (TV), 1971. **Page 176** 'I really didn't think they would come': author interview; 'I'm pretty movable as an artist': Cott, *Ballad of John & Yoko*, p. 152; 'He disappoints me': *Melody Maker*, 31 Jul. 1971. **Page 177** 'Someone had written the words': *The Write Thing* 43, 1984; 'I missed playing in a band': *Music Express*, Mar. 1982; 'Everybody can be artists': *International Times* 110, 1971; 'petty little perversion': Christie's auction catalogue, London, 2002. **Page 178** 'only just beginning': Dilello, *The Longest Cocktail Party*, p. 294; 'It's a bit sad now': Badman, *After the Break-Up*, p. 50; 'If I hadn't bought': *Frendz*, 19 Aug. 1971; 'I only decided to live there': interview by Francis Schoenberger, *Spin*; 'We figured McCartney': author interview. **Page 179** 'I felt he's a good example': *Frendz*, 28 Oct. 1971; 'I hope they're not after me': McCabe, op. cit., p. 75; 'I don't want that big house': ibid., p. 36; 'John was not trying': author interview; 'We told John he had': *Rolling Stone*, 9 Dec. 1971; '20 per cent of nothing': McCabe, op. cit., p. 40. **Page 180** 'When Paul's going out': ibid., p. 37; 'the others really dig': *Melody Maker*, 20 Nov. 1971; 'This does place me': *Guardian*, 12 Jan. 2002. **Page 181** 'if it would be possible': *New Musical Express*, 16 Oct. 1971; 'picked up the approximately': *Billboard*, 14 Aug. 1971; 'Has Eastman ever donated?': Christie's auction catalogue, London; 'the greatest achievement ever': *International Times*, 20 Dec. 1971; 'I don't think he deserves': McCabe, op. cit., p. 49; 'Repression is bad for you': *Ink*, 18 Aug. 1971. **Page 182** 'It became journalism': Cott, op. cit., pp. 152–3; 'After my exhibition': *Evening Standard*, 22 Mar. 1990; 'Klein was in a difficult situation': author interview; 'Spector insisted on making fun': author interview. **Page 183** 'We would launch a musical': Rubin, *Growing (Up) At 37*; 'It's really bad': *Melody Maker*, 6 Nov. 1971; 'Let's lay the guns down': *Club Sandwich*, winter 1994; 'He's talking about money now': *Melody Maker*, 20 Nov. 1971. **Page 184** 'I just want this thing settled': ibid.; 'but we couldn't sell them': author interview. **Page 184** 'Please publish, equal time': *Melody Maker*, 4 Dec. 1971, complete text in Christie's auction catalogue, London; 'He wanted to tell Paul': author interview. **Page 185** 'Happy Xmas!': Christie's auction catalogue, London; 'We saw John and Yoko': *Guardian*, 15 Jul. 1972. **Page 186** 'This appears to me to be': Wiener, *Gimme Some Truth*, p. 3; 'Something new is in the air': *Ink*, 21 Jan. 1972; 'I made John and myself': author interview; 'John Lennon does not give': Wiener, op. cit., p. 215; 'excessive use of narcotics': ibid., p. 213; 'If you were around them': *Goldmine*, 6 Nov. 1998. **Page 187** 'almost killed Yoko': Lennon, *Skywriting*, p. 32; 'I always used to think': *Rolling Stone*, 31 Jan. 1974; 'You know what's happening': McCabe, op. cit., p. 18. **Page 188** 'We brought along some rotten fruit': author interview. **Page 189** 'John and Yoko called me up': author interview; 'There was one guy who was smuggling': author interview; 'Lennon gave them this huge': author interview; 'I was over there': O'Hare interview with Johnny Rogan. **Page 190** 'I told him we were going to have a riot': author interview. **Page 191**

'irritating, embarrassing': *Cream*, Nov. 1972. **Page 192** 'George could be infuriating': Emerick, *Here, There & Everywhere*, p. 330; 'How much did EMI make': Christie's auction catalogue, London, Apr. 2007. **Page 193** 'Lennon had realised': author interview; 'It's rather like an obituary': *Radio Times*, 18 May 1972. **Page 194** 'So much emphasis is put': ibid.; 'We were friends': ibid.; 'We all wanted to play': *Beatlefan* tour special, 1990. **Page 195** 'The Beatles have definitely ended': *Melody Maker*, 15 Jul. 1972; 'What annoys me': *Guardian*, 15 Jul. 1972; 'I know we haven't got many friends': *Radio Times*, 18 May 1972; 'Geraldo wanted to help': author interview. **Page 196** 'The weird thing was turning': *Vanity Fair*, Nov. 2001. **Page 197** 'When I decided to make': *Rolling Stone*, 1 Mar. 1973; 'Not necessarily': *Melody Maker*, 27 January 1973. **Page 198** 'middle-class Jews': Sloman, *Steal This Dream*; 'I want to cut you': Goldman, *Lives of John Lennon*, p. 451; 'After we'd done the One': author interview. **Page 199** 'We're all friends': *Goldmine*, 29 Jul. 1988; 'Ringo, John, Klaus': *Rolling Stone*, 22 Jan. 1981; 'The three of us were there': *Melody Maker*, 3 Nov. 1973; 'Everyone in the room': Badman, op. cit., p. 92.

Chapter 7

Page 200 'I love him, you know': McCabe, *For the Record*, p. 43; 'He's a naughty boy': *Crawdaddy*, Nov. 1973. **Page 201** 'We separated ourselves': Badman, *After the Break-Up*, p. 95; 'There are many reasons': ibid.; 'No matter what anyone says': *Melody Maker*, 24 Jul. 1971. **Page 202** 'Things would happen': author interview; 'He made them feel': author interview; 'The only thing that has prevented': *New Musical Express*, 7 Apr. 1973; 'The chances are practically nil': Badman, op. cit., p. 95 **Page 203** 'George controlled the choice': *Melody Maker*, 3 Nov. 1973; 'I still haven't heard them': Gambaccini, *Paul McCartney in His Own Words*. **Page 205** 'It's costing too much bread': Christie's auction catalogue, New York, Dec. 2004; 'You have to remember': author interview; 'He worked very hard': author interview. **Page 207** 'I tried to call him': author interview; 'I was just having fun': author interview; 'The only talk about Beatle reunions': *Rolling Stone*, 19 Jul. 1973; 'I said, John and George': *Rolling Stone*, 17 Jan. 1974. **Page 208** 'There's always a chance': *Melody Maker*, 3 Nov. 1973; 'I don't suppose': Badman, op. cit., p. 98. **Page 209** 'She was the last person': Boyd, *Wonderful Today*, p. 174; 'George, in front of everyone': ibid., p. 177; 'He said it was just that': Davies, *Quarrymen*, p. 141. **Page 210** 'Yoko and me are in hell': Taylor, *Fifty Years Adrift*, p. 462; 'I got the impression': *Lennon* tribute magazine, 2005; 'just playing life by ear': *Melody Maker*, 3 Nov. 1973; 'He didn't used to drink': author interview; 'John would drink a bottle': *Daily Mail*, 18 Aug. 1988; 'Love John, President': National Archives. **Page 213** 'Just as I was going': Gambaccini, op. cit., p. 205; 'Klein made his way': ibid. **Page 215** 'I just got my visa': ibid. **Page 216** 'First they have to sever': *Rolling Stone*, 11 Apr. 1974; 'because lawyers for Mr Lennon': *New York Times*, 2 Mar. 1974. **Page 217** 'John came to a meeting': *Playboy*, Apr. 1984; 'Beatles Get Together!': *Melody Maker*, 16 Feb. 1974; 'My first impression of George': *Mojo*, Oct. 2006. **Page 218** 'It's not the pain': *New Musical Express*, 23 Mar. 1974; 'Linda or I said to her': Miles, *Many Years From Now*, pp. 589–90; 'I went there': ibid. **Page 219** 'It was a strange session': *Club Sandwich*, winter 1994; 'I remember Harry Nilsson': Miles, op. cit, pp. 589–90; 'There has been much talk': *New Musical Express*, 23 March 1974. **Page 220** 'With my personal life': *New Musical Express*, 8 Mar. 1975; 'We spent two or three nights': *Melody Maker*, 14 Sep. 1974; 'I didn't see John that much': Ono, *Memories of John Lennon*, p. 106. **Page 221** 'It seems that John had made up': *Daily Mail*, 18 Aug. 1988; 'I just got back into music': *Vanity Fair*, Nov. 2001; 'I'm going to be an ex-Beatle': *Melody Maker*, 14 Sep. 1974. **Page 222** 'Why not? It's history': ibid.; 'fourteen- and fifteen-year-old': *Rolling Stone*, 24 Oct. 1974; 'I think it's great': *Vanity Fair*, Nov. 2001; 'No! What for?': *Melody Maker*, 14 Sep. 1974; 'Together we would sound': *New Musical Express*, 12 Oct. 1974. **Page 223** 'You hear me saying': Peebles, *The Lennon Tapes*, p. 69. **Page 224** 'I thought, we'll form a label': Starkey interview with Ken Sharp.

Page 225 'the biggest break in my career': recording of press conference; 'How can we get together': *Melody Maker*, 23 Nov. 1974; 'I think the others are great': *Melody Maker*, 30 Nov. 1974; 'After I split up': *Rolling Stone* 289, Feb. 1979. **Page 226** 'They wanted a Beatle tour': radio interview; 'George didn't want to do': *Rolling Stone*, 19 Dec. 1974; 'Why do they want to see': ibid.; 'I learned that I should make sure': Badman, op. cit., p.197; 'were bulldozing all the rubble': *Rolling Stone* 512, 1987. **Page 227** 'Even [Lennon] was overwhelmed': *Melody Maker*, 7 Dec. 1974; 'They were all screaming': *Melody Maker*, 8 Mar. 1975; '[George] was pretty weird': ibid.; 'We had all arrived': *Playboy*, Apr. 1984. **Page 228** 'I didn't sign it': *Melody Maker*, 8 Mar. 1975; 'The numbers weren't right': *Playboy*, Apr. 1984; 'Somehow or other I was informed': *Melody Maker*, 8 Mar. 1975; 'I think [Julian] likes Paul': Lennon interview with Francis Schoenberger, *Spin*; 'We went on what must': Badman, op. cit., p. 146.

Chapter 8

Page 229 'I am an artist': Christie's auction catalogue, New York, Dec. 2004; 'What people don't realise': *Melody Maker*, 12 Apr. 1975. **Page 230** 'After I deal with this last batch': *New Musical Express*, 8 Mar. 1975. **Page 232** 'I know that Paul was desperate': *Playboy*, Apr. 1984; 'I don't care who gets': *Melody Maker*, 8 Mar. 1975. **Page 233** 'I'm getting calls from my Paul': Evans, *Beatles Literary Anthology*, p. 402; 'What would you think': Fields, *Linda McCartney*, p. 209; 'Bowies cutting': Taylor, *Fifty Years Adrift*, p. 463; 'I realise I've made some bum': *Melody Maker*, 30 Nov. 1974; 'I've lost all that negativity': *Melody Maker*, 8 Mar. 1975. **Page 234** 'told him she had a method': Fields, op. cit., 209; 'I was just going to visit': Lennon interview with Francis Schoenberger, *Spin*; 'It fell in place again': *Melody Maker*, 8 Mar. 1975; 'We sat trembling': *People*, 12 Jan. 1981; 'He was a different person': Fields, op. cit., p. 209; 'I was so numb': *Daily Mail*, 18 Aug. 1988; 'This is no disrespect': *Vanity Fair*, Nov. 2001. **Page 235** 'Yoko dominated John': *Daily Mail*, 18 Aug. 1988; 'I no longer have the dream': Christie's auction catalogue, New York, Dec. 2004. **Page 236** 'I meself have decided': Taylor, op. cit., p. 465; 'I was with them when Yoko': *Evening News*, 26 Apr. 1979; 'I am currently going through': Christie's auction catalogue, London, July 2008; 'As time went by': Baird, *Imagine This*, pp. 235–6. **Page 237** 'don't feel like dealing': Taylor, op. cit., p. 469; 'make me an offer': ibid.; 'Yes, it was a high old time': Christie's auction catalogue, London, April 2007; 'We might get over next year': Baird, op. cit., p. 253; 'Someone said, We weren't musicians': *Mojo*, Jul. 2001; 'It was to be a science fiction': *Guardian*, 6 Oct. 1979. **Page 238** 'He wants to be involved': Pythons, *Autobiography*, pp. 265–6; 'One can't escape the feeling': Palin, *Diaries*, pp. 258–9; 'I really ought to talk': *People*, 21 Apr. 1975. **Page 239** 'George is so straight': *Melody Maker*, 4 Oct. 1975; 'We were keen for Wings': *Record Collector*, May 2001; 'He had the basic idea': Asimov, *In Joy Still Felt*, p. 693. **Page 241** 'Should be a laugh': Taylor, op. cit., p. 465; 'Nothing is wrong': Mansfield, *The White Book*, p. 179; 'Mal was a big lovable bear': Miles, *Many Years From Now*, p. 601; 'Neil Aspinall called': Harry Nilsson interview with Ken Sharp. **Page 242** 'How about a cup of tea': *Record Collector*, Nov. 1995; 'a one-off charity concert': *New York Times*, 19 Sep. 1976; 'I wrote to him': *Record Collector* 195, 1995; 'He didn't know about it': Badman, *After the Break-Up*, p. 192; 'You can't reheat a soufflé': ibid. **Page 243** 'I think Sid is trying': ibid., p. 193; 'It couldn't have happened': *Mojo*, Oct. 2006. **Page 244** 'It's a perfect thing for parody': radio interview; 'Eric chose the right Beatle': Taylor, op. cit., p. 505; 'George occasionally attempts': *Mojo*, Oct. 1996; 'I loved the Rutles': *Rolling Stone* 289, 1979. **Page 245** 'I'd like some power': *Melody Maker*, 20 Sep. 1976; 'Sooner you than me': *People*, 7 Jun. 1976; 'It wasn't like that at all': Taylor, op. cit., p. 525; 'I happened to be on my way': *Rolling Stone* 482, 1986; 'There was a lot of alienation': *Rolling Stone* 512, 1987. **Page 248** 'I still remember vividly': *Daily Mail*, 18 Aug. 1988; 'When he went back to Yoko': Ono, *Memories of John Lennon*, p. 106; 'He said first of all': Davies, *Quarrymen*, p. 141; 'warm, funny and at peace': ibid., p. 142; 'In the background': ibid., p. 243. **Page 249** 'Everything we did was in the shadow': *Mojo*, Jul. 2001; 'Paul and Linda smoked': *The Sun*, 1984. **Page 250** 'It was so weird': Jack Douglas interview with Ken Sharp; 'looking tired and ill': Palin, op. cit., p. 309. **Page 251** 'What happened was that': Badman, op. cit., pp. 193–4; 'It's very difficult to just start': *Rolling Stone* 289, 1979. **Page 252** 'I don't see why they did that': Badman, op. cit., p. 197; 'Paul doesn't have to go': *Guardian*, 4 Dec. 1976. **Page 253** 'Somebody has to take care': Peebles, *The Lennon Tapes*, pp. 76, 78; 'It's true she settled with Klein': *Playboy*, Apr. 1984. **Page 254** 'I feel sorry for him now': *Rolling Stone*, 12 Jul. 1979; 'It's not very good': radio interview, 1979; 'We never wanted it out': *New Musical Express*, 29 Apr. 1978. **Page 256** 'On a personal level': ibid.; 'They're like leeches': radio interview, 1979; 'There is no such thing': *Mojo*, Nov. 2001; 'We didn't have any control': radio interview, 1979. **Page 257** 'People think we're giving all': *Rolling Stone* 289, 1979; 'I cannot see that either': *The Times*, 7 Apr. 1978; 'We've been nostalgia since 1967': *Rolling Stone* 289, 1979. **Page 258** 'I myself would be interested': ibid.; 'I know John was desperate to write': *Playboy*, Apr. 1984. **Page 259** 'Paul, George and It's Only Ringo': Lennon, *Skywriting*, pp. 13ff; 'When the Lennons go out': *Girl About Town*, 21 Jan. 1980. **Page 260** 'Julian was constantly': Lennon, *John*, p. 356; 'Remind Y.O. her teeth': Christie's auction catalogue, New York, December 2004. **Page 261** 'I made a mistake': *Rolling Stone*, 20 Oct. 1988; 'I'm 40 next': Badman, op. cit., p. 243; 'and then evenings': *Evening News*, 24 Apr. 1979; 'John later phoned me': Clapton, *Eric Clapton*, p. 200; 'It's lucky nobody made': *Record Collector*, Nov. 1995. **Page 262** 'I feel that I want to do one': ibid.; 'He's one of the few morally good': *Evening News*, 23 Apr. 1979; 'George had been thinking': Pythons, op. cit., p. 284; 'George paid for the whole thing': ibid., p. 285; 'no wonder they were nervous': ibid.; 'the bizarre journey': Palin, op. cit., p. 579. **Page 263** 'dependable Denis': ibid. **Page 264** 'The Beatles Are Back!': *New York Post*, 21 Sep. 1979; 'some dynamite weed': Badman, op. cit., p. 243; 'to keep our pockets clean': Steve Holly interview with Spencer Leigh. **Page 265** 'I didn't even have his phone number': *Record Collector*, Nov. 1995; 'The last time I asked John': Badman, op. cit., p. 249; 'I'm going to have a few songs': Jack Douglas interview with Ken Sharp; 'He wasn't sure if he could do it': ibid. **Page 266** 'George's not disowning the Beatles': King, *Beatlefan*, p. 702; 'because I'm still feeling that I'm supposed': Peebles, *Lennon Tapes*, p. 89; 'Why should they get a free ride': Jack Douglas interview with Ken Sharp. **Page 267** 'all the most interesting': *New Musical Express*, 22 Nov. 1980; 'Later I found that John's': Taylor, op. cit., p. 519; 'If George wants a million-seller': King, op. cit., p. 427; 'If that's what they want': Taylor, op. cit., p. 519. **Page 268** 'He was really up': *Tomorrow* (TV), 1981; 'I don't know': *Good Morning America* (TV), 1980; 'There was a writing session': Jack Douglas interview with Ken Sharp; 'It was just a very happy conversation': Evans, *Beatles Literary Anthology*, pp. 404–5. **Page 269** 'This is the way': *Rolling Stone*, 22 Jan. 1981; 'We were really celebrating': ibid.; 'There were some strange things': Jack Douglas interview with Ken Sharp; 'When I walked in': *Rolling Stone*, 22 Jan. 1981. **Page 270** 'They wanted to get something': ibid.

Chapter 9

Page 271 'It doesn't matter how many times': *Record Collector*, Nov. 1995; 'We had talked about living': *Los Angeles Times*, 11 Dec. 1980; 'Three or four days after': King, *Beatlefan*, p. 411; 'I kept telling my staff': ibid., p. 356. **Page 272** 'For ten years I was the devil': *Daily Mirror*, 12 Aug. 1981; 'I love you I miss you': *Rolling Stone*, 22 Jan. 1981; 'The only revenge': King, op. cit., p. 356; 'We all cried so hard': Fields, *Linda McCartney*, p. 215; 'Yoko was in a terrible state': *Daily Mail*, 7 Jan. 1981. **Page 273** 'John Lennon may well': King, op. cit., p. 326; 'After I finished': *Goldmine*, 6 Nov. 1998; 'We were constantly talking': *Donahue* (TV), 1981. **Page 274** 'Paul is a complex guy': *The Sun*, January/February 1984; 'strange conversations': Davies, *Beatles* [1985], p. 372; 'John and I were really': ibid.;

'I thought it all': *Nationwide* (TV), 1982; 'Eighty per cent of my power': *Mojo Special Edition*, 2000; 'People are offended': *Daily Mirror*, 12 Aug. 1981. **Page 275** 'John Lennon was the Beatles': *Good Morning America* (TV), 1981; 'I got a nasty letter': Jack Douglas interview with Ken Sharp; 'It's a total joke': undercover.com.au. **Page 276** 'He wrote two articles': *Playboy*, Apr. 1984; 'Paul is doing other things': King, op. cit., p. 359; 'I picked up the Evening Standard': Steve Holly interview with Spencer Leigh; 'We just picked the wrong people': *Playboy*, Apr. 1984; 'To me there was always a feeling': *Club Sandwich*, winter 1994; 'He thought it was worthwhile': *Music Week*, 26 Jul. 2008. **Page 277** 'He'd like to smile': *Donahue* (TV), 1981; 'the days of Beatlemania': UPI release, 27 Apr. 1981; 'Paul played the piano': author interview. **Page 278** 'They felt intimidated': Badman, *After the Break-Up*, p. 283; 'gentleman's agreement': King, op. cit., p. 675; 'I had so many responsibilities': author interview; 'I think I've misunderstood you': *Then and Now* (video), 1984; 'Look, I'm real nervous': *Music Express*, Mar. 1982; 'I gulped, thinking': *Record Collector*, Oct. 1995. **Page 279** 'Yoko's OK': *Daily Mail*, 27 Oct. 1981; 'Dad was always totally under': King, op. cit., p. 545; 'I don't intend to spend': *The Sun*, 27 Oct. 1981; 'as an assault on her person': *Daily Mail*, 25 Nov. 1981; 'could crash-land at any time': King, op. cit., p. 594. **Page 280** 'George was always worried': *Daily Mirror*, 31 Dec. 1999; 'George was finding fame': author interview; 'I would've liked to have seen': *Today* (TV), 1982; 'People like a loser': *Music Express*, Mar. 1982; 'A thing like that': *Today* (TV), 1982; 'One of the things we'd been consciously': *Newsnight* (TV), 4 Oct. 1982. **Page 281** 'psychosexual matrimony': *Popular Music* 6/3, 1987. **Page 282** 'The mistake most people': *People*, 14 Nov. 1983; 'being raped by these people': TV news bulletin, **Page 283** 'You'll never get them all': King, op. cit., p. 475. **Page 284** 'Don't be daft': *Daily Express*, 2 Dec. 1983; 'materialise on television': *Psychic Guide*, Sept.–Nov. 1983. **Page 285** 'We have filed complaints': *Good Day Sunshine*, 1989; 'they felt the quality of the work': ibid.; 'Amazing Beatles Bust-Up': *Sunday Mirror*, 24 Feb. 1985. **Page 286** 'This freaky guy shoots your dad': *Record*, Apr. 1985; 'but they declined': *Rolling Stone* 512, 1987; 'I was away at the time': ibid. **Page 287** 'Paul, it will look like': *Goldmine*, 6 Nov. 1998; 'I think in some ways': *People*, 24 Mar. 1986. **Page 288** 'My turn for some stick': author interview; 'As a joke': *Rolling Stone* 512, 1987. **Page 289** 'Paul probably suspects': *Musician*, Apr. 1992; 'There seems to be some consternation': press release; 'Paul's office had called me': *Musician*, Apr. 1992; 'The Beatles never did any of that': *Rolling Stone* 512, 1987. **Page 290** 'It was John's wish': author interview; 'The John Lennon I knew': author interview. **Page 291** 'It was all too convenient': *Rolling Stone* 512, 1987. **Page 292** 'The funny thing is': *Rolling Stone* 482, 1986; 'George wanted me to be in it': *Club Sandwich*, winter 1994; 'He'll always be my friend': *Guitar World*, c. Dec. 1987; 'Yeah, Paul and I are friends': ibid. **Page 293** 'We'll see that one in Sotheby's': *Observer*, 22 Nov. 1987; 'It didn't mean anything': Badman, *The Dream Is Over*, p. 365; 'I was keen to go': ibid., p. 366. **Page 294** 'There seem to be more of us': TV coverage of ceremony; '[Paul] was just trying to use': radio interview; 'Paul has suggested that maybe': recording of press conference, 28 Mar. 1988; 'Maybe it's because he ran out': *MuchMusic Live Interview* (TV), 28 Mar. 1988; 'We don't have a relationship': *Musician*, Mar. 1990; 'He wanted to be in a band': Zollo, *Conversations*, p. 119. **Page 295** 'It was about as much fun': ibid., p. 124; 'We wanted it to be something': ibid., p. 128; 'I don't really see the point': press conference, 19 Feb. 1990; 'There was always a lot of talk': Zollo, op. cit., p. 126; 'as long as John Lennon': press statement, 28 Nov. 1989.

Chapter 10

Page 296 'We are the only ones': *Q*, Dec. 1995; 'Boycott this book': *Rolling Stone*, 20 Oct. 1988; 'He ought to be ashamed of himself': Badman, *After the Break-Up*, pp. 410–11; 'genetic brain damage': *Time Out*, 24–31 Aug. 1988. **Page 297** 'The settlement was about ten': *Musician*, Mar. 1990; 'It doesn't wash away': ibid. **Page 298** 'Years I've lost': *Vox*,

Jun. 1992; 'Maybe on a good night': author interview; 'He wanted me to put it on hold': author interview. **Page 300** 'He's left it a bit late': *Sunday Times*, 1 Jul. 1990; 'George has taken the liberty': *CD Review*, late 1990. **Page 301** 'The significant thing': *People*, 21 May 1990; 'I don't think John would like it': *Sunday Times*, 1 Jul. 1990. **Page 303** 'a blackboard, with all these': Pythons, *Autobiography*, p. 311; 'I'd observed him': ibid., p. 310; 'When we got rid of Allen Klein': *Business Age*, Jul. 1995. **Page 305** 'No, it can't be possible': press conference, 29 Nov. 1991; 'I had to do something': ibid.; 'The press conference set the tone': *Mojo*, Apr. 1998; 'I only wish I could have been': Clapton, *Eric Clapton*, p. 312. **Page 306** 'to create a disease-free': NLP press release, 1992; 'I will vote for the Natural Law': ibid.; 'I've been up all night': Miles, *Many Years From Now*, p. 429; 'a Beatles tour': *Rapido* (TV), Dec. 1990; 'I'm always paranoid': recording of concert; 'I really enjoyed playing': *RCD* Vol. 1.4, 1992. **Page 307** 'We went through the stages': *Q*, Dec. 1995; 'None of the guys saw': *Record Collector*, Dec. 1995; 'We didn't want her talking': ibid. **Page 308** 'To have someone sit at your table': *Billboard*, Jun. 1999; 'an absolutely extraordinary individual': *Business Age*, Jul. 1995; 'a faithless and fraudulent manager': ibid.; 'an 18-page insult': ibid.; 'It's a help': *Billboard*, 9 Mar. 1996. **Page 309** 'We're getting together': Badman, op. cit., p. 492; 'John's spirit was in the studio': ibid., p. 508; 'I've listened to all the tapes': *The Times*, Mar. 1993. **Page 310** 'She was a little surprised': *Mojo*, Oct. 1995; 'We know we can't do anything': press conference, 19 Jan. 1994. **Page 311** 'It was all settled before then': Badman, op. cit., p. 518; 'I checked it out with Sean': *Q*, Dec. 1995; 'I remember how John always said': *Daily Mail*, 13 Nov. 1995; 'I told them I wasn't too happy': *Goldmine*, 6 Nov. 1998. **Page 312** 'There have been a lot of bad': *Record Collector*, Jul. 1995; 'I actually originally': *Mojo*, Oct. 1995; 'Maybe I'm peculiar': *Q*, Dec. 1995; 'I thought, Oh': ibid. **Page 313** 'It really sounds like a Beatles': *Record Collector*, Jul. 1995; 'It was one day': Badman, op. cit., pp. 527–8; 'It was a very sweet song': ibid. **Page 314** 'This German record label': author interview; 'this bad copy': *Billboard*, 9 Mar. 1996. **Page 315** 'I didn't like it as much': Badman, op. cit., pp. 527–8; 'He was saying to me': *The Times*, 11 Nov. 1995; 'He's still a Beatle': *Arena*, winter 1995; 'When Ringo said': *Q*, Dec. 1995; 'The most refreshing thing': author interview. **Page 316** 'there was so much Paul': *Mojo Special Edition*, 2000; 'He's been in the Beatles': *Record Collector*, Dec. 1995; 'has these voices in his head': *The Times*, 11 Nov. 1995; 'The point about this place': *Arena*, Autumn 1995; 'an imperious employer': *Independent*, 28 Oct. 1995; 'He'll never admit that he's wrong': author interview; 'He's charming to the people': author interview. **Page 318** 'Me and George Harrison': *Q*, Dec. 1995.

Finale

Page 321 'People still haven't gotten': *Oprah Winfrey* (TV), Sep. 1998; 'I should be more modest': *Love* (DVD). **Page 323** 'doesn't think he has cancer': *Beatlefan* 18/6, 1997; 'I'm not going to die': *Mail on Sunday*, 22 Jul. 2001; 'There is an inference': *Daily Telegraph*, 24 Apr. 1998; 'It was a decoy': ibid. **Page 324** 'The [Beatles'] demise': *The Times*, 20 Apr. 1998; 'crusading vegetarian': *Daily Telegraph*, 20 Apr. 1998; 'Nothing Paul McCartney wrote': *Daily Mirror*, 22 Apr. 1998; 'He is managing': *Goldmine*, 6 Nov. 1998. **Page 325** 'I know Paul thinks': BBC interview, 16 Jan. 1998; 'Linda and I did not': Fields, *Linda McCartney*, p. 269; 'There were those who think': TV interview. **Page 326** 'In my heart I am still': Apple press release, Sep. 1999; 'When I met him': *Sunday Times*, 12 Oct. 2003; 'Unless we do something': *Guardian*, 6 Nov. 1995; 'I got the short straw': *Daily Mail*, 7 May 1998. **Page 327** 'Unlike the experts': ibid.; 'That's total bullshit': *Vox*, Sep. 1992. **Page 328** 'There were security cameras': *Daily Mirror*, 31 Dec. 1999; 'I thought I was dying': court testimony; 'I was terrified': *Daily Telegraph*, 24 Jan. 2005; 'I spoke to Ringo': *Observer*, 9 Jul. 2000. **Page 329** 'George was still very disturbed': Clapton, *Eric Clapton*, p. 312; 'He is an indomitable spirit': *Mail on Sunday*, 22 Jul. 2001. **Page 330** 'He's been rescued': Martyn

Lewis, 'The Art of Dying', salon.com; 'He hadn't been well': *Mojo*, Dec. 2001; 'We were laughing': *People*, 17 Dec. 2001. **Page 331** 'where [George] was bedridden': *New York Post*, 7 Jan. 2004; '[George] had a look': *People*, 5 Dec. 2001; 'George aspired to leave': *Daily Telegraph*, 24 Jan. 2005; 'He was a very spiritual person': vnn.org, Jan. 2003; 'There was no urgency': *Mojo*, Dec. 2002. **Page 332** 'I am devastated': TV news bulletin; 'Thanks very much': *Concert for George* film. **Page 333** 'George was the funniest man': *Sunday Times*, 12 Oct. 2003; 'My job description': *Billboard*, 11 Mar. 2009; 'I've finally become everyone': Mansfield, *The White Book*, p. 222; 'Living sober was difficult': contactmusic.com, 2 Mar. 2008. **Page 334** 'I have this thing': *Sunday Express*, 24 Jan. 2005; 'I was never asked': *Independent*, 3 Oct. 2007; 'We never let Liverpool': *Liverpool Echo*, 21 Jan. 2008. **Page 335** 'He had a completely different': author interview. **Page 339** 'It's normal in any business': *Mojo Special Edition*, 2000. **Page 340** 'Why do I care': *Newsweek*, 15 Sep. 2003; 'It's actually just a very': *Mojo*, May 2003; 'This is like a drama': *Newsweek*, 28 Nov. 2005. **Page 341** 'Julian was devastated': Lennon, *John*, p. 388; 'John would say to me': speech at Q Awards, 10 Oct. 2005; 'It's the kind of challenge': *Mojo Special Edition*, 2000. **Page 342** 'You have to wonder': *Word*, Nov. 1995; 'I don't think it will add': Apple press release, Sep. 1999; 'In typical Apple fashion': *Love* (DVD); 'I knew I was the only one': ibid.; 'Apple wanted this to be': ibid. **Page 343** 'Ringo thought it was fantastic': *Music Week*, 4 Nov. 2006; 'The album puts the Beatles': *Love* press release, Nov. 2006. **Page 344** 'Let It Be with a fig leaf': *New York Times*, 6 Nov. 2003. **Page 345** 'We can't reach an agreement': *The Times*, 29 Sep. 2003; 'I am computer illiterate': court testimony, 2006; 'We have no plans': BBC news report, 14 Oct. 2003; 'even a moron in a hurry': court testimony, 2006; 'With great respect': press statement, 8 May 2006. **Page 346** 'the departure of Neil Aspinall': press statement, 4 Apr. 2007; 'Neil was great': *Music Week*, 23 Feb. 2008. **Page 347** 'I fear for the integrity': *Daily Mirror*, 11 Apr. 2007; 'If I'm unstable': contactmusic.com, 7 Feb. 2005; 'Paul Firing Me': *Sunday Mail*, 26 Mar. 2006; 'For 15 Years I Lied': *Daily Mail*, 12 May 2007. **Page 350** 'Nothing should have ended': author interview.

Bibliography

Asimov, Isaac, *In Joy Still Felt: The Autobiography of Isaac Asimov 1954–1978* (New York: Doubleday, 1980).

Badman, Keith, *The Beatles: After the Break-up 1970–2000* (London: Omnibus Press, 2000).

Badman, Keith, *The Beatles off the Record* (London: Omnibus Press, London 2000)

Badman, Keith, *The Beatles: The Dream Is Over: Off the Record 2* (London: Omnibus Press, 2001).

Baird, Julia, *Imagine This* (London: Hodder & Stoughton, 2007).

Baker, Glenn A., *The Beatles Down Under* (Ann Arbor: Pierian Press, 1985).

Beatles, The, *The Beatles Anthology* (London: Cassell, 2000).

Bedford, Carol, *Waiting for the Beatles: An Apple Scruff's Story* (Poole: Blandford Press, 1984).

Berke, Joseph (ed.), *Counter Culture* (London: Peter Owen, 1969).

Best, Pete, *Beatle!* (London: Plexus, 1985).

Bishop, Patrick and Mallie, Eamonn, *The Provisional IRA* (London: Corgi, 1983).

Blake, John, *All You Needed Was Love* (London: Hamlyn, 1981).

Booker, Christopher, *The Neophiliacs* (London: Collins, 1969).

Boyd, Pattie, *Wonderful Today: George Harrison, Eric Clapton and Me* (London: Headline Review, 2007).

Bramwell, Tony, *Magical Mystery Tours: My Life with the Beatles* (London: Robson Books, 2005).

Bresler, Fenton, *Who Killed John Lennon?* (New York: St Martin's Press, 1989).

Bromell, Nick, *Tomorrow Never Knows: Rock and Psychedelics in the 1960s* (Chicago: University of Chicago Press, 2000).

Brown, Mick, *Tearing Down the Wall of Sound: The Rise and Fall of Phil Spector* (London: Bloomsbury, 2007).

Brown, Peter and Gaines, Stephen, *The Love You Make: An Insider's Story of the Beatles* (New York: McGraw Hill, 1983).

Cadogan, Patrick, *The Revolutionary Artist* (lulu.com, 2008)

Carr, Roy and Tyler, Tony, *The Beatles: An Illustrated Record* (London: New English Library, 1975).

Castleman, Harry and Podrazik, Walter J., *All Together Now* (Ann Arbor: Pierian Press, 1976).

Christgau, Robert, *Any Old Way You Choose It* (Baltimore: Penguin, 1973).

Christgau, Robert, *Christgau's Guide: Rock Albums of the 70s* (London: Vermilion, 1982).

Christie's (South Kensington), *Rock and Pop Memorabilia* (London and New York: Christie's, various auction catalogues 1986–2009).

Cité de la Musique, *John Lennon: Unfinished Music* (Paris: Cité de la Musique, 2005).

Clapton, Eric, *Eric Clapton: The Autobiography* (London: Century, 2007).

Clayson, Alan, *George Harrison: The Quiet One* (London: Sidgwick & Jackson, 1989).

Clayson, Alan, *Ringo Starr: Straight Man or Joker?* (London: Sidgwick & Jackson, 1991).

Clayson, Alan and Leigh, Spencer, *The Walrus Was Ringo* (Chrome Dreams, 2003).

Coleman, Ray, *John Winston Lennon: 1940–1966* (London: Sidgwick & Jackson, 1984).

Coleman, Ray, *John Ono Lennon: 1967–1980* (London: Sidgwick & Jackson, 1984).

Coleman, Ray, *Paul McCartney: Yesterday & Today* (London: Boxtree, 1995).

Connolly, Ray, *John Lennon: 1940-1980* (Fontana, London, 1981).

Cott, Jonathan and Dalton, David, *The Beatles Get Back* (London: Apple, 1970).

Cott, Jonathan, *He Dreams What Is Going on inside His Head* (San Francisco: Straight Arrow, 1973).

Cott, Jonathan and Doudna, Christine (eds), *The Ballad of John & Yoko* (London: Michael Joseph, 1982).

Cott, Jonathan, *Back to a Shadow in the Night: Music Writings and Interviews 1968–2001* (Milwaukee: Hal Leonard, 2002).

Cunliffe, Marcus, *American Literature Since 1900* (London: Sphere, 1975).

Dallas, Karl, *Singers of an Empty Day: Last Sacraments of the Superstars* (London: Kahn & Averill, 1971).

Davies, Hunter, *The Beatles: The Authorised Biography* (London: Heinemann, 1968).

Davies, Hunter, *The Beatles* (revised edition; New York: McGraw-Hill, 1985).

Davies, Hunter, *The Quarrymen* (London: Omnibus Press, 2001).

Davis, Clive, *Clive* (New York: Ballantine, 1976).

Dean, Johnny (ed.), *The Best of The Beatles Book* (London: Beat Publications, 2005).

Dickstein, Morris, *Gates of Eden: American Culture in the Sixties* (New York: Penguin, 1989).

Dilello, Richard, *The Longest Cocktail Party* (Ann Arbor: Pierian Press, 1983).

Doggett, Peter, *Classic Albums: Let It Be/Abbey Road* (New York: Schirmer, 1998).

Doggett, Peter, *Are You Ready for the Country* (London: Penguin, 2000).

Doggett, Peter, *The Art and Music of John Lennon* (London: Omnibus Press, 2005).

Doggett, Peter, *There's a Riot Going On* (London: Canongate, 2007).

Draper, Robert, *The Rolling Stone Story* (Edinburgh: Mainstream, 1990).

Editors of Rolling Stone, *The Rolling Stone Record Review* (New York: Pocket Books, 1971).

Editors of Rolling Stone, *The Rolling Stone Interviews Vol. 1* (New York: Warner, 1971)

Editors of Rolling Stone, *The Age of Paranoia: How the Sixties Ended* (New York: Pocket Books, 1972).

Editors of Rolling Stone, *The Rolling Stone Interviews Vol. 2* (New York: Warner, 1973).

Editors of Rolling Stone, *The Rolling Stone Record Review Vol. II* (New York: Pocket Books, 1974).

Editors of Rolling Stone, *Harrison* (New York: Simon & Schuster, 2002).

Emerick, Geoff, *Here, There & Everywhere* (New York: Gotham, 2006).

Evans, Mike, *The Art of the Beatles* (London: Anthony Blond, 1984).

Evans, Mike (ed.), *The Beatles Literary Anthology* (London: Plexus, 2004).

Fawcett, Anthony, *John Lennon: One Day at a Time* (London: New English Library, 1981).

Fields, Danny, *Linda McCartney: The Biography* (London: Little Brown, 2000).

Finnis, Rob, *The Phil Spector Story* (London: Rock On, 1975).

Fong-Torres, Ben (ed.), *The Rolling Stone Rock 'n' Roll Reader* (New York: Bantam, 1974).

Gaar, Gillian, *She's a Rebel: The History of Women in Rock 'n' Roll* (Poole: Blandford Press, 1993).

Gambaccini, Paul, *Paul McCartney in His Own Words* (London: Omnibus Press, 1976).

Garbarini, Vic et al., *Strawberry Fields Forever* (New York: Bantam, 1980).

Ginsberg, Allen, *Spontaneous Mind: Selected Interviews 1958–1996* (London: Penguin, 2001).

Gitlin, Todd, *The Sixties: Years of Hope, Days of Rage* (New York: Bantam, 1997).

Giuliano, Geoffrey, *Dark Horse: The Secret Life of George Harrison* (London: Bloomsbury, 1989).

Giuliano, Geoffrey, *Blackbird: The Life and Times of Paul McCartney* (London: John Blake, 1991).

Giuliano, Geoffrey, *The Lost Beatles Interviews* (New York: Dutton, 1994).

Giuliano, Geoffrey, *Lennon in America* (London: Robson Books, 2000).

Giuliano, Geoffrey, *Revolver: The Secret History of the Beatles* (London: John Blake, 2006).

Goldman, Albert, *The Lives of John Lennon* (London: Bantam, 1988).

Goodman, Fred, *The Mansion on the Hill* (New York: Times Books, 1997).

Gould, Jonathan, *Can't Buy Me Love: The Beatles, Britain and America* (London: Piatkus, 2007).

Granados, Stefan, *Those Were the Days: An Unofficial History of the Beatles' Apple Organization* (London: Cherry Red, 2002).

Green, John, *Dakota Days: The Untold Story of John Lennon's Final Years* (London: WH Allen, 1984).

Green, Jonathon, *Days in the Life: Voices from the English Underground 1961– 1971* (London: Heinemann, 1988).

Green, Jonathon, *All Dressed Up: The Sixties and the Counterculture* (London: Jonathan Cape, 1998).

Guralnick, Peter, *Dream Boogie: The Triumph of Sam Cooke* (London: Little Brown, 2005).

Harrison, George, *I Me Mine* (Guildford: Genesis Publications, 1980).

Heylin, Clinton, *The Great White Wonder: A History of Rock Bootlegs* (London: Viking, 1994).

Heylin, Clinton, *The Act You've Known for All These Years: The Life, and Afterlife, of Sgt. Pepper* (London: Canongate, 2007).

Hoffman, Abbie, *Woodstock Nation* (New York: Pocket Books, 1971).

Hopkins, Jerry, *Yoko Ono* (London: Macmillan, 1987).

Humphry, Derek and Tindall, David, *False Messiah: The Story of Malcolm X* (London: Hart-Davis MacGibbon, 1977).

Janov, Arthur, *The Primal Scream* (London: Abacus, 1973).

Jones, LeRoi, *Black Music* (New York: Morrow, 1967).

King, Leslie T. (ed.), *Beatlefan Vols. 3 & 4: 1981–1982* (Ann Arbor: Pierian Press, 1986).

Kooper, Al, *Backstage Passes & Backstabbing Bastards* (New York: Backbeat, 2008).

Krassner, Paul (ed.), *The Best of the Realist* (New York: Running Press, 1984).

Krassner, Paul, *Confessions of a Raving Unconfined Nut: Misadventures in the Counter-Culture* (New York: Simon & Schuster, 1993).

Leng, Simon, *The Music of George Harrison: While My Guitar Gently Weeps* (London: Firefly, 2003).

Lennon, Cynthia, *A Twist of Lennon* (London: Star, 1978).

Lennon, Cynthia, *John* (London: Hodder & Stoughton, 2005).

Lennon, John, *Skywriting by Word of Mouth* (Pan, London, 1986)

Lennon, Pauline, *Daddy Come Home* (London: Harper Collins, 1990).

Lewisohn, Mark, *The Beatles: 25 Years in the Life* (London: Sidgwick & Jackson, 1987).

Lewisohn, Mark, *The Complete Beatles Chronicle* (New York: Pyramid Books, 1992).

MacDonald, Ian, *Revolution in the Head: The Beatles' Records and the Sixties* (London: Fourth Estate, 1994).

Madinger, Chip and Easter, Mark, *Eight Arms to Hold You: The Solo Beatles Compendium* (Chesterfield: 44.1 Productions, 2000).

Maharishi Mahesh Yogi, *On the Bhagavad-Gita: A New Translation and Commentary Chapters 1-6* (Harmondsworth: Penguin, 1969).

Mansfield, Ken, *The White Book* (Nashville: Thomas Nelson, 2007).

Martin, George, *All You Need Is Ears* (London: Macmillan, 1979).

Matovina, Dan, *Without You: The Tragic Story of Badfinger* (San Mateo: Frances Glover Books, 1997).

McCabe, Peter and Schonfeld, Robert D., *Apple to the Core: The Unmaking of the Beatles* (London: Martin Brian & O'Keeffe, 1972).

McCabe, Peter and Schonfeld, Robert D., *John Lennon: For the Record* (New York: Bantam, 1984).

McCartney, Mike, *Thank U Very Much* (London: Granada, 1982).

McCartney, Paul, *Composer/Artist* (London: Pavilion, 1981).

McKinney, Devin, *Magic Circles: The Beatles in Dream and History* (Cambridge, Mass.: Harvard University Press, 2003).

Melly, George, *Revolt Into Style: The Pop Arts in Britain* (Harmondsworth: Penguin, 1972).

Miles, Barry, *Paul McCartney: Many Years From Now* (London: Secker & Warburg, 1998).

Miles, Barry, *The Beatles Diary Volume 1: The Beatles Years* (London: Omnibus Press, 2001).

Munroe, Alexandra (ed.), *Yes Yoko Ono* (New York: Japan Society/Harry N. Abrams, 2000).

Neises, Charles P. (ed.), *The Beatles Reader* (Ann Arbor: Pierian Press, 1984)

Neville, Richard, *Hippie Hippie Shake* (London: Bloomsbury, 1995).

Noebel, David, *Communism, Hypnotism and the Beatles* (Tulsa: Christian Crusade, 1965).

Norman, Philip, *Shout! The True Story of the Beatles* (London: ElmTree, 1981).

Norman, Philip, *The Stones* (London: Penguin, 1993).

Norman, Philip, *John Lennon: The Life* (London: Harper Collins, 2008).

O'Dell, Denis and Neaverson, Bob, *At the Apple's Core* (London: Peter Owen, 2002).

Oldham, Andrew, *2Stoned* (London: Secker & Warburg, 2002).

Ono, Yoko, *Grapefruit* (London: Sphere Books, 1971).

Ono, Yoko (ed.), *Memories of John Lennon* (Stroud: Sutton Publishing, 2005).

Palin, Michael, *Diaries 1969–1979: The Python Years* (London: Weidenfeld & Nicolson, 2006).

Palmer, Tony, *Born Under a Bad Sign* (London: William Kimber, 1970).

Palmer, Tony, *The Trials of Oz* (London: Blond & Briggs, 1971).

Pang, May and Edwards, Henry, *Loving John* (London: Corgi, 1983).

Pythons, The, *The Pythons Autobiography* (London: Orion, 2005).

Peebles, Andy (ed.), *The Lennon Tapes* (London: BBC Books, 1981).

Peel, Ian, *The Unknown Paul McCartney* (London: Reynolds & Hearn, 2002).

Riley, Tim, *Tell Me Why: A Beatles Commentary* (London: Bodley Head, 1988).

Rosen, Robert, *Nowhere Man: The Final Days of John Lennon* (London: Fusion Press, 2000).

Rubin, Jerry, *Growing (Up) At 37* (New York: M. Evans & Co., 1976).

Salewicz, Chris, *McCartney: The Definitive Biography* (New York: St Martin's Press, 1986).

Sandercombe, W. Fraser, *The Beatles Press Reports* (Burlington: Collector's Guide, 2007).

Sandford, Christopher, *McCartney* (London: Century, 2006).

Schaffner, Nicholas, *The Beatles Forever* (New York: McGraw-Hill, 1984).

Schwartz, Francie, *Body Count* (San Francisco: Straight Arrow, 1972).

Seaman, Fred, *John Lennon: Living on Borrowed Time* (London: Wordsworth, 1991).

Sellers, Robert, *Always Look on the Bright Side of Life: The Inside Story of HandMade Films* (London: Metro, 2003).

Sheff, David, *Last Interview: All We Are Saying – John Lennon & Yoko Ono* (London: Sidgwick & Jackson, 2000).

Shipper, Mark, *Paperback Writer* (London: New English Library, 1978).

Shotton, Pete and Schaffner, Nicholas, *John Lennon in My Life* (London: Stein & Day, 1983).

Sloman, Larry, *Steal This Dream: Abbie Hoffman and the Countercultural Revolution in America* (New York: Doubleday, 1998).

Sotheby's, *Pop Memorabilia* (London: Sotheby's, 1986).

Spitz, Bob, *The Beatles: The Biography* (London: Aurum Press, 2005).

Starr, Ringo, *Postcards from the Boys* (London: Cassell Illustrated, 2004).

Sulpy, Doug and Schweighardt, Ray, *Get Back: The Beatles' Let It Be Disaster* (London: Helter Skelter, 2003).

Taylor, Alistair, *With the Beatles* (London: John Blake, 2003).

Taylor, Derek, *As Time Goes By: Living in the Sixties* (San Francisco: Straight Arrow, 1973).

Taylor, Derek, *Fifty Years Adrift* (Guildford: Genesis Publications, 1984).

Thomson, Elizabeth and Gutman, David (eds), *The Lennon Companion* (London: Macmillan, 1987).

Tobler, John and Grundy, Stuart, *The Record Producers* (London: BBC, 1982).

Turner, Steve, *The Gospel According to the Beatles* (London: Westminster John Knox Press, 2006).

Unterberger, Richie, *The Unreleased Beatles* (San Francisco: Backbeat, 2006).

Vollmer, Jürgen, *Rock'n'Roll Times* (Paris: Edition de Nesle, 1981).

Wenner, Jann S., *Lennon Remembers* (London: Verso, 2000).

Wexler, Jerry and Ritz, David, *Rhythm and the Blues: A Life in American Music* (New York: Knopf, 1993).

Wiener, Jon, *Come Together: John Lennon and His Time* (New York: Random House, 1984).

Wiener, Jon, *Gimme Some Truth: The John Lennon FBI Files* (Berkeley: University of California Press, 1999).

Williams, Allan and Marshall, William, *The Man Who Gave the Beatles Away* (London: Elm Tree, 1975).

Williams, Richard, *Out of His Head: The Sound of Phil Spector* (London: Abacus, 1972).

Wood, Ronnie, *Ronnie* (London: Macmillan, 2007).

Yogananda, Paramahansa, *Autobiography of a Yogi* (Los Angeles: Self-Realization Fellowship, 1974).

Zollo, Paul, *Conversations with Tom Petty* (London: Omnibus Press, 2005).

Among the periodicals consulted were *Arena, Beat Instrumental, The Beatles Book, Beatlefan, Berkeley Tribe, Billboard, Black Dwarf, Cashbox, Chicago Seed, Club Sandwich, Countdown, Crawdaddy, Cream, Creem, Daily Express, Daily Mail, Daily Mirror, Daily Sketch, Daily Star, Daily Telegraph, Dark Star, Disc & Music Echo, Down Beat, East Village Other, Evening News, Evening Standard, Free John Now!, Frendz, Friends, Fusion, Girl About Town, Goldmine, Good Day Sunshine, GQ, Guardian, Guitar Player, Guitar World, Hello, Hit Parader, Independent, Ink, International Times (IT), Jazz & Pop, Journal, Let It Rock, Life, Liverpool Echo, Look, Los Angeles Free Press, Mail on Sunday, Melody Maker, Mojo, Mojo Special Edition: John Lennon, Music Express, Music Week, Musician, New Musical Express (NME), New Statesman, New York, New York Daily News, New York Post, New York Times, New Yorker, Newsweek, Observer, Other Scenes, Oz, People, Playboy, P.O. Frisco, Popular Music, Psychic Guide, Q, Ramparts, RAT Subterranean News, RCD, Record, Record Collector,*

Record Hunter, Record Mirror, Record Retailer, Red Mole, Rolling Stone, Select, Sounds, Spin, the Sun, Sunday Mail, Sunday Mirror, Sunday Times, Time, The Times, Time Out, Uncut, Vanity Fair, Village Voice, Vox, Word, Write Thing, and *Zigzag.*

The National Archives in Kew, London allow public access to the complete transcript of the spring 1971 court action initiated by Paul McCartney to dissolve the Beatles' partnership. Also included in the Archives are several hundred pages of documents relating to the Official Receiver's work as effective boss of Apple Corps Ltd between 1971 and 1974; and several thousand pages chronicling the epic legal disputes between Apple and three of the Beatles, and Allen Klein's ABKCO organisation, between 1973 and 1976.

More than 100 hours of recordings of the Beatles at work and at loggerheads in January 1969 have been made available on unofficial, 'bootleg' CDs (most comprehensively on a 83-disc series entitled *The Complete A/B Road Sessions*). These records contain an often exasperating mix of lacklustre music and equally uninspired conversations, spiced with an occasional moment of artistry or emotional truth. They make agonising listening, in both personal and artistic terms, but provide a vivid exhibition of the parlous state of relations within the group just prior to the arrival of Allen Klein. Like all bootleg CDs, however, they are illegal to sell and distribute in any form.

Index